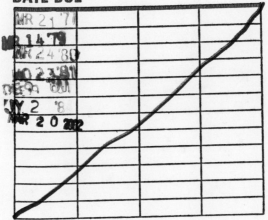

Education
of Exceptional
Learners

Education
of Exceptional
Learners

By FRANK M. HEWETT
Professor of Education and Psychiatry
University of California, Los Angeles

With STEVEN R. FORNESS
Associate Professor of Psychiatry
University of California, Los Angeles

Allyn and Bacon, Inc.
Boston • London • Sydney

To
Mike
and
Julie

Library of Congress Catalog Card Number: 73-89262

Printed in the United States of America.

Chapter opening illustrations were drawn for this text
by Steven D. McAdam.

ISBN: 0-205-04323-2
Third printing . . . June, 1975

Contents

v

Preface

This book is about learners, some of whom, by the way, happen to be different or exceptional and placed traditionally into various categories. It is not about rigidly categorized, handicapped individuals, some of whom, by the way, happen to be learners. The emphasis of the opening sentence establishes the approach of this text, in contrast to the intent of the second sentence, which reflects the focus of more traditional introductory books in special education.

Fifteen years ago, I became concerned with the secondary priority ranking given the learning and behavior problems of emotionally disturbed children as compared with the primary ranking given notions of psychic conflicts and mental illness. This concern resulted in a book on disturbed children that reversed these rankings and focused on such children as first and foremost learners ready at all times to learn something and on the "somethings" that were critical for them to learn. Over the years, it has become apparent to me that a similar reversal in priority ranking was long overdue for all children called "exceptional." This text is an attempt to apply it to nine categories of exceptional children.

In writing this book, I am deeply indebted to a number of graduate students and colleagues who shared in its conceptualization and organization, in assembling its content, and in critiquing the final product. In this regard my thanks go to Kenyon Chan, Ron French, Don Glass, Steve Saltzman, and Joe Ward. Janet Tegland deserves special appreciation and recognition for her important contribution to Chapter 1, "Historical Origins." Doug Palmer, Ray Parada, Mike Soloway, and Phil Watson were of great assistance at various stages along the way and in the final editing and rewriting phase of the project. Jim Coleman, George Fargo, Barbara Keogh, Sam Kirk, Francis Lord, and Herb Quay were colleagues whose advice and support were greatly valued during the course of the writing.

I have had the good fortune of working closely with the Santa Monica Unified School District and its Office of Special Services for the past seven years. During this time, the teaching and administrative staff of the district has participated in the continuous development of innovative programs for exceptional children, and I have been privileged to work with and learn from them. I am grateful to Alfred Artuso, Superintendent, for his strong support of these efforts and to Frank Taylor, Assistant Superintendent, for his much-valued working partnership in translating into public school reality many of the principles on which this book is based. Chapter 11 presents the Santa Monica Madison School Plan, which is the revision and extension of the engineered classroom design developed in the Santa Monica schools and presented in the earlier book.

My sincere appreciation is also given to Mary Hunt, who managed and prepared the entire manuscript during its many stages of development. Finally, my collaborating author and friend, Steve Forness, deserves a great deal of credit for helping to develop the overall plan and orientation of the book. He researched and wrote all the material related to mental retardation and joined me in the important decision-making regarding the rest of the content.

F. M. Hewett

Note to Reader

ED

LD

MR

SD

VH

HH

SH

PH

G

In this text we are concerned with children who fall into nine separate categories:

1. Emotionally disturbed children (ED)
2. Children with learning disabilities (LD)
3. Mentally retarded children (MR)
4. Socially and economically disadvantaged children (SD)
5. Visually handicapped children (VH)
6. Hearing handicapped children (HH)
7. Speech handicapped children (SH)
8. Physically handicapped children (PH)
9. Gifted children (G)

Traditionally, introductory texts in special education have treated the categories separately with a chapter or two devoted to each. In this book, we are going to combine the nine categories for much of our discussion. The reader desiring to review content in a particular category of exceptionality can utilize the index-band system illustrated on the right-hand margin of this page. Throughout this text, whenever a given category is under discussion, identifying initials will appear on the margin of the page, as shown. These will appear at different levels on the margin for each category. With the book closed, the darkened edges will be visible as continuous bands. By flipping through the pages marked by a given band at a given level, the reader can review content on a categorical basis.

Introduction

Children are different. Mrs. Thompson's third grade class descends on the school playground. It is recess. The children have marched in a more or less orderly manner from the classroom to the playground and are dismissed. What transpires from this moment on is a spectacle of difference, uniqueness, individuality, and, yes, conformity. But it is the differences that draw our attention.

Todd, who is a head taller than any of the other children, easily outdistances his classmates to the kickball diamond to tap first for "work-up." There he waits triumphantly for the others who finally assemble, including Mike, whose short legs and pudgy frame put him at a disadvantage. Mike, however, has the game ball which he proudly carries with him as a result of being selected ball monitor by Mrs. Thompson because of his consistently good behavior in the classroom.

Susan heads for the drinking fountain and is about to take a drink when she is shoved aside by Dora, who yells, "I'm first!" Susan steps passively back and waits until Dora quenches her thirst and saunters away. Susan watches as Dora bolts into a hopscotch game nearby and announces her intention to play. One of the girls in the group appeals to Mrs. Thompson to stop Dora from interrupting the game. A group of boys approach the fountain. They are laughing about Paul's pet white rat which had escaped from the cage that morning and was still loose somewhere in the classroom. Mark walks away from the group, not wishing to hear any more about it since he is scared that Paul's pet may yet turn up near his desk. Soon Susan is left standing alone. She moves toward the door to wait for the recess bell to ring.

Bill has brought his arithmetic test paper out to the playground with him. He proudly displays the "very good" comment, which Mrs. Thompson had written on it, to his friend, Henry, who shrugs his shoulders but appears impressed. Henry hadn't been able to do most of the problems on the test. A shriek of laughter goes up over on the ball diamond. Mike, who was up, has run for the ball, attempting to kick it, and has missed it altogether. The ball has rolled on by, and Mike has taken a spill. He is all right, but the players whoop it up at his expense. Todd helps Mike up and the game resumes. This time the pitcher rolls a slow ball and Mike makes a respectable kick that gets him safely to first base accompanied by "Atta boy, Mike!" shouted by Todd.

Mrs. Thompson watches the passing parade of freckled faces, tousled hair, shifting groups, random activity, and listens to the buzzing of voices punctuated with an occasional shout or screech. Yes, her children are different; both in the classroom and here on the playground, where their differences are perhaps more visible in certain respects. Over the year she has become well acquainted enough with the class so that she can readily engage in an informal, armchair ranking of their differences along a number of dimensions.

In terms of classroom behavior, Mike was the model student, eager to learn and cooperate. There is no question but that Dora with her bullying tactics and disregard for classroom rules and the rights of the other children was the most serious behavior problem. With respect to enthusiasm for new experiences and variety of interests, Paul with his endless collection of animals and many hobbies was outstanding, whereas Mark was just the opposite. He was absent frequently, avoided participation in class activities whenever possible, often daydreamed, and appeared to have many fears. Todd was clearly the class leader on the dimension of social adjustment. All the children liked him and admired his good nature and physical prowess. Susan had not made a single friend over the school year and was largely ignored by her classmates. Her shyness and withdrawal from all group situations placed her at the bottom of the class socially. Mrs. Thompson saw Bill as her brightest student, with Henry having the most difficulty keeping up in his work. Henry was very easily distracted, slow in grasping new material, and poor in handwriting. These were only a few of the dimensions Mrs. Thompson could consider. Physical size, general health, eyesight, hearing, stature, motor coordination, and language proficiency were some of the other possibilities.

Mrs. Thompson's third grade class actually consists of children who fall at various positions along physical, behavioral, and academic dimensions and who are far more heterogeneous as a class group than the designation "third grade" suggests. Some children may occupy rather extreme positions along behavioral and academic dimensions in contrast to the rest of the class. As Mrs. Thompson mulls over such children as Susan and Henry, she may find herself labeling them "emotionally disturbed," "socially maladjusted," or "borderline mentally retarded." In so doing, she would be placing them on dimensions of exceptionality that exist in the field of special education for purposes of categorizing differences found among children.

Individuals who are limited along dimensions of social adjustment, vision, hearing, physical-motor coordination, speech and language, and learning efficiency are called "exceptional children." Along the dimension of intelligence, children falling at either extreme are considered exceptional. That is, such children are particularly unique or "exceptional" along dimensions on which all children vary and which have particular relevance to learning and success in school.

Just when a position along a particular dimension leaves the range of difference found in regular classrooms such as Mrs. Thompson's and become truly "exceptional," resulting in a label and a possible special education program separate from the regular classroom, is easier to determine along some dimensions than others. For example, a blind, deaf, or crippled child is distinctly different from any child with problems of vision, hearing, or motor coordination in Mrs. Thompson's classroom. There would be little question regarding the need for special provision for such children (e.g., braille instruction, hearing aids, orthopedic braces) in school. In a similar manner, children unable to learn to care for their bodily functions, avoid hazards, and retain basic information would not be enrolled in a regular third grade classroom. But as we consider children who differ in terms of social adjustment and rate and efficiency of learning, the distinction between the uniqueness of children in Mrs. Thompson's class and those called "exceptional" is more difficult to define.

This book is about exceptional children who fall outside the range of differences found in Mrs. Thompson's class as well as about children like Henry, Susan, Mark, and Dora who might be found in any regular classroom in the United States today. All these children represent a valuable resource to our country, a resource that may be lost if the school does not find ways to help them develop and utilize their true learning potential. This is what the field of special education is all about. It is an extension of the good education we want to provide for all children to those who fall along the lower and upper ranges of critical dimensions related to learning.

This book is concerned with nine categories of children for whom an extension of good education is being attempted in the United States today. We will be concerned with their specific differences as well as with the problems they share in common that necessitate this extension of education. These nine categories of children are:

1. Emotionally disturbed children
2. Children with learning disabilities
3. Mentally retarded children
4. Socially and economically disadvantaged children
5. Visually handicapped children
6. Hearing handicapped children
7. Children with speech handicaps
8. Physically handicapped children
9. Gifted children

Traditional introductory texts in the field of special education devote a separate chapter to each category of exceptionality, often written by separate authors. What emerges is a separate consideration of each type of child that is in line with the practice of giving separate teaching credentials to teachers in the field and maintaining separate school programs for many of the children. This book aims at a collective orientation that cuts across the separateness traditionally found in other special education texts. This collective approach is not an ivory-tower notion undertaken for the sake of scholarship or theoretical inquiry, but a reflection of the times in which we live, which simply are moving us from isolating those who are different and toward including them more and more into the mainstream of the school and the society.

This text is conceived as offering a kind of transitional journey for the individual interested in special education today. This individual may be a beginning student commencing the study of children with learning and behavioral problems, a student in special education, a teacher working with such children in the school today, a student in teacher-training, a teacher like Mrs. Thompson concerned with so-called normal children but confronted with a myriad of differences among her students, an individual studying or practicing educational psychology, or an advanced student pursuing the field of psychology or education of exceptional children on a graduate level. For some of these individuals, we will be introducing the field for the first time, and for some we hopefully will be shifting their already established orientation toward exceptional children.

The transitional journey we will undertake begins in Part I with two chapters devoted to delineating our point of embarkation and considering where the field of special education has come from and what its traditional approaches and practices are. Chapter 1 is devoted to an historical overview of the attitudes toward and treatment of handicapped individuals during the past 3,000 years. Chapter 2 consists of a categorical presentation of nine categories of exceptional children that in many ways represents a condensation of much of the content found in traditional introductory texts in the field. In Part II, the transitional journey actually begins as we combine children in the nine categories into a single category as "learners" and discuss their similarities and differences across four psycho-social dimensions — flexibility, sociality, intelligence, and individualization. These broad dimensions allow consideration of the exceptional individual in relation to the total environment and set the stage for our narrower and more educationally relevant consideration of his characteristics in the learning situation and the school.

In Part III, we move into the classroom and examine the exceptional child as a learner on five levels of learning competence — attention, response-order, exploratory, social, and mastery. We also consider the importance of curriculum tasks, the instructional conditions under which they are presented, and consequences in his learning. In Part IV, we summarize a number of current issues confronting special education today and then consider a specific public school program for dealing with them.

Although we will be reducing categorical "separateness" throughout the book, we will acknowledge the established labels applied to exceptional children in our discussion by means of the index band on the margin. This index-band system will preserve a traditional framework while we gradually de-emphasize categorization in the content.

In essence, our transitional journey is directed toward three goals:

1. A conceptual and organizational rearrangement of knowledge and practice in the field of special education
2. A shift in point of view regarding exceptional children, which considers them first and foremost learners at varying levels of competence and which recognizes the similarities as well as differences that exist among categories
3. A merging of special and regular education with respect to increased understanding of all children who are different along critical dimensions relating to learning

In the course of our journey, we will maintain a link with tradition, yet, hopefully, we will have opened up new avenues for continued exploration by the time we reach our destination at the close of this text.

PART I

Background Dimensions

Jean-Marc-Gaspard Itard
1774 - 1838

Jean-Marc-Gaspard Itard
1774 - 1838

CHAPTER 1

Historical Origins

The roots of the field of special education can be traced to the beginning of man himself. They are linked to primitive times when men first became aware of those whose appearance and behavior differed from the expectations of the majority. Over the course of history, such differences have been reacted to in a variety of ways that have ranged from the cruel to the humane. Those who were different have been destroyed, tortured, exorcised, sterilized, ignored, exiled, exploited, and even considered divine. Their problems have been crudely explained in terms of superstition and levels of scientific understanding. They have been pitied, cared for, categorized, and accepted. And, finally, they have been educated. But in reviewing the history of attitudes toward, and the treatment of, exceptional individuals, we must initially leave the context of "education." This represents a fairly recent consideration. Long before the handicapped were understood, protected, accepted, and given the benefits of an education, they had to cope with survival in a world where the harshness of both nature and men threatened their very existence.

Special education in contemporary American society has evolved from man's basest to his highest nature, from his most irrational to his most rational behavior, and from his most ignorant to his most enlightened understanding of himself. As a starting point in the transitional journey of this book toward re-examination and reorganization of the field, we will review attitudes toward and treatment of the exceptional individual that are a part of man's history over the past three thousand years.

Our discussion will focus on four historical determiners that

9

are particularly relevant to the plight of the handicapped over the centuries.   The first determiner is the *threat to survival* due to harsh treatment by the physical and social environment.   Second, the determiner of *superstition* in relation to the appearance and behavior of the handicapped is of major significance.   Our third determiner, *science,* the direct opposite of the second, refers to the natural, lawful, and objective approach to exceptionality.   Fourth is the determiner of *service*, the direct opposite of the first, survival encompasses the care, humane treatment, and societal acceptance afforded the handicapped.   These four determiners are set forth in Table 1 with the major aspects of each listed.

Historically, we will follow a chronological order based on the following major periods:

Primitive and Ancient   3000 B.C.–500 B.C.
Greek and Roman   500 B.C.–A.D. 400
Middle Ages   A.D. 400–1500
Sixteenth and Seventeenth Centuries
Eighteenth Century
Nineteenth Century
Twentieth Century

During each period, we shall discuss the four historical determiners of the treatment of the handicapped using a swinging pendulum analogy.   History does not record an orderly progression of positive trends in relation to the treatment of individuals who were different, but rather it displays a highly variable and widely discrepant range of trends during most historical periods.   What accounted for the movement of the pendulum in relation to the treatment of exceptional individuals?   It was determined by nature,

Table 1: Historical Determiners of the Treatment of the Handicapped

SURVIVAL	SUPERSTITION	SCIENCE	SERVICE
harsh physical environment	sacrifice	natural explanation	exploitation
infanticide	witchburning	categorization	humane treatment
eugenics	torture	objective study	custodial care
harsh treatment	trephining	psychological theory	education
exile	exorcism	mental measurement	societal acceptance
	demonology	research	
	worship		

irrational and rational beliefs, social and economic conditions, religion, law, and, finally, by knowledge.   It also was determined by certain individuals whose convictions and contributions during critical moments of history had far-reaching effects, some negative and some positive.

Categorization of the handicapped is a fairly recent practice. Throughout most of history, perhaps the only categories that mattered were the weak, the odd, and the poor.   Children received little special attention or consideration separate from adults.   Most physically defective infants and children died early in life due either to infanticide or their inability to cope with the rigors of the environment.   Those who were peculiar in their behavior were treated no differently than adults.   As we shall see, the child has only recently become an individual in his own right, physically and emotionally. Most of our discussion in this chapter concerns the plight of individuals subjected to demands for survival and adaptation by the environment and judged, accepted, or rejected by others regardless of age or size.

In the following discussion, we will present the historical determiner dimension in relation to each time period and illustrate the range of the pendulum swings that took place during that time. In the figures accompanying each historical period, a solid line will indicate a marked trend, a broken line a moderate trend, and a dotted line a slight trend.   We will discuss the attitudes toward, and treatment of, exceptional individuals related to the positions of the pendulum and the agents responsible for its movement.

PRIMITIVE AND ANCIENT PERIOD (3000 B.C. to 500 B.C.)

PH

During primitive and ancient times, the pendulum largely swung between survival and superstition.   The natural elements, demonology, and religious beliefs were the primary agents of movement.   In the earliest primitive societies, physical abnormalities were not perhaps known beyond infancy since most tribes permitted the killing of a newborn if he was sickly or if the mother had died during the birth process.   Infants born under unlucky circumstances might also be killed.

For children who survived, adult life began at six or eight years of age when they left the family, set up their own huts, and took wives within only a few years.   The rigor of the natural environment soon eliminated the weak or infirm.   Courage and physical strength were the requisites for survival, not mental agility; and

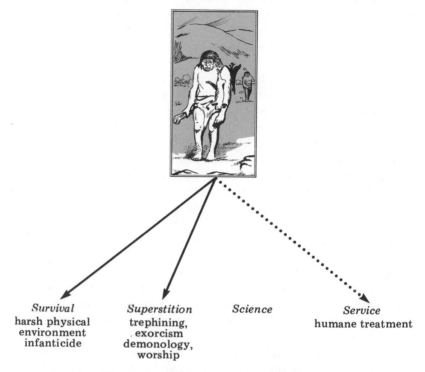

Survival	*Superstition*	*Science*	*Service*
harsh physical	trephining,		humane treatment
environment	exorcism		
infanticide	demonology,		
	worship		

Figure 1: Primitive and Ancient Period

primitive languages were largely limited to the sensual and particular and were uniformly poor in general or abstract terms (Durant, 1954).

In cases in which primitive man was physically sound yet became deranged and behaved differently from members of his community, he might be feared and considered the possessor of a supernatural power. If he was possessed by a good spirit, then he was naturally admired and revered; but if the spirit was considered evil, the man might be indulged in order to appease the spirit and prevent its revenge. This indulgence and reverence lasted only until man thought of driving out evil spirits through ceremonial rites conducted by individuals of high station, such as priests (Zilboorg & Henry, 1941).

The earliest "psychiatry" was practiced by Stone Age cavemen some half-million years ago. In cases of mental illness associated with severe headaches or convulsive disorders, a crude operation called *trephining* was often performed. A circular area of the skull was chipped away with a stone instrument, thus permitting the evil spirit that was responsible to escape.   Since it appears that some patients survived such treatment, the operation might have actually relieved a certain amount of pressure on the brain.

Early writings of the Chinese, Egyptians, and Greeks reflect a belief that mental disorders were the result of demons that had taken possession of an individual.   Among the ancient Hebrews, such disorders were thought to represent the wrath and punishment of God.   The primary treatment consisted of *exorcism,* an attempt to drive the spirit from the possessed through prayer, incantations, noisemaking, purgatives, flogging, or starving (Coleman, 1972).   It also appears that in some parts of China the tradition of kindness and understanding in relation to the mentally ill existed (Zilboorg & Henry, 1941).

The Babylonian world was filled with hostile demons who might hide in strange crannies or slip through doors and pounce on their victims in the form of illness or madness when the sacred protection of the gods was absent.   Giants, dwarfs, cripples, and particularly women sometimes had the power to turn "the evil eye" on their enemies, who might partially protect themselves with magic amulets, talismans, and charms.   Early Babylonian writings were largely devoted to describing magic formulas for eliminating demons and avoiding evil (Durant, 1954).

The ancient Egyptians were unique for forbidding infanticide; parents guilty of this crime were required to hold the dead child in their arms for three days and nights (Durant, 1966).   The Egyptians also believed profoundly in immortality and often engaged the services of blind individuals as professional mourners over the dead (Sigerist, 1943).

Thus early man accepted, rejected, and even worshipped the individual who was different in appearance or behavior, and he developed an elaborate demonological system to explain as well as treat such differences.

GREEK AND ROMAN PERIOD (500 B.C. to A.D. 400)

During the Greek and Roman period, the pendulum swung largely between survival and superstition, with the notable exception that attempts at scientific understanding, medical treatment, and humanitarian reform appeared for a significant, if brief, moment in history.

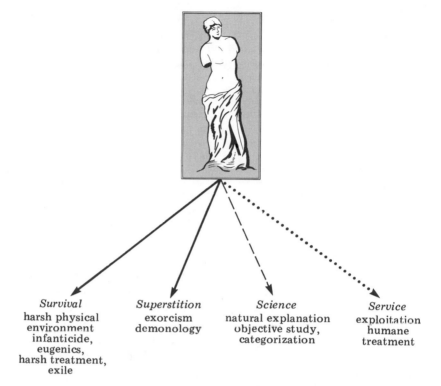

Survival	Superstition	Science	Service
harsh physical environment infanticide, eugenics, harsh treatment, exile	exorcism demonology	natural explanation objective study, categorization	exploitation humane treatment

Figure 2: Greek and Roman Period

The agents for moving the pendulum momentarily away from superstition and demonology were the scholars, philosophers, and physicians of Greece and Rome.

Ruthless eugenics were practiced in the Greek state of Sparta. Every child was vulnerable to his father's right of infanticide and to the judgment of a state council. Infants who appeared defective were thrown from a cliff on Mt. Taygetus and left to die on the jagged rocks below. The "survival of the fittest" doctrine of the state continued through early life, with Spartan infants experiencing much discomfort and exposure and male children at age seven entering a military regiment and school where they had to endure severe punishment and discipline (Durant, 1966).

The Greeks believed that mental illness was caused by the gods taking the mind away. Treatment of the mentally ill was attempted at the Aesculapian Temples where religious ceremonies were conducted calling upon the gods to appear and produce a miraculous cure (Zilboorg & Henry, 1941). All sickness was considered the result of possession by an alien spirit, and ceremonies of purification were considered essential. From time to time, homes, temples, camps, and even entire cities were "purified" by water, smoke, or fire (Durant, 1966).

During the fourth and fifth centuries B.C., Hippocrates moved the pendulum from its position of mythology and demonology in Greece toward scientific understanding and treatment of many exceptional individuals. He challenged the belief that illness was the result of the anger of the gods. He also dismissed the notion that epilepsy, considered "the sacred disease," was divinely caused. According to Hippocrates:

> It thus appears to me to be in no way more divine, nor more sacred than other diseases, but has a natural cause from which it originates like other afflictions. . . . If you cut open the head, you will find the brain humid, full of sweat, and smelling badly. And in this way you may see that it is not a god which injures the body, but disease (Zilboorg & Henry, 1941, pp. 43–44).

Plato, a contemporary of Hippocrates, suggested that the care of the mentally ill be assumed by the family:

> If anyone is insane, let him not be seen openly in the city, but let the relatives of such a person watch over him in the best manner they know of; and if they are negligent, let them pay a fine (Coleman, 19 2, p. 28).

In addition, Plato supported the practice of eugenics in his *Republic:*

> As soon as children are born, they will be taken in charge by officers, appointed for the purpose. The children of the better parents they will carry to the crèche to be reared in the care of nurses living apart in a certain quarter of the city. Those of inferior parents and any children of the rest that are born defective will be hidden away, in some appropriate manner, that must be kept secret (Cornford, 1945, p. 107).

Plato also advocated identifying children with superior intelligence at an early age and providing specialized instruction in science, philosophy, and metaphysics for them. These most intelligent and knowledgeable citizens would become leaders of the state. Plato felt survival of Greek democracy was contingent on the selection and education of gifted individuals for leadership (Kirk, 1972).

Infanticide continued to be practiced in Athens; infants who were of doubtful parentage or who were weak or deformed were left in large earthenware vessels near a temple where they would either perish from exposure or animal attack or be rescued for adoption by passersby. When a child was born, it was laid at the father's feet. If he acknowledged the child by lifting it up in his arms, he accepted the responsibility for retaining and nourishing it. If he did not pick it up, the child would be exposed to the elements (Durant, 1966).

Aristotle considered mental illness as a physical disorder and rejected the notion that psychological factors such as frustration and conflict could cause mental disorders (Coleman, 1972).

Even while agents of movement such as Hippocrates and Aristotle influenced the pendulum swing during this time, powerful forces lingering from man's primitive past and belief in demons were destined to periodically exert the dominant influence on the movement of the pendulum. Thus, the conflict over natural versus supernatural causes for physical and mental disorders was to continue for almost two thousand years.

The Roman practice of infanticide permitted the father to expose to death any child who was deformed or female. Eight days after birth, the child formally became a member of the most basic Roman institution, the patriarchal family, by means of a solemn ceremony. The father, however, had continuing power of life, death, and sale into slavery over his children. Abandonment of children was a widespread practice; Seneca records that professional beggars often collected such children, deliberately maimed them, and then used them to solicit alms from charitable passersby (Barclay, 1959). If this practice was truly profitable, it suggests that a compassionate attitude toward deformity must have existed among some of the Roman populace. The well-to-do Romans also began the practice of accepting "natural fools" or imbeciles into their homes, where they functioned as buffoons or objects of amusement at social gatherings (Wallin, 1955).

History suggests that at least four Roman rulers were mentally ill — Nero, Commodus, Heliogabalus, and Caligula (Wallin, 1955). Commodus was known periodically to gather crippled individuals together and use them for target practice with a bow and arrow (Durant, 1944).

The movement of the pendulum toward scientific understanding initiated by the Greeks continued in the days of the Roman Empire, although new and original contributions from the Romans themselves did not appear until the middle of the first century B.C. At that time, Asclepiades advocated humane treatment of the mentally ill including prescriptions of hydrotherapy, massage, sunshine, exercise, and abstinence from meat. He also violently objected to bleeding and placement of the deranged in dark cells and dungeons

(Zilboorg & Henry, 1941; Durant, 1944). In contrast, Celsus recommended harsh measures for controlling and treating the mentally ill individual:

> When he has said or done anything wrong, he must be chastised by hunger, chains, and fetters. He must be made to attend and to learn something that he may remember, for thus it will happen that by degrees he will be led to consider what he is doing (Zilboorg & Henry, 1941, p. 70).

Celsus also advocated keeping some patients in total darkness, shaving their heads, anointing them with rose oil, and the use of bleeding and morphine-like medications.

Aretaeus, in the first century A.D., was perhaps two thousand years ahead of his time when, in describing various disturbed mental states, he paid particular attention to what patients thought and felt. Soranus, in the second century, also considered the thoughts and feelings of the mentally ill important. He attacked those who placed patients in darkness, deprived them of food and water, and treated them as "ferocious beasts." His methods of treatment are handed down to us in detail:

> Maniacs must be placed in a moderately lighted room which is of moderate temperature and where tranquility is not disturbed by any noise. No paintings should adorn the walls. . . . Much tact and discretion should be employed in directing attention to their faults; sometimes misbehavior should be overlooked or met with indulgence; at other times it requires a slightly better reprimand and an explanation of the advantage derived from proper conduct (Zilboorg & Henry, 1941, pp. 81–82).

In his therapeutic procedure, Soranus reported that the sound of falling water often induced sleep and that warm sponges applied to the eyelids might induce relaxation. He also described a beginning type of psychotherapy in which laborers should be engaged in conversation about cultivation of the field and sailors in discussions of navigation (Zilboorg & Henry, 1941).

We see in the work of Aretaeus and Soranus a remarkable advancement in understanding and treating the mentally ill; but it did not persist or gain permanent acceptance. The Greek and Roman period is well suited to our pendulum swinging analogy. During this time, almost the full range of man's attitude toward, and treatment of, the mentally ill was apparent. The striking but tragically brief positions of naturalism and humanitarianism achieved by the Greeks and Romans were in marked contrast to the demonological traditions that were maintained. These traditions were to overshadow and dominate as agents of movement of the pendulum during the period of the Middle Ages.

MIDDLE AGES (A.D. 400 to 1500)

During the Middle Ages, the pendulum range again covers the extremes of our historical determiner dimension. With the rise of deep religious conviction throughout the world, the feebleminded and physically handicapped received more humanitarian care but the causes of deviate behavior were increasingly believed to be the influence of Satan himself. Thus, religion and religious beliefs become the major agents for movement of the pendulum during this period.

   The agonies brought about by war, poverty, and barbarism turned man toward seeking the hope of happiness beyond the grave and away from the thousand years of rationalism that had been

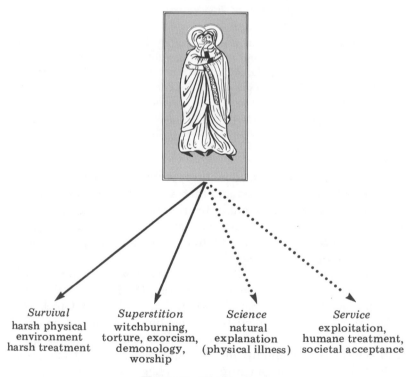

Survival	*Superstition*	*Science*	*Service*
harsh physical environment harsh treatment	witchburning, torture, exorcism, demonology, worship	natural explanation (physical illness)	exploitation, humane treatment, societal acceptance

Figure 3: Middle Ages

developing. In the early fifth century A.D., St. Augustine was a representative spokesman for the time. He believed that man's existence was due to original sin and that human will was from birth inclined to evil that could only be turned to good by a gratuitous act of God (Durant, 1950).

The influence of Christianity introduced commiseration, solicitude, and care for many handicapped individuals. The mentally defective often gained prestige as court fools or jesters. They were even exalted as "heavenly infants" or "infants of the good God" who enjoyed the special favor of the Almighty and whose jabberings were regarded as heavenly communication. The house in which a mentally defective was born was considered divinely blessed, and in Europe such individuals were often accorded special privileges and allowed to roam unmolested (Wallin, 1955). During the course of the Middle Ages, however, the treatment of the mentally defective became quite variable: they were favored as "innocents," tolerated as fools, or persecuted as witches (Doll, 1962).

The mentally ill, on the other hand, suffered uniformly from the new theology and the inevitable return to demonology and the many ancient superstitions that accompanied it. Hostility to science grew intense; psychiatry became the study of the ways and means of the devil and his cohorts. St. Gregory of Tours proclaimed that he who was worthy of "celestial" cures needed no help from "terrestrial" doctors for treatment of mental illness. In order to combat the evils of the devil, it was felt that his ways must be studied and signs of his influence determined. One such sign was based on *stigmata diaboli*, established in the third century. When an individual was suspected of being under the influence of Satan, his body would be pricked with a needle by inquisitors who hoped to find the insensitive area that was thought to be a vulnerable entry point for the devil and proof of his influence.

In Western Europe from the sixth to the eleventh centuries, the medieval mind was filled with superstitious beliefs involving trolls, elves, giants, fairies, goblins, gnomes, ogres, banshees, dragons, and vampires. Dead men walked the air as ghosts; men whose souls were sold to the devil roamed the woods as werewolves; and the souls of children dead before baptism haunted the marshes as "will-o'-the-wisps." Herbs, stones, amulets, rings, and gems were worn as protection against devils, and belief in witchcraft was next to universal (Durant, 1950).

Although the mentally ill were considered possessed by evil spirits, widespread torture and mass executions of "witches" and "sorceresses" did not appear for some time (Zilboorg & Henry,

ED

1941). Initially, prayer and religious ceremonies were seen as the logical curative approach. Gradually, the beliefs that physical illnesses were natural and that mental illnesses were mostly supernatural began to gain acceptance. To effect differential diagnosis, a passage from the Bible might be shouted into the ear of a patient having convulsions. A response was considered proof that the illness was the result of demoniacal possession because the holy words had frightened the demon. If, however, the patient remained unaffected, the illness was seen as natural (Zilboorg & Henry, 1941).

Treatment of the mentally ill, many of whom were abandoned by their families, was left largely to priests, and monasteries became refuges for many deranged individuals. There they were often treated with kindness and mild forms of exorcism such as "laying on of hands."

The Arab world, on the other hand, had inherited predominantly Greek scientific thought. Avicenna in the eleventh century stands as one of the rare enlightened individuals of this era who approached mental illness in a rational and remarkably creative manner. The case below shows his unique treatment of a mental patient:

> A certain prince . . . was afflicted with melancholia, and suffered from the delusion that he was a cow. . . . He would low like a cow, causing annoyance to everyone . . . crying, "Kill me so that a good stew may be made of my flesh." Finally . . . he would eat nothing. . . . Avicenna was persuaded to take the case. First of all he sent a message to the patient bidding him be of good cheer because the butcher was coming to slaughter him, whereat . . . the sick man rejoiced. Some time afterwards, Avicenna, holding a knife in his hand, entered the sickroom saying, "Where is this cow that I may kill it?" The patient lowed like a cow to indicate where he was. By Avicenna's orders he was laid on the ground, bound hand and foot. Avicenna then felt him all over and said, "He is too lean and not ready to be killed; he must be fattened." Then they offered him suitable food of which he now partook eagerly, and gradually he gained strength, got rid of his delusion, and was completely cured (Browne, 1921, pp. 88–89).

And in Europe, a bright spot was the shrine at Gheel in Belgium, where pilgrimages from every part of the civilized world were organized for the mentally sick. Many of the pilgrims remained in Gheel and lived with the inhabitants, who came to consider it a natural thing to accept them into their homes (Coleman, 1972). Throughout most of Western Europe, however, as theological beliefs concerning the cause of mental illness became more fully developed, mildness and gentle treatment gave way to the extreme measures of flogging, starving, chaining, immersion in hot water, and torture, all designed to punish the devil residing within the deranged individual.

Thus the stage was set for the cruel persecution not only of those who were deranged or who differed in religious belief but also of those who were different in any way — those who looked, acted, or thought differently.   The pendulum swing back toward the harsh treatment that had begun in the Middle Ages was to reach its most devastating positions during a portion of the next period.

SIXTEENTH AND SEVENTEENTH CENTURIES

The pendulum continued to swing during the next two centuries, beginning with a backward motion but moving in time to positions

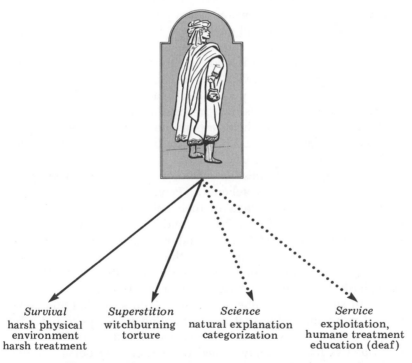

Survival	*Superstition*	*Science*	*Service*
harsh physical environment harsh treatment	witchburning torture	natural explanation categorization	exploitation, humane treatment education (deaf)

Figure 4: Sixteenth and Seventeenth Centuries

of humanitarianism, reform, and education. The agents of movement were more varied during this period than during the previous period. Initially moving in a climate of religious persecution, the pendulum gradually fell under the control of enlightened individuals whose increase in number resulted in the beginnings of more lasting hope and understanding for the exceptional individual.

On December 9, 1484, Pope Innocent VIII appointed two Dominican Brothers, Johann Spreager and Heinrich Kraemer, as "Inquisitors of Heretical Depravities." Their charge was to investigate all persons considered heretics without regard to rank or high estate. To bolster their position, the priests authored a text on witchcraft, *Malleus Maleficarum (The Witches' Hammer)*, which declared that anyone who did not believe in witches was either in honest error or polluted with heresy, described various types of witches and how they might be identified, and presented legal procedures for examining and sentencing witches. The book, published sometime between 1487 and 1489, went through nineteen editions during the next three-hundred years. It served as the keynote of the law for over two centuries and otherwise enlightened men endorsed its doctrine.

Although not all who were accused of heresy under the provisions of the *Malleus* were mentally ill, hundreds of thousands of deranged individuals fell victim to it because most such persons were considered witches, sorceresses, or bewitched. There were few arguments that could hold up against the book. Man was viewed as responsible for whatever he did. If he succumbed to an illness that perverted his perception, imagination, and intellectual functions, he did so of his own free will. Man chose to succumb to the devil and must be held responsible for his choice. He must be punished, eliminated, and his soul set free again. His body must be burned (Zilboorg & Henry, 1941).

The Spanish Inquisition was a well-organized, widespread attack on heresy and witchcraft. People were required by an "edict of faith" to inform against their neighbors, friends, and relatives. Torture was often used to establish guilt where evidence was uncertain. Girls of thirteen and women of eighty were subjected to torture on the rack, and the ultimate punishment was burning at the stake where crowds showed little sympathy and often hostility toward the victims (Durant, 1957).

In such an atmosphere of almost total suspicion and superstition, it is remarkable that any dissenting voice spoke out. But Reginald Scot, who wrote a book entitled *Discovery of Witchcraft*, published in 1584, daringly denied the existence of demons, devils, and evil spirits as the cause of mental disorders:

ED

> You must know that the effects of sickness on men, and still more on women, are almost unbelievable. Some of these persons imagine, confess, and maintain that they are witches and are capable of performing extraordinary miracles through the arts of witchcraft; others, due to the same mental disorders, imagine strange and impossible things (Castiglioni, 1946, p. 253).

King James I of England, however, personally condemned Scot's position and prolonged the course of demonology by ordering the book seized and burned (Coleman, 1972). Unfortunately, Scot's work had little effect as a result (Durant, 1957).

The tradition of the *Malleus Maleficarum* did not die easily or quietly. The Puritans carried it into the Commonwealth of Massachusetts, and, although the last witch was beheaded in Germany in 1775 and the last in Switzerland in 1782, as late as the twentieth century — in 1928 — a Reverend Montagne Summers, who translated the *Malleus Maleficarum*, supported its doctrine:

> There can be no doubt that had this most excellent tribunal continued to enjoy its full prerogative and the full exercise of its salutary powers, the world at large would be in a far happier and far more orderly position today (Zilboorg & Henry, 1941, p. 154).

During the seventeenth and much of the eighteenth centuries, science and medicine gave up preoccupation with the human mind and left it to the theologian and philosopher. Since the demonological tradition was still in existence, the physician avoided the perplexing problem of separating body and mind or relating them in attempts to explain mental illness. It was generally believed that a faulty functioning of body juices, particularly in the blood and brain, was the basic cause of mental illness, and bloodletting was the treatment of choice.

During this period, Herman Boerhaave wrote:

> If melancholy increases so far that from the great Motion of the Liquid of the Brain, the Patient be thrown into a wild Fury, it is called Madness. The greatest Remedy for it is to throw the Patient unwarily into the Sea and keep him under Water so long as he can possibly bear without being quite stifled (Zilboorg & Henry, 1941, p. 298).

A special twirling stool also was used to spin the patient into unconsciousness, thus rearranging the brain and restoring normalcy.

But the treatment of most mentally ill individuals had changed little since some two thousand years before, when Celsus

ED

MR

HH

had recommended chains as a useful form of restraint. Until the close of the eighteenth century, there were no real hospitals for the mentally ill. Custodial quarters, such as St. Mary of Bethlehem (Bedlam) in London, existed in 1547, but little actual treatment was provided. The most violent patients were put on public display for one penny a look; the more harmless inmates were allowed to seek charity on the streets (Coleman, 1972). Many mentally ill individuals wandered through the countryside seeking shelter in stables and pigsties. They were mocked and beaten and if apprehended were placed with murderers and other criminals in chains, and although the criminal served his term and was released, the mentally sick might never be set free.

In the sixteenth and early seventeenth centuries, special educators of the deaf appeared. Pedro Ponce de Leon taught reading, writing, arithmetic, astronomy, Spanish, Latin, and Greek to several deaf pupils from noble families. He apparently used an oral method of instruction. In 1620, Juan Bonet published a system of instruction for the deaf based on finger spelling which was the precursor of later manual alphabets. Also during this time, attempts were made to describe mental retardation and mental illness from a more psychological and educational point of view. In Fitz-Herbert's *New Nature Brevium*, a mental retardate is defined as follows:

> And he who shall be said to be a sot [i.e., simpleton] and idiot from his birth is such a person who cannot account or remember 20 pence, nor can tell who was his father or mother, nor how old he is, etc. so as it may appear that he hath no understanding or reason of what shall be for his profit nor what for his loss. But if he hath understanding, that he know and understand his letters, and do read by teaching or information of another man, then it seemeth he is not a sot nor a natural idiot (Hilliard, 1965, pp. 2–3).

In 1690, John Locke attempted to distinguish mental retardation from mental illness:

> Herein seems to lie the difference between idiots and madmen; that madmen put wrong ideas together and reason from them; but idiots make very few or no propositions and reason scarce at all (Doll, 1962).

Swinburne, in 1591, proposed a number of tests to diagnose mental retardation, such as measuring a yard of cloth and naming the days of the week (Hilliard, 1965).

During the sixteenth century, Suleiman the Magnificent searched the Turkish Empire for gifted Christian youth to provide with education in the Moslem faith, war, art, science, and philosophy. He conducted regular surveys and educated many superior individuals. Within a generation after the start of this widespread educational program for the gifted, the Ottoman empire became a great power in art, science, culture, and war and even attempted to conquer all of Europe (Sumption & Luecking, 1960).

In 1601, the Elizabethan Poor Law began to separate the poor afflicted, and unemployed or unemployable from the community and had them segregated in workhouses. The result was an increasing isolation of the mentally retarded from contact with normal life and a growing lack of understanding of their problems by the community that banished them (Hilliard, 1965). Jonathan Swift, a literary voice of the seventeenth and eighteenth centuries, was shocked by the number of child beggars on the streets of Dublin, and in 1729 wrote a satirical yet tragically reflective paper regarding the poverty of his time:

> *A Modest Proposal for Prescribing the Children of Poor People from Being a Burden to Their Parents or Country.*
> I have been assured that a young, healthy child, well nursed, is, at a year old, a most delicious, nourishing, and wholesome food, whether stewed, roasted, baked, or boiled; and I make no doubt that it will equally serve in a fricasee or ragout. I do therefore humbly offer it to public consideration, that of the hundred and twenty thousand children already computed, twenty thousand may be reserved for breed, whereof only one-fourth part to be males. . . .
>
> Some persons of desponding spirit are in great concern about the vast number of poor people who are aged, diseased, or maimed; and I have been desired to employ my thoughts what course may be taken to ease the nation of so grievous an encumbrance. But I am not in the least pain upon that matter; because it is very well known that they are every day dying and rotting, by cold and famine, and filth and vermin, as fast as can be reasonably expected (Durant & Durant, 1963, p. 361).

Although irrational and mystical beliefs were so deeply ingrained in men that the pendulum never left positions of witch burning, demonology, exploitation, and neglect, the sixteenth and seventeenth centuries saw an emerging trend toward scientific explanation, humanitarianism, concern of the state for the welfare of the individual, and care and education. These trends become more apparent as we move into the eighteenth century.

EIGHTEENTH CENTURY

The pendulum made much wider swings toward positions of acceptance of exceptional individuals during the eighteenth century. Witch burning finally ceased, and the world of demons was gradually overshadowed by a concern with the rights of man. The agents of movement were rationalism and enlightenment on the one hand and violent revolution on the other. Also, the contributions of certain bold individuals continued to exert influence on the positions of the pendulum.

The plight of children in the eighteenth century deserves special mention. Fifty-nine percent of all children born in London during this time died before reaching the age of five; sixty-four percent were dead before age ten. Many babies were abandoned at birth; those who were rescued and who survived were given to nurses at public expense and later placed in workhouses. Careless-

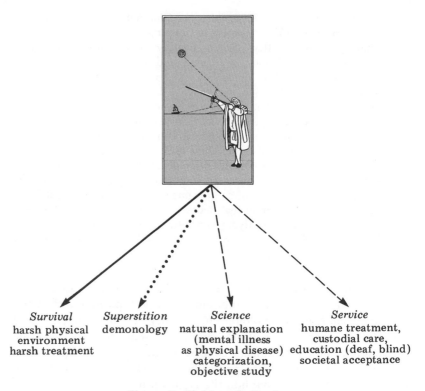

Survival	*Superstition*	*Science*	*Service*
harsh physical environment harsh treatment	demonology	natural explanation (mental illness as physical disease) categorization, objective study	humane treatment, custodial care, education (deaf, blind) societal acceptance

Figure 5: Eighteenth Century

ness of midwives and mothers caused a large number of physical deformities. From 1771 to 1777, 32,000 children were admitted to the Paris Foundling Hospital at the rate of eighty-nine per day. It is reported that eighty percent of these children died before completing their first year. Voltaire estimated that the average longevity of human life during his time was only twenty-two years.

The Industrial Revolution brought many women and children into factories as unskilled laborers. There were no safeguards for a child's welfare or his life, and work demands were often extreme. Discipline in the factories was maintained by blows and kicks. Many children were deformed as a result of heavy labor or accidents and some even killed themselves (Durant & Durant, 1965). The Ulster Institution for the Deaf and Dumb in Belfast recorded that "a little mute in his eighth year, a day scholar, was unfortunately killed at one of the factories before he could have known the revealed will of God" (Pritchard, 1963, p. 7).

A few men of conscience spoke out about the exploitation of child labor, but since conservatives of the day frowned on universal education, because it might lead to a surplus of scholars and a dearth of manual laborers, sending children to work instead of to school was not considered evil. The Durants (1965) conclude that child labor diminished not because men became humane but because machines became more complex. The cost of supporting orphans and paupers was in large part borne by the church, and parish authorities were often glad to farm out large numbers of children to industrialists in lots of fifty or one hundred. It is recorded that, in some cases, the church stipulated that the employer should take "one idiot to every twenty children."

Discipline was harsh for children in the home and community as well as in the factories. Some religious fanatics considered it permissible for a father to kill a disobedient child, since Calvin had written that "the Lord commands all those who are disobedient to their parents to be put to death," although his scriptural reference for such a pronouncement actually stated that parents had the right to accuse their son before the "elder of the city" (Durant & Durant, 1965). Children considered "incorrigible" might be sent either to prison or reform schools, where they became part of a group of criminals, mentally ill individuals, epileptics, and beggars. Mandeville, in 1723, commented that "Men who are to remain and end their lays in a Laborious, Tiresome, and Painful station of Life, the sooner they are put upon it first, the more patiently they'll submit to it forever after" (Despert, 1965, p. 96).

The mentally ill were increasingly looked upon as "sick" in-

ED

dividuals, although the causes of mental illness, so recently attributed solely to possession by the devil, were just beginning to be explored (Zilboorg & Henry, 1941).   Disturbed behavior demonstrated by children, however, was poorly understood.   Kanner relates an incident recorded by Gottfried Keller in 1713 which tragically portrayed the treatment of what was probably a childhood psychosis of that time:

> This seven year old girl, the offspring of an aristocratic family, whose father remarried after an unhappy first matrimony, offended her "noble and God fearing" stepmother by her peculiar behavior. Worst of all, she would not join in the prayers and was panic stricken when taken to the black-robed preacher in the dark and gloomy chapel.   She avoided contact with the people by hiding in closets or running away from home.   The local physician had nothing to offer beyond declaring that she might be insane.   She was placed in the custody of a minister known for his rigid orthodoxy.   The minister, who saw in her ways the machination of a "baneful and infernal" power, used a number of would-be therapeutic devices.   He laid her on a bench and beat her with a cat-o-nine tails.   He locked her in a dark pantry.   He subjected her to a period of starvation.   He clothed her in a frock of burlap.   Under these circumstances, the child did not last long.   She died after a few months, and everybody felt relieved.   The minister was amply rewarded for his efforts by Emerentia's parents (Kanner, 1962, p. 98).

We come now to an event that had far-reaching effects on the movement of the pendulum.   The French Revolution awakened the sense of an individual's social responsibility and, even more importantly, the sense of the community's responsibility toward its members, including children.   French medical men were among the first to reflect this awakening in their approach to the treatment of the mentally ill.   Noteworthy were the contributions of Philippe Pinel, who arrived in Paris eleven years before the French Revolution and served as physician-in-chief of two major hospitals for the mentally ill — the Bicetre and the Salpetrière — during this critical period of social upheaval.

To the revolutionaries, Pinel appeared a "madman" engaged in the liberation of animals when he sought and received permission to remove the chains of the mentally ill in the Bicetre.   He reorganized the administration, retrained the personnel of the hospitals, and collected perhaps the earliest psychiatric case histories.   Pinel was driven by the conviction that "the mentally sick, far from being guilty people deserving of punishment, are sick people whose miserable state deserves all the consideration that is due to suffering humanity. One should try with the most simple methods to restore their reason." He classified mental diseases simply as mania, melancholia, dementia, and idiocy and was opposed to bloodletting, "ducking" patients in water, and the use of drugs (Zilboorg & Henry, 1941, pp. 323–324).

While Pinel's reform was taking place in France, William Tuke established the York Retreat in England, where mental patients lived, worked, and rested in a kindly, religious atmosphere. In the United States, Benjamin Rush assumed direction of the Pennsylvania Hospital, where he brought about more humane treatment of the mentally ill and wrote the first comprehensive volume on psychiatry in this country (Coleman, 1972).

During this period of dramatic change in treatment of the mentally ill, the role of the humanitarian teacher or special educator was also established. In 1651, Harsdorffer in Germany had produced wax tablets on which the blind could write, and Bernouilli in Switzerland had invented a frame for guiding a pencil on paper. In the eighteenth century, Valentine Hauy introduced embossed print for use by the blind. Dedicated to proving that the blind could and should be educated, he opened a school in France. Even though the school survived the revolutionary turmoil, it closed in 1801 (Pritchard, 1963; Wallin, 1955). Diderot, in a 1749 paper entitled "Letter on the Blind for the Use of Those Who See," stated that our ideas of right and wrong are not derived from God but from our sensory experience. He also suggested that the blind might be taught to read by touch (Durant & Durant, 1965).

The 1600's saw development in communication techniques for the deaf. Bonnet published a system of teaching based on finger spelling that was elaborated by Pereira in the next century. Pereira also is credited with devising the lip reading method. In 1760, Abbé de l'Epée opened the first public school for handicapped children who were deaf and poor — the National Institute for Deaf-mutes in Paris. In this school Itard met and worked with Victor, the "wild boy," at the beginning of the nineteenth century. (This meeting will be described in detail in the next section.) Abbé de l'Epée was convinced that speech was not necessary in educating the deaf. Samuel Heinicke in Germany, however, believed that precise thought was possible only if speech was present and stressed that the deaf must develop language. The controversy surrounding the relation of speech and language to intelligence and to the education of the deaf is still in existence, as we shall see.

ED

VH

HH

Thus, by the close of the eighteenth century, schools for blind and deaf children had appeared; but little was done for the child with a physical or mental handicap. According to Pritchard (1963), public sympathy was more readily aroused by blindness and deafness than physical deformity, mental retardation, or deviant behavior. Children with physical handicaps were often repulsive to look at and, along with retarded and disturbed children, were sometimes considered examples of divine displeasure and chastisement of the parents. In addition, the borderline retarded individual was not noticeably backward in a day when few could read and write. Pritchard concludes that only as education became general was the problem of backwardness discovered.

Most of the recorded history from which the material in this chapter is drawn reflects the life and times of the Western world. Little is readily available concerning early attitudes toward, and treatment of, handicapped individuals in the East. However, one interesting historical reference relating to the beginnings of scientific concerns with physical deformity in Russia came to light during a visit the author made to Leningrad. In the city's Museum of Scientific Curiosities is a collection of large glass jars containing malformed fetuses and infants preserved in a formaldehyde solution. This collection was purchased from the Dutch by Peter the Great during one of his visits to Amsterdam in the early 1700's. Peter the Great, one of the few Russian rulers who maintained a deep interest in the affairs of the West, was convinced that Russia could greatly profit from the scientific advances being made in other countries. He attempted to buy the formula for formaldehyde, which was unknown in Russia, from the Dutch, but they refused to sell it to him. They did, however, agree to sell him their collection of specimens. On his return to Russia in 1718, Peter issued a formal decree directing his people to bring to the attention of governmental authorities any deformed animal or human specimen so that these might be gathered and studied. The actual decree is translated below:

> As is known, it sometimes happens in the human race, as it does among beasts and birds, that monsters are born, which monsters, that is, freaks, have always been collected as rarities in all states, concerning which a decree was issued several years ago ordering that these be turned in and promising payment for such, and some have indeed been turned in.
>
> However in a huge country such as ours, there may be more of these monsters, but ignorant people are concealing them, believing that such monsters are born in consequence of diabolical acts

effected by means of witchcraft and the evil eye, which is not possible; but it does come about as the result of internal injuries to the
mother, or in consequence of her fright and notions during pregnancy, and there are many examples of a child bearing the marks of
whatever frightened the mother; the same can happen if the mother
gets hurt or ill, and so forth.

Hence this decree is being renewed and reissued to the effect
that such monsters, whether they be human, cattle, beast, or bird,
be brought to the commandant of the town, for which payment will
be made, specifically, for dead monsters, ten rubles apiece for
humans, five for cattle and beast, three for birds, and for live monsters, one hundred rubles for humans, fifteen for cattle and beasts,
and seven for birds; and if a monster is unusually strange, then the
payment will be more; on the other hand if the abnormality is slight,
the payment will be less.

The following is added, that should the parents be of nobility
and should they be unwilling to bring a monster in out of shame,
then this method is to be used: he who brings the monster in is not
obligated to say whose it is and the commandant must not ask, but
on accepting this monster must pay the money and allow the person
to go.

And should anyone try to obstruct this law, he must be exposed; and should anyone be proven guilty, he will be fined ten
times the price set for the monsters, and money should not be given
to informers.*

This attempt on Peter's part to introduce the scientific study of
physical deformity in Russia may be one of the early landmarks in
the development of what is the field of "defectology" or special
education in the Soviet Union today.

The role of sensory experience in learning also was receiving
increased attention during this era. Locke asserted that all knowledge came through the senses, and Rousseau echoed the importance
of using the natural curiosity of the child rather than books as a
basis for learning. Rousseau's position of allowing the child's
capacities and interests to develop in a natural, unrestricted environment rather than being confined by artificial societal standards
has been periodically re-examined and reasserted in educational
practices with normal and exceptional children (Pritchard, 1963).

The eighteenth century stands as a critical transitional period
for all mankind, including the handicapped. The dignity of the
individual, including the child, was established, and fear, supersti-

*The author is indebted to Mrs. Collette Schulman of the Johnson Foundation,
Racine, Wisconsin, for the translation of this decree.

tion, and hostility toward those who were different began to give way to attempts at rational understanding, humanitarian care, and education. Thus the climate for the true emergence of special education in the nineteenth century came into existence.

NINETEENTH CENTURY

During the nineteenth century, the pendulum swung within the most restricted range in the history of man. The range was predominantly at the positive end of our historical determiner dimension, and the agents of pendulum movement were individuals — physicians and educators — who carried the momentum of the late 1700's into a remarkable period of reform and service for the exceptional individual.

The early nineteenth century underscored the need for care and education of the handicapped, including child paupers. Street

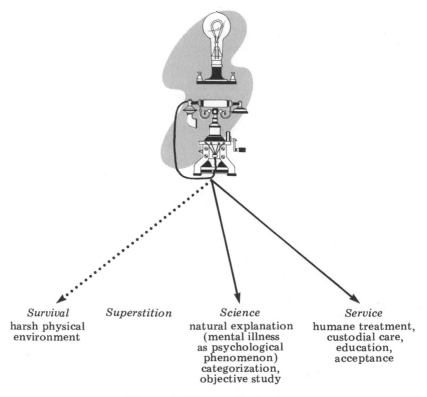

| *Survival* | *Superstition* | *Science* | *Service* |
| harsh physical environment | | natural explanation (mental illness as psychological phenomenon) categorization, objective study | humane treatment, custodial care, education, acceptance |

Figure 6: Nineteenth Century

begging was widespread in England and elsewhere, and children were exhibited by their parents in an effort to excite pity because of their rags and deliberately produced sores. The blind and physically handicapped were particularly vulnerable to such abuses. Mentally defective children of the poor were often placed in workhouses if the parents could not pay for institutionalization in an asylum (Pritchard, 1963).

The physician of the eighteenth century was still preoccupied with anatomy and physiology, and mental illness continued to be viewed as the result of a disease of the brain. Thus medical men were strongly opposed to psychotherapy and psychological explanations of mental illness. In the work of Charcot and Bernheim in France, however, a greater understanding emerged of the role of psychological factors and the mentally ill patient's inner life. This psychological viewpoint was finally to achieve prominence near the turn of the century in the contributions of Janet and Freud (Zilboorg & Henry, 1941).

Reform in the treatment of the mentally ill, given impetus by Pinel in the previous century, was widespread. Ferrus, in France, introduced a revolutionary procedure at the Bicetre when he selected patients capable of working and assigned them to a large farm which included a dairy, animals, and workshops. Yet, he considered non-restraint for mental patients, in general, impractical and idealistic. The issue of restraint was widely debated throughout Europe and America in the 1830's. In the United States, Isaac Ray stated that although non-restraint might be successful with Europeans, who traditionally are accustomed to obeying orders, it would not work with Americans, whose belief in liberty would cause them to assert themselves if they were not physically restrained.

One of the most spirited voices for reform in the United States was that of Dorothea Dix, a retired school teacher described as having "staggering grit." Her mission was to have hospitals built for the mentally ill, and in a presentation to Congress in 1848 she stated that she had seen:

> More than 9,000 idiots, epileptics, and insane in the United States, destitute of appropriate care and protection . . . bound with galling chains, bowed beneath fetters and heavy, iron balls attached to drag chains, lacerated with ropes, scourged by rods and terrified beneath storms of cruel blows; now subject to jibes and scorn and torturing tricks; now abandoned to the most outrageous violations (Zilboorg & Henry, 1941, pp. 583–584).

Dorothea Dix believed the deplorable conditions in Ameri-

ED

can institutions "were due to an antiquated, ignorant, and callous system of public policy based upon theories and practice which must be revolutionized out of respect to Christianity and advancing civilization" (Zilboorg & Henry, 1941, p. 583). Between 1841 and 1881, she established thirty-two modern mental hospitals. In England, Daniel Tuke wrote extensively on the subject of reform, but society at large was slow to rid itself of the impulse to shut out the criminal and the mentally ill rather than to treat and rehabilitate them (Zilboorg & Henry, 1941).

MR

In 1829, Louis Braille, a young student of the Paris School for the Blind, adapted an existing military code that had been constructed for night-time communication to the needs of the blind. This code adaptation was first called *sonography* and later *braille* (Robbin, 1955).

In the latter part of the nineteenth century, Alexander Graham Bell and his invention of the telephone opened up new channels for teaching speech to the deaf. The hearing aid was developed

VH

and greater emphasis was placed on using amplification of sound in teaching speech to children with severely defective hearing. Oral methods of teaching the deaf advanced as a result and many children who had never understood speech or language were now able to do

HH

so (Kirk, 1972).

The onset of the nineteenth century is perhaps a most visible landmark in the history of special education because of the work of Jean-Marc-Gaspard Itard, a young, ambitious physician who was medical advisor to the National Institute for Deaf-mutes in Paris. The story of Itard and his contribution to the field begins in the forest of Aveyron in Southern France in 1799 when a "wild boy" of eleven or twelve years of age was seized by hunters after apparently having lived most of his life as a primitive forest creature. The boy, animal-like in appearance and behavior, was naked, dirty, scarred, unable to speak, and selected food by smell. He was brought to Paris and placed in the National Institute for Deaf-mutes where his presence elicited much interest and curiosity. Some of this may have stemmed from comparison of the boy to the "noble savage" described earlier by Rousseau. But Rousseau's concept of the ideal man, unbound by the stifling conventions of society and free to make his own way in a natural environment, was hard to accept when the revolting appearance of the boy was considered. He was a "disgustingly dirty child affected with spasmodic movements and often convulsions who swayed back and forth ceaselessly like certain animals in the menagerie, who bit and scratched those who opposed him, who showed no sort of affection for those who attended him, and who was, in short, indifferent to everything and attentive to nothing" (Itard, 1962, p. 4).

Itard obtained permission to care for the boy and was convinced that with proper training in the ways of civilized man, the boy could become normal. Thus the stage was set for an extremely significant event in the history of special education. It involved more than an ambitious training program, for it was to embody an idealism and optimism that would have far-reaching effects even to our present time. Itard was reflecting the post-French Revolutionary belief in the individuality and dignity of every human being and the right and potential of man to rise above any obstacle. He was also reflecting the belief that environmental experience — education and training — could alter the seemingly unalterable. The significance of such beliefs increases immeasurably as we look back over the centuries of oppression, superstition, and fear that preceded the nineteenth century and that had fostered pessimism and a sense of hopelessness. However, Itard's confidence was not shared by all of his colleagues. Leading medical authorities of the day, such as Pinel, considered the boy a "hopeless idiot" and thought very little could be gained by Itard's efforts.

Itard, on the other hand, considered the boy simply wild and untaught. Much interest focused on the experiment because of a philosophical controversy of the day between the nativists and the sensationalists. The nativist theory assumed the individual is born with innate ideas that gradually unfold with the developing mind. The sensationalist theory, to which Itard subscribed and based on the work of John Locke, believed the mind a *tabula rasa* waiting to receive all of its impressions from sensory experience. Itard reasoned that he only had to give the wild boy the necessary training to supply the mental content that he lacked, and he would become a normal individual. Pritchard (1963) concludes that Itard may have only had a cursory knowledge of Locke's thesis, for he seemed to overlook the fact that while experience is necessary to produce mental development, so is a mind capable of using this experience. It was in the conviction that he would completely normalize or "cure" the boy that Itard's idealism was unfortunate.

During a five-year period of intensive training, Itard certainly "made a difference" in the life of this boy, whom he called Victor. In two reports published in 1801 and 1806, Itard described his program, designed to develop the senses, the intellectual functions, and the emotional faculties of the boy. There were five principal aims:

1. To make him social through gradual transition from the life he had led in the forest
2. To arouse his nervous sensibilities by intense stimulation
3. To give him knowledge of ideas through environmental interaction
4. To assist him in learning to speak through imitation
5. To channel mental activity associated with meeting physical needs into the educational process (Pritchard, 1963)

MR

The first nine months of the program, covered in the 1801 report, resulted in the boy's developing normal habits of sleeping, eating, and personal hygiene. He also became more sensitive to touch, taste, and smell and displayed affection for and dependence on his governess. Even though speech was not attained, he learned to voice certain monosyllables such as *lait* (milk) and *O Dieu,* and finally acquired the vowel sounds as well as *d* and *l*. He also learned to place objects together in proper order, such as arranging the letters of the alphabet to spell *lait*.

With these evidences of progress, Itard launched into four more years of training, which were described in the 1806 report. First, greater attention was given to development of the senses. By blindfolding Victor so that hearing would not be distracted by sight, Itard taught him to distinguish gross difference in sounds, such as that between a drum and a bell. Gradually he taught him to respond to the varying tones of his teacher's voice. After much work, Victor was able to visually identify various written words without understanding their meaning and to distinguish colors. The sense of touch was developed by teaching the boy to distinguish between chestnuts and acorns hidden in a bag. He also learned to select certain block letters by touch alone. Victor's sense of taste was likewise developed, and he learned to differentiate between sweet and tart.

Itard expected mental development rapidly to follow the sensory training. Victor was trained to connect an object with its name and use. He also learned to distinguish between action verbs written on a blackboard and later was able to carry out the action indicated. Itard keenly wished to teach Victor to speak, but despite painstaking training, the boy did not progress beyond the utterance of a few monosyllables and remained essentially mute.

Itard hoped Victor's mental development would rapidly progress with the onset of puberty, but the major effect of this period was to bring out all the wild and uncontrollable elements in the boy. He became violent and eventually unmanageable, and Itard's experiment ended with Victor being given over to the care of his governess with whom he resided and received kindly care until his death at age forty in 1829.

Itard was bitterly disappointed over his failure to make Victor normal. He reluctantly was forced to admit that the boy was indeed mentally retarded, as Pinel had diagnosed, and is said at one point during the frustrating five-year training program to have cried out to Victor in a fit of despair:

> Unfortunate! Since my pains are lost and my efforts fruitless, take yourself back to your forests and primitive tastes; or if your new wants make you dependent on society, suffer the penalty of being useless, and go to Bicetre, there to die in wretchedness (Davis & Ecob, 1959, p. 13).

MR

Despite his disappointment, Itard was praised by the French Academy of Science in its 1806 report:

> The Academy acknowledges that it was impossible for the institutor to put in his lessons, exercises, and experiments more intelligence, sagacity, patience, courage; and that if it has not obtained a greater success, it must be attributed not to any lack of zeal or talent, but to the imperfection of the organs of the subject upon which he worked (Davies & Ecob, 1959, p. 15).

History was to add its commendation to Itard's work, for he was among the first to show that even a seriously retarded individual can be helped to improve his level of functioning through appropriate training. Itard was also perhaps the first educator to apply a completely individualized and clinical method (patterned after a medical approach) to the study, observation, and education of a pupil (Wallin, 1955). Itard's dedication, ingenuity, persistence, and optimism were to remain as a legacy for the special educator from the beginning of the nineteenth century to the present time. The French director Francois Truffaut has made a moving and detailed film depicting Itard's work with Victor, "L'Enfant Sauvage" or "The Wild Child."

Itard's accomplishments were instrumental in stimulating the instruction of the retarded at the Bicetre and the Salpetrière in the 1830's when it was firmly established that the retarded could learn and be improved (Doll, 1962). Itard's work led to the contributions of Edouard Seguin, whom Doll has described as the man who reflected the most significant thinking of previous generations and who consolidated and built a unique educational system out of it and as "perhaps the greatest teacher ever to address his attention to the mentally deficient." Seguin was Itard's protégé.

His concept of education was the promotion of the harmonious physical, intellectual, and moral development of the child.

Talbot (1964) summarizes Seguin's place in special education and his contribution to a theory of pedagogy that was based on previously isolated medical, physiological, and philosophical tenets as follows:

1. That observation of the individual child preceded and was the foundation for the child's education.
2. That education dealt with the whole child and that the things taught must likewise be kept whole.
3. That activity was the basis for and the means of learning; that sensory learning was included in activity.
4. That the child learned best and most economically from real things and that he remembered in proportion to his opportunity to compare.
5. That even the most defective child has some spark of understanding upon which learning could be built (p. 15).*

In his emphasis on the person as a whole, Seguin recognized the existence of a mind that could be taught to attend to, compare, and make judgments about sensory learnings, whereas Itard had tended to separate sensory experience as an end in itself. Seguin's "physiological method," as it was called, included the development of techniques and materials, many of which had not been directly used in teaching previously. He prescribed music training to develop controlled behavior and intelligent response, use of art media for symbolic stages, and use of child-originated academic materials. The tangible teaching aids he designed included pegboards, buttoning and lacing materials, object collections, series-type tangible materials, tools for sensory experience, and visual training devices such as shutters, colored glass, silhouette slides, and a giant kaleidoscope. Seguin's contributions have extended to the entire field of education, as was his desire.

Seguin established the first successful school specifically for training the feeble-minded in Paris in 1837 and continued his pioneering efforts in their behalf for the next ten years. The success he enjoyed with young mental defectives was vividly described in a letter written by George Summer to Samuel Howe in 1847:

During the past six months, I have watched with eager interest the progress which many young idiots have made in Paris, under the

*Talbot, M. E. *Edouard Seguin: A study of an educational approach to the treatment of mentally defective children.* New York: Bureau of Publications, Columbia University, 1964. Reprinted by permission.

direction of M. Seguin, and have seen with no less gratification than astonishment, nearly one hundred fellow-beings who, but a short time since, were shut out from all communion with mankind, and who were objects of loathing and disgust — many of whom rejected every article of clothing — others of whom, unable to stand erect, crouched themselves in corners, and gave signs of life only by piteous howls — others, in whom the faculty of speech had never been developed — and many, whose voracious and indiscriminate gluttony satisfied itself with whatever they could lay hands upon. . . . These . . . I have seen properly clad, standing erect, walking, speaking, eating in an orderly manner at a common table, working quietly as carpenters, and farmers, gaining by their own labor the means of existence, storing their awakened intelligence by reading one to another; exercising, toward their teachers and among themselves, the generous feelings of man's nature, and singing in unison songs of Thanksgiving.   There is nothing either visionary or impracticable in the attempt . . . for republics, it is an imperative duty, the necessary result of the principle on which they are founded, and by which they are sustained — the principle of justice, that accords to everyone, not as a privilege, but as a right, the full development of all his faculties (Talbot, 1964, p. 66).

In 1848, Seguin emigrated to the United States due to his unhappiness with the French government and at the urging of individuals such as Samuel Howe who saw in his particular method of teaching a way of restoring severely retarded children to normal functioning.   Seguin assisted in setting up the first state residential facility for the retarded in the United States, and hopes were high that residential schools offering a strong training emphasis would literally cure the retarded.   Seguin, in his dedication speech for the first educationally oriented facility for the mentally retarded at Syracuse, New York, in 1854, clearly expressed his deep convictions about his work:

God has scattered among us — rare as the possession of genius — the idiot, the blind, the deaf-mute, in order to bind the rich to the needy, the talented to the incapable, all men to each other, by a tie of indissoluble solidarity.   The old bonds are dissolving; man is already unwilling to continue to contribute money or palaces for the support of the indolent nobility; but he is every day more ready to build palaces and give annuities for the indigent or infirm, the chosen friends of our Lord Jesus.   See that cornerstone — the token of the new alliance between humanity and a class hitherto neglected — that, ladies and gentlemen, is your pride; it is the greatest joy of my life; for I, too, have labored for the poor idiot (Davies & Ecob, 1959).

But by the end of the nineteenth century, hopes that training would normalize the retarded had faded. Despite important and significant contributions that "made a difference" in the lives of the retarded, Seguin's methods did not produce the sought-after miracle, and the view of residential schools as training institutions gave way to one of custodial facilities for children and adults who were hopelessly dependent (Dunn, 1963a).

In the last decade of the nineteenth century, Dr. Maria Montessori obtained a copy of Seguin's book, *Idiocy and Its Treatment by the Physiological Method,* translated it, and modified many of the methods and materials that were described (Montessori, 1912). She first applied her approach to the mentally retarded, but her techniques were less well received in the United States than in some countries of Europe and Asia because of the pessimism that swept the country following Seguin's efforts (Dunn, 1963a). From that point, Montessori extended her methods to the teaching of normal children, thus doing what Seguin had hoped would be done in merging special education practices with the mainstream of regular education.

The beginning of the nineteenth century was particularly noteworthy in the field of special education because of the teacher-pupil relationship between Itard and Victor and the development of training procedures that were aimed at educating the seemingly uneducable. A striking parallel to this event occurred in the latter part of the same century in the teacher-pupil relationship between Anne Sullivan and Helen Keller and the training program that made such a remarkable difference in the life of a young deaf and blind child. Helen Keller was born in 1880, a normal child, but nineteen months later she was striken with a still undiagnosed illness that left her deaf and blind and led to muteness. Some considered her an idiot, but her parents sought help from Alexander Graham Bell, who referred them to the Perkins Institution for the Blind in Boston. At the Perkins Institution some fifty years earlier Samuel Howe had demonstrated that a deaf-blind child could be taught to read and write by means of a finger alphabet and could learn to communicate with the seeing and hearing world. His work with Laura Bridgman had received wide attention, yet no skilled teacher had been able to replicate it with other deaf-blind children.

Anne Sullivan was visually handicapped and had entered the Perkins Institution for her education at the age of fourteen, the same year Helen Keller was born, and graduated in 1886. As a result of a series of eye operations, she had acquired partial sight. After studying Dr. Howe's reports on Laura Bridgman for several months, Anne Sullivan departed for Tuscumbia, Alabama, and the

Keller household, where she began her intensive efforts to teach Helen to understand and communicate with the world around her. By the end of the first month, Anne Sullivan had achieved a breakthrough; while pumping water over the child's hands and fingerspelling the word "water," Helen revealed that she had made the association between the physical and symbolic experiences. From that moment on Helen's progress was remarkable. She quickly learned the names of objects and events in her environment, and by the age of ten began oral speech when she learned to say aloud, "I-am-not-dumb-now." The story of the astonishing results of Anne Sullivan's work with Helen received widespread publicity. Some considered it a "miracle." Others gave complete credit to the teacher and viewed Helen as an automaton. Still others were skeptical as to whether Helen was really handicapped in the first place and accused Anne Sullivan of being a fraud.

The truth of the matter, as stated by Alexander Graham Bell, was that the combination of a gifted, intuitive teacher and an eager and very intelligent pupil had contributed to the success. There were many obvious differences between Helen Keller and Itard's Victor, but the most significant was probably Helen's nineteen months of normal experience as a child before losing her sight and hearing and her unquestionable superior intellectual potential. Helen Keller went on to graduate *cum laude* from Radcliffe College and to write a number of books, several of which provide us with vivid, moving accounts of her life with Anne Sullivan (Keller, 1955). The stage play and later motion picture "The Miracle Worker" describes Anne Sullivan's dedicated efforts to teach Helen Keller.

In reviewing the implications of the nineteenth century for special education, Doll (1962) concludes that with the exception of mental testing, Freudian psychology, and biochemical techniques, almost every current point of view in the education of exceptional children had by then found some level of expression. Between 1818 and 1894, residential institutions for the mentally retarded and other exceptional children had appeared in the United States, and by 1890 state responsibility for the care of the retarded was generally accepted and supplementary private agencies were appearing. Institutional segregation on either a temporary or permanent basis was seen as most effective, but the special class movement first to gain impetus in Germany was being considered in America as well. Educational theory reflected developmental concepts and concern with the child's total personality, and the importance of individualization of instruction was recognized. The profoundly retarded were considered in need of lifetime cus-

todial care, but the less severely retarded were seen as candidates
for some level of gainful employment.

The nineteenth century was indeed the beginning of special
education. Building on fragments of knowledge and understanding accumulated over thousands of years and further dismantling
centuries of cruelty, superstition, and neglect of the handicapped,
the 1800's firmly established care, treatment, and education as the
mandate for the twentieth century.

TWENTIETH CENTURY

As shown in Figure 7, the pendulum swing along our historical determiner dimension was similar to that evidenced during the nineteenth century with the exception of a eugenics movement. The
agents of movement were varied — individuals in fields of educa-

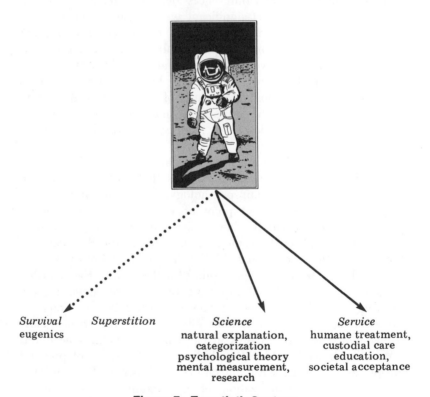

Survival	*Superstition*	*Science*	*Service*
eugenics		natural explanation, categorization psychological theory mental measurement, research	humane treatment, custodial care education, societal acceptance

Figure 7: Twentieth Century

tion, psychology, and medicine; social reform; war; public sentiment; and increased federal, state, and local concern.

The quest for measurement devices to identify and classify individuals according to intellectual potential began seriously at the turn of the century. In 1890, Cattell had advocated the establishment of norms in psychological testing. He devised a series of sensory and motor tests, but these proved poorly suited to the differentiation of intellectual abilities. In 1893, Jastrow developed memory tests; and in 1897, Ebbinghaus produced a completion test based on his concept of verbal synthesis as a test of intelligence.

These peripheral views of intelligence were in contrast to the central concept of Alfred Binet, whose landmark contribution in developing a scientifically reliable means for evaluating intelligence was to have a lasting effect on diagnosis, classification, and educational planning (Doll, 1962). Binet was commissioned in 1904 by the French Ministry of Education to develop a test to determine if a child suspected of mental retardation should be transferred to a special class. The label "mentally deficient" would be applied when a child demonstrated such limited intelligence that he was unable to profit from regular class instruction.

In developing his intelligence test, Binet, along with his collaborator, Simon, was concerned with measuring central or native intelligence rather than peripheral or acquired ability. A fundamental aspect of this central intelligence was seen as the ability to exercise judgment. Binet rejected Seguin's emphasis on sensory and motor activities in training the mentally retarded and instead recommended training in memory, reasoning, perception, problem-solving, and attention, which he called "mental orthopedics" (Doll, 1962). He was complimentary regarding Seguin's "great personal talent" and "good sense" but critical of the "obscurities" and "absurdities" in his work (Pritchard, 1963).

Binet also severely criticized Seguin's optimism and stated that attempts to educate some retarded children were fruitless. His position was part of what Pritchard (1963) has described as the rising tide of opinion which was in marked contrast to the earlier optimism introduced at an idealized and somewhat unrealistic level by Itard, and carried along during the 1800's by Seguin. Such opinion resulted partly from the disappointment and discouragement associated with Seguin's failure to cure the retarded in this country with the increasing study of eugenics and partly from fears that a degeneration of the race was at hand unless segregation and sterilization of mental defectives were practiced. In the United States, Goddard and Dugdale traced the descendants of the Juke and Kallikak families in which there were identifiable mentally defective individuals and revealed that a large number of their ancestors had been criminals, prostitutes, and paupers. The eugenics movement eventually resulted in sterilization laws that presently apply to the mentally deficient in all states, to the psychotic in all but two states, and in about two-thirds of the states to the epileptic (Wallin, 1955).

A second aspect concerned the Binet testing movement itself and the belief that an intelligence test score was infallible and not subject to change. Such a belief led to the notion that the mentally retarded could not really profit from an education in the usual sense of the word. Although Binet himself had questioned Seguin's optimism regarding the educability of the retarded, he was to demonstrate a tempered optimism himself regarding efforts to teach them to read and write.

> It has been remarked, and justly, that reading is the triumph of abstraction, and that a defective may require two years to learn to read by syllables, and very poorly even then. No matter if this is possible, even with considerable effort, such a defective ought to learn to read. This is demanded not by the state of the child's intelligence, *but by the society in which he lives,* where illiteracy would bring shame on him (Pritchard, 1963, p. 179).

In 1916, Lewis Terman revised the Binet-Simon test and restandardized it on American children. Terman also introduced the concept of the I.Q. or intelligence quotient, which differed from the Binet-Simon measurement of mental age. Binet had reported a given child's intelligence in terms of the age of the average child in the standardization group who performed in a similar manner on the test, whereas Terman related mental age to actual chronological age and produced an intelligence quotient that was to become the quantitative criterion for mental retardation. It also made possible a description of mental retardation in statistical terms of probability (Farber, 1968).

The Binet testing movement was criticized and attacked in the 1910's. William Healy of the Chicago Juvenile Court claimed it was necessary to increase the range and type of items for adequate diagnosis; W. E. Fernald saw the problem of borderline diagnosis as still unsolved; and S. D. Porteus, in 1915, contended that the Binet test reflected previous training and that it unfairly penalized children with emotional and sensory problems. Lightner Witmer called for a broader definition of mental retardation and emphasized the role of emotional deprivation, lack of experiential stimulation, functional nervous disease, improper nutrition, sensory defects, physical illness, and improper discipline in determining intellectual functioning. In 1911, he stated:

> Mental retardation is not a disease, it is not a brain defect. It is not even a condition with a definite number of assignable characteristics. It is a mental status, a stage of mental development (Doll, 1962, p. 35).

These protests and qualifications have continued to the present day, and Binet's central theory of retardation as deficiency in judgment has been revised and extended by measurement efforts designed to cover individual variation in terms of sensory-motor functioning, special abilities and disabilities, emotional patterns, and environmental deprivation. However, the overall impact on the field of mental retardation by Binet's test was revolutionary. In 1910, the American Association on Mental Deficiency extended the traditional classification system involving "idiot" and "imbecile" to include "moron." The older categories, which had earlier been differentiated merely by the criterion of presence of speech, were now distinguished by the upper limit of a mental age of two years. The new category of "moron" (coined by Goddard from the Greek term for "foolish" with a deficiency in judgment, sense, or intelligence) covered the mental range of from eight to twelve years and reflected Binet's emphasis on social adequacy as the basis for intelligence.

Goddard's category of "moron" covered thousands of mildly retarded individuals among the general population who, prior to establishment of the intelligence test movement, were largely unrecognized. The more seriously retarded included in the "idiot" and "imbecile" categories had been provided with institutional care for some time, but this borderline group had been neglected and only recently aided by the beginnings of special classes in the public school. The identification of the "moron" group prompted a differentiation of institutional programs for the retarded, and the "colony" came into existence. A colony consisted of a number of mentally retarded individuals capable of living outside the control of an institution who, with institutional supervision, could work and support themselves with group earnings. In 1916, Bernstein organized a colony in the Rome State School in New York where boys and men in the moron category "lived freer, happier, and more productive lives than in the institution" (Doll, 1962).

The first special class for mentally retarded children living outside an institution was developed in Germany as early as 1860. By 1905, Saxony had enrolled 10,000 children in 492 special classes in 180 cities. The curriculum was based on the Froebelian notion

ED

of the educational value of play as well as on Seguin's physiological methods. In the United States, special classes for the retarded were held in Cleveland in 1875 and again in 1893. By 1905, classes had been initiated in Chicago, New York, Providence, Springfield, Philadelphia, Boston, and Portland (Doll, 1962). By 1911, there were public school classes for the retarded in ninety-nine American cities, and by 1922 some 23,000 children were enrolled across the country.

MR

The early public school programs for the retarded in the United States often included a mixture of problem children, and the optimism and dedication of the teachers may not always have been matched by adequate preparation and experience. Steinbeck (1918) cites the case of one such class in the Cleveland public schools:

> About 14 of the most serious cases of imbecility in the most congested quarters of the city were gathered together and a superior, conscientious teacher placed in charge. The good folk responsible for this inauguration were united in their belief that the pupils would soon become as normal children, once they were properly taught. The teacher heroically attacked the problem, but before the close of the school year, all were aware that their experiment was doomed to failure. At the close of the term, the class was disbanded — the imbeciles returned to their homes, probably not much the worse for their "schooling" but the poor teacher suffered a mental collapse which necessitated a sojourn at our capitol State Hospital.

VH

HH

Special programs for the retarded declined during the depression, but after World War II, they rapidly increased: 1948 — 87,000; 1958 — 213,000; 1963 — 390,000 (Farber, 1968).

SH

Wallin (1955) reports the development of special classes for those other than retarded in the United States in Table 2:

PH

Table 2: Special Classes in the United States

TYPE OF CLASS	YEAR	CITY
Deaf	1869	Boston
Unruly or truant boys	1874	New York
Blind	1896 (or 1899)	Chicago
Orthopedically handicapped	1899 (or 1900)	Chicago
Speech defective	1908	New York
Pre-tuberculosis or malnourished	1908	Providence
Epileptics	1909	Baltimore
Partially sighted	1913	Roxbury, Mass.
Hard of hearing	1920	Lynn, Mass.

Systematic provision for identifying and teaching children with superior intelligence did not appear until near the turn of the century when the Elizabeth, New Jersey, schools adopted a multiple tract system in 1886 whereby pupils were grouped according to the academic pace they could maintain, with the brighter students advancing at an accelerated rate.   The Cambridge Plan, which was developed in 1891, permitted the gifted pupil to cover the first six grades in four years.   The history of special education of gifted children has been divided into three eras: 1867–1899 — flexible promotions; 1900–1919 — concern with child's maturity in relation to accelerated programs; and 1920's to present — enrichment of the curriculum (Sumption & Luecking, 1960).

Beginning in 1917 and continuing into the Hitler era, Germany experimented with educational programs for *hoffnungskinder* — "children who show promise."   Special schools and classes were organized and children assigned on the basis of psychological tests. Hollingworth (1926) considers the official recognition given by Germany to the significance of mental measurement as a basis for special education to be greater than that given by any other country. She sees this partly as a reflection of Germany's lack of indoctrination with the theory that all are born equal.

Two names stand out for their pioneer work in the United States for sufferers from cerebral palsy — Winthrop Phelps and Earl Carlson (who was afflicted with cerebral palsy).   These physicians each approached the treatment and education of the crippled child according to his own special standpoint: Phelps from the approach of physiotherapy and the use of braces; Carlson from the study of the whole child with emphasis on understanding his psychological life.   Carlson paid particular tribute to the doctors who urged his mother to concentrate on his mental development rather than on a physical cure which was impossible (Schonell, 1956).

The work of Sigmund Freud has played a large part in increasing our understanding of mental illness as a psychological phenomenon.   His significant contributions to psychiatry, which broke from the organic tradition of the field of medicine in the nineteenth century, have been summarized by Coleman (1972, p. 56):

1. Development of techniques for becoming acquainted with conscious and unconscious aspects of the mental life of the patient.
2. Demonstration that abnormal mental phenomena were simply exaggerations of normal phenomena.
3. Development of a therapeutic technique — psychoanalysis — for the psychological treatment of the mentally ill.

Freud must also receive recognition for aiding in the estab-lishment of the child as a unique individual in his own right rather than merely a miniature adult. The nineteenth century had seen rapid change with regard to the reduction of physical abuses, ex-ploitation, and neglect of children, but an understanding of the psychology of childhood and concern for the effects of early experi-ences in personality development had been slow in emerging. The nineteenth century saw increased respect for the physical and social rights of the child, and respect for his psychological and emotional rights increased in the twentieth century, with Freud making a major contribution.

Kanner (1962) reports that around 1900 a number of publi-cations described psychiatric phenomena as occurring in childhood, in contrast to the historical tradition that considered mental illness a condition of the post-childhood years. This approach, followed by Freud's theory of infantile sexuality presented in 1905 and Beer's contention in 1908 that behavior deviations should be treated at the time of their earliest appearance, provide further evidence of the child's emergence as a unique individual and the importance of early experiences and events in later life. It was not until the 1930's, how-ever, that consistent efforts were made to study children with severe emotional disturbances in terms of diagnosis, etiology, therapy, and prognosis. From that time on, controversy arose as to whether there was one all-inclusive type of childhood psychosis, such as suggested by Beata Rank's notion of the atypical child, or specific types of psy-chotic disorders, such as Kanner's early infantile autism, Mahler's symbiotic infantile psychosis, or Bender's three types of childhood schizophrenia — pseudodefective, pseudoneurotic, and pseudopsy-chopathic.

The scientific study of animal and human behavior also began in the twentieth century. In Russia, Ivan Pavlov, while studying the salivary response in dogs, discovered the conditioned reflex, which paved the way for a great amount of experimentation in modern psychology, including applications to human learning. In the United States, John Watson combined Pavlov's conditioning prin-ciples with ideas of his own and developed a point of view called "behaviorism." Child-rearing practices of the 1920's and 1930's were influenced by Watson's view, which emphasized the effects of social stimuli on learning and behavior. Beginning in the 1940's, such practices began to reflect the influence of Freudian psychology, with its emphasis on the inner life of the child and the critical periods of emotional development during the early years.

Cruickshank (1967b) has pointed out that both World Wars I and II made a positive contribution to the cause of the handicapped

due to the compulsory military physical examinations and the return
of injured and disabled veterans to their homes after the wars.   The
physical screenings revealed tens of thousands of men who were
physically impaired, yet who had led previously normal lives, and
this discovery tended to contribute to greater understanding and
acceptance of handicapping conditions.   Disabled veterans who
had been accepted previously in their communities tended to be
viewed as normal when they returned even though they had suffered
physical impairment.   Cruickshank sees this attitude as being unconsciously extended to physically handicapped children and gradually
to all types of exceptionality, mental as well as physical.

The 1920's and 1930's saw increased study of the individual
variability of the mentally retarded and of statewide coordination of
a number of services for their care.   Bernstein, at the Rome State
School in New York, continued his efforts aimed at returning the care
of the mentally deficient to society rather than to the institution.   He
advocated more work colonies and paroles, and by 1921 had one-
third of his institutional population functioning on a largely self-
sustained basis in colonies, on parole, or on leave.   In New York
City, the Vocational Adjustment Bureau was established as a private
agency to locate employment for mentally retarded, disturbed, or
delinquent girls.   Beginning in the 1930's, placement of the retarded
in families in the community for care and supervision was also
introduced.

Also in the 1920's and 1930's, the field of medicine began investigation of brain injury at birth, mongolism, and endocrine disorders as they related to mental retardation.   The Depression and
World War II delayed progress in all fields of special education;
but by the late 1940's the demands of parents, the enthusiasm of
professionals, and federal, state, and private funding gave new
impetus to progress in the area of mental retardation.   The current
developments linked to this post-war impetus include a revival of
anatomical and biochemical research, advances in the study of sensory deprivation, application of principles of Freudian psychology,
special interest in the problems of the severely retarded, the cerebral
palsied, and the vocationally trainable, and increasing cooperation
between professional disciplines, parents, administrators, and the
general public in attacking the problem of mental retardation (Doll,
1962).

As early as 1851, Howe had stressed that blind children should
be educated in regular schools because of the social advantages of
such a setting.   But the idea was not put into effect until 1900, when
Hall opened the first special class for blind children in a Chicago
public school.   Blind students and educators were enthusiastic, but

ED

MR

VH

seeing teachers were cold despite the fact Hall had put on an impressive demonstration showing he could "braille" the poetry of Milton almost as rapidly as the lines were read to him.   He also demonstrated that he could read back the material at approximately the same speed as a sighted individual.   Unfortunately, the professional consensus was that he had memorized the text, and it was not until two years after his death that the placement of blind students in regular schools was widely accepted (Ross, 1951).

The 1950's began a significant era in special education in the United States when a series of federal legislation provisions established grants for research and training of personnel in education of the handicapped.   In 1961, President John F. Kennedy boldly committed the country's resources to the cause of handicapped individuals in general and to the mentally retarded in particular:

> The manner in which our Nation cares for its citizens and conserves its manpower resources is more than an index to its concern for the less fortunate.   It is a key to its future.   Both wisdom and humanity dictate a deep interest in the physically handicapped, the mentally ill, and the mentally retarded.   Yet, although we have made considerable progress in the treatment of physical handicaps, although we have attacked on a broad front the problems of mental illness, although we have made great strides in the battle against disease, we as a nation have for too long postponed an intensive search for solutions for the problems of the mentally retarded.   That failure should be corrected (President's Committee on Mental Retardation, 1962, p. 196).

President Kennedy's mandate established a President's Committee on Mental Retardation made up of leading professionals in a variety of fields related to special education.   The Committee surveyed the national scene with regard to the problems of the mentally retarded and the need for increased services.   Its recommendations, as well as the impetus of the surging special education movement, were reflected in Public Law 88-164, which allocated federal funds for training professional personnel in areas of the handicapped and for supporting research and demonstration projects in special education.   In 1967, a Bureau for Education of the Handicapped was established in the United States Office of Education to administer research, educational, and training programs supported by the federal government across the country.

Thus in a little more than a century and a half, the flame kindled by countless individuals and events over the course of history and fanned by the optimism and dedication of Itard, Seguin, and others in the 1800's and early 1900's came to burn brightly on behalf of the handicapped in the United States in the 1960's. Never before in the history of man had so many agents and resources contributed to movement of the pendulum at the positive end of our historical determiner dimension.

ED

SUMMARY OF HISTORICAL DETERMINERS

Looking back over the course of history that we have briefly traced in this chapter in relation to events and individuals that have influenced attitudes toward and treatment of handicapped individuals, we can summarize our discussion in terms of the four major historical determiners — *survival, superstition, science,* and *service.*

Survival

Throughout most of history, the demand for survival was a primary determiner of the fate of the physically handicapped individual. The harshness of nature eliminated the physically infirm in the days of primitive man. During the Greek and Roman periods, the practice of exposure and infanticide further threatened their existence. War, poverty, barbarism, and disease continued to take their toll through the Middle Ages, and, as late as the eighteenth century, more than half the children born in London died before reaching age ten. Thus few physically handicapped children survived, and of those who did who were poor we can imagine their plight as paupers and street beggars. As stated in our introduction, the two broad categories of exceptionality — weak and poor — suffice to describe the handicapped through much of history. The chances for survival for individuals in either group were indeed meager.

PH

Superstition

Man's fascination with and fear of the unexplained, whether in the natural world about him or in the behavior of his fellows, was perhaps the primary determiner of the fate of mentally handicapped individuals throughout much of history. The superstitious beliefs that have been generated over the centuries stand as testimony to man's limitless imagination and desperation in the face of the unknown. Primitive man viewed deranged behavior as caused by good and evil spirits that were revered, worshipped, and appeased.

ED

MR

As civilized man developed, elaborate demonological concepts appeared in most ancient societies, and rites of exorcism and measures for protection against evil spirits are described in great detail in some of the earliest writings, which have been handed down from both pagan and early religious sources. Greek mythology provided a complex system for conceptualizing and treating mental illness. Despite the bold, naturalistic position of Hippocrates, the metaphysical and moralistic continued to dominate Greek thought.

With the onset of the Middle Ages in the fifth century, man was plunged into an era of darkness and demonology, in large measure the result of the polarization by early Christians of the good and evil components of his nature. The mentally retarded, exploited as court fools or jesters, seem to have been viewed as enjoying the favor of God. The mentally ill, with their bizarre behavior, strange utterances, and distorted beliefs, were often considered possessed by Satan himself and thus were targets for cruel and inhumane treatment inflicted by God-fearing, righteous individuals. A thousand years later, such treatment was to culminate in the mass persecution of witches, many of whom were mentally ill, but some of whom were probably individuals with beliefs and behavior that were simply out of step with church, state, and community expectations. These thousand years or so did not pass without a dissenting voice regarding the inhumanity of such persecutions and pleas for more rational, scientific understanding of mental illness, but such voices were not to achieve prominence until near the end of the eighteenth century.

Science

Science has stood through the centuries in opposition to the irrational and superstitious and has attempted a lawful explanation of natural events and man's behavior through observation, study, and experimentation. Hippocrates, four centuries B.C., considered mental illness a disease brought on by natural causes rather than the anger of the gods. Although his medical explanation for the ills of the mind and body were based on intuition and clinical observation rather than fact, he was the first to attempt separating medicine from demonology, religion, and philosophy. The conflict between natural versus supernatural causes for mental and physical illness was to continue for centuries. In the second century A.D., the medical advancement of the Greek and Roman period came to a halt, and science was clearly overshadowed by superstition for more than a thousand years.

During the Middle Ages, when physical illness gradually came to be considered the result of natural causes, mental illness was still largely viewed as the result of possession by demons and spirits. By the eighteenth century, the physician returned to the tradition of Hippocrates and left questions of separating mind and body and the influence of evil spirits to the theologian and philosopher.

During the nineteenth century, psychiatry emerged as separate from medicine, and the physical disease framework for explaining mental illness adhered to by the physician of the eighteenth century was gradually extended to include the role of psychological factors. In the educational realm, Itard's documentation of his work with Victor was the beginning of the development of special education procedures based on observation and study that were to have far-reaching effects.

The early twentieth century saw scientific approaches applied to the measurement of individual differences by Binet, the formulation of theories of learning by Pavlov and Watson and others, and the medical investigation of genetic and biochemical factors in mental retardation. Our historical journey has been particularly noteworthy with respect to man's struggle with natural and supernatural explanations of physical and mental phenomena. The rapid emergence of scientific enlightenment during the past two centuries has greatly contributed to the trend for the pendulum to reside more and more in positions of science and service in relation to handicapped individuals.

ED

MR

Service

PH

Our summary of historical trends is not complete without consideration of the treatment and service that handicapped individuals have eventually come to receive. In primitive days, the physically defective were ignored or killed. The mentally ill were targets for worship or rejection since they were viewed as possessed by good or evil demons. During the Greek period, Plato advocated family care for the mentally ill and isolation for other defectives. The wealthy Romans exploited certain retarded individuals as buffoons and objects of amusement. Humane understanding and treatment of the mentally ill was advocated by some, but punishment with hunger and chains was seen as necessary by others.

The influence of Christianity during the centuries after the Greek and Roman periods brought about commiseration, solicitude, and care for some of the handicapped; but mental defectives were

still exploited as court fools or jesters, and the mentally ill were subjected to religious rites of exorcism, rejection, torture, and even
death.   In some cases, monasteries were places of refuge for the
deranged, and kindness and attempts at primitive medical treatment
were provided.   Gheel, Belgium, stands out as testimony to the
multi-variable nature of man at all times throughout the ages.   Here
an entire community accepted the mentally sick into its homes as a
natural course of events, and pilgrimages from all parts of the
civilized world came to the shrine established there.   In the sixteenth
century, treatment of the mentally ill was influenced by the almost
universal hysteria generated by belief in witchcraft, and extremely
cruel and inhumane treatment was seen as a justifiable means of
driving out the devil.   Once again, however, voices of reason spoke
out, if only softly and briefly, for compassion in treating the mentally
ill and removal of chains and force.   However, bloodletting, twirling
on stools, and "ducking" under water were advocated by some as
treatment methods.   Custodial care for the mentally ill was initiated
in London at St. Mary of Bethlehem (Bedlam), but little treatment
was offered.

    The seventeenth century saw the beginnings of the develop-
ment of special instructional techniques for the blind and deaf and
attempts to describe mental retardation and mental illness from
psychological and educational points of view.   During the eighteenth
century, children suffered from shockingly high mortality rates and
abuses in factories and were sentenced to harsh prisons if they
broke the law.   Their lot was destined to improve, as was the fate
of many of the weak and handicapped, with the French Revolution
and the dramatic awakening it created with regard to the individuality of man and his rights.   Pinel struck off the chains of the
mentally ill in France, Tuke established a humanitarian retreat for
them in England, and Rush brought about more humane treatment
in the United States.   Schools for the blind and deaf appeared by
the end of the eighteenth century, but little was done for the physically handicapped, retarded, or disturbed until the nineteenth century.   Reform in the treatment of the mentally ill was a major issue
during the 1800's.   Dorothea Dix attacked the deplorable conditions
in American institutions.   The work of Itard and Seguin in the
nineteenth century reflected not only a dedication to educate the
handicapped but also an enthusiasm and optimism that every child,
no matter how extreme his problem, could be taught "something."
With their work began an era of creative individualization of instructional materials and techniques that can be considered the true
beginning of the field of special education.   This optimism diminished at the turn of the century with the alarmist eugenics movement

and the notion of fixed intelligence, but it appeared again in the 1960's with a national commitment to handicapped children and youth.

ED

Special schools for exceptional children began to appear in 1818; by 1890, state responsibility for the care of the retarded was accepted. Special classes were established in public schools for the mentally retarded in Germany in 1860 and appeared in America toward the turn of the century; classes for other exceptional children appeared as early as 1869 in the United States. The twentieth century has seen improved and increased services to the handicapped in this country. Freudian psychology contributed to the understanding of the psychological basis for mental illness and the importance of early experience in the development of the child. In the early 1900's, Binet's testing movement revealed thousands of mildly retarded who had previously been overlooked, and isolated state institutions were modified to include work colonies. Gifted children were provided with accelerated programs. After World War II, a gradual but steadily increasing delivery of services to handicapped individuals occurred, and with the 1960's and President Kennedy's efforts on behalf of the retarded, special education entered an accelerated period of growth in research, training, and programs.

MR

As we look back, it is apparent that the handicapped individual's chances for survival, the enlightened understanding of his problems, the scientific contributions to his welfare and development, and the range of services available to help him develop and utilize his true potential exist in greater measure today than ever before. We have recaptured some of Itard's and Seguin's enthusiasm and optimism regarding the parts that education and training can play in improving the functioning level of the handicapped, particularly the retarded. Our present level of optimism does not naively assume that the mentally retarded can be cured through training procedures, but we are firmly convinced that special education can make an important difference in their lives and the lives of all handicapped children. Such optimism is reflected in the philosophy of this book — that all exceptional children are, first and foremost, learners — ready at all times to learn something and only secondarily handicapped by conditions that limit learning. With this historical journey behind us, we turn to the present and an introduction to nine contemporary categories of exceptionality.

G

CHAPTER 2

Contemporary Practices

ED

LD

MR

SD

VH

HH

SH

PH

G

Our historical journey in the last chapter introduced us to many descriptive terms and labels that have been applied to individuals whose appearance and behavior differed from the majority of those around them. We found the mentally handicapped described as having mania or melancholia, as insane, as idiots, imbeciles, simpletons, witches, sorcerers, madmen, infants of God, sots, and morons. Many other exceptional individuals probably fell into such general classifications as the weak, odd, and the poor. During the past century, however, as our concern with the treatment and education of the handicapped has markedly increased, the categories used to describe the range of exceptionalities have been extended and made more specific. As stated, we will consider nine such categories in our discussion of exceptional learners:

1. Emotionally disturbed children
2. Children with learning disabilities
3. Mentally retarded children
4. Socially and economically disadvantaged children
5. Visually handicapped children
6. Hearing handicapped children
7. Speech handicapped children
8. Physically handicapped children
9. Gifted children

These labels describe the major categories into which exceptional

ED

children have been placed and most of the categories can be further broken down. Nine categories cover a wide range of differences, and it will be difficult in this text to do justice to the large body of descriptive data available on each. As if this were not problem enough, there is always the possibility that a given exceptional child will fall into more than one category. For example, a child may be mentally retarded, demonstrate serious emotional problems, suffer from a speech handicap, and live in an economically disadvantaged environment. What category does he fall into? Such a child is multi-handicapped, and special educators have increasingly recognized the fact that a large number of such children exist.

Combinations of handicapping conditions are so numerous that we must chart a reasonable course for ourselves at the outset of this book. In this chapter, we shall restrict our discussion to children whose major handicap falls in one of the nine categories. However, beginning with Part II and continuing through the remainder of the book, we shall move to collective consideration of exceptional children along behavioral dimensions that relate to adaptation to the physical and social environment in general and to the school environment in particular. Such an approach not only will provide an opportunity for comparing various exceptionalities along common dimensions, but also will allow us to consider the types of problems that are faced by children with more than one handicapping condition.

In the following sections we will separately consider the nine exceptionalities in terms of definition and classification, incidence, causal conditions, identification and diagnosis, treatment, and educational provisions. And once we have established the exceptional child in his traditional guise we shall move to collective consideration in Parts II and III.

EMOTIONALLY DISTURBED CHILDREN

Most children are emotionally disturbed from time to time during the course of growing up. Longitudinal studies reveal that a surprisingly large number of so-called normal children exhibit such disturbed behaviors as fearfulness, destructiveness, and hyperactivity (Macfarlane, Allen, & Honzik, 1955). But most of these children are never labeled "emotionally disturbed" because their problem behavior is moderate in degree, infrequent in occurrence, and not definitely patterned. Just when a given child qualifies for such a label is often difficult to determine and is related to the setting in which he is being observed and the expectations of the observer.   In the classroom, a child who is inattentive, withdrawn, or nonconforming to such a degree that he consistently fails to meet the expectations of the teacher and the school is a likely candidate for the label "emotionally disturbed."

ED

Definition

Formal definition of the term "emotional disturbance" reflects the theoretical orientation of the labeler.   Some orientations are:

Psychiatric approach: primary behavior disorders, psychosomatic disorders, and psychoses (Watson, 1959)

Psychodynamic approach: impairment of emotional growth during some stage of development with resultant distrust toward self and others and hostility generated from anxiety (Moustakas, 1953, 1955)

Psycho-social and psycho-educational approach: socially defective children, children with neurotic conflicts, and children with psychotic processes (Morse, 1967)

Neurological approach: brain damage behavior syndrome, hyperkinetic-impulse disorder, Strauss syndrome, and postencephalitic behavior syndrome (Clements & Peters, 1962)

Legal approach: behavior that violates specific legal norms with such seriousness or frequency that it constitutes arrest or court action and results in the label "juvenile delinquent" (Kvaraceus & Miller, 1959)

Ecological approach: what is considered deviant, how it is designated, interpreted, and treated is viewed as much a function of the perceiver as of the behaver (Rhodes, 1967)

Behavioral-educational approaches: disorders that consist of inadequate or inappropriate behavior that is learned and can therefore be changed through application of learning procedures (Dupont, 1969)

The child who cannot or will not adjust to the socially acceptable norms for behavior and consequently disrupts his own academic progress, the learning efforts of his classmates, and interpersonal relations (Woody, 1969)

A socialization failure whose behavior is maladaptive and deviates from what is expected for his age, sex, and social status (Hewett, 1968)

Classification

ED

Even though we cannot discuss each definition or point of view in detail here, we can present them as a means of introducing the emotionally disturbed child as the complex individual he has come to be in the literature. His behavior has been considered the result of mental illness, ego deficits, inadequate socialization, neurological impairment, and learned maladaptive behavior. In this text we will focus on the emotionally disturbed child as a learning and behavior problem; but in order to provide a more traditional background, we will first review a psychiatric classification system. The psychiatric approach as described by Watson (1959) organizes emotional disturbance into primary behavior disorders (habit disturbances, conduct disturbances, and neurotic traits), psychosomatic disorders, and psychoses.

Among the primary behavior disorders, habit disturbances involve problems in the performance of some major biological function, such as eating, sleeping, elimination, and sex. These may include thumbsucking, nail biting, eating too much or too little, vomiting, bedwetting, soiling, inability to sleep, night terrors, faulty speech development, and sexual disturbances. Conduct disturbances normally occur at a later age than habit disturbances and reflect aggressive, destructive, nonconforming, and delinquent behavior. The child with a conduct disturbance is seen as attempting to coerce the world into meeting his needs on his own terms. Whereas conduct disturbances relate to a conflict between the child and his environment, neurotic traits are at least partially internalized and show a conflict within the self. They are manifest in such problems as jealousy, withdrawal, inhibition of aggression, and phobias which are related to fear of animals, the dark, or strangers and which are often accompanied by intense anxiety.

Psychosomatic disorders result when increasing psychological tensions are reflected through anatomical and physiological channels; they include gastrointestinal pain, fever, headaches, allergic conditions, and ulcerative colitis. Psychotic reactions are more severe disturbances than primary behavior disturbances and are more all-encompassing in relation to the child's behavior. Personality disorganization is extensive and often the child's development has been atypical and irregular since early infancy. There are disturbances in the most basic interpersonal relationships. In addition, there are usually many areas of inadequacy that can involve speech disorders, deviant thought processes, bizarre preoccupations, low frustration tolerance, and excessive fantasy, often to the point of in-

ability to separate fantasy from reality.   Childhood schizophrenia is
a severe psychotic reaction.

The most profoundly disturbed child is the child who evidences early infantile autism.   The autistic child may exhibit extreme
problems in the areas cited above.   Among the behaviors commonly
seen among autistic children are constant rituals, head banging,
rocking, and total withdrawal from contact with others.   These children also often fail to develop any communicative speech and
demonstrate an intense concern for "sameness" in the environment.

One behavioral-educational approach to the classification of
emotional disturbance was based on an analysis of teacher ratings of
children's problem behaviors.   Morse, Cutler, and Fink (1964)
gathered ratings on 441 children made by sixty different teachers
using a rating scale developed by Peterson (1961).   The sample of
teachers, from all over the country, represented a wide range of
placement and program philosophies.   These ratings were subjected
to a factor analytic study (Quay, Morse, & Cutler, 1966).   Three independent clusters or dimensions of behavior were found to account
for the major variance.   These three dimensions are summarized as
follows:

1. Conduct disorder: includes children described as defiant, im-
   pertinent, uncooperative, irritable, and boisterous
2. Inadequacy-immaturity: covers problems such as sluggishness,
   laziness, lack of interest, preoccupation, dislike for school, and
   inattentiveness
3. Personality problem: includes "inferiority feelings," "self-
   consciousness," "lack of self-confidence," "fearfulness," and
   "depression"

These dimensions cannot all be directly related to the psychiatric
classification presented earlier, but the first and third appear to
relate to conduct disturbances and neurotic traits, respectively.   The
second may be a variant on psychotic traits.

Another type of child described in this study but whose traits
did not point to a single distinguishing factor is the socialized
delinquent.   Quay (1963b) considers the socialized delinquent outside the realm of the "emotionally disturbed" since the child's
socially maladjusted behavior in school may well represent appropriate behavior in his "street world."   We have not included
social maladjustment or delinquency as a separate category but
rather will consider many of the characteristics of children with such
problems within the categories of the emotionally disturbed and the

ED

disadvantaged. The psychiatric and related psycho-educational approaches to classification tend to focus on the inner life of the disturbed child, including the conflicts and dynamics underlying his problems. They ask the question: Why is this child disturbed? Behavioral-educational approaches are concerned with the observable manifestations of the child's problems and consider the questions: What maladaptive behavior does the child manifest, how are environmental events related to the maintenance of such behaviors, and how can the environment be altered so the child develops more adaptive behavior? These two approaches are not mutually exclusive and can be largely distinguished by emphasis and priority ranking of goals.

One attempt to relate the problems of emotionally disturbed children directly to learning and success in school uses a developmental sequence of educational goals as a framework for viewing maladaptive behavior (Hewett, 1968). The developmental sequence includes six levels of competence required for learning:

1. Attention   4. Exploratory
2. Response   5. Social
3. Order   6. Mastery

Emotional disturbance is defined as a lack of competence at one or more levels. Part III of this text expands on this approach and extends it to all nine categories of exceptional learners.

Incidence

Because of the numerous classification systems used to describe emotionally disturbed children and the lack of clarity that results regarding specific types of problems described by a given label, studies to determine actual incidence of emotional disturbance vary in their estimates. This problem has been discussed by Woody (1969), who states that whereas one investigator may consider "timidity" and "withdrawal" as separate behaviors, another might group them together. In addition, definition of such terms as "introverted" and "aggressive" often are impossible to state with precision. The United States Office of Education (1970) estimates that some two percent of the school-age children in the nation are emotionally disturbed. Some previous estimates, however, have ranged from ten to twenty-five percent (Bower, Tashnovian, & Larson, 1958;

Ohio Commission on Youth and Children, 1956; the Ford Foundation, 1958; and the American Psychiatric Association, 1964). Schultz,
Hirshoren, Manton, and Henderson (1971) reported wide discrepancies among state prevalence estimates of emotional disturbance
which are used for special education purposes.   While eighteen
states used an estimate of two percent, the total range nationally was
from .05 percent to fifteen percent.   White and Harris (1961), in
reviewing studies between 1928 and 1958, concluded that the incidence of serious maladjustment is somewhere between four and
seven percent but that incidence of mild maladjustment is impossible
to estimate due to problems and inconsistencies in definition, sampling, and assessment.   With respect to sex, boys are consistently
found in greater number in populations of disturbed children with
estimates ranging from sixty-six percent (McCafferey & Cumming,
1967) to eighty percent (Quay, Morse, & Cutler, 1966).

The validity of incidence estimates arising from single surveys has been questioned by McCafferey and Cumming (1967).
They followed a group of children, classified as emotionally disturbed by their teachers in the second grade, to the fifth grade level
and found the majority of the children were no longer classified as
disturbed by that time.   Such spontaneous improvement over time
also has been reported by Glavin (1968) and Clarizio (1968).
Lewis (1965) reviewed the literature on the effect of psychothera-
peutic intervention on the status of children considered emotionally
disturbed and concluded that two-thirds improved whether they
received therapy or not.   He therefore regarded maturation rather
than therapeutic treatment as the key factor in accounting for
improved adjustment.

These findings suggest that emotional disturbance is a transient phenomenon in the lives of most children so classified and that
an orientation toward them as "learners" on their way to improving
their adjustment may be more valid, particularly in the educational
realm, than one that considers them ill or disabled.   Viewed in such
a context, incidence figures are largely meaningless.

Causes

The American Psychiatric Association (1952) classifies mental illness
into two major categories:

1.   Organic brain disorders
2.   Functional disorders, including psychiatric, psychophysiologic,

and visceral, psychoneurotic, personality (character), and transient situational personality disorders

Thus emotional disturbance can result from organic brain dysfunction or experiential factors such as family, cultural, and social influences or a combination of both. Experiential factors, some of which begin early in childhood, determine the majority of emotional disturbances seen among school-age children. The role of neurological problems also has received increasing attention. Clements and Peters (1962) have stated that "most" childhood psychoses are based on brain deviation. Among the evidence they cite to relate behavior and learning problems to brain dysfunction are the positive correlations between complications of pregnancy and later behavior and learning problems, the good response of children with suspected brain damage to drugs and training without psychotherapy, and differences between siblings reared in similar environments. Since such problem behaviors as impulsivity, hyperactivity, and distractibility frequently found among children considered brain damaged are also seen in emotionally disturbed children, the question often arises as to whether the child's primary difficulties are organic or functional in origin. Reger (1965) has concluded that the only way a diagnosis of minimal brain damage can be made with certainty is through autopsy. In contrast to this position, Clements and Peters (1962) claim that there are definite behavioral similarities between some children with questionable histories and adults with known brain damage and that these symptoms often cluster into recognizable entities.

Thus the etiological or causal puzzle is complex to assemble; what pieces are selected and how they are related is often determined by the theoretical orientation or professional discipline of the individual who attempts to explain the "why" of behavior and learning problems. In two California school districts within twenty miles of each other, the author observed marked differences in explanations of causality offered by district consultants working with educationally handicapped children. The state of California uses the category "educationally handicapped" to describe both the emotionally disturbed child and the child with a learning disability. One district utilized the consultative services of a physician who was thoroughly convinced that most behavior and learning problems were neurologically based. This district reported that eighty-five percent of its educationally handicapped children's problems were organic in nature. In the other district in which the physician did not share this bias, only ten percent of the educationally handicapped was estimated as suffering from neurological impairment.

Identification and Diagnosis

ED

In identifying emotionally disturbed children, the judgment of class-room teachers is a common criterion.   A casual observer in any classroom can usually select several children who appear out of step with their peers and the expectations of the teacher.   A classroom teacher who has become familiar with the typical range of learning and behavioral differences found among children in a certain age group is in a better position to single out children with special prob-lems, much as Mrs. Thompson did in our Introduction.   Bower (1960, 1961) found that teachers were surprisingly accurate in their designation of emotionally disturbed children when compared to selections made by psychologists and psychiatrists.   Maes (1966) analyzed Bower's data and found that teacher ratings of behavior had the highest predictive value with regard to the ratings of clinicians.   Once the emotionally disturbed child has been identified he may be referred for an evaluation to a school psychologist or other professionals in the manner described in our examples of Susan and Henry in the Introduction.   Woody (1969) has discussed in detail the detection, referral, and psycho-educational diagnostic procedures commonly used with behavioral problem children.

Treatment

In attempting to aid the disturbed child in improving his learning and behavior in school, psychotherapy or some form of counseling may be recommended for him and/or his parents.   This is most often provided outside the school by a psychiatrist, clinical psychol-ogist, or social worker on a private or clinic basis.   Some school dis-tricts, however, have offered group and individual counseling to students as a part of their psychological services program.   The effects of psychotherapy on the child's school performance are not clear from studies that have been done.   As noted earlier, two-thirds of children labeled disturbed in several investigations improved over time without therapy.   Therefore, studies on the effect of psycho-therapy are apt also to reflect spontaneous improvement.

Phillips (1960) compared short-term, non-depth therapy with traditional psychoanalytically oriented therapy with children from three to eleven years of age, matched for I.Q.   The short-term approach gave parents "common sense" explanations of the child's problem and included the teacher in an information-giving-and-taking role.   Based on ratings of children's behavior at home and in school, ninety-two percent of the non-depth group and sixty percent

ED

of the depth therapy group were judged as improving significantly.

Glavin and Quay (1969) reviewed the recent literature with respect to the effects of therapeutic efforts undertaken with the disturbed child and/or his parents. They concluded that such interventions are more effective if they involve the parents also, rather than just the disturbed child. Slatoff (1968), however, has reported that many parents of disturbed children strongly resist getting actively involved in therapy since they prefer to deny the existence of the child's problem.

Educational Provisions

Most emotionally disturbed children remain in regular classrooms. A visit to almost any classroom will reveal two or three such children in a class of thirty. Whether these disturbed children are referred for a diagnostic evaluation and possible placement in a special class will depend, among other things, on the classroom teacher's range of tolerance for behavioral and academic differences. This range often varies markedly from teacher to teacher. Some teachers are comfortable with "acting out" or disruptive students; others tolerate little deviance from expected standards of behavior. Shy, fearful children may seem to "disappear into the woodwork" in some classes, whereas in others the teacher will be deeply concerned with such withdrawal.

In an early study, Wickman (1928) found that teachers rated "acting out" children as having more serious problems than children who were timid and shy. These ratings were opposite of those made by mental hygienists who saw the withdrawn child as having the most serious problems. Recent studies (Bower, 1957; Beilin, 1959), however, show that contemporary teachers are very aware of the possible seriousness of withdrawal.

The child who falls outside the range of tolerance for behavioral differences of the teacher is most apt to be placed outside the regular classroom. In general, the author has observed that teachers' ranges of tolerance for academic differences among children are much greater than their range of tolerance for behavioral differences. The underachieving, disturbed child may be maintained for the major portion of his school career if his teachers accept and can deal with his behavior.

The issue of placing exceptional children in special classes as opposed to integrating them in the regular school program will be dealt with in Chapter 10. But here we will point out that there is conflicting evidence regarding the social, emotional, and academic advantages of either setting to the disturbed child. Special classes are set up for "emotionally disturbed" children in many school districts and a variety of labels are attached to them (e.g., social adjustment classes, classes for the educationally handicapped, classes for behaviorally disordered children). These classes may contain from six to fifteen students and be under the supervision of a teacher holding special credentials, with special training, or neither. Many such classes are self-contained with the child spending his entire school day in the class. However, resource rooms under the supervision of a "crisis teacher" offering part-time help for children with behavior and learning problems are appearing on the scene (Morse, Cutler, & Fink, 1968).

In a national survey of educational programs in the public school for disturbed children, Morse, Cutler, and Fink (1964) classified such programs into seven categories: psychiatric-dynamic, psycho-educational, psychological-behavioral, educational, naturalistic, primitive, and chaotic. The first two approaches are concerned with underlying psychological problems relating to the child's difficulties in school, whereas the second and third are more interested in manifest behavior problems and academic deficiencies. Most teachers reviewed the primary problems of their students in behavioral and educational terms and academics were listed as occupying more than fifty percent of the class time in seventy percent of the programs evaluated.

Some districts maintain separate schools for emotionally disturbed children and others assist parents with tuition costs for private day schools. Residential schools that offer twenty-four-hour supervision may be the most desirable placement for a child whose family and home situation is poor. A major effort in organizing a residential treatment program with a strong educational emphasis has occurred with Project Re-Ed (Hobbs, 1966; Lewis, 1967). In this program, the child receives the benefit of a therapeutic milieu in which his daily life is organized and supported by a wide range of professionals, including special educators, social workers, psychologists, and psychiatrists. The goal is to re-establish the child as quickly as possible in his home, school, and community. The average stay per child is six months, and a success rate of between seventy-five and eighty-seven percent has been reported.

Placement in a state institution for the mentally ill is usually the last resort for those children who are so severely disturbed that they need twenty-four-hour care and for whom residential schools are unavailable due to scarcity of facilities or funds. The Neuropsychiatric Institute at the University of California, Los Angeles, is an institutional setting that provides extensive diagnostic and treatment service, including a full-time school program for disturbed children for limited periods of time. Eventual referrals cover the full range of possible placements from return to public school to long-term care in a residential state institution.

Schultz, Hirshoren, Manton, and Henderson (1971) identified twelve types of services to emotionally disturbed children provided by school districts across the nation. These are:

1. Special class
2. Resource-room
3. Crisis intervention
4. Itinerant-teacher program
5. Academic tutoring
6. Homebound instruction
7. Guidance counselors
8. School social workers
9. Psychotherapy provided by school psychologists
10. Psychiatric consultation
11. Transportation provided by district to nonschool agency
12. School district payment of private school tuition

The special class placement was found to be utilized by the most states, followed by resource-room programs and homebound instruction.

This introduction to the emotionally disturbed child has reviewed definition and classification approaches, estimates of incidence, possible causal conditions, identification and diagnostic procedures, as well as treatment and educational programs available. More detailed information, as well as a clearer understanding of what the disturbed child is really like at home, in the community, and at school will follow.

CHILDREN WITH LEARNING DISABILITIES

When a child displays an educationally significant discrepancy between his estimated intellectual potential and actual school performance that cannot be explained in terms of intellectual, experiential, sensory, or physical problems, he may be labeled as having a "learning disability."

Definition

Kirk and Bateman (1962) define this category as follows:

> A learning disability refers to a retardation, disorder, or delayed development in one or more of the processes of speech, language, reading, writing, arithmetic, or other school subjects resulting from a psychological handicap caused by a possible cerebral dysfunction and/or emotional or behavioral disturbances. It is not the result of mental retardation, sensory deprivation, or cultural or instructional factors.

LD

This definition describes a child advancing toward educational goals at a slower rate than would be expected in terms of his ability, a child who may need specialized remedial help to overcome his difficulties. The underlying basis for his learning disability either may be neurological or it may result from emotional or behavioral disturbances. Definitions of children with learning disabilities are apt to differ considerably with reference to this latter assumption. For example, the National Advisory Committee on Handicapped Children of the United States Office of Education proposed the following definition (1968) for use in the congressional bill entitled "The Learning Disabilities Act of 1969":

> Children with special (specific) learning disabilities exhibit a disorder in one or more of the basic psychological processes involved in understanding or in using spoken or written language. These may be manifested in disorders of listening, thinking, talking, reading, writing, spelling, or arithmetic. They include conditions which have been referred to as perceptual handicaps, brain injury, minimal brain dysfunction, dyslexia, developmental aphasia, etc. They *do not* include learning problems which are due primarily to visual, hearing, or motor handicaps, to mental retardation, emotional disturbance, or to environmental disadvantage (p. 73).

This definition narrows the category to exclude children with emotional or behavioral disturbances. Historically, the notion of specific learning disabilities emanates from the 1860's and 1870's, when the prediction of functional loss as a result of specific brain lesions or injuries became meaningfully accurate (Gearheart, 1973). In recent decades, special educational strategies related to the instruction of brain-injured children, as contrasted with the genetically retarded, began to evolve and have continued to the present day. One notable proponent of a special educational program for certain types of children with presumed brain injury was Dr. Alfred Strauss,

whose expertise in the medical/physiological aspects of the problem
was fostered by his efforts to re-educate brain-injured veterans of
World War II in Germany (Gearheart, 1973). Strauss, working in
conjunction with Laura Lehtinen, a special educator, described the
endogenous or genetically retarded child as contrasting dramatically
with the exogenous or brain-injured child. They described the
brain-injured child according to four behavioral characteristics: perceptual disorders, a greater tendency to perseverate upon one activity, conceptual alienations in organization of thought, and unusual
or inappropriate social or behavioral style. Strauss and Lehtinen
also described three biological characteristics of the brain-injured
child, but these are of limited usefulness for classification purposes
since a child may not exhibit any of them yet may still qualify for
the label of brain injury based on his demonstrating the four
behavioral characteristics (McIntosh & Dunn, 1973). The exogenous or brain-injured child has come to be known as the Strauss
syndrome child. Strauss and Lehtinen's work with these children
is described in their book, *Psychopathology and Education of the
Brain-Injured Child* (Strauss & Lehtinen, 1947). Even though many
children with unexplained learning problems demonstrate characteristics associated with brain injury, establishing the presence of
definite neurological impairment rarely occurs, due either to the
subtle nature of the impairment, or to the limitation of present-day
medical diagnostic techniques, or to the fact that many such children actually have motivational or emotional problems that account
for their hyperactivity and distractibility. Efforts to resolve this
controversy will undoubtedly continue; but in the context of the
field of special education in general and the philosophy of this book
in particular, the argument has more theoretical and academic than
practical educational relevance. The Kirk and Bateman definition
wisely sidesteps this issue, for what really matters is that some
children simply are not efficient, capable learners in line with their
capacity; and since their basic disorders in the learning process
persist and can be specified, we try to remedy them quickly.

Classification and Incidence

How many children with learning disabilities are there in the
nation today? Since our statement of the necessary conditions for
placing a child in the category is imprecise, so also will be our estimates of incidence. Gruenberg (1964b), however, attempts logically to divide into three groups the population of children who

display symptoms of brain injury and who may be said to manifest learning disabilities:

1. Children with established neurological impairment
2. Children with purely functional impairment (based on non-organic problems)
3. Children with suspected but unconfirmed neurological impairment

LD

Children who clearly have central nervous system damage, such as cerebral palsy and epilepsy (to be discussed in our section on the physically handicapped), account for one percent or less of the school population. Children with functional problems might include fifteen to twenty percent, if the full range of children having difficulty in school as a result of educational deficits and cultural factors were included; Kirk and Bateman exclude these as does the National Advisory Committee on Handicapped Children. The actual incidence of the unconfirmed group is unknown, but estimates of five percent of the school-age population are not uncommon. The United States Office of Education (1970) offers a conservative estimate, as it did with emotional disturbance. According to their estimate, only one percent of school-age children are seen as having learning disabilities. And again, boys substantially outnumber girls.

Causes

Depending on our definition of a learning disability, questions regarding etiology or causality will be answered differently. Gruenberg's first and second types of children are considered elsewhere in this chapter with respect to causal factors. Children in the third group (those presumed to have an actual dysfunction of the central nervous system and a resultant learning disability) typically have had problems related to the birth process. Defects in germ plasm, noxious influences affecting embryonic, fetal, or infantile development, or chemical and mechanical factors that may irreversibly damage the neural tissue of the neonate may be involved, as may be neurological damage suffered as a result of postnatal trauma or infection.

McCarthy and McCarthy (1969) point out that not all types of cerebral dysfunction lead to learning disabilities, and conversely, that not all school learning problems can be classified as learning disabilities. They use the model of two overlapping circles, one representing presumed cerebral dysfunction and the other representing actual learning problems in school. Children may either suffer from cerebral dysfunction or have learning problems without a relationship existing, but the areas in which the circles overlap represent the group with learning disabilities.

Identification

Clements (1966) reviewed many recent publications concerned with the characteristics of children with learning disabilities. In order of frequency mentioned, the ten most cited were:

1. Hyperactivity
2. Perceptual-motor impairments
3. Emotional lability
4. General orientation defects
5. Disorders of attention (e.g., short attention span, distractibility)
6. Impulsivity
7. Disorders of memory and thinking
8. Specific learning disabilities in reading, arithmetic, writing, and spelling
9. Disorders of speech and hearing
10. Equivocal neurological signs and electroencephalographic irregularities

Hyperactivity, leading this list, is a general description for many other characteristics, including emotional lability and impulsivity, which are also on the list. Shrager, Lindy, Harrison, McDermott, & Wilson (1966) report that the teachers, social workers, psychiatrists, psychologists, and pediatricians that they surveyed reached a consensus on six behaviors most characteristic of hyperactivity in children: (1) fidgety and restless, (2) inattentive, (3) hard to manage, (4) unable to sit still, (5) easily distracted, and (6) unable to take frustration. Underlying all these terms is the notion of an activity level that is quantitatively above normal and qualitatively different as far as appropriate social behavior is concerned.

Keogh (1971) has enumerated three possibly interrelated hypotheses regarding etiology and intervention for the hyperactive-type behavior complex. The first hypothesis assumes that some maladaptive behaviors reflect neurological impairment. Keogh's

second hypothesis assumes that the hyperactive child may be neu-
rally intact, but that the nature and extent of his motor activity disrupts the accurate acquisition of information especially during
crucial points of learning.   Hypothesis number three concerns a
speeded-up decision-making process in hyperactive children that
may cause them to make decisions before they consider all relevant
information, even though the incomplete information used for the
decision is relatively accurate.   Although Keogh cautions that these
etiological hypotheses may not be mutually exclusive, it is clear that
they generate different treatment methodologies that may be useful in future efforts to validate them.   For example, a hyperactive
child envisioned as organically impaired might best be helped by
drug therapy, whereas the same child, alternatively viewed as an
impulsive rather than reflective decision maker, might profit from
instruction that reduced the amount of information available for
decision making.   Empirical measurement of the effect of different
treatments might well lend support to one hypothesis or the other,
or possibly their interaction.

     According to McCarthy and McCarthy (1969), identifying a
child with a learning disability involves eliminating children whose
problems can be explained as something other than cerebral dysfunction.   Thus the field tends to adopt the guidelines of the definition proposed by the National Committee on Handicapped Children.

Diagnosis

If viewed as "diagnosis-by-elimination," the diagnosis of learning
disabilities must involve comprehensive medical, psychological, linguistic, and educational evaluation.   Clements (1966) has outlined
such an evaluation to include medical, developmental, and family-
social history taking, general physical and neurological examination
to assess vision and hearing, routine laboratory tests, and special
tests such as electroencephalographic brain wave tracings when indicated.   Also recommended are a behavioral assessment, involving
a study of cumulative school records for information about behavior,
school progress, and achievement; psychological evaluation with an
individual intelligence test; visual-motor-perceptual tests; personality tests; speech and linguistic evaluations to assess the child's ability
to communicate and think in language symbols; and achievement
testing in reading, arithmetic, and spelling.   The same evaluation
procedure might be recommended for any exceptional child, since
it will provide valuable information about the nature and extent of
his problems.

LD

True differential diagnosis, that is, ruling out the effects of all factors except presumed cerebral dysfunction, is an idealized concept not easily attained and perhaps not necessary in the long run. The goal of all evaluation in special education is as complete an understanding of the child as possible, so that educational intervention can be as specific and efficient as possible. McCarthy and McCarthy (1969) state that the significant concern for education is not the fact of brain injury but rather the presence of certain behaviors in the child's repertoire that make learning difficult or impossible.

Treatment and Educational Provisions

The broad range of characteristics identifying children with learning disabilities indicates that the problem areas given highest priority and the specific techniques utilized in the educational programs differ according to the theoretical bias of the special educator. Some of the approaches utilized are: linguistic (Bateman, 1964), motoric (Kephart, 1971), movement (Barsch, 1965), neurological reorganization (Delacato, 1963), visual-perceptual (Frostig & Horne, 1964), and the application of kinesthetic, tactual techniques (Fernald, 1943). These approaches stem from concern with fundamental pre-academic aspects of learning, which are thought to underlie the learning disability child's problem in achieving competence in complex skill areas such as reading, written language, and arithmetic. We will elaborate on some of these approaches in Part III.

Actual programs for children with learning disabilities reflect both the orientation of the special educators who run them and the specific problems of the children involved. McCarthy and McCarthy (1969) describe three types of programs: a visual-perceptual-motor program stressing body balance, movement, and positioning, and visual, auditory, and tactual training; a linguistic program, stressing talking, listening, and reading; and a diagnostic-remedial program, which undertakes an intensive individual assessment with each child, arrives at a remedial plan, and transmits this to the regular classroom teacher, who implements it with the continuing consultant help of an itinerant learning disabilities teacher. In contrast to the consultant and resource nature of the third program, other programs may enroll the child for part or full day, and most aim for a return to full-time regular class placement as early as possible.

An additional area that should be included at this point concerns the use of drug therapy with children with learning disabilities. Two classes of drugs commonly used with such children are tranquilizers and stimulant, sympathomimetic amines. Chlorpromazine, a major tranquilizer, has been used under a variety of conditions and seems to quiet hyperactive children, although, regrettably, unpleasant side effects may often interfere with learning (Freeman, 1966; Hartlage, 1965). Chlordianepoxide (Librium) and diazepam (Valium) are minor tranquilizers that have also been recommended for control of behavior disorders. Freeman (1966), however, cautions against uncritical use of any medication with children with learning and behavior problems. Amphetamines, such as Benzedrine and distroamphetamine (Depadrine) are widely used stimulants that paradoxically induce a quiescent rather than excitatory effect in prepubertal, hyperkinetic children. Another effective, "paradoxical" stimulant is methylphenidate (Ritalin), which has been demonstrated to improve significantly the task attention of hyperactive children in two studies by Sykes and his collaborators (1971, 1972). Nevertheless, Conners (1972) found considerable heterogeneity both physiologically and psychologically within his sample of assumed "minimal brain dysfunction" children treated with methylphenidate and other drugs. He concluded no particular syndrome of hyperkinesis was uniquely responsive to drug therapy and that reduction of motor activity level was not among the more important types of changes observed.

The child with a learning disability has existed in the school for many years, but in the past his difficulties may have been simply attributed to emotional disturbance or mental retardation. Despite our imprecision in definition and the preoccupation with presumed cerebral dysfunction as a cause of the problem, the emergence of the learning disability area has resulted in a focus on basic and specific disorders in the learning process rather than on global, medically based categories. This focus may eventually offer a unifying concept for the entire field of special education.

MENTALLY RETARDED CHILDREN

Definition

Within the past few years, the study of mental retardation has been subject to a knowledge implosion of unprecedented dimensions. As a result, some of our previous notions about the retarded child are being seriously questioned; there is increasing appreciation about the complicated nature of mental retardation; and, even as this text is being written, approaches to the mentally retarded are undergoing rapid change.

What is mental retardation? The definition accepted by the American Association of Mental Deficiency (AAMD) is that mental retardation "refers to subaverage general intellectual functioning which originates during the developmental period and is associated with impairment in adaptive behavior" (Heber, 1961, p. 499). Thus a person must meet three criteria in order to be considered retarded:

1. *Subaverage intellectual functioning,* generally determined on an individual intelligence test by performance at least one standard deviation below the mean.
2. *Onset during the developmental period,* that is, anytime before the seventeenth year of life which is regarded as the period during which intellectual potential is determined.
3. *Impairment in adaptive behavior.* During preschool years "adaptive behavior" refers predominantly to the rate of development of sensory motor skills, for example, sitting up, walking, and talking. During school years, it refers basically to academic achievement and, at the adult level, to the person's social and economic adjustment. However, all three factors — maturation, learning, and social adjustment — are considered important at every age as indices of adaptive behavior.

An important aspect of the definition is its emphasis on both intelligence and behavior. A school-age child who performs below average on a test of intelligence but still manages to succeed in the regular classroom, even on a marginal level, could not strictly be considered retarded according to this definition. The assumption is that the child's adaptive behavior reflects a higher level of intellect than is recorded by the test. A child who is not able to adapt to the regular classroom but who has measured intelligence in the normal range would not be considered retarded either. Impaired adaptive behavior, in his case, might be the result of some factor other than low intellectual ability, such as emotional disturbance. Thus a system of checks and balances is established to avoid such practices as labeling children as mentally retarded on the basis of a single criterion. As we shall see in Chapter 5, the questionable validity of intelligence test scores, especially with very young children or children from environmentally deprived backgrounds, makes it essential that such checks be maintained.

It is also important to realize that, under the AAMD definition, a person might be considered retarded at one time in his life but not at another. A child with low intelligence who does poorly in academic work would most likely be considered mentally re- tarded. As often happens, however, he may be able, upon gradua- tion from high school, to support himself independently at an unskilled or semi-skilled job, especially if he has had good voca- tional preparation. Society, at that point, would not necessarily consider him retarded. Social competency has, in fact, been con- sidered by some (Doll, 1941; Tredgold & Tredgold, 1952), as one of the most important diagnostic criteria for mental retardation. Thus numerous changes which occur over time in a person's life situation often play an important part in determining whether he will wear the label of mental retardation. This is particularly true in cases where the level of retardation is severe and more likely the result of some central nervous system pathology.

Classification

Though there are several ways to classify retarded children, the method generally favored by educators is to classify by educational potential. Retarded children are divided into four groups:

1. *Slow learners or borderline retarded* children (I.Q. 75–85) tend to be capable of marginal success in the regular classroom. Though many become school drop-outs, some manage to gradu- ate from high school. Most go on to become self-supporting and socially adjusted adults.
2. *Educable mentally retarded* children (I.Q. 50–75) are for the most part normal in appearance but can be said to function at an intellectual level which is approximately one-half to three- fourths that of normal children. EMR children will usually not be ready for academic skills such as reading and math in the first grade but can eventually be expected to attain anywhere from a second to sixth grade level in academic achievement. Most be- gin school in the regular classroom, but low achievement or adaptive behavior make it necessary for many to be placed in special classes. As adults, most will be capable of working at unskilled or semi-skilled jobs; yet some, particularly at the lower I.Q. levels, will need marginal assistance in economic and social adjustment.
3. *Trainable mentally retarded* children (I.Q. 25–50) function at a level which is one-fourth to one-half that of normal children. Most can be expected to have physical or sensory impairments

and tend to "look" different in terms of facial features or physical characteristics.   Unlike EMR children, TMR children's developmental problems emerge quite early in infancy or preschool years.   Normally placed in special day schools, TMR children need training in self-care activities and language development and, in most cases, are not capable of any but the most rudimentary skills at the first grade level.   Most will be capable only of limited economic usefulness, perhaps in a sheltered workshop.   As adults, many may ultimately have to live in residential institutions when parents or relatives are no longer able to provide for them.

4. *Profoundly mentally retarded* children (I.Q. below 25) are for the most part totally dependent on others for their existence, are institutionalized quite early in life, and are not presently considered in the purview of special education.

It should be noted that the I.Q. ranges given above are quite arbitrary and are mentioned only as a frame of reference.   There is also considerable overlap among I.Q. categories, and some school districts may not admit to their EMR classes any children who have I.Q.'s below 60.   Likewise some slow learners may be placed in EMR classes, and EMR children may well remain in regular classes because of their good adaptive behavior or simply because not enough special classes are available; in fact, only about half of all retarded children needing special education are currently being served (U.S. Office of Education, 1970).   It should also be noted that the educational system of classification does not completely correspond to the AAMD system (Heber, 1959), which classifies retardation accordingly: borderline (I.Q. 70–84), mild (55–69), moderate (40–54), severe (25–39), and profound (below 25).

Incidence

Three percent of the population of the United States are identified as mentally retarded (President's Committee on Mental Retardation, 1967).   The United States Office of Education places the percentage of school-age retarded children at 2.3.   It should be mentioned that if I.Q. were the only criterion used to determine mental retardation, we would expect statistically that some sixteen percent of the population would be considered retarded.   When the AAMD criterion of adaptive behavior is added, the incidence is, of course, dropped to three percent or less.   The prevalence of retarded children, however, is not the same at every age level.   Figure 8 is an

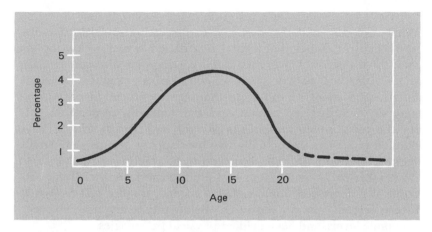

**Figure 8: Estimated Percentage of Mentally Retarded Persons
by Chronological Age**

illustration of the incidence of retardation by age of persons identified as retarded, and is a smoothed-curve adaptation of epidemiological data reported in Gruenberg (1964a).   It can be seen that
only a small percentage of children are diagnosed as retarded before
school age, and these are usually the more severely retarded who
are more easily identified.   Mildly retarded children, who comprise
the largest percentage, are usually not identified until after school
entrance when their intellectual differences are most obvious.   As
these persons leave school, their differences become less evident to
society and the percentage of identified mentally retarded persons
decreases.

The incidence of mild mental retardation also varies with
socio-economic class.   Kirk (1972) has indicated that, according to
the normal curve distribution, the number of educable mentally
retarded should be around 21 per 1,000 school children but that the
figure may range from 10 per 1,000 in areas of high socio-economic
status to 50 per 1,000 in poverty areas.   The number of trainable
retarded children (4 per 1,000) remains relatively constant across
socio-economic class since pathological conditions rather than socio-
environmental factors are primarily responsible for more severe
cases of retardation.   In fact, if a strict definition of mental retardation were used, employing precise measures of adaptive behavior
and eventual social competence, the exact incidence of mental
retardation would probably be closer to *one* percent overall (Dunn,
1973).   As we have seen with other exceptionalities, boys outnumber girls by a slight margin.

Causes

What causes mental retardation? In discussing etiology, it is important to remember that mental retardation is merely a symptom and not a disease. Over two hundred different diseases or other states of medical pathology are known to cause mental retardation, but these account for no more than ten to fifteen percent of all mentally retarded individuals and are generally responsible only for the more severe cases. As Wright and Tarjan (1963) have pointed out, there are actually two overlapping groups of mentally retarded individuals. The first tend to be mildly retarded with no discernible pathological signs and often come from socially or economically depressed families; but a second, smaller group (ten to fifteen percent) usually have I.Q.'s below fifty, come from all socio-economic levels, and have evident physical pathologies.

Organic or physical causes of mental retardation can occur before birth, during labor, or after birth. Among the more well known are: chromosomal disorders such as Down's syndrome, in which the child is born with characteristic "mongoloid" stigmata; inborn errors of metabolism such as phenylketonuria (PKU), in which the child is born lacking an enzyme necessary to metabolize phenylalanine and from which brain damage results unless a corrective diet is initiated early in infancy; and infections during fetal life such as rubella (German measles), which may cause serious damage to the fetus if the mother is infected during the first trimester of pregnancy. Mental retardation is also sometimes associated with prematurity, prolonged loss of oxygen during birth, and sustained high fever during childhood illness.

For nearly ninety percent of mentally retarded persons, however, it is impossible to pinpoint precisely what caused the retardation. In most cases, such individuals have I.Q.'s over fifty, are relatively normal in appearance, and tend to come mostly from lower socio-economic classes. Though controversy exists as to whether these individuals are simply the lower end of the polygenetically determined distribution of intelligence (Freeman, 1970; Jensen, 1969), Dunn (1973) has pointed out that mild mental retardation most likely results from the complex interplay of familial and societal factors in which heredity tends to set limits on intellectual potential while environment determines to what extent such potential will be fulfilled.

By way of illustration, one study by Wolf and Drillien (reported in Masland, Sarason, & Gladwin, 1958, p. 64) indicated that a prime predictor of prematurity in children (a condition that is sometimes associated with later mental retardation) was the maternal grandfather's income. It is not difficult to see why the amount of money a grandfather earns might be related to eventual mental retardation in his grandson. His financial ability to provide good nutrition, health care, and a minimal amount of education for the child's mother may ultimately be found to relate to mental retardation in a variety of complex and subtle ways: the socio-economic class which the mother herself attains, the community in which she lives, her health and ability to carry the fetus to term, her awareness of and willingness to seek child health services, the amount of cognitive stimulation she can provide for the child in formative years, her interest in preschool experiences for the child, and her reinforcement of his school efforts. These factors, among others, have been found to relate to a child's intelligence (Hurley, 1969; Hunt, 1961; Sarason & Gladwin, 1959).

Although subtle and as-yet-undiscovered biological factors may be the actual causes of mild mental retardation, the problem of a large percentage of the mildly retarded remains, at present, a non-medical issue. Unlike more severe mental retardation where medical sciences become the primary (though, of course, not the only) focus, solutions for the problems of mild retardation remain with behavioral scientists in such disciplines as psychology, psychiatry, sociology, anthropology, and special education. Preventive efforts, in which parents are taught to provide early environmental stimulation for their infants or in which early preschool experiences are available, can overcome, at least in part, the social and educational deficits which often occur in children from deprived backgrounds. School programs for both types of retarded children (excluding the more severely or profoundly retarded) are discussed below.

Identification, Diagnosis, and Educational Provisions

Educable mentally retarded (EMR) children are usually not identified as such before reaching school age. Although EMR children may well have problems in communication, physical development, and socialization during preschool years, differences tend to be moderate and may not cause undue concern until the child begins formal schooling. Where he might have been able at one time to function marginally at home or in his neighborhood, he now has to function in an environment which demands increasingly more than he is able to give. A child with an I.Q. of seventy may not be ready to begin reading until he is eight years old, while his normal peers will be reading well before that.

In most cases the potential EMR child may not be identified until he has spent one or more years in the regular classroom. Although elementary teachers are usually not prepared to teach the mentally retarded, many may not have even had an introductory course in exceptional children. Unless the school district has a group testing program in the early grades, the potential EMR child may remain in the regular class competing with normal peers. The EMR child whose learning problems are severe or whose behavior problems interfere with classroom management eventually becomes too difficult for his teacher to ignore.

At that point, the teacher seeks help, and the child is referred to a school psychologist. After giving the child a battery of tests designed to explore his functioning in areas of intelligence, perception, and personality, the school psychologist makes a decision as to the child's potential. Other professionals, such as pediatricians, may be consulted but usually an admissions team composed of the school psychologist, the teacher, the school nurse, and the principal makes the final determination. If the child's inability is due primarily to low intelligence and not to other factors, and if he cannot be expected to make satisfactory progress in the regular grades, the child is then referred for special education.

The most common form of special education for the EMR child is the special classroom, which is usually located within a regular public school. EMR classes are generally grouped according to the following levels: primary, elementary or intermediate, and secondary. Class enrollment may average fifteen to eighteen pupils, depending on the range of ages and mental abilities. Since *mandatory* education in many states may not begin for the EMR child until he is six or eight years old, preschool classes are seldom available. When they are, preschool classes provide experiences for the child to improve his school readiness much as normal preschools do for younger children but at a somewhat slower pace.

Special education classes at the primary level (ages six to nine) provide experiences in oral language and speech development, sensorimotor development, self-awareness, group membership and social adjustment, self-care, safety, manipulation of materials, work habits, direction following, and reading readiness. Academic tasks are not greatly emphasized except, perhaps, for beginning to count and recognize letters or words. By the elementary level (ages nine to thirteen), EMR children have begun learning tool skill subjects such as reading, writing, spelling, and math. Units in basic social studies and practical science are also taught not only as academic subjects but as activities in which tool skill subjects can be applied and practiced.

The secondary program provides consolidation in the use of tool subjects learned earlier but with increasing emphasis on preparation for work and home-living. Stress is given to civic responsibility, news media, use of leisure time, homemaking, consumer education, finances, practical law, social roles, travel, and vocational choice. The EMR typically has more opportunity for interaction with normal peers at the high school level in that he or she will be increasingly able to attend regular classes in physical education, industrial arts, home economics, and fine arts. Toward the end of his formal school career, the EMR youth will also become involved in a work-study program, a vocational training program run by an agency other than the school, or even a trial job on a part-time basis.

The focus of special education for EMR children, then, is on (1) developing basic academic skills, (2) social competence, (3) personal adjustment, and (4) occupational adequacy. Recent statements regarding education for the educable mentally retarded stress that they will ultimately need two basic skills which cut across all curriculum areas: (1) *thinking critically* or being able to weigh the facts of a given situation together with their implications, and (2) *acting independently* or making a decision based on these facts and following it through (Goldstein, 1969; Heiss & Mischio, 1971). Thus in order to become an independent adult, the EMR youngster may well have to be taught and given experience in problem-solving methods which will apply in generic fashion to a multitude of academic, personal, social, vocational, financial, and leisure situations.

Trainable mentally retarded (TMR) children are usually identified before reaching school age. The mongoloid stigma of Down's syndrome, for example, can be identified almost at birth, as can a number of other cases of mental retardation which feature abnormal physical characteristics. Even when gross physical abnormalities are absent, retardation may be so marked that the child fails to develop normally during the first years of life. Children who appear listless, fail to smile or babble, or are unable to sit up, walk, or talk within a normal length of time are all suspect. A pediatrician is usually the first person to whom concerned parents come for advice. Most pediatricians are not experts in mental retardation and will often refer parents to child development and evaluation clinics specializing in mental retardation where various professionals such as pediatric neurologists, social workers, and child psychologists working together in the same setting will be

MR

able, in most cases, to arrive at a definitive diagnosis and treatment plan.

In most cases the child can gain from systematic training in dressing, feeding, and toileting. Nursery schools or day-care centers have been established in limited numbers to provide habit training and language development programs for young TMR children. With the aid of other professionals, such as specially trained public health nurses who visit the home and provide guidance in child care and management, parents can usually maintain the child at home through the school years. The more severely retarded tend to present problems in medical and behavioral management and may have to be placed in residential facilities as they grow older, in many cases because of the debilitating effect the presence of a retarded child has on other family members (Farber, Jenne, & Toigo, 1960). Only about five percent of all the mentally retarded are in residential institutions, and the trend is toward keeping more retarded individuals in community settings wherever possible (President's Committee on Mental Retardation, 1971).

As trainable mentally retarded children reach school age, public education facilities are available but still in limited numbers. Special education is typically provided for TMR children in a special day school. Emphasis is on (1) oral language development, (2) self-help skills, (3) socialization, and (4) preparation for living and working in sheltered environments (Dunn, 1973; Johnson, 1967; Kirk, 1972). School activities include practice in listening, following directions, communicating with others, reading or recognizing signs and labels that are commonly encountered, counting, and telling time. Self-help activities include lessons in dressing, grooming, eating, care of personal belongings, toileting, and safety. TMR children also engage in arts and crafts, motor and recreational activities, some vocational experiences, and practice in home-living. Since many trainable mentally retarded children can ultimately be expected to live at home and, perhaps, work in a sheltered workshop, special education programs are generally geared, with increasing emphasis as the child grows older, to prepare them to function optimally in such situations.

SOCIALLY AND ECONOMICALLY DISADVANTAGED CHILDREN

As suggested in the last chapter, perhaps one of the oldest handicapping conditions, and one involving the largest number of individuals in history, is poverty; the social tragedy of child pauperism is reflected in our account of several historical periods. Although the socially and economically disadvantaged have not always been included in discussions of exceptional children in the past, possibly because they do not clearly fall into traditional medical and psychological problem areas, it is most appropriate that they be included here. For when the concept of exceptional *learner* is considered within a distinctly educational framework, the socially and economically disadvantaged child represents one of the greatest domestic social problems that must be dealt with today.

Definition

Havighurst (1964) considers the term socially disadvantaged as a relative term implying that the individual has a disadvantage relative to some other child for some kind of social life. The socially disadvantaged child, then, is handicapped in relation to growing up to lead a competent and satisfying life in American society. In our category we have included "economically disadvantaged," as a definite relationship often exists between socioeconomic status and social disadvantageness of children. Yet not all socially disadvantaged children come from poor families, and not all low income families produce socially disadvantaged children. With respect to the latter, approximately sixty-five percent of American children live in working class families in which their mother or father does manual work for a living. The great majority of these homes are adequate. The children are properly fed and clothed and receive love and protection from their parents. They learn to like and respect the teacher and the school. Most working class families participate in most aspects of American mass culture and as such are not culturally deprived.

SD

Classification, Incidence, Causes, and Identification

Havighurst places the number of socially disadvantaged children in this country at fifteen percent of the child population, although he admits it is a "personal" rather than "scientific" estimate. This incidence figure may vary not only according to socially disadvantaged and socio-economic criteria but also according to geographical location. Havighurst estimates that some thirty percent of children living in the major cities of New York, Chicago, Philadelphia, Washington, D.C., Detroit, Cleveland, and Baltimore fall into the socially disadvantaged category.

If the socio-economic factors alone are not sufficient to explain the problems of the socially disadvantaged child, then what are the underlying causes? Havighurst attempts to describe them in terms of social group characteristics. Socially disadvantaged children:

1. Are at the bottom of American society in terms of income.
2. Have a rural background.
3. Suffer from social and economic discrimination at the hands of the majority of society.
4. Are widely distributed in the United States. They are most visible in the big cities, and are also present in all except the very high income communities. There are as many of them in rural areas.

SD

In racial and ethnic terms, Havighurst views these groups as about evenly divided between whites and nonwhites; they consist mainly of:

1. Blacks from the rural South who have migrated recently to Northern industrial cities.
2. Whites from the rural South and the Southern mountains who have migrated recently to the Northern industrial cities.
3. Puerto Ricans who have migrated to a few Northern industrial cities.
4. Mexicans with a rural background who have migrated into the West and Midwest.
5. European immigrants with a rural background from Eastern and Southern Europe.

According to Havighurst, these groups make up about fifteen percent of the population of the United States; but since they tend to have large families, their children make up as much as twenty percent of the child population. In again emphasizing the lack of any simple and direct socio-economic, geographical, cultural, racial, or ethnic explanation for the problem of the socially disadvantaged child, Havighurst concludes that not all socially disadvantaged children come from these groups, but the great majority do and that not all children in these groups are socially disadvantaged, but the great majority are.

The characteristics of the socially and economically disadvantaged child that handicap him in the American school setting will be discussed in greater detail in Parts II and III. Here, we will only briefly describe some of them. The family setting of the disadvantaged child may not be verbally oriented and encourage questions, offer answers, develop adequate language understanding or usage, or reflect a belief in the value of education and school achievement. It may not set the example of reading or provide toys and play materials that stimulate and challenge the child. Thus, entrance into school, with its reliance on verbal communication and expectations that children are oriented toward exploring and learning about their environment, may take for granted experiences and attitudes that the disadvantaged child simply does not possess. The work of Deutsch (1963) has revealed that the family environment of disadvantaged children also does not prepare the child to pay attention or listen to what is going on around him, and this may markedly interfere with his chances of success in school.

SD

Treatment and Educational Provisions

Treatment and remediation of the problems of socially disadvantaged children involve more comprehension and complex undertakings than might be necessary with any other exceptional learner. To begin with, the number of these children is greater than those with any other handicapping condition. In addition, the problem stems from a number of major social ills, and corrective measures must necessarily affect many levels of the society. Nevertheless, the matter of effecting change in the American educational system so that the benefits of an education are not denied disadvantaged children is receiving increased attention today. Passow (1963) has reviewed some of the issues that are involved in bringing about such change. First are needed coordinated, multi-level approaches that take into account the child, the family, the neighborhood, the school, teacher, and classroom, as well as agencies and institutions in the community, city, and larger metropolitan areas. An innovative classroom program may be attempted by a single teacher of an inner city school but may be futile unless supported by the climate of the school, neighborhood, and family. Second, attacks on the problems that can be prevented must be distinguished from problems that are compensatory and can be helped. A junior high student may need intensive academic remediation because of a long history of school failure, whereas a preschool or kindergarten child may primarily need help with his cultural limitations, short attention span, underdeveloped abstract thinking ability, and lack of motivation for school success. Third, major curriculum modifications are essential. Preschool programs must offset early impoverishment in verbal and cognitive experiences and enter into more intensive training than found in traditional nursery school programs. Project Head Start, launched in 1965, has provided a major national program during the summer months aimed at these goals. The development of language skills and reading during the elementary years may have to include experimentation with methods, materials, groupings, and special personnel.

Employment experience, such as that found in work-study programs for potential drop-outs, can be coordinated with work-oriented English, social studies, mathematics, and guidance, and can provide an alternative pathway to adulthood as early as age thirteen or fourteen. Automatically assuming, however, that every disadvantaged child is a candidate for semi-skilled or unskilled work is undesirable, and efforts must be made to offer such a child intellectual opportunities which are meaningful and which contribute to both immediate and long-range development. Indeed, curriculum enrichment for more able disadvantaged students has been attempted in such programs as the Higher Horizons Program of New York City. Upward Bound, a related type of program begun by the United States Office of Education in 1965, aims to "rescue" high school students with poor academic records who might, with special assistance, be directed toward college or a more constructive future.

Curriculum modification for disadvantaged children also involves creating instructional materials that are exciting and interesting. The bland, middle class oriented, traditional basal reading programs are often poorly suited. New materials, which present easily recognized experiences and focus on problems of everyday living, such as how to make sound purchases or apply for a job, can be more meaningful. Programmed instructional material, with its small increments of learning, systematic progression, and individualized, self-pacing qualities, as well as other types of audio-visual learning aids, also may prove useful.

Reorganizing the classroom arrangement, as in ungraded classrooms or through team teaching situations, may hold promise for dealing with the great range of skill and ability levels found among disadvantaged children. In addition, extension of diagnostic and remedial programs drawing on a number of professionals and involving clinics and agencies in the community will aid in helping disadvantaged children with learning and adjustment problems more serious than those that can be dealt with in the classroom.

A major effort may be necessary in relation to the parents of disadvantaged children. The school program and its stress on educational achievement and motivation may need careful interpretation and clarification for parents who have had little formal schooling themselves and who may be indifferent and apathetic toward education. Formal parent-teacher conferences in the school may be less desirable than informal contacts in the neighborhood or home, where practical suggestions can be made regarding day-to-day problems the parents face.

In dealing with the problems associated with education of the socially and economically disadvantaged, the concept of special education truly merges with general or regular education. Far from an easily identifiable category, the disadvantaged population is representative of a critical social dilemma facing the entire American society today. As we continue our discussion of the disadvantaged child throughout this book, we will find problems associated with the first three categories in this chapter — emotional disturbance, mental retardation, and learning disabilities — singly and collectively appearing within groups of these children. For example, a poor child in the United States has fifteen times the chance of being labeled mentally retarded than does a child from the middle or upper classes (Hurley, 1969). The relationships of social and economic disadvantage to these problems, which are found among children along the full range of the social advantage-disadvantage and high-low socio-economic continua, will be one of our particular concerns.

MR

SD

VH

VISUALLY HANDICAPPED CHILDREN

Visually handicapped children are categorized into two groups, the partially seeing and the blind. From an educational point of view, the partially seeing are distinguished from the blind in that they possess a degree of useful vision in relation to reading and doing school work. Blind children possess so little useful vision that they must use braille in the reading process.

Definition and Classification

The American Foundation for the Blind (1961) provides the legal definition of blindness used for educational purposes:

> 20/200 vision or less in the better eye with the best possible correction or a restriction in field of vision to an angle subtending an

arc of twenty degrees or less. The partially seeing are defined as those who have remaining visual acuity between 20/200 and 20/70 in the better eye with the best possible correction or who, in the judgment of eye specialists, can benefit from either temporary or permanent use of some type of special educational program.

To understand these definitions we must first discuss visual acuity — sharpness or clearness of vision. Visual acuity is frequently measured by a wall chart of block letters such as the Snellen chart or another vision test utilizing the same principles. The test distance for using the Snellen chart is twenty feet, and the basic unit of measurement is the visual angle of one minute of arc, which is a visual distance clearly distinguishable by the normal eye at two hundred feet. The large letters on the top of the chart appear to be the same size from two hundred feet away, while a standard sized letter appears from a distance of twenty feet. During the test, the individual is asked to read the letters or symbols on the chart to the best of his visual ability from a twenty-foot distance. This distance becomes the top number in the visual acuity index (e.g., 20/200) cited earlier in the definitions. The location number describes the size of letters that are read successfully. If the individual from a distance of twenty feet can correctly read the line of letters read by a person with normal vision from that distance, he is said to have 20/20 vision. If, however, from a twenty-foot-distance, he can only read letters that a normally sighted person is capable of reading from seventy feet, his visual acuity is described as 20/70. A person, therefore, is legally blind when he can only read from twenty feet a letter size which can be read by a normally seeing individual from a two hundred-foot distance (visual acuity index — 20/200). Ashcroft (1963) points out that there are many more complex aspects to vision than can be measured by a Snellen chart test and at best it reflects only a very small sample of an individual's visual behavior.

Incidence

Using the legal definition for blindness of the American Foundation for the Blind, an incidence estimate of one in every 3,000 school age children (.03 percent) is generally accepted; the number of partially seeing children with visual acuity between 20/70 and 20/200 is estimated to be one in 500 (.02 percent). As a group, the visually handicapped constitute the smallest area of exceptionality (Ashcroft, 1963). The United States Office of Education (1970) reports a total incidence figure of .1 percent for visually impaired school age children.

Causes

Forty-nine percent of the visual deficits found among partially see-ing children are due to refractive errors.   These errors involve light rays focusing in back of the retina (hyperopia or farsighted-ness), in front of the retina (myopia or nearsightedness), or par-tially in back and partially in front of the retina (astigmatism), instead of directly on the retina as in the mature normal eye.   Struc-tural defects of the eye, such as cataracts or albinism, account for twenty-two percent of visual defects, and defects of muscle function for seventeen percent.   Defects of the eye due to infection and injury cause eleven percent of impaired vision among the partially seeing (Kerby, 1952; Kirk, 1972).

With respect to causes of blindness, forty-seven percent are due to prenatal causes, the majority of which are undetermined; thirty-three percent to poisonings; seven to eight percent to in-fectious diseases and neoplasms; and two percent to injuries.   The percentage of blindness caused by poisonings includes retrolental fibroplasia, a disease with a spectacular history.   This disease did not exist before 1938, was not diagnosed as a clinical entity until 1942, and had virtually disappeared by 1955, leaving behind thousands of blinded children.   The disease occurred only in premature babies; in 1952 evidence finally emerged pointing to the increased concentration of oxygen, routinely used in incubators with premature infants, as the cause.   It was then established that concentration and duration of oxygen therapy could be markedly reduced without endangering the infant's life and the disease began to disappear.   However, the thousands of children blinded by this "man-made" disease are now growing up, and schools and institu-tions in the country have had to provide increased services for them (Kirk, 1972).

Identification and Diagnosis

The child with a serious visual problem is usually identified dur-ing the preschool years, but the partially seeing child may not be singled out until the elementary school period, when vision becomes important in the performance of school work.   The National Society for the Prevention of Blindness (1965) says that these ten behavioral signs may be indicators of visual defects:

1. Attempting to brush away blurs, rubbing eyes excessively, frowning
2. Shutting or covering one eye, tilting head, or thrusting it forward when looking at near or distant objects
3. Difficulty in reading or in other work requiring close use of eyes
4. Blinking more than usual, crying often, irritability when doing close work
5. Stumbling or tripping over small objects
6. Holding books or small objects close to eyes
7. Inability to participate in games requiring distance vision
8. Excessive sensitivity to light
9. Red-rimmed, encrusted, or swollen eyelids; recurring sties; inflamed or watery eyes; crossed eyes
10. Complaints of not seeing well; of dizziness, headaches, or nausea following close eye work; of blurred or double vision

VH

Any child manifesting one or more of these signs consistently should be referred to the school nurse or an eye doctor for intensive examination. The ophthalmologist is a medical doctor who specializes in diagnosis and treatment of defects and diseases of the eye. He may perform surgery and also prescribe other types of treatment, including medication and glasses. Another eye specialist who can examine a child having visual difficulty is the optometrist, who is a licensed, non-medical practitioner. He measures refractive errors and eye muscle disturbances and prescribes glasses, prisms, or exercises for the eye.

Treatment and Educational Provisions

Educational provisions for blind and partially seeing children have been described by Ashcroft (1963) in terms of six general types of administrative plans. Some visually limited children remain in regular classrooms in which little if any formal special education is provided. If the child makes optimum progress toward his goals, this arrangement may be satisfactory, although it probably is best for older children, for those with mild impairments, for late blinded individuals, or for those with considerable previous training in braille and other special learning techniques.

Some programs for the visually handicapped use the services

of an itinerant teacher who periodically works directly with visually limited children and may offer consultative assistance to classroom teachers who have children with visual problems in their rooms.   The itinerant teacher plan has been used more widely with partially seeing children and is increasing for children who are blind.   It may be most feasible for visually limited children at the secondary level, particularly if the child has had good earlier training.

The resource teacher or resource room plan maintains the child almost all the time in a regular classroom.   The child periodically goes to the resource teacher in a separate room where tutorial assistance, training, and special materials are provided. Resource teachers typically serve a maximum of twelve partially seeing or eight blind children or some combination of the two. This plan is probably the most common type of administrative provision for educating the visually handicapped while maintaining them in regular classrooms.

The cooperative plan enrolls the child in a special classroom where he does close eye work (partially seeing) or reading and writing in braille (blind).   The visually limited child may participate with his seeing peers in the regular classroom during activities when he does not need special assistance.   There is also a special class plan in which the visually handicapped receive all their instruction in a self-contained class from a special teacher while participating to some degree in activities with seeing children.

The residential school plan is the oldest educational plan for the visually handicapped.   It has been primarily provided for the blind, although partially seeing children can be enrolled in areas where no special public school facilities are available.   The residential school provides a complete educational and boarding school program.   Unlike the twenty-four-hour residential facilities for the mentally retarded, it functions on a school-calendar-year basis, is not oriented toward custodial care, and does not involve the legal commitment of children.

In general, the content and methods of instruction for both the blind and partially seeing are the same as those used with seeing children except that the media (braille, audio presentation, tactual aids, and large type) are different.   One important additional emphasis in school programs involving the visually handicapped relates to mobility and orientation training to assist the child in coping with the physical and social environment through use of his remaining vision and/or other senses.   Ashcroft (1963) stresses the importance of such training by citing the example of the blind child who can play Chopin flawlessly but cannot locate the piano efficiently. The goal of mobility and orientation programs for blind children is the achievement of some level of optimum, independent functioning. These programs go beyond training in "navigation" to include development of self-care and social skills. They will be discussed in further detail in Chapters 7 and 8.

Braille is taught in the same sequence as reading instruction is with sighted children. Readiness is emphasized during kindergarten and much of first grade, and a mental age of six to six and one-half is considered necessary for a successful beginning. In the early grades, in which emphasis is on oral reading, the blind child is not overly disadvantaged with respect to speed; but when reading becomes largely silent, such a disadvantage appears.

No more efficient and useful means of reading and writing for the use of the blind has been found than braille. Six raised dots constitute the braille cell, and the sixty-three possible combinations of these dots can be utilized to present almost any literary, musical, numerical, or scientific material to the blind. Even though braille actually has attributes of a "code," it should be treated as a complete reading and writing medium with the same concerns for meaning and understanding (Ashcroft, 1963).

HEARING HANDICAPPED CHILDREN

Definition and Classification

Children who are hearing handicapped are traditionally classified into two groups: the hard of hearing and the deaf. The two groups are distinguished by the degree to which hearing loss affects the normal and spontaneous development of spoken language. Using this language development reference, the hard of hearing are those individuals whose hearing loss does not rule out language development during or after the prelingual period. The deaf are those individuals who have such a severe hearing loss at birth and in the prelingual period (before two to three years of age) that language development does not occur (McConnell, 1973).

Myklebust (1964b) considers these definitions limited since they confuse degree of hearing loss and age of onset. A child who loses his entire capacity to recognize auditory stimuli at ten years of age would be classifiable as hard of hearing rather than deaf if he had previously undergone normal language development. This seeming inconsistency with the common usage of the term "deaf," reflecting a functional educational rather than sensory deprivation focus, has led Wooden (1963) to propose consideration of deaf children within two groups, according to the age of onset of "functional" hearing loss. Prelanguage deaf would be those in whom deafness preceded firm establishment of language and speech, while postlanguage deaf would include those who are hard of hearing according to language but "functionally" incapable of recognizing auditory stimulation. The Committee on Nomenclature of the Executives of American Schools for the Deaf has been concerned with the importance of considering the age of onset as well as the ability to speak and hear in formulating a definition of deaf and hard of hearing (Silverman & Lane, 1970).

In determining degree of hearing loss, we are concerned with an individual's sensitivity to frequency and intensity of sound. Frequency is perceived subjectively as pitch, while intensity is perceived as loudness. In regard to frequency, the range needed for practical listening purposes is considered. This is from 250 Hertz (Hz) or cycles per second (roughly middle C) through the five octaves above (500, 1000, 2000, 4000, and 8000 Hz). Speech is intelligible for the most part if one hears normally in the range from 500 to 2000 Hz, and the three frequencies in the middle range of 500, 1000, and 2000 Hz are considered the speech frequencies. Hearing, however, is usually measured audiogrammatically at frequencies from 125 through 8000 Hz. Intensity is measured in terms of decibels (dB), a logarithmic unit of sound intensity above an arbitrary reference point. This reference point is established as the average level at which normally hearing young adults, using both ears, can detect the faintest sound of which they are capable (Davis, 1970). The average whisper requires about 20 dB of sound intensity, moderate conversation about 60 dB, and 130 dB of sound begins to produce discomfort to the listener.

McConnell (1973) has classified the hearing handicapped into five classes according to their average hearing level for 500, 1000, and 2000 Hz in the better ear. Slight hearing problems begin when the level is more than 26 dB, but not greater than 40 dB, and difficulty is encountered only with faint speech. Mild hearing difficulty involves an average hearing level of 41 dB, but not greater than 55 dB, and may present problems in hearing speech at normal loudness. Marked hearing problems occur when the level of average hearing is more than 56 dB, but not greater than 70 dB, involving difficulty even with loud speech. Severe hearing loss requires more than 71 dB, but not more than 90 dB, for hearing, and individuals so handicapped will only understand shouted or amplified speech. Extreme hearing problems require more than 91 dB of sound intensity, and such a loss usually precludes the understanding of even amplified speech. In this classification the lower limits of the average hearing levels for each group correspond with the dB hearing levels established by the International Standards Organization (ISO).

Incidence

Myklebust (1964b) estimates that five percent of school age children have hearing losses that require some kind of attention. He includes in this group those children who will need special educational assistance unless further loss of hearing is prevented. This overall estimate is in line with that of Silverman and Lane (1970), who did an extensive and detailed study of Pittsburgh school children. They report that one-half percent to one percent of these children will require some type of special education. Their study did not include children who were already enrolled in special schools and classes for the hearing handicapped. The estimates of Myklebust and Silverman and Lane confirm and extend earlier estimates of O'Connor (1954) and Hardy (1952) that up to one and one-half percent of school age children are at least minimally handicapped educationally by hearing problems. McConnell (1973) states that prompt medical help should be adequate for aiding the remaining three and one-half to four percent who may fail screening tests and for remedying the hearing problem before it becomes a handicapping condition. McConnell concludes that those with "slight" or "mild" hearing problems as specified earlier under "Definition and Classification" would not normally be enrolled in special classes or schools but may well be educationally handicapped to the extent that they need some type of attention, ranging from special seating in the regular classroom to part-time tutoring in communication skills. The United States Office of Education (1970) estimates the percentage of school age deaf children to be .075 while the percentage of hard of hearing is reported to be .5.

Causes

Causes of deafness can be organized under two general headings: endogenous and exogenous. Endogenous deafness is the result of an inherited defect while exogenous deafness is caused by disease or injury. Myklebust (1964b) surveyed 777 boys and girls in residential and day schools throughout the United States and found

22.6 percent were deaf due to endogenous factors while 27.8 percent had deafness of exogenous origin.   He separated meningitis as a separate cause, and deafness in 11.3 percent of the children in the survey was linked to that disease.   The largest single cause was listed as "undetermined" and 38.3 percent of the children fell into this category.   Wooden (1963) points to this substantial figure as an example of the inadequacy of medical histories for children who are hearing handicapped.   Exogenous causes of deafness include infections such as German measles (rubella) in early pregnancy, as well as influenza and mumps.   Childhood diseases of scarlet fever, mumps, measles, whooping cough, typhoid fever, and pneumonia may also cause injury to the mechanism of the ear.   Otitis media, a chronic infection of the inner ear, was once an important cause of hearing loss but has declined recently due to use of antibiotics and improved surgical techniques.   However, McConnell (1973) reports that misuse of antibiotics may actually cause hearing loss through damage of the inner ear (Hawkins, 1967), although little is actually known about what dosage may cause damage to hearing in the infant as compared to the adult.   On an ecological basis hearing loss may occur today through frequent exposure to very high intensity noise associated with occupational and other environments.   Although major hearing problems in childhood may not be caused by such sounds, certain toys, such as cap guns and toy rockets, may produce noise levels sufficient to damage hearing (McConnell, 1973).   Rock and roll music presented in public places has also been shown to be played at intensity levels above the damage-risk level (Lipscomb, 1969).

Types of hearing defects can also be described according to locus: conductive hearing loss which reduces the intensity of sound reaching the inner ear, sensory-neural loss caused by defects of the inner ear or auditory nerves, and central deafness due to dysfunction of the central nervous system (Kirk, 1972).

Identification and Diagnosis

In identifying hearing handicapped children, teacher referrals and parent requests for evaluation uncover some children who need help.   But the majority may not be detected since they hear conversational speech and learn to talk at an average age.   A loss of thirty or forty decibels often goes unnoticed, and the deviant behavior that develops may be attributed to low intelligence or emotional problems.   Kirk (1972) recommends that a periodic group screening test be given to all school children.   For those who ap-

pear to have a hearing loss on a screening test, an individual evaluation is recommended. This test is conducted by an otologist, a
physician who can determine the exact nature of the hearing difficulty and if necessary administer or prescribe treatment. He may
discover wax in the child's ear, infected adenoids or tonsils, or some
other abnormality that can be corrected. The otologist also may
determine the type of hearing aid that will improve the child's
hearing or may recommend a special treatment program.

Treatment and Educational Provisions

Hard of hearing children were once taught largely in special classes;
but with the advancement in hearing aids, it has been found that
most such children gain more from being integrated in regular
classrooms. They are not very different from their age mates and
not seriously retarded academically except possibly in areas of
speech, language, and reading. Itinerant teachers may work with
hard of hearing children on a part-time basis and instruct the child
in appropriate use of a hearing aid, provide auditory training to
help him listen to and discriminate different sounds, teach him lip

reading skills so that he may fill in sounds and words that are in-
distinct by using certain cues in lip and facial movements, and,
finally, assist him in improving his speech.
     As we consider educational provisions for the deaf, we en-
counter the controversy over the use of either oralism or manual-
ism. The oral method requires communication through speech and
lip reading without reliance on signs or gestures. The manual
method provides communication by using conventional gestures of
the hands or arms to express thoughts, and it includes the use of a
manual alphabet which employs fixed positions of the fingers or
hands to designate the various letters of the alphabet. Both methods are used today, and most authorities agree there is a place for
each or for a combined method. Some schools, however, are strictly
oral in their approach and discourage any use of sign language and
finger spelling. Other schools use both methods. It is often found
that the children themselves, particularly those living together in
residential units, communicate mostly by the manual method.
     One of the most difficult communication areas for the deaf
is developing abstract language skills. Although the normal child
may come to imitate adult language forms that he has heard, more
subtle forms of language, different shades of meaning of the same
word, and complex grammatical functions may have to be systematically taught to the deaf child. One well-known system of instruc-

tion is the Fitzgerald Key (Fitzgerald, 1954), in which plates bearing guide words and symbols are used to supplement the child's understanding of language patterns.

Education for deaf children is provided in residential schools, day schools, and special classes in public schools. Approximately two-thirds of the deaf children in educational programs go to residential schools that are operated either privately or publicly. In public school special classes, some five to ten children are assigned to work with a special teacher. According to Kirk (1972), the decision as to whether a deaf child should be placed in a day school or residential school program cannot be made on the basis of which is the most effective educational setting, but rather on what is most beneficial for a particular child in a particular community. If adequate resources at home are available, such children are probably best placed in a day school. Since the normal hearing child benefits from a great deal of incidental learning *before* he enters school, parent education can be quite useful in helping parents of preschool deaf children provide simple but necessary learning experiences prior to school entrance.

SPEECH HANDICAPPED CHILDREN

Definition and Classification

Speech is the tool which assists in developing a formalized language. It involves the ability to pronounce sounds, assimilate these sounds into words, and combine these words into meaningful units. Its aim is to convey a constellation of ideas to the listener. Speech develops initially with the birth cry, which soon gives way to differentiated crying, cooing, and babbling over the first few weeks of life. Within four to six months, the infant begins to repeat and imitate sounds, and by nine months can put syllables together. The child's "first word" is generally spoken at the end of the first year, and meaningful speech occurs early in the second year. By the time he is two, the child is combining words, and by three years is well on his way to expressing himself in sentences. The rate of development depends greatly on how parents respond to and reinforce the child's efforts at speech.

Although there are a number of definitions of speech disability in the literature, one of the most widely adopted has been proposed by Van Riper (1972), who states that "Speech is defective when it deviates so far from the speech of other people that it calls attention to itself, interferes with communication, or causes its possessor to be maladjusted." Speech problems occur among many types of exceptional children. The estimated prevalence of speech disorders accompanying other types of handicapping conditions is: 9.5 percent — partially hearing (Hull, Mielke, Timmons, & Willeford, 1971); 50 percent — cerebral palsy (Wilson, 1973); 8–37 percent — mild mental retardation (Dunn, 1973); 94 percent — moderate mental retardation (Matthews, 1971). In fact, such problems cut across categories in much the same way as behavioral and emotional problems, thus making the category of the speech handicapped far from restricted in the sense of the retarded and the visually, hearing, and physically handicapped. Speech defects may be grouped in the following categories:

1. Disorders of articulation
2. Disorders of voice
3. Stuttering
4. Delayed speech development
5. Cleft palate
6. Disorders associated with cerebral palsy
7. Disorders associated with impaired hearing

SH

Disorders of articulation involve substitution, omission, distortions, and additions of sounds. Typical substitutions are *w* for *r* (as in "wight" for "right") or *th* for *s* (as in "yeth" for "yes"). Such errors are commonly found among young children with immature speech. Omissions, if excessive, tend to make a child's speech almost unintelligible, as consonants are often dropped from the beginning, middle, or endings of words. Distortions in speech reflect an attempt to approximate a correct sound such as with a "whistling" *s*. These are more readily corrected than substitution problems, while omissions are the most difficult to correct. Additions appear in unintelligible speech and jargon and in the speech of deaf children who may say "sumber" for "summer" or add a vowel between other syllables as "on-a the table."

Disorders of voice are not found as often as disorders of articulation and include problems in (1) vocal quality, (2) vocal pitch, and (3) vocal intensity. Defects in vocal quality appear in the production of sound and include breathiness, hoarseness, or huskiness. Resonance of sound may occur largely in the nasal cavity producing a nasal, twangy quality or outside the nasal cavity, in which case instead of "Spring has come" we hear "Sprig has cob." Problems in vocal pitch are often related to the fact that the growing larynx may develop at a faster rate than the rest of the body, with pitch remaining at a high key level into adolescence. Such problems as "falsetto voice" can be corrected once a boy enters late adolescence. The intensity, loudness, or softness of the voice may reflect attention seeking, lack of control of vocal power, or immaturity and insecurity.

Stuttering has probably received more study than any other speech problem. It has been distinguished from stammering but the problems are essentially the same (Ainsworth, 1967). Stuttering is generally considered a disorder of rhythm or fluency, but as Johnson, Brown, Curtis, Edney, and Keaster (1967) suggest, disfluency alone does not adequately describe stuttering. Young children are often disfluent in the early acquisition of language and any "normal" speaker will also experience moments of disfluency. It is not until the disfluences occur with such frequency and severity that they become noticeable to the listener and irritating to the speaker that the condition is called stuttering (Hull & Hull, 1973).

Delayed speech occurs when the child does not develop speech according to his age level or develops only a partial understanding of language or vocal expression. Causes of such delay include hearing loss, mental retardation, environmental deprivation, cerebral dysfunction, and glandular irregularities. The term "aphasia" has been used to denote loss of speech specifically associated with cerebral dysfunction. Aphasia among children has been termed "childhood aphasia" and "congenital" or "developmental aphasia." "Childhood aphasia" usually refers to a language dysfunction associated with some form of central nervous system damage that resulted after language had begun to develop; "congenital" or "developmental aphasia" implies that damage to the central nervous system occurred prior to the development of language.

If the bone and tissue of the palates fail to fuse during the second and third months of pregnancy, the child will be born with a cleft in the roof of the mouth and sometimes in the lip. Some such conditions can be remedied through surgery and adequate speech is possible. In other cases where the condition cannot be corrected, the speech may be so defective that the person is judged mentally retarded by the layman. Typical characteristics of cleft palate speech are hypernasality, nasal emission, and misarticulation (Morley, 1967; Westlake & Rutherford, 1966).

The child with cerebral palsy may develop either perfect speech or no speech at all. He may display problems in almost every aspect of speech. Wolfe (1950) found seventy percent of a group of cerebral palsied children had inadequate articulation, forty percent of which was related to the condition of cerebral palsy and twenty-six percent of which was functional in nature. Respiratory deviations and constriction and tension of the vocal cords may produce vocal disorders.

The hard of hearing child often has articulation problems in his speech. Depending on the severity and kind of hearing loss, there may be omissions and distortions of sounds in the high frequency range, omissions and indistinctness of word endings, and poor discrimination between voiced and voiceless sounds. Frisina (1967) found that if a child has a mild hearing loss, the sounds *s, sh, z, th, t, ch,* and *f,* which are of high frequency and low acoustic power, are those most likely to be misarticulated. Fewer and less severe articulatory disorders are found among individuals with a conductive hearing loss, who can hear their own speech through tone conduction, than among those with a sensory-neural loss.

Incidence

Over the last fifty years, a number of studies, designed to estimate the prevalence of speech disorders in the United States, have had discrepant findings. Three factors may have contributed to this discrepancy: (1) the use of different criteria to define various speech and language problems, (2) the fact that surveys are conducted in restricted geographical areas, and (3) the recognition that maturation plays an important role in the quality of speech performance. Recognizing and attempting to control for these problems, Hull, Mielke, Timmons, and Willeford (1971) collected prevalence data on a national sample of 38,000 public school children. They found that 1.19 percent of the males in their sample had an articulation disability, compared to only .66 percent of the females. They also found that 1.21 percent of the males had a stuttering problem compared to .41 percent for the females. Results from this survey also showed that the percentage of children, both males and females, judged to have articulation problems drops sharply during the first two years of school and continues to become smaller through the twelfth grade. The U.S. Office of Education (1970) places the total percentage of school age children in the nation with speech handicaps at 3.5.

Causes

The causes of disorders of articulation may be found in malfunctioning of any part of the intricate vocal system, including breathing, vocal cord vibration in the larynx, auditory discrimination, sound reception and perception in the central nervous system, tongue, pharynx, lips, teeth, palate, and jaws.   As with other disorders, a distinction must be made between causes that are functional and those that are organic in nature.   Some individuals have impaired functioning of the vocal system and no speech problems; others have such problems but no structural defects.   Impoverished environment, immaturity, bilingualism, and emotional problems may all contribute to a functional speech problem.

Stuttering, which has the next highest incidence after disorders of articulation, may be attributed to either an organic or psychological cause depending on one's theoretical orientation.   No single causal explanation has gained professional consensus. Organic theories center around the difficulty in neural flow which produces incoordination, hesitation, and repetition in the muscular activity of speech.   Psychoanalytic concepts and learning theory have also been utilized to explain stuttering.   Parental anxiety or overconcern may result in a child who, passing through a normal state of language development with repetitions and hesitations, becomes fearful of displeasing his parents, anticipates stuttering, becomes tense while dreading the situation, and consequently stutters.   Van Riper (1954) views stuttering as having a multiple origin, and as such the search for a single theory to explain all cases may be futile.

Identification and Diagnosis

SH

According to Sommers (1969), the methods chosen for identifying children with speech and/or language disabilities should meet the criteria of "effectiveness" and "efficiency."   "Effectiveness" refers to successfully identifying those children who need remediation, and "efficiency" refers to the use of diagnostic procedures that do not waste time, effort, or information.   A review by Hull and Hull (1973) found that two methods of identification, the survey method (Ainsworth, 1948) and the teacher referral method, when used in combination, probably met Sommers' criteria more closely than any other method.   The survey method as described by Ainsworth (1948) involves the use of brief speech screening procedures with each child in the entire school (when a speech correction program is being initiated) or in certain selected classes (when a speech correction program is ongoing).   The teacher referral method involves having teachers listen to and observe their students and refer those with noticeable deviations for further screening and testing procedures to determine the specific problem.

Several tests are available for speech clinicians that will assess articulation. Most articulation tests assess the spontaneous production of each consonant sound in three positions — initial, medial, and end — by means of pictures. Examples of such tests are the Hejna Developmental Articulation Test (1959), the Goldman-Fristoe Test of Articulation (1969), and the Templin-Darley Tests of Articulation (1960).

Treatment and Educational Provisions

The classroom teacher plays an important role in the remediation program for the child who has speech and/or language problems. A teacher may carry out a program of remediation in the classroom or reinforce the work of the speech clinician. Van Riper (1972) describes a procedure which a teacher can use in introducing sounds which involves listening rather than student reproduction. In Chapter 7 we will further discuss the role the classroom teacher may assume in relation to problems of articulation or stuttering. Lindamood and Lindamood (1969) have designed a program for teaching auditory discrimination as an aid to the development of auditory perception, reading, spelling, and speech skills. Publications are available to the teacher that can be used to help the child improve his articulation (Black, 1964; Egland, 1970).

The speech therapist or correctionist who works in the schools may have a master's degree and the majority have done graduate work beyond the bachelor's level. Many will hold a state certificate, since thirty-two states have speech certification requirements. According to Hull and Hull (1973) there are three broad areas in which the speech therapist can be of service in the total educational program:

1. To act as a resource person by providing consultant services to the classroom teacher and other staff members in regard to the improvement of communication skills in the classroom
2. To provide direct services for students with speech disabilities
3. To serve as a program administrator working with the school administrator in planning and operating the speech correction program

Speech correctionists assigned to schools find that approximately eighty to eighty-five percent of their cases display articulatory impairments. Articulation problems are particularly common in young children, although with maturation many of these problems disappear.   Unless the young child shows extreme difficulties, the speech therapist usually gives time and nature a chance to work. However, as Kisatsky (1967) states, a major problem for the speech clinician is to be able to predict which child will develop without correction and which one will need correction at an early age.

Speech correction for children with articulation problems may be provided by a speech clinician on either an individual or group basis for sessions held at least twice a week.   The cooperation of both the parent and the regular classroom teacher is important for extending practice and effecting transfer of the speech correction program to the child's total life situation.

There have been many theories and approaches to the treatment of stuttering.   West (1966) describes seven approaches that have been utilized:

1. Psychoanalysis
2. Mental imagery, i.e. developing visualization ability
3. Classical or Pavlovian conditioning
4. Negative practice, i.e. removal of stuttering by consciously practicing stuttering
5. Diagnosogenic theory (Johnson, 1956)
6. Hemispheric dominance
7. Physiological approaches to treatments

In addition to the approaches mentioned, two relatively new emphases are developing:

1. Treatment with behavior modification techniques
2. Sheehan's (1970) role-conflict theory

Van Riper (1970) notes that correct speech therapy for the stutterer aims at several goals:

1. To improve the morale of the patient
2. To reduce the situational and phonic anxiety
3. To reduce the stereotyped stuttering responses
4. To reduce the reinforcement of stuttering responses that occurs through avoidance, repression, and escape reward
5. To give the individual's existing fluency some stimulus value

Since speech is so fundamental to the communication process, and communication is so fundamental to learning and adapting to the demands of the environment, concern with speech problems ranks high on the priority list of the special educator.   Problems of language usage and understanding were not discussed in this section, but they are also of critical concern across all categories. We shall discuss the significance of such problems in relation to other exceptional children in Parts II and III of this text.

PHYSICALLY HANDICAPPED CHILDREN

We come now to considering a group of exceptional children who may clearly be categorized as medical problems. This group is comprised of the physically handicapped whose difficulties are the result of neurological, orthopedic, or chronic health disorders. Although the term "physically handicapped" might also include children with visual and hearing handicaps, we shall use it only with reference to children whose major problems are non-sensory in nature. The present text will not attempt to cover the physically handicapped as broadly as has been done in some other special education texts (Connor, 1967a, 1967b; Kirk, 1972; Dunn, 1973), and we will restrict our discussion to an example of one crippling condition, cerebral palsy, and one chronic health problem, epilepsy.

Crippling Conditions (Cerebral Palsy)

SH

PH

A crippling condition of major concern to the special educator is cerebral palsy — a complex, neuromuscular disability due to injury to the brain before, during, or after birth. It is characterized by disturbances of voluntary motor function, especially of the arms and legs, and has been described according to the principal area of the brain that was damaged and the type of motor dysfunction manifested. Types of motor dysfunction include *spasticity* (involuntary contraction of affected muscles producing tenseness and lack of accurate movement), *athetosis* (involuntary contraction of successive muscles resulting in poor coordination and almost constant uncontrolled motion of the extremities), *ataxia* (poor body balance and spatial orientation), *rigidity* (widespread, constant muscle tension), and *tremor* (small rhythmic movements or uncontrolled shaking). In terms of frequency of occurrence it is estimated that spasticity accounts for almost half the cases of cerebral palsy, with athetosis found in about one-fourth of them, and rigidity, ataxia, and tremor in that order of frequency appearing in the remainder of the cases (Hopkins, Bice, & Colton, 1954).

Estimates of the prevalence of cerebral palsy are variable.

Wishik (1956) estimated five persons per 1000 under twenty-one years of age had cerebral palsy; Morgenstern (1964) reported three per 1000; and Friedman and MacQueen (1971) reported that 1.7 per 1000 children with cerebral palsy were in need of special attention.   Woods (1963) noted an apparent trend toward a lower incidence of cerebral palsy in recent years and an increase in milder subclinical cases.   Cerebral palsy may be accompanied by visual defects (about fifty percent of the cases), hearing handicaps (approximately twenty-five percent), and speech defects (about fifty to seventy-five percent) (Cardwell, 1956).   It also appears that approximately seventy-five percent of children with cerebral palsy are below average in intelligence and that some fifty percent are seriously retarded (Miller & Rosenfeld, 1962).

Cerebral palsy refers to a number of neuromuscular disabilities which are characterized by disturbances of motor function resulting from damage to the central nervous system.   This damage may take place prenatally, paranatally, or postnatally (during the early years of life).   According to Wilson (1973) prenatal factors that may predispose the fetus to damage include:

1. Blood-type incompatibility, especially the RH factor
2. Maternal infections, particularly rubella, and occasionally other virus diseases
3. Toxemia, a condition associated with presence of toxic substances in the blood of the mother
4. Conditions that cut off the supply of oxygen to the brain of the fetus or affect oxygen-carrying properties of the mother's blood, such as severe anemia
5. Prematurity
6. Diabetes
7. X-ray therapy

Paranatal conditions which can cause central nervous system damage are:

1. Prolonged labor
2. Difficult or abnormal birth, such as breech birth
3. Anoxia
4. Obstetrical procedures

Factors that may be responsible for central nervous system damage in the early years of life include:

1. Infections of brain tissue, such as encephalitis

2. Accidents that have resulted in central nervous system damage
3. Lead poisoning
4. Progressive neurological disorders

Since cerebral palsy is often a multiple handicapping condition, a variety of specialists in speech, recreation, physical education, and medicine are involved in its treatment. Orthopedic surgery and the use of braces and prosthetic aids may aid the child in gaining better control over his arms and legs. Masland (1967) reported that some symptoms of cerebral palsy can be relieved through operations on the brain itself. Physiotherapists trained in providing exercises for muscle re-education, ambulation, and balance may work with the child as does the occupational therapist who offers activities of high interest designed to improve muscle coordination and self-help skills such as feeding, dressing, and undressing.

A number of school programs exist for the cerebral palsied child depending on the extent of his handicap and the presence of additional handicaps. Home instruction may be provided if the child has normal or near normal intelligence and is severely physically disabled. Home-to-school telephone units in which several children are connected simultaneously with a teacher, or in which one child is connected to a regular classroom, are also well established as media of instruction for physically impaired children. Hospital schools offer short-term diagnostic and treatment periods during which special attention is provided, and long-term care is available in institutions for the mentally retarded where totally dependent children with all degrees of physical handicaps may reside on a twenty-four hour basis. Perhaps the most common type of educational facility for the cerebral palsied child is the special day school or class. Here children with mild or moderate physical handicaps and normal or near normal intelligence may receive their schooling; but the majority of children with cerebral palsy who have mild handicaps and normal intelligence are probably found in the regular classrooms of the public school where slight modifications in school buildings and classrooms can greatly compensate for such children's physical impairments.

The list of crippling conditions that may affect children due to skeletal deformities, infection, metabolic disturbances, accidents, and other causes is a sizeable one. Wilson (1973) has related these conditions to the actual problems they present in school, such as limiting the ability to sit or move about the classroom or manipulate materials required for learning. We have focused on cerebral palsy as a major crippling condition and will utilize it as representative of a number of related physical handicaps in our later discussions.

Chronic Health Problems (Epilepsy)

Chronic health problems which afflict children are also numerous. Rheumatic fever, congenital heart defects, tuberculosis, cystic fibrosis, and diabetes are a few examples. Epilepsy, as we found in the previous chapter, has been of considerable historical significance. The essence of the definition of epilepsy comes from the Greek work, epilepsia, which means "a taking hold of, a something seizing the subject as though that something were outside himself." Torres (1969) proposed a classification system for seizures based upon (1) clinical characteristics, (2) electrical manifestations, and (3) response to treatment. He divides the types of seizures into two main groups: (1) those that are generalized over the entire body (grand mal, petit mal, and akinetic myclonic), and (2) those that are focal at the onset although they may progress to a generalized major motor seizure (motor, sensory, psychomotor, and autonomic).

The witnessing of a grand mal seizure may be particularly upsetting to an individual who has never seen one. A number of individuals afflicted with epilepsy experience a warning (called an aura) of an impending seizure. An aura may be olfactory, visual, or auditory in nature. The aura may precede the seizure by an instant or it may allow sufficient time for some safety precautions such as the removal of sharp or hard objects. During the actual seizure, the child may exhibit a rolling and jerking of the eyes, rapid pulse movements, changing facial color, gnashing of the teeth, and laborious breathing. He may utter a shrill cry and begin spasmodic movements and convulsions of the body and slump or fall to the floor. This may be followed by drowsiness, headache, or nausea. Unconsciousness may be prolonged but seldom for more than half an hour. Approximately two-thirds of the cases of epilepsy are of this form (Best, 1967). During the actual seizure there is little that can be done to help the child. If he is in a precarious position, he may be gradually eased to the floor, moving with his bodily rhythm rather than holding him tightly. Placing something soft like a coat or blanket under his head may prevent discomfort and turning the head to one side may ease the discharge of saliva.

A less serious form of epilepsy involves the petit mal seizure in which there is mental confusion, a blocking of consciousness perhaps accompanied by vacant staring, twitching eyelids, a nodding head, and a sigh or gasp.   Such a seizure can take place during a pause in conversation or during an activity such as bicycle riding or playing.   Some petit mal seizures last but a few seconds and may resemble daydreaming or lack of attention.   Others may occur for a duration of two to three minutes with the child unconsciously making sucking noises, moving his hands aimlessly but with force, or walking around in a daze.   Following such a seizure the child characteristically has no recollection of what has happened.

Approximately seven epileptics are found in every 10,000 school children (Harlin, 1965).   The causes of epilepsy are produced by a variety of neurological disorders, but the actual seizure is due to a disturbance in the electrochemical activity of the discharging cells of the brain.   Peterman (1953) studied 2,500 children with convulsive disorders and found thirty-three percent caused by acute infection, twenty-six percent of unknown origin, and fourteen percent as the result of actual pre- or postnatal injury to the brain.   Factors that precipitate seizures can include emotional disturbance, sleep, menstruation, drug withdrawal, hyperventilation (rapid and intensive breathing), fever, environmental change, light stimulation, drugs, chemicals, allergy, and alcohol (Livingston, 1963).

Crowther (1967) estimates that with appropriate medical or surgical treatment some fifty percent of those afflicted with epilepsy may become seizure-free and that twenty percent may experience such a reduction in frequency that they are able to maintain an adequate social adjustment.   Epilepsy is seen predominantly as a disorder of youth, with at least three-fourths of all cases beginning before age twenty, and in the majority of these the epilepsy is only temporary (Lennox & Lennox, 1960).

With the advent of increased control of epilepsy by drugs, most afflicted children can participate in regular classroom programs.   Educationally, the most significant problem this disorder and other chronic health conditions may present in school is temporary or chronic lack of strength, vitality, and alertness (Wilson, 1973).   In the classroom the primary concern of the teacher may be the attitude of the other class members toward an occasional seizure. If the teacher moves slowly yet deliberately to aid the child at such times and communicates that it is just another event in the school day rather than a major crisis, undue alarm may be prevented.   Also, during instruction devoted to health and hygiene, discussion leading to a more realistic understanding of the disorder can be presented.

Epilepsy is only one of the chronic health problems found

among physically handicapped children.   The United States Office of Education (1970) estimates that some .5 percent of school age children in the nation are afflicted with crippling conditions or health impairments.

In Parts II and III we shall review in more detail the psychological, social, and educational problems faced by the physically handicapped learner.

GIFTED CHILDREN

In our discussion, we have tended to use the terms "handicapped" and "exceptional" interchangeably since the individuals we have been describing were limited in terms of social-emotional functioning, learning efficiency, intelligence, school success, sensory functioning, speech and language adequacy, physical condition, or health. We come now to consideration of the concept of exceptionality as "superior" rather than "limited" and to the gifted individual.

Definition

Since a person can be gifted or talented in any number of areas, such as music, art, athletics, or intellectual ability, a problem arises in the establishment of criteria for giftedness.   Some definitions have included outstanding ability or attainment in any field of endeavor; others have focused on creative imagination and intellectual superiority.   Because of the difficulty in obtaining a quantitative measurement in many areas and due to the widespread acceptance of intelligence tests, the I.Q. score is often used in defining and identifying the gifted individual.

PH

G

Incidence

In determining the actual incidence of gifted children in the population using the I.Q. measurement, we must not only be concerned with selecting a cut-off point, but also recognize that the intellectual and cultural level of a community will greatly influence the number of gifted children identified.   Thus our population estimate will be strongly influenced by geographical and socio-economic factors. Such cultural influences were also found with the socially and economically disadvantaged and to some extent the mentally retarded.

Gallagher (1959) compared proportions of high I.Q. school children in an average and in a superior socio-economic community. Using the Stanford-Binet Intelligence Test, he found that sixteen to twenty percent in the average community had I.Q.'s above 115; in the superior community, the range was from forty-five to sixty percent. If we accept the cut-off of 140 I.Q. in our definition of giftedness, then Gallagher's findings show one-half to one percent of children above that level in the average community and two to three percent in the superior community.

Kirk (1972) suggests that the early experiences of children in families representing higher socio-economic and educational levels are conducive to the development of reasoning ability and understanding abstract concepts that are generally considered indicative of intellectual capacity and emphasized on the predominantly verbal and abstract intelligence tests in use today. He also points out that we could do more to cultivate giftedness than we are doing today by improving the early experiences of children from less advantaged backgrounds and by locating the potentially gifted among them by other than conventional tests.

Causes

The causal factors related to giftedness are difficult to determine due to the extreme significance of environmental experiences. Gifted individuals of every color, race, or creed and in every social class and culture can be found. Pressy (1960), in a review of the lives of geniuses throughout history, suggests several factors common to their early childhood. They had early encouragement from parents, intensive instruction, opportunity to practice skills learned, stimulating social contacts, and cumulative success experiences. When discrepancies among racial and ethnic groups with respect to numbers of gifted individuals are reported, we cannot speak with any certainty of inherent intellectual differences but must consider both the kinds of intelligence tests and other methods of identification used, and the socio-economic, cultural, value-system, and experiential differences existing among such groups.

Lewis Terman, who in 1916 revised the Binet-Simon tests of intelligence for use in the United States, followed a group of 1,528 gifted children in California for thirty-five years (Terman & Oden, 1959). An I.Q. of 140 in the 1916 Stanford-Binet Intelligence Test was used as a final criterion for selection. The ratio of boys to girls was 116 to 100. Among his subjects were one hundred percent more Jewish children, twenty-five percent more children of native-born parents, and a slight excess of Scottish children, with fewer Italian, Portuguese, Mexican, and black children than in the general population. The homes from which these children came were at higher socio-economic levels, and the parents averaged four to five years more schooling than the general population in the United States. The children in Terman's study were superior in physique and general health as compared with standards for average American children. They were heavier at birth, manifested greater height and strength, and walked and talked earlier. They also had fewer problems, such as sensory defects and malnutrition, during childhood. In a study involving 929 gifted students in elementary and secondary schools, Martinson (1961) further confirmed the findings of Terman that the true portrait of the gifted child is on the whole one of physical superiority. Their physical superiority was maintained throughout the years, and at average age forty-four, Terman's subjects had a mortality rate of four-fifths that of the general population.

Martinson (1961) found that the gifted as a group develop reading skills early. Terman (1925) also found that the gifted in his sample exhibited advanced learning achievement. They reported that the highest levels of school achievement were found in areas that required verbal comprehension and usage, whereas the fields that primarily required manual dexterity, such as writing and art, were the weakest areas for the gifted.

An area of study relating to giftedness that has received increasing attention is creativity and productive thinking. Tests based on Guilford's (1956) theory of the structure of intellect indicate that elementary and secondary age children identified as "high creative" but not "high I.Q." achieve equally well in school as children rated "high I.Q." (Getzels & Jackson, 1962; Torrance, 1959).

Identification

When identification of gifted children is left to the classroom teacher, studies suggest that many children will be selected who are not gifted and that many truly gifted children will be overlooked. Pegnato and Birch (1959) found that 31.4 percent of teachers' choices of gifted children were in error and that they missed more than half of those who had superior ability. Academic and social success with talent in areas such as drama or art tend to promote identification as gifted, whereas underachievement, shyness, and nonconformity can result in an individual's being excluded from consideration. Dunlap (1967) suggests fourteen positive characteristics that can help teachers identify gifted children. In a congenial setting, gifted children are likely to:

1. Learn rapidly and easily
2. Retain what they learn without much drill
3. Show much curiosity, as indicated by the kinds, depth, scope, and frequency of their questions
4. Have rich vocabularies marked by originality of thought and expression
5. Enjoy reading, usually at a mature level
6. Show interest in words and ideas, as demonstrated by their frequent use of dictionaries, encyclopedias, and other sources
7. Reason things out, think clearly and precisely, and be quick to comprehend
8. Have the ability to generalize, to see relationships, and to make logical associations
9. Examine, tabulate, classify, collect, and keep records
10. Be interested in the nature of man and his universe at an early age
11. Know and appreciate many things of which other children are unaware
12. Seek older companions among children and enjoy adults
13. Possess a good sense of humor and be cheerful
14. Have a strong desire to excel

Dunlap also says that such negative characteristics as restlessness, carelessness with handwriting, impatience with subjects requiring rote learning and drill, indifference toward uninteresting classwork, and a critical attitude toward themselves and others often characterize gifted children.

   Gallagher (1959) places teacher observation well down the list of effective approaches as a method of identifying gifted children. The type of information that has been predominantly used to supplement teachers' observations are scores on group achievement and intelligence tests. However, studies have indicated (Pegnato & Birch, 1959; Terman, 1925) that group tests are about as accurate as teacher nominations (approximately fifty percent in each case) in the identification of the gifted. Most desirable is the individual intelligence test, although it is expensive, time consuming, and impractical to administer to all children in school districts with limited psychological services. The group intelligence test is generally good for screening, but it can penalize children with reading problems and emotional or motivational difficulties, as will reliance on group achievement test batteries. Identification of gifted children is usually accomplished by a variety of procedures, including teacher referral, school achievement, and group and individual intelligence measures.

Educational Provisions

Among the approaches to the education of gifted children are acceleration, enrichment, and special classes. Acceleration is designed to decrease the time a child spends getting through school and can be accomplished by early grade school admission, skipping grades, telescoping grades by covering the regular curriculum in a shorter time, and early admission to college. In general, gifted children profit from acceleration, and the traditional concern regarding effects of social and emotional factors when a child is displaced from his normal age-mates appears to be largely unfounded. Worcester (1956) found that children admitted to school early on the basis of mental age did as well or better academically than their older classmates, were socially and emotionally better adjusted than their classmates, and had as good or better physical coordination. Kirk (1972), however, emphasizes that no conclusion can be drawn from research studies regarding the group of gifted children as a whole and that decisions related to acceleration must be made for each individual, taking into account his deviation from the class into which he will be placed and the variability in growth patterns within himself.

In place of accelerating gifted children to advanced levels, some schools attempt an enrichment of the regular grades. This can be done by challenging the gifted child with additional or advanced work and can help him develop independence, initiative, and creativity. This approach is advantageous since it allows the child to remain with children of his own age and to develop leadership potential, making every teacher a teacher of the gifted with the end result of raising the quality of instruction for all children, as well as minimizing costs related to running a special program. Kirk (1972), however, points out that the advantages may not be realized due to teacher limitation in terms of time, knowledge, and skill.

Special class placement for gifted children can occur on a part-time basis, in a totally separate public school program, or in a special school. The latter two provisions are not accepted by many school systems, and there is a lack of research evidence to suggest that full-time special class placement yields better results than acceleration or enrichment in the regular grades.

At the secondary level, the rotating scheduling of classes

makes flexible assignment of gifted students to classes in line with their interests and abilities simpler and more practical than is possible in the self-contained elementary level program. In addition, increased counseling and guidance services, extracurricular activities, advanced classes such as honors programs for superior students, heavier course loads to facilitate early graduation, and part-time enrollment in nearby universities and colleges for advanced work before high school graduation are adaptations included in some secondary programs for the gifted.

Some individuals with handicapping conditions, such as visual or hearing impairment, physical handicaps, or chronic health problems, possess superior intelligence and require unique approaches to their education. Helen Keller is perhaps the best known in this category. Our understanding of the relationship between superior intelligence and handicapping conditions discussed throughout this chapter will increase as we consider it in the psycho-social context of Part II.

SUMMARY

This chapter has briefly presented exceptional learners as they have been traditionally categorized. We have not aimed for a comprehensive discussion of causation or etiology, identification and diagnostic procedures, or treatment provisions. Also we have become more involved with the learning and behavior problems of children who are emotionally disturbed, handicapped by a learning disability, mentally retarded, or socially and economically disadvantaged than of children in the other categories. This emphasis will continue throughout the book.

The problems of the physically handicapped learner, including the visually and hearing handicapped, the child with a crippling condition or chronic health problem, and the gifted child, are by no means viewed as unimportant. Our increased focus on the four categories mentioned above, however, stems from the fact that the problems these children present in school appear more a part of the current educational crisis facing the nation and that the largest number of exceptional learners is found within these categories. However, in the next two parts of this book, we will refer to children in all nine categories whenever relevant as we attempt our collective portrait of the exceptional learner, first in the larger social environment in Part II and second, in the learning and school environment in Part III.

PART II

Dimensions of Difference

CHAPTER 3

Determiners of Difference

The members of our cast were assembled and introduced in Part I. In Chapter 2 they were presented in their traditional roles and categories and identified by specific names and labels. In Part II, we are embarking on a transitional journey.

ASSESSING THE PROBLEM

As a first step, let us return to Mrs. Thompson and her concern with Susan's isolation and withdrawal in class and with Henry's continued failure to improve in reading and arithmetic. Let us speculate on what might happen within the traditional special educational realm described in Chapter 2 to help her gain a better understanding of their problems and obtain help for the children themselves. Does Susan have an emotional problem that underlies her poor adjustment in class? Is Henry a mentally retarded child who just cannot be expected to keep up with the class, or does he have some specific learning disability or problem in sight or hearing that accounts for his poor functioning? The search for answers to these questions would probably start with Mrs. Thompson's discussing the problem with her school principal. School records would be reviewed and possibly Susan's and Henry's parents would be asked to visit the school and provide additional information.

If the problems appeared to warrant further study, the district psychologist may be asked in for consultation. He may admin-

ister certain tests in an attempt to determine the intelligence level
of the children, their academic functioning level, and any special
problems they may have in perception and motor coordination.   In
turn, the psychologist may request the services of other special consultants associated with the school district, such as the physician,
psychiatrist, pediatrician, or neurologist.   Armed with reports and
recommendations from all the consultants who had reviewed the
problems of Susan and Henry, the special education staff of the
district would consider (1) what to tell Mrs. Thompson to do to
increase her understanding of the problem of her students, and (2)
what to tell Mrs. Thompson to do to help the children, including
the possibility of removing them from her class and placing them in
a class for the "emotionally disturbed" or "children with learning
disabilities" or for the "educable mentally retarded."

    The first consideration would include some direct and useful
information: a physician's or pediatrician's report of general health,
physical development, and vision and hearing assessment; a psychiatrist's evaluation of the seriousness of emotional difficulties; a neurologist's discussion of the presence or absence of signs possibly
related to impaired brain functioning; and a psychologist's assessment of I.Q. level and academic and special learning problems.
This information makes up the traditional base for special educational decision-making with unique children like Susan and Henry.
This base is built with the contributions of professionals in disciplines outside the field of education and is essential because the
problems that limit the exceptional child in learning and school are
often partly medical, psychiatric, neurological, or psychological in
nature.   There is no question that establishment of this multi-
disciplinary base increases the educator's understanding of the problems of exceptional children.

BUILDING THE BRIDGE

However, such a base must be looked at in perspective.   In actuality it may be viewed as standing on one side of a chasm that separates theory from practice, diagnosis from treatment, and clinical
description from a definitive educational program.   This chasm
must be bridged in order to link the multi-disciplinary base with the
educational operations base on the other side.   For it is this latter
base that is Mrs. Thompson's primary concern.   It is the classroom
with children lined up at the door day after day waiting to enter and
be taught.   What can be offered Susan and Henry to help them with

their school problems will largely take place here, even though medical treatment, special training, and psychotherapy can be important benefits offered on the multi-disciplinary side. In this text we are going to focus on this educational operations base and the benefits that exceptional children can derive directly from the school.

The problem of building a bridge that consists of relevant and translatable information across the chasm and connecting the multi-disciplinary and educational operations bases is a sizeable one. Traditionally, the locus of such bridge building has been from the multi-disciplinary side. Elaborate diagnostic and descriptive information has been assembled and reported to the classroom teacher who, despite increased understanding of the problem, still waits for help in doing something about it. The implications for such help are the essence of our bridge.

Let us consider the bridge building efforts that might have been made by the multi-disciplinary group associated with evaluating Susan and Henry. After considerable examination, evaluation, report writing, and conferences, the children may be re-introduced to Mrs. Thompson as follows:

"Mrs. Thompson, this is Susan. She is in good health with no physical problems. Her verbal I.Q. is 90, her performance I.Q. is 100, with a full scale I.Q. of 95. Thus, she falls within the normal range of intellectual functioning. Her reading is at low fourth grade level, and her arithmetic level is low third grade. Her major problem appears to be in the inter-personal area, where she is fearful of others and feels very inadequate. She has a negative self-concept and an immature fantasy life. In summary, she appears a child with certain neurotic traits and a schizoid personality development."

"Mrs. Thompson, this is Henry. His general health is good, and there are no problems with hearing or vision. His verbal I.Q. is 85 and his performance I.Q. is 75 with a full scale I.Q. of 80. This places him at the borderline level of the dull-normal range of intelligence. His reading and arithmetic are on low second grade level. There are suggestions of minimal neurological impairment in the rotations and distortions he made in a geometric figure copying task."

These are brief introductions. In actuality, Mrs. Thompson would have detailed information and test protocols to review. But the overall impression she may come away with might rely on the highlights presented above. Even though no one can debate the value of some of this information, when we picture Mrs. Thompson waiting by the classroom door as Susan and Henry file in for another day in class, we cannot help but wonder if she is truly in a better position to offer them the help they need than she was the day she stood observing them on the playground.   In short, did any useful, practical bridge emerge from the evaluations of Susan and Henry?

Mrs. Thompson and many other regular and special teachers often experience a sense of abandonment as they wait at the educational operations base of the actual classroom for guidelines with respect to what to do with children who are different.   A further illustration of this dilemma can be provided by means of an elaboration of an analogy suggested by Schwitzgebel (1965).

Teachers who must deal with children with unique behavior and learning problems stand on unfamiliar terrain like strangers in a city with a destination in mind but few directions for how to arrive there.   The destination is a practical educational solution, a set of educational objectives and methods, to guide them in teaching children like Susan and Henry.   This destination we will call "the corner of First and Main."   If you are lost in a strange city and wish to get to a certain destination the logical thing is to ask for directions.   Surely the chances of finding your way will be increased if you get the assistance of an informed, local resident who knows the surroundings.   The teacher approaches the first person to walk by.   It is a physician.

"Pardon me," she says, "but can you help me get to the corner of First and Main Streets?"

The physician smiles and says, "Of course.   I just happen to have a map with me."   He produces the map, hands it to the teacher, nods, and is gone.

The teacher expresses appreciation, takes the map and starts on her way.   But as she opens the map, a puzzled look comes over her face.   Yes, it is a map but not the one she expected.   The physician has given her a geological map depicting accurate and important information about certain physical aspects of the area.   However, the map says nothing about First and Main.   Perhaps another person will be able to help.   A psychiatrist happens by and the teacher asks again for assistance.

"Here is a map," he says.   "I think it will be of use to you."   But as the teacher unfolds the map she again is puzzled.   She has been given a political map, which provides useful information about persons in the area but makes no direct reference to First and Main.

The teacher feels a growing concern.   Certainly someone must know how to get to First and Main.   At this point, a psychologist comes along.   Again another map and again a puzzled look on the teacher's face.   This time the map is a topographical map, and although relevant to certain major aspects of the area, it is irrelevant to finding the corner of First and Main.

Without overextending our analogy, the point should be obvious. Educators may look long and hard for the professional ally who possesses a street map clearly and directly stating the location of First and Main and how to get there. But in truth, the teacher will probably have to take whatever clues she can from the maps of her colleagues in other disciplines and find First and Main largely on her own. This book was written in order to provide more direct clues in relation to this quest. Although admittedly not offering a simply stated street map pinpointing the destination, it will, hopefully, aid the field of special education in general and teachers specifically in getting closer to the vicinity of First and Main.

Returning to our earlier example of bridge building, what is being suggested here is initiating the bridge *from the other side*. That is, Mrs. Thompson may need to take a closer look at Susan and Henry, describe them along the behavioral and learning dimensions that she understands and has control over, explore some possible instructional approaches, and then build a bridge back across to the traditional multi-disciplinary base. Thus Susan and Henry may be introduced to the physician, psychiatrist, and psychologist as follows:

"This is Susan. She excels in reading and keeps up with most of the class in her school work but needs help with her multiplication facts. She hasn't made any friends, and I see this as her biggest problem. I have been pairing her for reading each day with another girl who is also shy but who is having a problem in reading. Susan appears to enjoy helping out and does a good job. I think it makes her feel important. She still withdraws and seems to like dolls and games the other children have outgrown. I am trying to get her interested in some activities she can share with others."

"This is Henry. Henry takes longer to learn most things than anyone in the class. He has started reading but needs constant help. He tries hard in arithmetic and is making some progress here. Henry's handwriting is so poor I have let him continue with manuscript printing, but will introduce cursive writing when he is ready. Since he likes to write stories and is anxious to succeed, I don't feel handwriting drill is too important to stress right now."

Bower (1969b) describes the notion of *building the bridge from the other side* in relation to the emotionally disturbed child:

My first serious exposure to the world of work came as a teacher of emotionally disturbed children. About the only thing I had going for me at the time was youth, ignorance, and a determination to survive at all costs. Nothing in my experience and education had prepared me for this. I sought help from my learned colleagues in education and mental health, from great books, from my puzzling students. I ran eagerly to case conferences with all cerebral and sensory neurons quivering and ready, and came away with much interesting stuff. Every once in a while there was a psychic click that led me to try something new in the classroom. After two years, however, I began to sense that the gap between knowing a person's state of mind and knowing how to help him learn in school were difficult "knowings" to bridge. I also began to sense that emotionally disturbed children were, like other children, action-oriented, competence-seeking animals interested in learning and in learning how to learn. Why not start from this side of the bridge and ask the clinicians to zero in their skills on educational as well as therapy goals? As a teacher responsible for doing something with these children for several hours a day, I — along with my colleagues — wanted some practical ways to think and act about my job.*

A comparison of the multi-disciplinary summaries cited earlier with Mrs. Thompson's comments reveals definite similarities, and that is how it should be. We are all looking for First and Main, but perhaps Mrs. Thompson's educational-operations-based start is going to help us get there more quickly and effectively. For in formulating the educational problems of Susan and Henry, Mrs. Thompson was viewing them with a relatively open mind rather than with one narrowed by ominous medical and psychiatric diagnostic terminology, which all too often results in attachment of a label.

THE CHILD AS A LEARNER

The philosophy of this book stresses a single label for all children — normal, exceptional, unique, or different. That label is stated in the title and it is **learner**. The exceptional child is first and foremost a learner, ready at all times to learn something. He is secondarily handicapped by medical, psychiatric, neurological, or psychological problems. This is the cornerstone of the bridge built from the *other side*, from the educational operations or classroom side over to the

*Bower, E. M. Review of F. M. Hewett, *The emotionally disturbed child in the classroom. American Journal of Orthopsychiatry*, 1969, 39, 855–856. Copyright, The American Orthopsychiatry Association, Inc. Reproduced by permission.

traditional multi-disciplinary base. It also offers the most relevant and direct single clue to finding First and Main Streets — a truly effective educational program for all children.

However, this position with respect to building the bridge from the educational operations side is not without risk to the teacher. For if you truly consider every child a learner at all times, ready to learn something, and if he learns nothing, then the implication is clear. Children who learn nothing are not child failures, but the result of teaching failures. The "learner" orientation removes the protective refuge of the diagnostic label with its convenient use as a self-fulfilling prophecy. For if Susan learns nothing and Henry learns nothing, Mrs. Thompson could explain it by simply stating: "How could any child with a schizoid personality or neurological impairment be expected to learn in a third grade classroom?"

Viewing exceptional children first as learners and second as handicapped physically or psychologically places the approach of this book in a behavioral framework in contrast to the medical model, which has traditionally dominated the field of special education. That is, it is not what the child *cannot do* and the multitude of physical and psychological factors that may be related to his problem that are emphasized, but rather what the child *can do* and his observable behavior in a learning situation. Thus, we will shift from "disease" to "level of competence," from "handicap" to "stage of readiness to learn," and from "specific diagnostic category" to "learner." The behavioral orientation utilized in the book is a pragmatic one, not rigorously theoretical in nature. This is an important point to clarify at the onset. Emphasizing what children can do and their observable behavior is not denying the existence of possible underlying physical and psychological factors that may obviously limit what they can do. It is simply avoiding preoccupation with these factors and their undesirable side-tracking effects that have been discussed earlier. To set an educational objective for a child, based on everything known about him, which appears reasonable and appropriate, and to expect him to move toward it is just *good teaching*. It is an approach emanating from the educational operations base and may be influenced by any understanding obtained from bridge building efforts taking place from the multi-disciplinary base. Analogies such as our bridge building and varied map examples are limited in the final analysis because of their over-simplicity and concreteness. We are talking about a point of view, a degree of emphasis, a focus, an orientation, not about closed-minded dogma.

What is a *learner*? The term is a dynamic one. It suggests

movement, development, change, progress, and achievement. As a starting point, we can simply define a learner as *an individual in the process of acquiring knowledge and skill.* And as we look in on Mrs. Thompson's classroom during an arithmetic lesson, we can observe some of the contributing factors that determine an individual's effectiveness as a learner.

> As Mrs. Thompson surveys the group before her, she can select three children who are poor candidates for the role of learner in this lesson. First, there is Henry, who just doesn't seem to grasp even basic number concepts. Mrs. Thompson questions whether Henry really has the ability to keep up with the academic expectations of the third grade. Then there is Mark, who has moved three times over the past two school years and has ended up in Mrs. Thompson's class with almost no preparation for work with fractions. Susan is looking out the window apparently daydreaming, and despite several reminders to "pay attention," she is continually distracted from the lesson.

CAPACITY AND EXPERIENCE

Henry, Mark, and Susan are learners in the process of acquiring knowledge and skill. But they are not identical learners; they are different with respect to what they bring to Mrs. Thompson's classroom. Henry may be an ineffective learner because he lacks the intellectual *capacity* necessary for third grade work. In addition to intellectual capacity, children vary in terms of the basic potential they possess for receiving sensory stimuli, perceiving it accurately, and eliciting motor and verbal responses. This potential may be largely determined at the time of birth, but injury and illness can alter it throughout an individual's lifetime.

Mark, on the other hand, may well possess the capacity necessary for learning at the third grade level but may lack the *previous experience* necessary for success. Experience can be defined as the *range* and *nature* of opportunities that an individual has had for learning about the physical properties and social expectations of the environment and for development of motor, language, and intellectual skills.

Susan's problems may also primarily relate to previous experience rather than to capacity, but whereas Mark suffered from a limited range of experience, Susan's behavior may reflect the *nature* of previous experience. Continued frustration and failure in the school setting could have resulted in Susan's seeking an escape through excessive daydreaming and withdrawal.

Thus, differences in capacity and differences in the range and nature of previous experience can account for the problems of Henry, Mark, and Susan in Mrs. Thompson's classroom. It is precisely such differences to a more marked degree that account for the problems of exceptional learners in the American school.

Actually pinning down the relative contributions of basic capacity and previous experience in determining the functioning level displayed by individuals such as Henry, Mark, and Susan is not easy. In fact, few issues in the entire field of human growth and development have received such persistent attention.

In Chapter 1, we saw the issue reflected in the *nativist* versus *sensationalist* position of scholars of the eighteenth and nineteenth centuries. According to the nativist Pinel, Victor, the "wild boy," clearly lacked the capacity for being normalized. But to Itard, a sensationalist, normalcy for Victor was initially viewed as possible if proper sensory and training experiences could be provided. Victor did not become a normal boy, but he certainly was a different individual at the end of Itard's training program than he would have been if he had been left in the forest or merely been given custodial care in an institution. Both Pinel and Itard were partly correct — capacity does set limits in terms of learning, but experience plays a most significant part in determining the level of competence an individual actually attains.

Today we are not as polarized with respect to the either-or contribution of heredity and environment or nature and nurture. We have come to recognize that the functioning level we see — what Mrs. Thompson sees as she attempts to teach Henry, Mark, and Susan — is the result of capacity and experience in interaction with, not versus, one another.

Thus, a simple equation to summarize this relationship can be stated:

$$\text{capacity} \times \text{experience} = \text{functioning level}$$

This equation essentially expresses the same relationship between heredity and environment presented in the more fundamental statement of Dobzhansky (1950):

$$\text{genotype} \times \text{environment} = \text{phenotype}$$

Here genotype represents the sum total of the individual's hereditary properties. The interaction of the genotype with the environment results in the phenotype, or "all external and internal structures of the organism" (p. 161). Our use of capacity, experience, and functioning level instead of more basic terms will enable us to apply this equation to the educational and adjustment problems of the exceptional learner in a simpler and more direct manner.

In our discussion of the characteristics and behavior of exceptional learners in the remainder of this text, we will find capacity and experience contributing in varying degrees to a child's functioning level at any time. Several examples illustrate the relationship of these determiners to functioning level:

> The blind child clearly lacks the capacity to see the picture being held up by the teacher in front of the class. The child from a disadvantaged background can see that it is a picture of a red barn and a farmer plowing a field, but his lack of previous experience with such content may preclude the picture having any real meaning for him. The child with a learning disability may be inattentive to the entire lesson partly because of some capacity-based, neurological dysfunction and partly because learning, school, teacher, and lessons have become negative for him due to previous experience.
>
> The child with a hearing handicap may lack the capacity to hear the teacher's question about the picture. The gifted child eagerly blurts out the answer because he has been studying agriculture on his own and has planted a productive garden at home. When a question is directed toward the speech handicapped child, he may not respond because he is afraid he might stutter and be subjected to ridicule by his classmates, as has been his previous experience.
>
> As the teacher makes an assignment to the class, the mentally retarded child may lack the capacity to recall the sequence of directions given after a few moments have passed. The child with a chronic health problem, such as a cardiac condition, may have been absent so much during the preceding weeks that he does not understand what to do due to a limited range of experience. The emotionally disturbed child may willfully tear up his worksheet and throw it on the floor, and wait defiantly for the teacher to do something about it. Based on the nature of his previous experience, and frustration with academic tasks and teachers he has come to hate, this type of behavior is an established routine.

How do we determine what proportion of a child's functioning level is the result of capacity or experience? Even though we recognize the inevitable interaction effect discussed earlier, in setting expectations, selecting tasks, and actual teaching, we are concerned with whether the child has the capacity to see, hear, speak, respond motorically, perceive accurately, and comprehend. When we are confronted with a child who does not learn, we are in the position of the driver who turns the ignition switch on in his car and finds the starter does not turn over. He, too, is concerned with capacity — in this case the capacity of the battery to turn over the starter. Is the battery dead or does the problem lie somewhere between the battery and the ignition switch? In terms of our automotive analogy, the problem of capacity can be dealt with directly. We can attach a voltage meter and directly measure the capacity of the battery. But in the special educational realm, such direct and precise measurement is not possible. In most cases, we are forced to rely on indirect behavioral measures, such as speech evaluation and psychometric tests.

With children who have marked problems in vision and hearing, obvious mental retardation, speech defects, severe neurological impairment, and motor handicaps, our indirect measurement efforts may have a fair degree of accuracy. But the emotionally disturbed child, the child who is socially and economically disadvantaged, the mildly retarded child, the child with a learning disability, and the gifted underachiever can confound the picture with problems related to previous experience and functioning. When we attempt to measure indirectly such children's intellectual capacity or perceptual-motor proficiency by means of a test, for example, we can be easily fooled. Perhaps the child was not paying attention; perhaps he refused to try; perhaps he was confused with the directions given him; or perhaps he lacked the previous experience necessary to demonstrate his actual capacity. This is only the beginning of our problem of accurate measurement of capacity. Perhaps he was afraid, angry, preoccupied with recalling a fight he had on the school bus that morning, hungry, or sleepy. In short, we have a difficult time knowing what a child is actually capable of doing as compared with the effects of his previous experience.

But we must do the best we can. Despite our position earlier in this chapter that elaborate medical and psychological diagnostic efforts may be of questionable usefulness when the child and teacher meet face to face and the business of teaching and learning must get underway, the importance of assessing capacity in visual, auditory, motor, speech, perceptual, and intellectual areas as a screening procedure cannot be minimized. It is a necessary first step in the realistic formulation of expectations for the child. But we must not overlook the dissimilarity between direct measurement of the capacity of the car battery and indirect measurement of the learning capacity of the child. There will always be some who approach measurement of a child's capacity as if a given technique of assessment could be applied with the directness and certainty of the voltage meter to the car battery, and this we must guard against.

SUMMARY

In this chapter, we have presented a learner as an individual in the process of acquiring knowledge and skill. All learners vary in terms of the interaction of basic capacity and previous experience. This interaction determines the functioning level they bring to the learning situation. Exceptional learners are primarily unique because of capacity and experiential differences which distinguish them from normal learners and which account for their broad range of functioning levels. We are limited in obtaining precise measurement of capacities for learning, and what we actually measure is the present functioning level of the child partly determined by the effects of the range and nature of his previous experience.

The next two chapters concern the functioning levels of exceptional learners as they move through, interact with, and learn about the world around them. The functioning levels or dimensions we will be concerned about are related to flexibility, sociality, intelligence, and individualization. These dimensions have been described by Simpson (1949) as defining the most important features of man in nature and have been utilized by Martin and Stendler (1959) in their text on child behavior and development.* They describe man in relation to his total environment and offer an opportunity for conceptualizing the nature of exceptionality and what it actually means to be different. **For if man can be viewed as truly unique in nature because of his level of functioning along the dimensions of flexibility, sociality, intelligence, and individualization, then men can be regarded as truly unique in relation to other men as they demonstrate greater or lesser competence along these dimensions.**

Such is the premise for the discussion of exceptional learners in Chapters 4 and 5. Our task is first to sketch in the broad outlines of a collective portrait of the exceptional child as he moves through the total environment and then to detail our work in Part III with an emphasis on the school and learning. Thus from general questions of how the child adapts to a changing, physical environment (flexibility), how he gets along with and is perceived by others (sociality), how adequate he is intellectually (intelligence), and what becomes of him as he matures and moves toward adult life (individualization), we will consider specific questions related to

*Simpson uses "socialization" in place of "sociality." We will use the latter term, as do Martin and Stendler in their text.

increasing his competencies in learning in the classroom.   We will expand our basic equation to include these dimensions of difference or functioning levels:

$$\text{capacity} \times \text{experience} = \text{functioning level} = \begin{array}{l} \text{flexibility} \\ \text{sociality} \\ \text{intelligence} \\ \text{individualization} \end{array}$$

In our discussion, the relative contribution of capacity and experience in determining these functioning levels will be obvious at times and not as apparent at others.   We shall, however, refer to these determiners wherever appropriate in relation to each of the nine categories and utilize them in our summary discussions to emphasize similarities and differences between categories.

CHAPTER 4

Flexibility and Sociality

In this chapter we begin our collective considerations of exceptional children as learners and turn to the dimensions of flexibility and sociality.

FLEXIBILITY

Flexibility essentially refers to adaptation to a changing physical environment. Children notice things, hear things, touch things, and smell things. They crawl, walk, run, and jump. They are constantly interacting with the world around them. They go in the shade if the sun gets too hot; they put on a jacket if it turns cold; they come in the house when it begins to get dark; they avoid picking a rose because of the thorns on the bush or because a bee hovers nearby. They find their way home independently from the movies, avoiding traffic hazards, but perhaps taking a detour after hearing a fire engine siren appear to stop around the block. Children are flexible — paying attention, doing, following directions, exploring, and learning in a multitude of situations.

What do we know about exceptional learners in relation to flexibility? As we stated earlier man's unique attributes along this dimension give him, in part, a special place in the world. We will now consider exceptional learners in terms of their adaptation to the physical environment.

133

The dimension of flexibility is particularly relevant to the problems of many emotionally disturbed children who participate in everyday events in a maladaptive manner. Some approach the activities and experiences of childhood at home, in the neighborhood, and in school with impulsive, uncontrolled behavior; others draw away, preferring to remain uninvolved, isolated, and withdrawn. As we mentioned in Chapter 2, Quay, Morse, and Cutler (1966) found that three factors or sets of behavioral characteristics discriminate between types of behavior problem children found in the public school:

Conduct problem
Inadequacy-immaturity
Personality problem

From their summary statements with regard to each characteristic, we can infer the flexibility problems of many emotionally disturbed children.

The conduct problem child is seen as "aggressive, hostile, and contentious." Such a child moves through the environment freely and directly, participating in a wide range of experiences. But he often does so in a random, coercive, or even destructive manner, failing to profit or learn from any experience and attempting to set the rules and limits himself. Toys are broken before utilized creatively, interest span varies greatly, and participation in games is contingent on domination and having things his own way.

The inadequacy-immaturity child exhibits "sluggishness, laziness, lack of interest, preoccupation, dislike for school, and inattentiveness." Here the problem may be one of holding back from new experiences and developing singular interests. The child often prefers to stay home and watch television for long periods rather than to seek out play activities with others, and he often engages in excessive fantasy. The personality problem child has been described as demonstrating "inferiority feelings, self-consciousness, lack of self-confidence, fearfulness, and depression." This child views new experiences as threats, worries about his inadequacy to perform as well as others and is generally unhappy much of the time. Such withdrawal can greatly limit the number and kind of activities he engages in and can lead to distorted beliefs about the world in which he lives.

An inflexible child with an emotional disturbance particularly related to school participation is the child with so-called "school phobia." He is similar to the personality problem child just de-

scribed. Levison (1962) considers such a child in an acute panic
state when in school. He might turn pale, begin to tremble, become
immobilized, or feel a strong urge to run away. Psychosomatic
symptoms such as abdominal pain and dizziness also can occur.
These problems do not occur on days the child does not have to go
to school. Much has been written about the faulty family relationships, particularly between mother and child, which appear basic to
school phobia. In our discussion, however, we are concerned with
establishing the problem as seriously limiting the child's range of
experience and particularly his participation in school.

Autistic, schizophrenic, or psychotic children, seldom found
in the public school, have extreme flexibility problems. Often such
children have largely retreated from reality and participation in
everyday events and live in a fantasy world of their own. Instead of
playing with appropriate toys and seeking the stimulation of others,
they sit and endlessly rock back and forth or crouch fearfully in a
corner. Their high degree of inflexibility denies them the involvement with sights, sounds, objects, and events that are essential for
normal childhood development to occur. In a study aimed at
analyzing specific factors associated with disturbed behavior,
Spivack and Swift (1966) found that one factor separating disturbed
children from normals was "inability to self-initiate a course of
action." Independence, goal-directedness, and efficiency often are
not found among emotionally disturbed children. The lack of
these three characteristics may account for much of their confusion,
experiential deprivation, and lack of free movement in the
environment.

The emotionally disturbed child, in general, has the capacity
for an active, involved, and highly flexible relationship to the physical environment. The fact that he often functions in an inflexible
and maladaptive manner probably relates to the faulty nature of his
environmental experience, much of it in the interpersonal realm,
which we shall consider in the next section of this chapter.

Even though the problems of the child with a learning disability
are often most visible and disruptive in the confines of the classroom,
it is interesting to follow such a child outside to the playground,
down the street to his neighborhood, and into his home, and then
to consider how flexible he is in adapting to the larger environment.
Hyperactivity, perhaps the most commonly recognized characteristic
of children with learning disabilities, may go unnoticed in the world

of running, jumping, tumbling, climbing, and playing. Rappaport, Hirt, and Decker (1964) have speculated that hyperactive behavior is not necessarily bad, but that the fact that there is so much of it causes problems in the classroom. Outside, where demands for conformity and control are lessened, this problem may not occur. Cruickshank (1967a) has included hyperactivity along with hyper-distractibility, disinhibition, and impulsivity under the general problem heading of distractibility in describing such children. He views the basic difficulty as stemming from the child's inability to refrain from reaction to extraneous external or internal stimuli. As a result, such a child often is a poor participant in games requiring prolonged concentration and attention, readily being drawn away by noise and activity around him or irrelevant thoughts about past or future events. A sign stating "wet paint" may be an open invitation for touching, and a knothole in a fence may be irresistible in terms of finger poking. Clements and Peters (1962) have reported that parents of children with learning disabilities often express concern with the child's tendency to "not concentrate for more than a few minutes at a time," "jump from one thing to another," and "mind everybody's business but his own."

Characteristics such as hyperactivity, distractibility, and impulsivity are often observed in emotionally disturbed children who do not exhibit specific learning disabilities. Conversely, children with learning disabilities are often found to be emotionally unstable in a variety of ways. Bender (1949) says that such instability results from the child's lack of successful contact with the world around him and from the frustrations, misinterpretations of reality, and bizarre behavior patterns that can result. Clements and Peters (1962) found parents of children with learning disabilities reporting such problems as daydreaming, nervousness, and frequent temper outbursts, sometimes for no apparent reason.

Problems in accurate perception of visual, auditory, and tactual stimuli can lead to much of the frustration and misinterpretation of reality found among these children. Unlike sensory defects, such as blindness and deafness, which preclude the individual's receiving visual and auditory stimuli, perceptual disorders refer to a lack of ability to recognize, or decode, such stimuli in an accurate manner. Myklebust (1964a) defines perceptual disturbance as "inability to identify, discriminate, and interpret sensation." Geometric forms often are incorrectly copied, figure-ground confusion can exist (difficulty in discriminating central figures from the background context in which they are placed), and the child may not be able to identify familiar objects by touch alone. Particular difficulties in auditory discrimination (e.g., recognizing tunes or differentiating between various sounds) can be at the root of some of the learning disability child's problems (Kass, 1969) and can subtly affect his attempts to relate to his environment.

Children with learning disabilities also may exhibit poor spatial orientation and demonstrate motor problems such as clumsiness and awkwardness in activities requiring a high degree of coordination. There often is difficulty in maintaining balance, and the child may fall or stumble frequently.

In terms of our consideration of capacity, experience, and functioning level, the child with a learning disability is presumed to have a neurological basis for his difficulties. Thus the characteristics in relation to functioning level we have discussed may be attributed to a problem in capacity present at or shortly after birth. But what about the effects of environmental experience? Garrison and Force (1965) have suggested that deprivation of psychological needs due to inadequate or harsh environmental experience can damage personality development as much as can organic disorders. Many of the problems associated with learning disabilities could conceivably reflect such experience or be greatly aggravated by it.

One concept which relates to how well the mentally retarded child moves through and interacts with his environment is the notion of "rigidity." This term here refers to the persistence of a response or behavior beyond the point where it is appropriate or correct. It was Lewin (1936) who first advanced the notion that retarded children are more "rigid" in their thought processes and thus are more apt to persist at monotonous tasks for longer periods of time than normal children. In experiments on this concept, Kounin (1941a, b) gave retarded and normal ten-year-olds the task of drawing simple cat figures and then drawing figures of bugs. Normal children drew cats up to a point, became bored, and then switched, but retarded children persisted and continued to draw cat figures long after the others had stopped. Kounin also gave retarded children a deck of cards to be sorted, first by form and then by color. Retarded children seemed to persist in sorting according to the first principle and could not as readily shift to sorting by the second. Kounin suggested that such inflexibility would affect the development of adequate intelligence in retardates since it makes the occurrence of cognitive change more difficult.

The concept, however, was not entirely accurate. Later experimental studies in which retarded individuals and normals were given similar satiation tasks (Green & Zigler, 1962; Zigler, 1963) did not verify the supposed presence of rigidity among retardates. Some retarded children could make the necessary shifts in activity; this seemed to depend more on their experience and background than on the fact that they were retarded.   The difference seemed to be that all retarded children in Kounin's studies were institutionalized.   Zigler (1966) suggested that retarded children living in institutions are more apt to have been deprived of social contact, and that persistence in tasks given by an adult may occur due to the child's high motivation to secure adult contact.   Such children may have sensed that by continuing at the task, boring as it was, they could maintain the adult's presence; but if they changed the situation by shifting to another task, the session would be terminated and the adult would "go away."   Thus, in a situation where an adult assigns a task and directs the child to "keep doing it as long as you wish," the institutionalized retarded child may actually persist in an effort to maintain social contact and thus only *appear* to be inflexible. Retarded children living at home, on the other hand, are not significantly different from normal children in flexibility, since they are not subject to the same degree of social deprivation (Green & Zigler, 1962).   Apparent discrepancies in flexibility between retarded and normal persons, therefore, seem to reflect *motivational* and *experiential* differences rather than a true cognitive deficit.

There are, of course, some areas in which the retarded are deficient, and those deficiencies become more obvious the lower the I.Q.   The more severely retarded a child is, for example, the more likely it is that he will have accompanying physical handicaps, since the possibility is greater that the same disease or organic factor that caused his retardation has affected his physical functioning as well. Mentally retarded children have been found to be less proficient in physical motor behavior than normals of the same chronological age (Cratty, 1969; Francis & Rarick, 1960), but the differences are not as marked in gross motor areas or when the task is relatively simple. Hearing problems tend to occur more frequently among retarded children than normals (Lloyd, 1970), although this may be less the case with visual handicaps (Benton, 1964).   Retarded children have also been found to respond more slowly on reaction time tests (Baumeister, Urquhart, Beedle, & Smith, 1964; Berkson, 1961), and appear to have particular problems in the area of speech, with a high percentage having disorders in articulation (Tarjan, Dingman, & Miller, 1960; Webb & Kinde, 1967).   Speech disorders not only may impede the child's social relationships but also may make it particularly difficult for him to make his needs known effectively. Difficulty in these areas render it less likely that the child will be as flexible in dealing with his environment as a normal child who can express a discomfort, pinpoint a dissatisfaction, ask a question about something he does not understand, or move freely, quickly, and alertly through his surroundings.

Though mentally retarded children may not move as freely and openly through their environment, this may not be a totally inborn characteristic. When such children select the familiar (well-understood games, favorite toy, neighborhood play area) rather than the unfamiliar (games with new rules, complex toys or objects, play area with strangers or new hazards), they may be exhibiting wariness of others — particularly adults with whom they have had negative experiences in the past (Zigler, 1966), immature personality development (Cromwell, 1967), difficulty in relating language concepts to physical acts (Luria, 1963; Hermelin & O'Connor, 1963), or lack of previous experience (Hunt, 1961). Thus as we begin to review current knowledge, it would appear that the flexibility of the retarded child may, in some areas, be determined less by capacity than by experience.

This is not to say, however, that the child who is truly retarded will not have problems in flexibility. Simply because of his lowered intelligence, he has what we might call "fewer options" in relating to the physical world than the normal child, i.e., he may not as readily consider *all* the alternatives in getting from one place to another or he may not think as critically about the consequences of certain physical acts as a normal child might. Thus, when a normal child is confronted with a problem in relating to or interacting with his environment, he is more apt to come up with alternative solutions and try different ways of approaching a problem. The retarded child, on the other hand, may perceive fewer strategies and is much more apt to be thwarted by obstacles in his physical environment and subject to greater frustrations because of decreased flexibility.

The socially and economically disadvantaged child who lives in the middle of a large city often has a more limited range of experience than the child from a middle-class home located in the suburbs. Narrow sidewalks, busy streets, back alleys, deserted buildings, and crowded, impoverished living quarters impose limits on what the child can do and how he can do it. As stated in Chapter 2, the disadvantaged child can emerge from a wide range of cultural, social, and economic backgrounds. In our discussion regarding such children in this text, we will use the references (e.g., lower class, disadvantaged, urban, slum) used by the author cited and will not attempt to define each reference with respect to its range.

Goldberg (1967) refers to the "constricted world" of children living under such conditions and states that some children in the inner city have never been more than a block or two away from their own neighborhoods. Deutsch (1963) characterizes the lower-class child as having limited opportunities to explore the outside world, a lack of esthetically pleasing surroundings, a scarcity of books, toys, puzzles, pencils, and paper, and a lack of guidance and encouragement in their use. Among the many deficits he brings with him to school is a limited understanding and knowledge of the physical, geographical, and geometric aspects of the environment.

Hunt (1964) has considered the effects of crowded living conditions on the child's early life. In infancy, being surrounded by a large number of individuals and exposed to a constant bombardment of sights and sounds, may actually be advantageous. But during the second year, when a youngster typically begins to move about constantly, to throw objects, and "get into everything," he may be sharply curtailed in what he is allowed to do because of these same crowded conditions.

The flexibility of the Pueblo Indian child has been described by Zintz (1962). It is partly determined by cultural values, which often contrast markedly with those held by the teacher and school. The Indian child is oriented toward maintaining harmony with nature rather than attaining mastery over it. He may not be totally committed to a scientific explanation of natural phenomena, and a belief in myths and sorcery, as well as fear of the supernatural, may greatly alter the types of experiences he seeks and what he learns as a result. In addition, he may be "present time" rather than "future time" oriented and not respond to long-range tasks that hold promise of an eventual goal.

A number of writers have described the physical, concrete style of the lower-class child as he moves through and interacts with the environment. Goldberg (1963) compares this motoric, "thing oriented," and non-verbal style of the lower-class child with the more abstract, symbolic, "idea oriented" verbal style of the middle-class child. Eisenberg (1963–1964) speculates that this concrete approach to learning limits the child's flexibility and makes generalizations and transfer difficult. In addition to having a physical style, the lower-class child appears more visually than auditorily oriented. He would rather look than listen. Since so much listening is associated with words spoken by others, the language problems of the lower-class child, which we shall discuss in Chapter 9, may be, in part, a reflection of his non-auditory orientation.

Despite these limitations, Eisenberg and others have credited the lower-class child with a number of adaptive strengths, such as being able "to negotiate the jungle of the slums." Cuban (1970) summarizes such strengths, which have appeared in the literature, and concludes that lower-class children have a realistic "know-how" and demonstrate responsible, adaptive behavior under difficult circumstances. They also appear to possess a high degree of self-reliance and a sense of autonomy and independence.

Thus, what the socially and economically disadvantaged child learns about the world may be restricted by the nature of the setting in which he lives. How he learns to move through the world may handicap him in the formal school environment, where he may lack certain adaptive skills, but viewed in terms of the real world in which he must live and play, his behavior may be highly adaptive and flexible.

The visually handicapped child who is born blind or who has lost his vision during the early years must rely on the remaining senses of hearing, touch, and, to a lesser extent, taste and smell for knowledge of the world around him and for clues for successful adaptation to it. Even though hearing alerts us to the distance and direction of an object that has made a sound, it does not provide a concrete idea of the object itself. A large part of accurately knowing and successfully adapting to a changing environment is based on seeing. The visual sense allows us to examine a spider's web, to contemplate the changing colors of a sunset, to survey a giant oak tree in terms of its size, shape, distance from us, and position in relation to other objects, and to study its component parts such as leaves, branches, twigs, and bark. It permits us to recognize hazards such as an approaching automobile, an open ditch, or an obstacle in our path. The blind individual must depend on hearing and touch experiences for such concrete knowledge. Yet the spider web can only be partially experienced by touch alone, the sunset not at all, and the giant oak only in limited aspects. Traffic and other hazards can only be partially avoided by sensory experiences other than the visual.

Among the visually handicapped, the most seriously disabled individual in terms of visual flexibility is the one who became blind before the age of five. Such an individual will not have or retain any useful visual imagery (Schlaegel, 1953) or have any real idea of color (Lowenfeld, 1963). Thus, his dreams will be non-visual and will largely reflect auditory, tactile, and kinesthetic experiences, in that order of experience (Blank, 1958). Paivio and Okovita (1971) found that congenitally blind adolescents recalled more word pairs with high auditory imagery than pairs with high visual imagery. The reverse was true for the sighted control group.

With so much dependence on the non-visual senses, it has been postulated that blind persons are endowed with or develop hyperacute sensitivity of the senses of hearing, touch, taste, and smell. Telford and Sawrey (1967) conclude that studies do not support this notion and that seeing individuals are equal or actually superior to the blind in identifying the direction or distance of a sound source, discriminating relative pressures, temperatures, or weights, or in sensitivity to smell, taste, or the vibratory sense. Likewise, no superiority has been demonstrated by the blind in either rote or logical memory. Whatever superiority certain blind individuals might display in any of these areas is seen as the result of increased attention to small cues and greater reliance on such cues for information and guidance rather than hyperacute sensitivity.

Despite the lack of visual imagery, blind individuals do develop concepts of form, space, and distance beyond those seemingly provided by experiences of touching and movement alone. Lowenfeld (1963) reports that blind individuals are able to reproduce all kinds of objects, large and small, in clay modeling and artwork and that they can recognize an object through touch on the basis of previous contact. Such unification of separate perceptions into the total concept of an object is evidence of a level of conceptual development based on tactual experiences normally attained by the sighted individual primarily through the visual modality. This is not a fully understood phenomenon; Lowenfeld concludes that the entire area of space and form perception in the blind needs further investigation.

Experiencing the real world is only one aspect of flexible adjustment to it. Moving efficiently through it is another important aspect. Safe and independent travel is one of the most difficult tasks for the blind or severely visually handicapped individual to perform. Determiners of mobility of the blind are reliance on auditory cues, motivation, and previous experience. The normally sighted individual does not have to rely on hearing when moving about, but the blind individual does.

Perhaps the most comprehensively researched area relating to the mobility of the blind concerns the so-called obstacle sense. It has been observed that many totally blind individuals can actually sense obstacles in their paths. This observation led to a continuing series of experiments begun in the 1930's. These studies have established the following facts:

1. Individuals who are both deaf and blind do not possess, and seem incapable of acquiring, the obstacle sense, and, in general, auditory stimulation is both a necessary and sufficient condition for the perception of obstacles (Worchel & Dallenbach, 1947)
2. Change in the pitch of a sound or echo is a necessary condition for the perception of obstacles
3. At normal walking speed, sound frequencies of about 10,000 cycles and above are necessary for obstacle perception (Cotzin & Dallenbach, 1950)
4. Blind subjects lacking this perception can develop it with practice (Worchel & Andries, 1950)
5. Blindfolded, normally sighted subjects can, with practice, develop the obstacle sense (Worchel & Mauney, 1951)

The accumulated knowledge gained from these studies indicates that the obstacle sense is based on small unrecognized auditory cues such as echoes. There appears nothing supersensory or mystical about the phenomenon.

In addition to reliance on auditory cues for mobility, the blind child needs to develop motivation and curiosity and to engage in active exploration of his world. The visual incentives that promote crawling, creeping, standing, walking, and running in the sighted child are not available to the blind child. In addition, the falls, bumps, and bruises he experiences can induce anxiety in both himself and those around him.

Blind children tend to score lower on tests of gross motor performance as compared with normals or the partially sighted (Buell, 1950). Some of this inferiority may be attributable to limited experiences in body movement. Many normal playground activities can be safely engaged in by blind children with supervision, and they can swim, dance, and participate in many sports. Buell found overprotection on the part of parents a significant determiner of visually handicapped children's performance in sports and concluded that, as far as motor performance was concerned, neglect was preferable to overprotection.

In terms of independent travel, the blind have been assisted by human guides, seeing-eye dogs, and the use of long white canes. Human guides are costly, and reliance on them restricts travel more than use of dogs or canes. Blind individuals with seeing-eye dogs actually travel more than those using human guides or canes (Finestone, Lukoff, & Whiteman, 1960), but it has been estimated that they are practical for only about five percent of the blind (Ashcroft, 1963). The use of the long white cane and the technique of moving it in a pendulum-like, scanning motion in order to locate obstacles is generally recognized as superior to other techniques, and specific courses of training have been developed to teach it.

The problems of the partially seeing individual in relation to flexibility are quite different from those of the blind individual. His spatial orientation and conceptual development may not differ significantly from those of sighted individuals, and he is usually capable of independent travel without special aids or techniques. The totally blind individual, however, is a unique problem in terms of capacity. With visual experience irrevocably denied him, he must learn about and adapt to his world using other sense modalities. He may lack visual imagery of any type but is quite capable of compensating for this in part in perceptual and conceptual areas. Mobility, a critical problem, can be overcome to a considerable degree with appropriate early stimulation and experience and continued training during later life.

What effect does impaired hearing have on the flexibility of the hearing handicapped child? To answer this question it is useful to consider the role of hearing in relation to exploration and adjustment in the environment. Myklebust (1963) has described hearing as non-directional and as scanning the environment in all directions simultaneously. It is a necessary sense since we do not cease hearing even in sleep; its importance in self-preservation is obvious. When deafness occurs, the individual loses his basic sense for environmental contact and exploration and must use vision for both foreground and background scanning. Vision is not an efficient monitoring sense for the environment since the individual must look up and leave what he is doing and thinking about in order to maintain awareness of what is going on around him. Sensory deprivation limits the world of experience. Reality is perceived less effectively, and as a result perception, conception, imagery, and thought are affected.

Elsewhere, Myklebust (1964b) has described the playing pattern of a deaf child who periodically looks up from his toys in order to scan the environment and assure himself that changes going on around him are not threatening. This matter of environmental change is of critical importance for deaf children because early in their lives startling and frightening experiences often occur that could not be predicted or monitored visually. Thus, vibrations felt through the floor may place the deaf child "on guard." Also, when an unfamiliar object is introduced into the environment, he may immediately move to explore it further by touching, smelling, or even tasting it. Myklebust views such behavioral consequences of deafness as having important implications for learning and adjustment and suggests that unnecessary visual and vibrating sensations be avoided in creating an effective learning environment for deaf children. Even though deafness accounts for some physical insecurity, Heider (1948) suggests that deaf children may actually have fewer fears than normal children because fewer tales are spread to them of imaginary dangers (such as witches and bogey men) and of accidents and fires.

The two major contemporary news media, radio and television, are not directly useful to the individual with impaired hearing. Thus newspapers become a primary source of information. In a portion of a survey made of the New York State deaf population (Baroff, 1969), seventy-nine percent of the deaf individuals in the study stated that they read a newspaper every day; only three percent claimed they had never read a newspaper. This latter group probably represented individuals with extremely poor reading ability.

The child with hearing impairment appears considerably handicapped in exploring and interacting with the environment. Lacking the capacity to *hear* effectively, he must direct much of his energy and attention to orienting himself and monitoring events going on around him visually. Even though this may partially compensate for his deficit, it also creates interference and inefficiency in his everyday life. Because the experiences of noise, sounds, warnings, music, and voices are unavailable to him, his knowledge of the environment and of many of its critical features is seriously limited.

In terms of flexibility — moving, looking, listening, adapting — in the physical environment, the sensory and motor abilities of the speech handicapped child have been studied. One area to receive attention is the relationship of auditory discrimination to defects in articulation. Hall (1938) found that children and young adults with articulation problems did not differ from normal speakers with respect to auditory acuity, auditory discrimination of either simple or complex patterns, or in regard to auditory memory of speech sounds. Hansen (1944), Reid (1947), and Spriesterbach and Curtis (1951) also take the position that problems of articulation are not necessarily associated with clear-cut auditory defects. Van Riper and Irwin (1958), however, maintain that the crudeness of techniques for testing sound discrimination is responsible for the inconsistent results in the literature, and Van Riper (1954) prescribes specific exercises for improving auditory discrimination. Eisenson (1963) also considers speech defective children with retarded language development defective in auditory memory (the ability to recall words and sequence them into phonetic and meaningful units).

SD

Children with stuttering and articulation disorders not associated with observable organic defects were found more likely to have motor problems in use of appropriate rhythm, coordination, and application of strength, although no single specific type of physical disability characterized all speech defective children (Belto, 1941). Jenkins and Lohr (1964) believe that the performance of speech impaired children is slightly below that of normals on tests of motor proficiency, and that children whose speech problems persist are more inferior on such tests than those who outgrow their problems.

SH

Telford and Sawrey (1967) suggest that children from lower socio-economic levels are represented disproportionately in studies relating to the physical characteristics of the speech handicapped. Many children in such studies had severe articulatory disorders, and these are more common and persistent among children of the lower class. Poor nutrition and inadequate medical care may partly account for inferiority in physique and motor proficiency. Also, children who do not outgrow speech problems may simply not have models of good speech available to them. The availability of such models is usually more restricted in lower-class than in middle-class homes and communities.

The term "delayed speech" is used to describe children whose language development is significantly below what would normally be expected on the basis of age and intelligence estimates. Eisenson (1963) has observed such children in a play situation in a speech clinic and reports on their frequent physical striking out at objects or individuals as a means of making their wants known. They may isolate themselves from others and play with a single toy or object for long periods of time. Some appear to seek out close physical contact with older persons and inanimate objects. They may rub their bodies along walls or their faces against toys. Emotional lability is seen in the behavior of many delayed speech children. They throw and break toys, pull down block houses, throw pencils, chalk, and crayons, tear paper, and, in general, keep things stirred up around them. Of course, such behavior can reflect a primary problem of emotional disturbance with the delayed speech development symptomatic of the disturbance.

It is difficult to define clearly the child with a speech handicap in the context of flexibility. Since speech problems often occur in combination with other handicaps, they cannot be easily separated and discussed. For children with no other handicapping condition, however, the presence of a speech problem may have little to do with his flexible adjustment to the physical environment.

ED

Crippling conditions and chronic health problems greatly limit the physically handicapped child's exploration of his environment. Natural interests in moving, jumping, running, touching, holding, climbing, throwing, and catching often can never be satisfied because of restricted body movement, poor coordination, or lowered strength, vitality, and alertness. From the early years, physically handicapped children are often denied the simple but significant experiences of crawling on the floor, tumbling on the grass, helping mother or father around the house, playing with intriguing toys, or entering into games with their friends. Many physically handicapped children can never function independently in the environment and must rely on others to help them move and care for themselves. Some achieve a measure of independence with the help of orthopedic braces and wheelchairs or medication. The issue of independence-dependence in relation to adapting to the demands of a changing environment is particularly critical with the physically handicapped. Well-meaning adults who spend too much time compensating for the child's handicap, anticipating his needs, and extending sympathy can actually prevent the child from utilizing his potential for independent functioning. On the other hand, the child's problem must be faced realistically and efforts must be made to protect him from endangering himself.

SH

PH

The child with epilepsy can often enter into most of the normal activities of his age group; but sports, where the risk of an unexpected fall exists, and unsupervised swimming may have to be avoided. Setting such realistic limits in terms of the range or type of activities in which physically handicapped children can engage is often more difficult as the child matures and enters adolescence. The desire to be like one's age mates is intense, and watching others play basketball and football can be very frustrating.

The author recalls work with two adolescent boys afflicted with hemophilia (a condition of the blood in which normal clotting does not occur) who, despite constant warnings from their parents and physicians, went out of their way to play tackle football or engage in fist fights. Bleeding problems were inevitable when they were injured, and only with extensive psychotherapy was each boy finally able to accept and realistically deal with his handicap.

Koegler (1960) has studied the emotional reaction of physically handicapped children during adolescence and found that this group resents sympathy and instead seeks understanding. For crippled children and adolescents who desire athletic participation and whose conditions make such participation appropriate, wheelchair tennis, basketball, and baseball can offer exciting experiences and important physical exercise.

Capacity sets rather fixed limits for many physically handicapped children, yet the importance of understanding rather than pity and the exploration of ways to provide some degree of active, independent functioning makes experience a vital determiner of such children's flexible adjustment to the physical environment.

PH

G

In our description of gifted children in Chapter 2, we listed some of their characteristics that have bearing on the dimension of flexibility. As they survey and move through the world about them, they learn rapidly and easily; they show much curiosity; they examine rather than merely show cursory interest, and they appreciate many things of which other children are unaware. The Terman study (Terman & Oden, 1959) collected data on the interests of gifted children in activities, games, and play in general. Although there were some exceptions, it was reported that the typical gifted child likes active games requiring much exercise, likes to play with tools and machinery, enjoys the companionship of others, and shows no unusual fondness for solitude or study. Thus, the sometimes-expressed belief that gifted children seek isolation, withdrawal from physical exertion, and preoccupation with books was not confirmed.

Interest in making collections appeared in twice as many of the gifted subjects as in those in the control group, and these collections tended to be large and more often of a scientific nature. In terms of play interests, gifted boys tended to be more masculine than unselected boys at all ages between eight and twelve years of age. After this period, there was little difference between the groups. Thirty-five years after the initial study, more than four-fifths of the subjects reported an interest in two or more avocational pursuits and more than one-half had three or more. Although no general population norms are available for comparison, the breadth and diversity of the gifted adults' interests is impressive.

Dunlap (1967) suggests that the possibility of failure causes some gifted children to shun new experiences. If they are not wholly secure, they may participate half-heartedly, seek excuses, or give up altogether. Dunlap sees this as a reflection of the gifted child's keen sensitivity to possible eventualities not typically found among the less gifted.

When discussing the broad area of flexibility and gifted individuals, the concept of creativity is relevant. Indeed, Guilford (1959) considers flexibility as one of several traits contributing to creativity; others include: originality, fluency, and motivational and temperamental traits. His use of the term is probably more narrow and specialized than our use of it in Part III. The definition of creativity has differed according to personal or phenomenological, as compared with societal and cultural, frames of reference. In terms of the former, a product is creative if it is new or novel to the individual involved, regardless of whether it is useful or unique (Maslow, 1959; Rogers, 1959). The latter considers an activity or product truly creative if it is culturally as well as individually novel and useful (Torrance, 1962).

Unfortunately, the Terman study did not establish the degree of creativity existing among the gifted subjects as children. The follow-up data revealed a lack of outstanding accomplishment in such areas as fine arts, music, and, to a lesser extent, literature; but due to a lack of original assessment in relation to creative potential, little can be said regarding the correlation between high intelligence and creativity on the basis of that study.

In developing tests of creativity, considerable attention has been given to divergent thinking processes. The subject may be asked to give as many uses as he can for a common object, such as a brick. The subject who states a brick can be used as a bed warmer is demonstrating more originality than one who answers that bricks can be used to build houses. Divergent thinking involves exploring the number, diversity, and uniqueness of possible alternatives; convergent thinking is directed toward more restricted, obvious, and practical solutions (e.g., bricks can be used to build houses). Even though the originality inherent in divergent thinking links it clearly to creativity, the creative process must also entail convergent thinking. Unlimited associations, hypotheses, and solutions are not sufficient for true creativity unless they also have a certain amount of personal acceptability and social usefulness.

Guilford and Merrifield (1960), Getzels and Jackson (1962),

and Torrance (1962) have developed tests to measure creativity. How valid these approaches are can only be ascertained when children scoring high on uniqueness and novelty of responses are followed into adult life, and their actual level of attained creativity studied.

This discussion of creativity leads to a consideration of the relationship between the intellectually gifted individual versus the intellectually creative one. As mentioned in Chapter 2, Getzels and Jackson (1962) found that adolescents scoring in the top twenty percent on a creativity measure did just as well in academic work as adolescents who scored in the top twenty percent on an intelligence test. The creativity group, moreover, tended to have a better sense of humor and was more unconventional, original, and predisposed to take risks, whereas the high I.Q. group was more conforming, stereotyped, and conservative with respect to risk-taking. One conclusion from the study is that there is little relationship between scores on tests of creativity and intelligence quotients since the most creative individuals were not the most intelligent and vice versa. However, statistical treatment of the Getzels and Jackson data has been criticized (Burt, 1962; De Mille & Merrifield, 1962; Marsh, 1964; McNemar, 1964; Ripple & May, 1960), and Marsh concludes that I.Q. may still be the best predictor of creative potential.

In this discussion, we are surrounded by unresolved problems relating to definitions of both creativity and giftedness, actual validity of tests employed for the measurement of creativity, and research methodology in studies undertaken. Once these problems are resolved, we will be in a better position to understand and predict the relationship between intellectual giftedness and creativity. Aside from the creativity issue, intellectually gifted individuals appear highly flexible in relation to adaptation to the physical world around them.

G

Conclusions

The characteristics of exceptional learners along the dimension of flexibility can be summarized under three main headings:

1. Reception and perception of sensory stimuli
2. Degree of active and independent participation in the physical environment
3. Acquisition of knowledge and skill in relation to the physical environment

We will discuss our conclusions making reference, where possible, to the effects of capacity and experience in accounting for similarities and differences among exceptional learners.

Reception and Perception of Sensory Stimuli.   The blind child and the deaf child are denied major sensory experiences due to their lack of capacity for seeing and hearing.   Of all our exceptional learners, they are at the greatest disadvantage when it comes to receiving sensory stimuli.   Both must compensate for their sensory deficits by relying on intact senses — touch and hearing for the blind, vision for the deaf.   For the blind, keen sensitivity to auditory cues is a learned ability that greatly aids mobility.   Visual monitoring of the environment is relied on by the deaf, but it is in many ways inefficient.   The child with a learning disability has the capacity to see and hear but may be unable to accurately identify, discriminate, and interpret sensory stimuli.   This may be a problem stemming from early neurological impairment and may be complicated by hyper-distractibility.   Some problems of the learning disability child appear among emotionally disturbed children.   The distractibility, impulsivity, and hyperactivity of the disturbed child seem to be the result of anxiety, preoccupation with fantasy, or a negative orientation toward learning that is related to previous experience.

The disadvantaged child is often a selective attender; evidence suggests he may be more visually than auditorily oriented.   Speculation might lead us to consider such a child's experience as the primary determiner.   Listening is in many ways intimately involved with the words of others; and in a home and neighborhood environment that is restricted in language usage, reliance on visual rather than auditory experience quite logically develops.   In contrast to the disturbed child's "tuning out" because of fear or daydreaming, the disadvantaged child may be simply selectively oriented on the basis of a learned *modus operandi.*

The role of experience in aggravating the child with a learning disability problem cannot be overlooked.   Whatever the limitations imposed by capacity in terms of distractibility and perceptual dysfunction, continued frustration and failure undoubtedly contribute to development of avoidance patterns of behavior that can aggravate and eventually overshadow the initial neurologically based difficulty.

Gifted children appear sensitive and alert to what is going on around them and demonstrate superior ability to profit from experience and to anticipate eventualities.

In regard to receiving and perceiving sensory stimuli, ex-

ED

LD

SD

VH

HH

G

ED

LD

MR

SD

VH

HH

SH

PH

G

ceptional learners cover a wide range: total lack of capacity (blind and deaf), presumed capacity-based deficits (learning disability), experientially determined problems of anxiety and avoidance (emotional disturbance and learning disability), a visual orientation due to previous experience (disadvantaged), and superior capacity and functioning (gifted).

Degree of Active and Independent Participation. Active and independent participation in the environment are critical aspects of flexibility. Martin and Stendler (1959) consider independence and self-reliance major socialization goals of the American society. The exceptional learner's ability to approach these goals is most significant in terms of his overall adjustment. The blind child again faces serious problems here. Even though he has the vitality and ability to move freely through his environment, he cannot do so without relying on special aides such as human guides, seeing-eye dogs, or scanning techniques involving use of a cane. The crippled child can take in the environment visually but is confined to a wheelchair, enclosed in braces, or dependent on crutches. He may also experience serious problems in terms of attaining independence. Children with lowered vitality due to chronic health problems are similarly limited. For the blind, crippled, and chronically ill child, capacity sets some rather definite limits, but pity, overprotectiveness, and failure to motivate and to provide opportunities for independent functioning are attributes of experience that can greatly increase such limits.

The deaf can achieve relative independence through use of visual monitoring systems but have to devote a disproportionate amount of energy and time to visually "sizing up" possible threats in the environment. Motor coordination problems possibly linked to capacity are found among the mentally retarded and children with learning disabilities. The latter are often hyperactive, particularly in confining learning situations. Children with speech handicaps tend to do poorer on tests of motor proficiency, but establishment of the role of capacity and/or experience here is unclear.

The disturbed child may have all the sensory and motor capacities necessary for active and independent participation but fail to use them adequately because of faulty early experiences and resultant impulsive, disorganized, destructive behavior, or shyness and withdrawal. Retarded children may resist new experiences and seek the familiar more on the basis of negative previous experience and anxiety than of capacity. Disadvantaged children may excel in this area of flexibility as a result of successfully learning to "negotiate the jungle of the slums," where self-reliance and independence are requisite for survival. However, in the "sanctuary of the classroom," such autonomy can run head on with demands for conformity to authority made by the teacher and school. Gifted children are active participants in their environment. Their superior health and physique combined with curiosity and an ease of learning place them at an advantage in achieving independence and self-reliance.

Active participation and independence can be primarily precluded by capacity (blind, crippled, chronic health problems) but aggravated by lack of stimulation, pity, and overprotection. It can be limited by the necessity of monitoring with another sense (deaf) and affected by motor coordination problems linked to capacity (mentally retarded, learning disabilities). Experience can account for faulty participation or lack of independent functioning (emotional disturbance) or attainment of a high degree of autonomy and self-reliance (disadvantaged). Both capacity and experience combine to make the gifted child successful in these areas.

Acquisition of Knowledge and Skill. As children look and listen and move through their environment, they learn about it. The blind child is again at a serious disadvantage here because of his lack of capacity to see and difficulties in undertaking independent travel. However, concepts of form and space usually considered dependent on vision apparently can develop to some degree through tactual and auditory experience. The crippled child shares the problem of lack of mobility with the blind child, but when physically transplanted he may acquire considerable knowledge and skill through observation not possible for the blind child. The same is true in part for the child with a chronic health problem. The deaf child perceives reality less effectively because of sensory deprivation.

Children with learning disabilities may lack the capacity to interpret the real world accurately because of perceptual problems. The rigidity seen among mentally retarded children that can preclude their easy transition to new situations or active seeking of new experiences is seen as related to motivation, anxiety, and previous failure. In this respect, some emotionally disturbed children's hesitancy to undertake the unfamiliar or to vary from established routines may have a similar experiential basis.

The disadvantaged child is restricted in terms of the knowledge and skill he acquires by the narrow confines of his environment. His motoric or physical style, in contrast to the more verbally oriented approach of the middle-class child, may reflect the limited language emphasis found in his home. Gifted children are usually

ED

LD

MR

SD

VH

HH

PH

G

ED

LD

MR

SD

VH

HH

PH

G

eager to learn all they can about the world in which they live, asking questions, seeking answers, and independently engaging in hobbies. Since much of our knowledge of gifted children comes from studying those with social and economic advantages, environmental opportunities probably support such curiosity and independent pursuits.

Learning about the world can be considerably restricted due to lack of sensory capacity (blind) or in terms of reality perception (deaf, learning disabilities) and mobility (blind, crippled, chronic health problems). Rigidity relates to capacity (learning disability) or to motivation and previous experience (mentally retarded, emotionally disturbed). Actual environmental restrictions limit the scope of learning opportunities and foster a physical rather than verbal orientation (disadvantaged). Gifted children with environmental advantages are avid students of the world about them.

We turn now to a review of the range of functioning exhibited by the children in our nine categories across the dimension of sociality.

SOCIALITY

Sociality is a characteristic related to flexibility but concerned with participation in and adaptation to the world of people. The biological helplessness of early infancy initiates a dependence on others and the beginning of a lifetime relationship with them, giving and taking, obeying and challenging, pleasing and displeasing, accepting and rejecting. Children learn to fit into a society with rules, traditions, expectations, beliefs, and values determined by others. They form close attachments and are influenced by parents, siblings, neighbors, peers, teachers, television personalities, sports heroes, scoutmasters, clergymen, and politicians. Man is a highly social creature and intimately involved with others around him.

If the emotionally disturbed child is handicapped by his disorganized and inflexible behavior in the environment at large, his problems substantially increase when we view him in the world of people. Woody (1964) reviewed teacher referrals of 133 elementary age boys and thirty-nine girls to a special education program. Of some twenty-one behavioral characteristics, poor social relations was the primary reason for referral for forty-seven percent of the boys and forty-six percent of the girls.   Among other writers who have recognized the problem of getting along with others as central to the school difficulties of emotionally disturbed children are Bower (1969a) and Rubin, Simson, and Betwee (1966).

We can extend our discussion of the three types of children described by Quay, Morse, and Cutler (1966) in the last section to the area of sociality.   The conduct disorder child may be the "bully," relating to others through force and intimidation; even though he gains some control and prestige as a result, he may always operate on the fringe of the group.   The inadequacy-immaturity child may have so few interests in line with those of his peers that they have little in common.   In addition, he may not go out of his way to make friends and engage in play activities.   The personality problem child may greatly fear the competition, give and take, and unexpected adjustments involved in group interaction and hence will avoid others at all costs.   The autistic, psychotic, or schizophrenic child is likely to represent extremes in social malad-justment in relation to the inadequacy-immaturity and personality problem child.

The child with a learning disability will probably not experience failure and frustration in a formal learning situation until he enters school.   But since the basis for such a child's problem may be some degree of neurological dysfunction present at birth, many aspects of his early development, including interpersonal relationships, will be affected.

Rappaport (1966) has discussed how the stage can be set for a faulty mother-child interaction if the child lacks the sucking reflex at birth or is hypersensitive or hyperactive during the early years.   The feeding experience that normally promotes pride, love, and gratification on the mother's part can become an unpleasant and frustrating affair if the child cannot suck and alternately screams and falls asleep.   Such a beginning can have a marked effect on how the mother handles the child on other occasions; in place of warmth and affection, she may develop a helpless or outright rejecting attitude toward him.

As the child achieves mobility and begins to move freely about the house, he may be into everything with a frequency and determination not seen in average toddlers.   As his own worst enemy in a family where his disruptiveness, constant movement, and seeming belligerence are negatively reacted to by others, he

LD

experiences little success, receives little praise, and fails to develop a healthy and adequate concept of himself. Rappaport speculates that over the years this interaction continues and becomes more vicious and futile from the child's point of view. The child comes to expect the loser's role; as he sees others succeed and receive the admiration and affection of adults he may become bitterly jealous and defeated.

Rappaport (1964) sees children with minimal neurological difficulties as perhaps eventually developing several maladaptive patterns of behavior that markedly interfere with their getting along with others. One of these is a low frustration tolerance. When the child is not immediately successful, he may lash out and attack the object, person, or situation seen as responsible for his failure. Such lashing out may be physical in the earlier years and eventually expressed more on a verbal level and accompanied by tears. In the classroom an arithmetic problem marked with a red pencil "X" may precipitate an outburst of anger and a defiant claim that the answer was right and the teacher who corrected it wrong.

Another maladaptive behavior observed in some children with learning disabilities is referred to as flight from challenge. This involves attempts by the child to avoid situations that hold a promise of failure, such as refusing to attempt a class assignment, which he in fact cannot do, saying it is much too easy and not worth his time. Some children demonstrate overcompensation in an effort to cover up their deep feelings of inadequacy. Rappaport gives the example of a child who memorized all the Gilbert and Sullivan operettas and sang them in situations in which he could not compete successfully. Another boy, who lacked the physical skill for playing baseball, was able to recite the names and complete records of most major league players.

The child who continually feels threatened by demands he cannot handle may attempt to control and manipulate others. Exaggerated helplessness or imaginary physical complaints often bring parents and others running to cater to the child's every whim. Problem situations also can precipitate a power struggle in which the child stubbornly refuses to comply or even goes out of his way to do the exact opposite of what is expected.

These kinds of maladaptive behavior patterns are the result of the continuous and often subtle interaction between capacity and experience. The possible neurological impairment that underlies the problems of the child with a learning disability is not the direct determiner of such behavior patterns. Rather, it sets the stage for excessive failure and frustration and places the child at a distinct disadvantage in coping with the expectations of others.

The world of the child is largely composed of people, and it is their reactions and expectations which are especially critical in the lives of the mentally retarded and which often create particular problems in sociality. The more severely retarded, who tend to have multiple handicaps, short stature, and other physical disparities, are often shunned because they "look different." The mildly retarded child may be relatively normal in appearance, thus creating the problem of people expecting him "to act his age." His mental age, of course, is slightly lower than his chronological age, and thus his behavior may not match his appearance in that he may have the cognitive capacity and social awareness of a much younger child. Though the notion of "a child's mind in a grown-up body" is a simplistic one and not always adequate to explain the retardate's behavior, it should be kept in mind, particularly as we begin to expect certain "mature" responses to social situations.

MR

What about the social and emotional adjustment of mentally retarded children? Do they exhibit more disturbances than normals do in getting along with others? Beier (1964) states that such disturbances do occur with a higher incidence among the retarded than among the general population. The retarded individual is viewed as subject to greater stresses, frustrations, and conflicts and consequently is liable to develop behavioral disorders. In order to be effective in social interaction, an individual must be sensitive to the requirements of the environment and responsive to appropriate ways of dealing with these social demands. These are, of course, requisites for social competence for all of us, but there are a number of reasons why they become problematic for the retarded child. Because of maturational lag, the mentally retarded may be slower to incorporate values of right and wrong and to develop internal controls. As a result, he may frequently exhibit inappropriate or anti-social behavior. Increased incidence of speech disorders, mentioned earlier, also impede the retarded child's social relationships and prevent him from obtaining reinforcement from others for his efforts in language. Many behavioral patterns of the retarded come from reactions by parents and siblings who may tend either to overprotect the child, thus preventing him from realizing his potential, or to reject him in subtle, often unconscious, ways, thus lowering his feelings of self-worth (Farber, Jenne, & Toigo, 1960; Meyerowitz & Farber, 1966; Wolfensberger, 1967).

Retarded children, particularly the mildly retarded, tend to be overrepresented in lower socio-economic classes and thus have a great deal in common with the children we will discuss in the next section. This often means that they come from broken families or families in which parents, for a variety of reasons, are not always able to serve as good adult models. Thus the retarded child has less of an opportunity to learn social skills and modes of social inter-action than a child in a family where both adults are present and available. Tymchuk (1972) has suggested the existence of a per-sonality structure peculiar to the socio-culturally retarded child and characterized by a lower self-concept and higher manifest anxiety, particularly with reference to school situations.

MR

The retarded child is further characterized by a motivation to interact with adults, a trait that actually depends more on past experience than on the fact of retardation. Research experiments on retarded children deprived of meaningful social contact, such as those in state hospitals or those from culturally deprived back-grounds (Harter, 1967; Zigler, 1966; Zigler & Butterfield, 1968), in-dicated that these children were actually more interested in social contact with the adult experimenter than they were with the experi-mental task itself. The presence, in fact, of an attending adult often decreased the child's performance on a task. Normal children, whose needs for social attention have usually been met, are free to complete the task at hand; but retarded children are not. Whereas the normal child views such situations as an opportunity to solve a task or learn new information, the retarded child's agenda is often different. He uses the task situation as an opportunity to meet his needs for social attention and affection. He may often see the class-room situation as social rather than cognitive, an important concept for prospective teachers to bear in mind.

The retarded child has also been found to look to adults to interpret reality for him (Cromwell, 1967; Zigler, 1966). His own judgment or cognitive ability naturally tends to be somewhat unre-liable, and therefore he may look to others for answers rather than trust his own judgment. As Carlson and MacMillan (1970) have shown, retarded and normal children made similar predictions about the outcome of an event, but when an adult experimenter made a counter-suggestion, the retarded children more readily changed their initial predictions. The retarded were more willing to trust an adult's prediction since their own judgment may have let them down in the past. As a matter of fact, mildly retarded adults followed by Edgerton (1967) tended to rely heavily on an-other adult in their lives for support and social adaptation. The adult "benefactor" was often a spouse, employer, or landlady; and less than twenty percent of the retarded persons in Edgerton's study were in any way independent of their benefactor for assistance in their daily lives.

It should be noted that this social motivation is complicated by the fact that retarded children are also wary of adults (Zigler,

1966). Their hesitancy arises from previous encounters in which adults may have reprimanded them or otherwise reacted unfavorably because of their failures or inadequacies. The paradox of wanting to interact and at the same time being hesitant to do so is one that may be overcome, as MacMillan (1971a) suggests, through initial acceptance and support.

Equally difficult for the mentally retarded are his social relationships with peers. Jones, Gottfried, and Owens (1966) have indicated that normal children's attitudes toward the retarded are even less favorable than their attitudes toward other categories of exceptional children. Retarded children are thus often subject to rejection and ridicule by their peers, particularly in school and carrying over into their neighborhood. For example, Meyerowitz (1967) found that retarded children attending special classes were just as well known as other children on their block but were not played with as often. Even in experimental situations in which normal children were given the opportunity to choose a partner for a game, retarded children were chosen significantly less often (Gottlieb & Davis, 1971). It is not clear how much of this peer rejection depends on the retardate's being placed in special classes or being left in the regular grades (Goodman, Gottlieb, & Harrison, 1972). Retarded children may be seen by their peers as subject to a different standard of behavior if they are in special classes and therefore be treated with special consideration, while retarded children in regular classes who are not *formally* labeled may not be as readily excused for low performance or immature behavior. Quay (1963a), however, suggested that retarded children might actually prefer rejection in regular classes to segregation in a special class. There is some wisdom in this view since the mildly retarded child in particular is going to be expected to live and compete in a world filled with normal peers. Jones (1972) reported that retarded children were extremely concerned about the effect special class placement had on their friendships. It is significant that one of the factors affecting whether or not a retarded child was identified as such and placed in a special class was whether or not he had a friend in the regular class he was attending (Mercer, 1971).

Particular difficulties are imposed on the retarded child in the highly social, formal school situation. An interesting observation to this effect was made by the President's Committee on Mental Retardation (1969), which noted that the most demanding time and place that must be dealt with by the retarded child occurs with his arrival at school in the morning and entrance into a classroom. The "six hour retarded child" is their descriptive term for the child who may function within normal expectations at home and in his immediate neighborhood but who, upon entrance into school, is viewed as mentally retarded and therefore functions as retarded perhaps only for six hours a day. This view applies most directly to children from low socio-economic backgrounds. It has further-more been shown experimentally that, when teachers are told that a child has "low ability," they tend to teach him less and expect less of him even when the child actually has a normal I.Q. (Beez, 1968), and that teacher expectancy may indeed be a powerful phenomenon (Rosenthal & Jacobson, 1966, 1968). Though evidence is by no means conclusive and does not apply to all retarded children, it demonstrates that the notion of retardation is often a relative one and is based on social expectations in a given time and place.

MR

SD

The family life of the disadvantaged child in the inner city has been described by Eisenberg (1963–1964) as marked by a "degree of cooperativeness and mutual aid" not typically found in the middle-class home. He views lower-class children as enjoying each others' company more freely and fully than may be the case with individu-alistic and self-oriented, middle-class children. In addition, there is a diffuseness in the family situation which, according to Eisen-berg, lessens the occurrence of sibling rivalry or competition for mother's or father's love. Reissman (1962) has acknowledged this lessened rivalry and also sees a lack of strain accompanying com-petition and an ease in separating from parents as other benefits emerging from the lower-class home.

Eisenberg points out that the inner city child has collective rather than individualistic values. The family is oriented toward making advances through social group forces, not individual activ-ity. This may be due to the feeling that "the odds are stacked against you" and "if we are going to get anywhere, all of us have to do it at one time." The home and neighborhood of the lower-class child are seen as maintaining a different reward system than that of the school (Goldberg, 1967). At home, physical prowess and physical aggression in the face of frustration are rewarded, as is physical work done well. In school, most rewards are not re-lated to the physical realm but to conceptualization, verbal re-sponse to frustration, and intellectual work done well.

Warden (1968) concludes that the literature supports the generalization that socio-economic status is at least partially respon-sible for friendship choices. Newgarten (1946) found that both elementary and high school students followed class lines in choosing friends and that among younger children, rejection of peers was

linked to social class discrimination. Goldberg (1963), in reviewing studies of teacher ratings of pupil acceptability, concludes that
school performance is a more consistent determiner of a favorable
teacher rating but adds that it is "highly probable" that the lower-
class poor achiever is viewed more negatively than is his middle-
class counterpart. With regard to self-concept, lower-class children,
particularly blacks, evidence a greater degree of self-derogation, of
seeing themselves as ugly, stupid, or inferior than non-disadvantaged children or even than lower-class white children (Goldberg,
1967). Since how one comes to view himself is largely determined
by the appraisal of others, we see some of the detrimental effects of
negative social experience.

The values relating to getting along with others brought to
school by Pueblo Indian children may markedly contrast with the
teacher's expectation. The culture from which the children come
supports anonymity and submissiveness rather than individuality
and aggression. They would rather follow along in traditional ways,
maintain the status quo, and not engage in competition or any
steady quest for success (Zintz, 1962). Erikson (1950) has written
about the exasperation of white teachers working with Indian children in government schools when, at the start of a footrace, the
runners hesitate and ask why they should run when it is already
certain who is going to win.

The disadvantaged child is often caught between two social
environments — one supported by his home and neighborhood, the
other maintained by the school. Even though he may be socially
acceptable and respected in the former, his contrasting values and
experience may place him in an unfavorable position in the latter.
Thus in discussing sociality and the social world of the disadvantaged child, we are actually concerned with two worlds, one in
which the child may be largely a winner, and one in which there is
a good chance he will be a loser.

When a visually handicapped individual enters a room filled with
people, his hearing enables him to gain information and maintain
communication, but he is at a serious disadvantage in many respects. People may not talk at all; they may move away or enter
the room after him without being heard; comments directed toward
him may go unnoticed unless he is specifically addressed by name.
Thus the social world of the blind can be an uncertain and frustrating one.

We will begin our discussion of the relationship of blindness to sociality by considering social attitudes toward the blind. Then we will review the resultant effects of such attitudes on the personality development of the blind. Gowman (1957) asked high school seniors to rank five potential injuries with reference to severity of personal impact; four-fifths placed blindness in the first position. Teachers and administrators selected the visually handicapped as the least preferred for teaching (except for aggressive delinquents) from among eight categories of exceptional children and described them as the group they knew the least about. Some special educators, however, tend to place the visually handicapped in a more favorable position than do educators in general, and knowledge about a group of handicapped individuals appears to relate to the type of attitude held (Murphy, 1960).

Sighted individuals have been found to be naive, lacking in understanding, and overly pitying of blind individuals (Lukoff & Whiteman, 1961), but not as negative about their capabilities as the blind themselves believe them to be. Sommers (1944) found blind children most aware of their handicap in such social situations where people discuss their blindness, express feelings of sympathy, or attempt to help them too much. They also are aware of it when crossing streets and traveling. In a situation in which a blind person must ask a stranger for assistance, Cutsforth (1951) describes the emotional conflict that can ensue. On the one hand, the kindhearted guide must be thanked in line with societal expectations, but on the other, the frustration such necessary dependence creates in the blind individual might lead to a desire that the guide be cursed or beaten down with the cane.

Sommers' study also revealed a number of conflicts encountered by parents of blind children, including having a blind child viewed as a visitation of divine disapproval or a personal disgrace. She found five patterns of parental reaction to the child's handicap. In many ways these patterns of reaction can be found in the reaction patterns of parents of a child with any serious handicapping condition:

1. Acceptance and genuine love and high regard for the child
2. Denial of the child's problem and unrealistic expectations
3. Overprotectiveness and a tendency to infantalize the child
4. Disguised rejection manifested by overconcern and a tendency to exaggerate the role of being a good mother
5. Overt rejection with the child openly rejected and others (e.g., physician, teachers, society at large) given the blame for being prejudiced against blindness

The personality adjustment of blind and partially seeing individuals has been studied through questionnaires, experimental reactions to stress, behavioral inventories, projective methods, and interview techniques.   The question of whether a visual handicap actually contributes to social and emotional maladjustment has not, however, been conclusively answered.   Cowen, Underberg, Verillo, and Benham (1961) reviewed the literature in this area and uncovered many design and methodological problems in the research investigations that have been conducted.   In a study of the adjustment of three groups of children — blind children in day school programs, blind children in residential school programs, and comparable sighted children — the authors found that no basic differences emerged among the three groups.   There were also no differences when the attitudes and levels of understanding of their parents were compared.   Better adjustment was, however, associated with greater visual disability, and the findings suggest that partially seeing children may actually have greater adjustment problems than do the blind.

The authors caution acceptance of an "inevitable" relationship between visual handicap and maladjustment.   Ashcroft (1963) sets forth his "opinion" that limitation in vision does not necessarily produce social and emotional maladjustment and that such maladjustment does not always occur in a direct relationship to severity of visual limitation.   He does, however, concede that negative attitudes toward the visually handicapped and negative self-regarding attitudes by the visually handicapped themselves are frequently found and that such attitudes can produce a disproportionate amount of maladjustment.

The hearing handicapped individual is often at a serious disadvantage when interacting with others.   Myklebust (1964b) has considered the effect of varying degrees of impairment and age of onset on social relationships.   A loss of thirty to forty-five decibels makes conversation difficult without amplification.   The child can communicate, however, by having sound amplified and by getting close to the speaker.   This level of hearing loss appears to affect basic awareness and monitoring rather than socialization.   A loss of forty-five to sixty-five decibels clearly affects social interaction.   Even though amplification makes conversation possible, the child must give all sound equal attention and thus often is limited to interacting with one person or a small group.   There is a sense of detachment from others, and social relationships with those who have similar hearing problems may be preferred. When the hearing loss involves a sixty-five to eighty decibel loss, amplification is less satisfactory for maintaining social relationships. Reliance on visual and tactual senses becomes considerable. The child may suffer from a lack of identification and find relationships with similarly impaired individuals most satisfying. Profound hearing impairment is associated with a loss of eighty to one hundred decibels. Here amplification maintains intelligible speech and attention to loud environmental sounds. Visual and tactual senses become mandatory for functioning in the environment, and the difficult task of interacting with others may preclude relationships with any but the profoundly deaf.

Age of onset of deafness can have a marked effect on the ability to communicate and on social adjustment. If profound deafness occurs prenatally or before age two, the child may be extremely isolated and very dependent on visual and tactual senses. Also, the most serious problems in communication and identification present among the deaf may develop as a result. McConnell (1973) points out that the identity of self depends on the knowledge that our own feelings and attitudes are similar to those of our peers, and the inability of the deaf child to profit from the many subtleties of language regarding sex roles and interpersonal relationships may create serious problems in this area. Deafness itself does not cause emotional problems or mental illness, but if present from early childhood, it may create considerable stress and adversely affect personality development, as evidenced by the fact that schizophrenia occurs with the deaf population almost two and one-half times as often as in the hearing population (Altshuler, 1967).

If a child hears normally for the first two years of life, he has oral language advantages and reflects fewer detrimental psychological effects than the child who has never heard. Helen Keller, whose remarkable accomplishments were discussed in Chapter 1, had the advantage of almost two years of normal hearing before illness resulted in total deafness and blindness. The advantages of normal hearing are even greater if the child has hearing to age five or six. When hearing loss occurs during the school years, the child's language problems diminish, but friendships and identification with the majority group are difficult to maintain. Myklebust sees individuals who suffer hearing impairment during this period as often becoming leaders in the deaf community. Once the individual reaches early adulthood, onset of hearing loss may not alter personality problems but may aggravate undesirable traits. In addition, social relations, including marital plans, educational goals, and vocational levels can be severely disturbed.

In a review of investigations concerning the social maturity of deaf children, largely based on the use of the Vineland Social Maturity Scale, Myklebust concluded that they are some ten percent retarded as compared with hearing children. This appears the result of the higher levels of social competence required with advancing years and the fact that deaf children often encounter difficulty in attaining the self-help and self-direction skills needed to meet such levels of competence. Myklebust considers the degree of inferiority in social maturity by age twenty-one as high as fifteen to twenty percent among deaf individuals.

Baroff (1969) found deaf individuals in New York State capable of establishing effective personal contacts. Seventy-five percent of those interviewed claimed they had close friends and a higher percentage reported being with others on a social basis at least once a week. Almost half reported hearing as well as deaf friends; one-third of the deaf individuals interviewed, however, felt that hearing people had negative feelings toward them. In view of the many friendships claimed, Baroff concluded that this did not support the presence of paranoid-like thinking among the deaf. In a study of hospitalized, psychotic individuals who were deaf, Altshuler and Baroff (1969) also found there was no preponderance of paranoid symptoms.

HH

SH

The child with a speech handicap is constantly frustrated in his attempts to relate to other people. Van Riper and Irwin (1958) have described the speech defective's tendency to react with either aggression or withdrawal to such frustration. Attempts at reducing the anxiety that is aroused often include preoccupation with health problems and worries about a job or grades in school. In this way, the individual may come to attribute his basic difficulties to problems in these areas rather than to the speech defect itself.

The personality and social problems of stutterers have received considerable attention. Goldstein (1958) and Sheehan (1958), in surveying the literature over a twenty-five-year period found a wide range of opinions and descriptions. On one hand, the stutterer was viewed as an essentially normal individual except in speech, and on the other hand, he was seen as maladjusted with a basically neurotic personality. Overall, these surveys did not support the notion that stutterers have a unique personality pattern, are neurotic, or severely maladjusted. They are, however, more tense, anxious, and withdrawn, with lower levels of aspiration and significantly more personal and social problems than non-stutterers. It is not known whether such problems were responsible for the stuttering in the first place or are actually a consequence of social reactions to it.

As a group, children with speech problems tend to be less well accepted by their peers than are children with normal speech (Woods & Carrow, 1959), and those with articulation problems appear to have significantly more conduct and behavior disorders than do normal speaking peers (Fitzsimons, R. M., 1958). Such problems as temper tantrums, showing off, refusing to obey, shyness, and destructiveness are found more frequently among children with speech difficulties.

Many speech problems are associated with the child's relationship to his parents. Johnson, Curtis, Edney, and Keaster (1956) consider the essential difference between the child who begins to stutter and the one who does not to be the parental reaction to the way the child speaks. Parents of young children who begin to stutter appear to have a specific anxiety with respect to the child's speech, a generalized anxiety in relation to this total behavior, and unrealistic expectations regarding what normal speech and normal behavior actually should be. Similar findings have been reported by Bloodstein, Jaeger, and Tureen (1952) and Moncur (1952). The latter's study described a syndrome of environmental factors that appeared related to the precipitation or aggravation of stuttering. The syndrome includes such parental reactions as "domination by disciplinary action, domination by oversupervising and overprotecting the child, domination by holding the child to excessively high standards, and domination by adverse parental criticism." Moore, Soderberg, and Powell (1952) engaged a group of male adolescent stutterers in conversation about such topics as their parents, future hopes, and fears and found severity (duration) of stuttering significantly greater when they talked about their parents than about any of the other topics.

Although some speech defects are clearly organic in origin, many are the result of faulty social experiences. Where inadequate speech models exist, such as in the home and neighborhood of some disadvantaged children, defects of articulation and/or of voice can develop. In addition to imitative causes, the child's experience with others, particularly his parents, may be so negative that speech defects occur as symptoms of general maladjustment. Even though many speech defects have both organic and functioning components, opinion appears to be shifting from the organic to the functional factors as to which is most significant (Van Riper & Irwin, 1958).

The social problems of physically handicapped children are largely the result of the impact of the reaction of others to the handicap, of the child's interpretation of this in relation to his own limitations, and of conflicts that arise as a result of aspiration level versus actual capacity. Broida, Izard, and Cruickshank (1950) and Smoch and Cruickshank (1952) have reported on the basic insecurity of the crippled child in social relationships. Insecurity and fear appear to result in defensive reactions of blame and hostility when he is appraised or criticized. Frustration and dissatisfaction toward the role of constant bystander, while classmates run ahead, move with ease, and surpass him with accomplishments, also contribute to the crippled child's social insecurity.

Dissatisfaction with his crippled body can produce a basic insecurity in the physically handicapped child. Meerloo and Meerloo (1950) state that the child with cerebral palsy has a different body image than the normal child in that he views and experiences his body primarily as a "frustrating object." Perkins (1963) reports on differences found among children with athetoid and spastic types of cerebral palsy with respect to personality make up. Children with the athetoid condition were seen as having no unusual fears, as being loving but quick to anger, outgoing, relatively unconcerned with their handicap, and oriented toward social participation. Spastic children, on the other hand, were described as filled with many fears, limited in display of affection, slow to anger, withdrawn, markedly concerned with their handicap, and slow to make friends and engage in group activities. Haring (1959), however, considers the problems that afflicted children have with parents, peers, and other individuals in their lives are of greater influence than is the type of cerebral palsy. Force (1956) studied sixty-three physically handicapped children enrolled in regular classroom programs and found their status as friends, workmates, and playmates significantly lower than for non-disabled children. Children with cerebral palsy ranked lowest on a social value scale.

The social aggravation of a handicapping condition is clearly seen in the case of the individual with epilepsy. Livingston (1966) considers the hazards associated with seizures of secondary importance to the emotional disturbances developing out of mistreatment in the home, school, and community. The main anti-social characteristics that many epileptics exhibit are irritability, temper outbursts, and aggressiveness, along with a moodiness and emotional change-ability.   Such problems can result from deprivation and maltreat-ment (Keating, 1961).   Scientific understanding and control of epilepsy have probably proceeded at a faster rate than social under-standing and acceptance.   Caveness and Merritt (1965) have summarized the findings of an American Institute of Public Opinion survey relating to adult attitudes toward epilepsy throughout the United States in 1949, 1954, 1959, and 1964.   When asked if they had knowledge of epilepsy, 92 to 95 percent of those sampled re-sponded in the affirmative over the fifteen-year period.   To the question, "Would you object to your child playing with epileptics?" 57 percent answered "no" in 1948, 68 percent in 1954, 67 percent in 1959, and 77 percent in 1964.   When asked if they thought epilepsy was a form of insanity, 59 percent said "no" in 1949, 68 percent in 1954, 74 percent in 1959, and 79 percent in 1964.   The question, "Should epileptics be employed?" was answered "yes" by 45 percent in 1949, 60 percent in 1954, 75 percent in 1959, and 82 percent in 1964.

In the case of both the child with a crippling condition and the child with a chronic health problem, the reactions of others toward the handicap and their acceptance or lack of it can over-shadow the actual physical handicap itself in terms of effect on the child's adjustment.

One misconception regarding the gifted child has him sitting alone far off from his peers, looking disdainfully out through his horn-rimmed glasses at their immature play antics, shrugging off their taunts that he is a square, and calmly reflecting on some aspect of Newtonian physics that he finds more satisfying than social inter-action.   Such a picture simply cannot be drawn from what is known of the social behavior of gifted children.   To begin with, their general social status among peers is high.   Gallagher (1958) in-vestigated the social popularity of high I.Q. elementary level chil-dren in a Midwestern town and found them chosen as friends far more often than were classmates falling in the average range of in-telligence.   A positive relationship between I.Q. scores and popu-larity has also been shown by Miller (1956) and Grace and Booth (1958).

In terms of interest in play activities involving varying de-grees of social participation and organization, the gifted children in the Terman study (Terman & Oden, 1959) were assigned lower sociability scores than the control group. This was viewed as inconsistent with other data secured on the social and activity interests of the gifted and was explained on the basis of the gifted child's attraction to mildly social games such as checkers and chess that were less popular with average children because of the demands they made on intelligence. Also, since the gifted child may be a year or two younger than his classmates, he is more handicapped in strenuous competitive sports such as football and basketball and may not rate them as high among his social play interests.

Strang (1963) has described the social awareness and sensitivity found among many gifted children. If academic achievement is not accorded prestige by his classmates and if superior work on his part may put him in a visible, non-valued position with them, he may actually do poorer work in order to maintain acceptance. Also, Strang suggests that public praise by the teacher may actually decrease the learning efforts of a gifted child if he senses that it will be detrimental to his relations with his classmates.

The child with an I.Q. well over 155 may, however, encounter serious social adjustment problems. Terman and Oden (1947) found the highly gifted in their study to be poor mixers and solitary children. The Terman and Oden study as well as Hollingworth (1942) concluded that the ability range that is most adaptable in the school today is probably around I.Q. 125 to 155. Within this range, enough peers with similar interests and abilities can be found to avoid intellectual isolation, and the gifted child is not so different that positions of leadership in various activities are denied him.

The mental health of the gifted individuals in the Terman study was consistently superior in relation to rates of mental illness within the general population. Gallagher (1964) states that social and emotional problems can and do occur among gifted children. These problems stem from the same general sources as those found among disturbed average ability children. However, since there is a tendency for the high I.Q. child to come from a more adequate family than the average and to possess superior physical health, the probability of such adjustment problems occurring is lessened.

Compared to the home life of the average child, the family situation of the gifted child has been found to be more intellectually stimulating. The family pattern is less autocratic, more reading occurs, and better books and magazines are available. Travel is undertaken more often, and, overall, the family demonstrates greater energy and stability. The cultural patterns of such a family directly support education and achievement (Stouffer & Shea, 1959).

Conclusions

Perhaps no socialization goal is as emphasized in American society as "getting along with others" (Martin & Stendler, 1959). From early childhood, we are made keenly aware of the expectations of others; if we fail to meet these expectations, rejection and self-devaluation often ensue. The exceptional learner can be adversely affected by overemphasis on conformity. His problem may assume a greater visibility, and he may be subjected to the intolerance of others around him who are mirroring the opinions and attitudes of the majority because "what others think" has become such a guiding force in their lives.

The effects of negative social experience with family members, peers, classmates, teachers, and others in the environment can aggravate capacity-based problems of the exceptional individual. They also can largely create the major problems of such individuals on a transient or persistent basis. Of course, positive social experiences can have the reverse effects. In our summary discussion on sociality, we will consider three relationships that seem to exist between the social environment and the problems of exceptional learners. Social experience is seen as:

1. An aggravation of capacity-based problems
2. A cause of persistent problems
3. A cause of transient problems

Social Experience as an Aggravation of Capacity-based Problems. Blindness, deafness, crippling conditions, chronic health problems, and mental retardation are capacity-linked problems that place an individual at a serious disadvantage, often from birth. The presumed cerebral dysfunction associated with learning disabilities also may contribute to "setting the stage" for a difficult and stressful life for the child.

The reactions of others toward the handicapped individual can greatly aggravate the problems associated with the handicapping condition itself. The blind and the crippled child may be frustrated by too much help or pity. The fact that he never seems to measure up to the expectations of others may be most devaluing to the mentally retarded child or to the child with a learning disability. More behavior problems than are found among the population at large appear in the mentally retarded, deaf, speech handicapped, and learning disability child. We can assume that these behavior problems result largely from frustration and failure. Parents of handicapped children, faced with an admittedly difficult role, may accept the child and his problem, deny the existence of the problem, set unrealistic expectations, overprotect the child, project the blame for the problem onto others, or reject the child to varying degrees. The guilt, frustration, and feelings of failure associated with being the parent of a handicapped child produce stress that can be expressed in a variety of ways. Pity and overprotection are in many ways no better than outright rejection. The optimal social environment for a child with a capacity-based handicap recognizes his strengths and weaknesses, attempts to understand and respect him as a person, and offers him every possible opportunity for realizing his potential. Such conditions might be cited as optimal for any non-handicapped child as well. They are more difficult to achieve when the child's handicap makes attainment of such valued goals in our society as independence and conformity most difficult. In the case of the gifted child, capacity can be positively reacted to by the home and school, and recognition, encouragement, and enrichment can be provided.

Social Experience as a Cause of Persistent Problems. For some exceptional children, the experiences they have from birth in the social environment actually produce the handicapping condition. Even though we recognize subtle problems in capacity that can be associated with learning disabilities and speech handicaps or even with emotional disturbance, we know that prolonged failure and negative experiences with parents and others in the environment can cause serious problems of adjustment that themselves become a primary handicapping condition. Emotionally disturbed children who develop persistent patterns of maladaptive behavior, such as over-aggressiveness, withdrawal, or daydreaming, are often reacting against an environment that they simply cannot handle. The anxiety that is generated due to the consistent threat of failure, imagined or realistic fears, and faulty relationships with others may be expressed in many ways from nail-biting to a psychotic retreat from reality.

Speech handicapped children can exhibit a variety of social and personal problems, but their distinguishing characteristic is specific to the communication process. A breakdown in the critical communication mode of speech places one in a highly visible and vulnerable position with others. Speech problems can result from lack of capacity, but the importance of environmental experience has been increasingly recognized. Parents of speech handicapped children are often overanxious regarding the child's speech development. They may make unrealistic demands and exert considerable

ED

LD

SH

G

domination over him.   The speech problem itself, then, becomes a symptom of a faulty parent-child relationship.

Social Experience as a Cause of Transient Problems.   Still another relationship between social experience and the problems of handicapped children can be described.   In this relationship, the social environment does not produce problems in the way faulty parent-child relationships can — by causing emotional difficulties that persist and generalize.   Rather it produces them on a transient and environment-specific basis.   The socially and economically disadvantaged child is a case in point.   Such a child's home and neighborhood environment may consider him anything but handicapped, different, or exceptional.   He adapts to this environment and may be admired and respected for his physical prowess, physical aggression in the face of frustration, and physical work well done.   However, a few blocks away from this environment, in which he may admittedly have problems but not be a perpetual loser, is another environment called school, in which he suddenly becomes a candidate for all sorts of labels and placement into any number of categories such as culturally deprived or socially maladjusted.   While he is in this environment, he may get into serious problems with the teacher, fail to meet most of the school's expectations, and eventually be suspended or expelled.   Once back in his neighborhood environment, he ceases to be an exceptional individual in terms of the criteria of the school.

Some children, particularly those from poverty areas, have been characterized as "six hour retarded children."   These children function within normal expectations at home and in the immediate neighborhood, but as they walk through the classroom door to begin participating in a six-hour daily school program, they are viewed as mentally retarded.   Indeed, in terms of the academic and social expectations of the school setting, their functioning may be retarded, but in reality only relatively so.   In Chapter 1 we found that, historically, some mentally ill and mentally retarded individuals went largely unnoticed in the larger social environment with their "exceptional identity" coming into being only with the advent of mass education.   Early in this century, thousands of heretofore unlabeled children were suddenly discovered in the United States with the widespread use of intelligence testing and formulation of the "moron" category for the mildly retarded.

Some gifted children may also function as "six hour children" if their home environments do not recognize or appreciate their superior abilities.   This is probably a rare occurrence, since many of our studies regarding the gifted reveal that they generally come from homes and families that are well above average in terms of intellectual stimulation and enrichment. The "six hour handicap" concept might also be extended to some emotionally disturbed children, particularly those with school phobia, and some children with learning disabilities whose particular problems in paying attention, sitting still, and learning academic subjects are classroom specific.

The social environment plays a critical role in the lives of exceptional children. Problems stemming from capacity (blind, deaf, crippled, chronic health problems, learning disabilities, mental retardation) may be aggravated by faulty social experiences. Such experiences may actually produce handicapping conditions of a persistent nature (emotional disturbance, speech handicaps) or produce them on a transient basis (disadvantaged, mildly mentally retarded, some emotional disturbance, some learning disabilities).

In this chapter, we have begun our collective review of the problems of children in nine categories of exceptionality across the dimensions of flexibility and sociality. In the next chapter, we complete our broad psycho-social survey by examining these children along the dimensions of intelligence and individualization.

ED

LD

MR

SD

VH

HH

SH

PH

CHAPTER 5

Intelligence and Individualization

In Chapter 4, we established exceptional learners as having differences and similarities in their ability and efficiency to receive incoming stimuli, to participate effectively in the physical environment, and to learn about the world around them (flexibility). We also examined the effects of social experiences (sociality) on their lives. In this chapter, we will consider the exceptional learner with discussions related to intelligence and individualization.

INTELLIGENCE

Intelligence essentially refers to the unique characteristics of learning efficiency, problem solving capacity, and language facility made possible by the relatively great size and complexity of the human brain. Children profit from experience, attach labels to events and objects with which they come in contact, learn to read, master number concepts, recall information in test situations, and develop extensive vocabularies. Some children demonstrate more intelligence than others: they "catch on" more quickly, generalize from one experience to another more efficiently, plan for the future more adequately, and develop academic skills more rapidly and extensively.

From the simple operational answer, "It is what an intelligence test measures," much has been theorized about the nature of intellectual ability. Freeman (1962) classifies the various definitions of intelligence into three different groups. Group I definitions stress "adjustment or adaptation of the individual to his total environment." Group II definitions stress that "intelligence is the ability to learn," and Group III definitions center on "the ability to carry on abstract thinking." Wechsler (1958), who has developed intelligence test instruments that are widely used with children and adults (Wechsler Preschool and Primary Scale of Intelligence (Wechsler, 1967), Wechsler Intelligence Scale for Children (Wechsler, 1949), Wechsler Adult Intelligence Scale (Wechsler, 1958), defines intelligence as: **"Intelligence, operationally defined, is the aggregate or global capacity of the individual to act purposefully, to think rationally, and to deal effectively with his environment."** This is a broader, more encompassing definition than many others and reflects a trend that began in the 1940's (Burton, 1967).

Our introduction to this discussion of intelligence must begin with another look at the capacity and experience determiners of functioning level. When we speak of a child's intelligence, are we speaking of his capacity or innate ability for behaving in areas covered by the above definition? The answer is related to the problem of direct and indirect measurement discussed in the previous chapter. We simply have no direct way of measuring the capacity for adaptation to the environment and the ability to learn and carry on abstract thinking other than inferring such capacity from a behavioral measurement such as provided by means of an intelligence test. Thus what we actually measure is the child's functioning level in these areas as determined by both capacity and previous experience. Burton (1967) emphasizes that intelligence as dealt with by psychologists is not the innate ability of the individual; but she adds that this view of intelligence does not preclude the influence of factors attributable to hereditary and genetic structures.

Strang (1963) has summarized much of what is known about the relationship of heredity to intellectual development. Identical twins display a close resemblance in physical and mental traits, as would be expected from their identical genetic inheritance. Children of the same parents less closely resemble each other than do identical twins, but such resemblance is considerably higher than found among unrelated children. When identical twins are reared apart, the effects of differing environments appear in areas of social behavior and school achievement more than in relation to personality structure or general mental ability.

The inherited intellectual capacity present at birth greatly determines how an individual will select, react to, relate, integrate, organize, and profit from environmental experience.   From the moment of birth, however, such capacity is supported or restricted, nurtured or suppressed, enhanced or neglected to varying degrees by the multitude of environmental interactions that constitute life itself. Estimates of the relative influence of innate and inheritable factors that determine intellectual capacity have ranged from seventy-five to eighty percent (Burke, 1928; Jensen, 1969).   Thus, every individual has both potentialities that he can develop and certain limitations due to hereditary or genetic factors that he cannot transcend.

In determining what behaviors are considered "intelligent," the culture and society in which the individual lives become extremely important.   Eisenberg (1963–1964) provides us with an amusing, yet telling, example of this importance:

> Some years ago, a prominent psychologist went to Africa to study the chimpanzee.   He took along some geometric form tests which are standard for cross-cultural studies.   During the rainy season, he found, as had been demonstrated by others before him, that primitive peoples do poorly on the form boards.   If you were to use American standards, they would be mentally defective.   When the rains stopped, he went out with his guides to look for the chimpanzees.   Day after day, the native guides deduced where the chimps would be found that day and led him to the right spot.   They did this by observing details of the environment that the psychologist could not learn to see in all the time he was there.
>
> Obviously these people were not mentally defective as you might have concluded from the test score.   They hadn't learned the geometry of Euclid that is in our environment from the beginning — houses with square corners, streets built in straight lines — they hadn't seen triangles and diamonds.   What they learned is a kind of non-Euclidean geometry with relation to Nature about them.

Intelligence, then, is linked to both the individual's innate ability and to his previous experience, and is measured by his functioning level on a test.   An intelligence test is based on extensive sampling.   First, a sample of the behavior deemed intelligent by the society is selected (e.g., problem solving, abstract thinking) by the test constructor or psychologist.   Next are selected a sample of possible test items that will measure an individual's level of functioning in relation to these critical behaviors (e.g., how many apples are two apples and six apples or how are a cat and a dog alike).   Once these items have been put together in a test, complex sampling must be undertaken by giving the test to a large representative group of individuals for whom the test is intended in order to standardize it and establish norms.   Finally, an individual's actual functioning level is sampled by selecting a time, place, and setting for administration of the test (e.g., the school psychologist says to the teacher, "Miss Jones, I would like to schedule Johnny Adams for intelligence testing on Wednesday morning at 9:30 in the counselor's office"). Sampling, then, is a key consideration in answering the question, "How does a test actually measure intelligence?" Burton uses the analogy of cake baking in this regard:

> If one is baking a cake and wishes to know if the cake is done, the usual procedure is to insert a straw, a toothpick, or some such item into the cake and make a judgment as to whether or not it is done. If this is thought about for a moment, it will be apparent that what one is literally doing is taking a sample of perhaps a thousandth part of the whole cake and forming a judgment on the basis of that one sample and applying this judgment to the entire cake. (This is probably a good operational definition of a test.) However, the success or failure of "jabbing the cake" and drawing an inference from this is going to be a function of the part of the cake sampled. Through a long history of trial and error, most people know that the best place to "jab the cake" is in the center. In other words, the attempt is to get the best sample possible on which to base a generalization to the rest of the cake. If one is a little off on the "sample," there is a good possibility of ending up with a slightly overdone or slightly underdone cake. The process of "testing" in test construction is really no more mysterious than this. The psychologist has a concept, culturally based, of what intelligence is, and he tries to evolve a series of items that will sample the kinds of behaviors that are encompassed in this concept of intelligence. The degree to which he "hits the center of the cake" is the degree to which he has a valid test of intelligence. We must admit that there are some slightly overdone and some slightly underdone intelligence tests currently on the market.*

From this example and the preceding discussion we can begin to appreciate the distance traveled from the ideal of direct measurement of the innate capacity of intelligence to the indirect, best estimate measurement of intellectual functioning with a test. This distance must be kept in mind as we label and classify children along the dimension of intelligence.

In practice, there are three categories of intelligence tests:

1. Group and individual tests
2. Language and non-language tests
3. Culture-bound and culture-free tests

Group and individual tests include the paper and pencil tests administered to groups without special tester training for administration, scoring, or interpreting. Some commonly used tests in this category are the California Test of Mental Maturity (Sullivan, Clark, & Tiegs, 1957), Kuhlman-Andersen (1963), and SRA Test of Primary Abilities (Science Research Associates, 1962). Individual tests are given in a one-to-one situation with verbal and performance responses required of the child being tested. These tests require advanced training on the part of the examiner and include the well-known Stanford-Binet (Pinneau, Terman, & Merrill, 1960), Wechsler Intelligence Scale for Children (Wechsler, 1949), and the Wechsler Preschool and Primary Scale of Intelligence (Wechsler, 1967). Language and non-language tests include tests requiring visual or auditory knowledge of language (e.g., Stanford-Binet) and also tests using verbal directions on the part of the examiner but only requiring the child to respond to non-language material, for example, the Peabody Picture Vocabulary Test (Dunn, 1959), and various other reading readiness tests. Culture-bound tests consist of tests developed in a particular society, standardized on individuals living in that society, and dependent on the learning and experience available to them; they are not applicable or "fair" to use in other societies. The ideal of a culture-free test, totally non-dependent on specific past experience, has been difficult to achieve, although efforts continue toward this end.

Each test in the three categories ultimately aims at assigning a score to the functioning level of the individual tested. The I.Q. or Intelligence Quotient is the best known example of such a score. In Chapter 1, we briefly traced its development from the work of Binet to Terman. Binet initiated a sampling sequence similar to the one described earlier in relation to intelligence test construction by:

1. Selecting a number of tasks he considered relative to success in school work (e.g., memory tasks or naming common objects)
2. Testing groups of children to see if they demonstrated a range of abilities on these tasks
3. Combining a final selection of tasks
4. Giving the test to large numbers of school children at various age levels

As a result of the final stage, Binet found that ability to do his tasks varied among children at each age level and between children at various age levels. From this, he derived the notion of mental age (MA). Mental age reflects the average score or level of intellectual functioning on Binet's test for a child of a given chronological age (CA). For example, an eight-year-old child would be assigned a mental age of eight years if his score equaled the average score on the test attained by children in the standardization sample who were eight years old. But as Binet observed, some children attained scores equal to the scores of children who were younger or in some cases older than they were. Knowing the child was eight years old (CA) was one thing, but recognizing that he could only attain a score on the test equal to, say, the average six-year-old's perform-ance (MA) was something else. This relationship between the chronological age and mental age was conceived by Terman to determine the actual intelligence quotient (I.Q.).

In practice, the I.Q. is calculated by dividing a child's mental age by his chronological age. To avoid decimals, the resulting quo-tient is multiplied by 100. Thus, our eight-year-old, whose test score is in line with other eight-year-olds, is assigned an I.Q. of 100, whereas another eight-year-old, whose score was identical to that of the average six-year-old, is given an I.Q. of 75. Even though there are some statistical differences in calculating I.Q.'s on the two most widely used individual tests (Revised Stanford-Binet Intelligence Scale, Wechsler Intelligence Scale for Children), the basic con-cept of relating MA to CA has been retained.

We now consider the question of the validity of group versus individual tests and the concept of fixed versus changing I.Q. Group intelligence tests are limited in their use with children with learning problems due to the tests' reliance on reading skills. If the child cannot read the directions or individual items in the test, we are hardly obtaining a true picture of his intellectual functioning. Indi-vidual tests require little independent reading ability, as the ex-aminer presents individual directions orally. Group tests usually have only one correct answer to items, whereas individual tests can give a child partial credit for a variety of answers. Group tests also sample a more limited range of behaviors than do individual tests. Add to this the possibility for distraction and confusion during a group-administered intelligence test, and it can be seen that the group test is probably a less valid measure than is the individual test.

In addition to the general categories of intelligence tests dis-cussed above, there are special versions of such tests and uniquely constructed tests for children with severe visual, auditory, and lan-guage problems. Examples of these special tests are the Hayes-Binet Intelligence Test for the blind and the Leiter International Per-formance Test used with some deaf individuals and with others with serious problems in language development.

A major issue that arises with respect to intellectual assessment with all children, and exceptional children in particular, centers around the constancy of the I.Q. score. In other words, "Does intelligence change?" According to Hunt (1964), the notion of fixed intelligence can no longer be supported. He also states that early experience has a crucial effect on cognitive development. Burton sees the problem of assigning a fixed I.Q. score to a child as arising from the widely held assumption that "intelligence" and "I.Q." are synonymous with "innate ability." From our discussion of the impossibility of directly measuring capacity and from our reliance on indirect functioning level measures as a basis for arriving at an I.Q. score, it should be clear that such an assumption is false. In a group of middle-class children followed over a ten-year period, Sontag, Baker, and Nelson (1958) found that many were consistent in their I.Q. test performance and resultant scores; but some showed a steady, continuous increase and some showed just the reverse. Thus, intelligence as measured by the I.Q. test can and does change.

We have devoted considerable space to a background discussion of intelligence because it bears so critically on our understanding of children who are called emotionally disturbed, socially and economically disadvantaged, mentally retarded, and gifted. Let us, then, begin our review of the characteristics of these and our other exceptional learners across the dimension of intelligence.

How do emotionally disturbed children do on intelligence tests? Bower (1960) found lower intelligence test scores among emotionally handicapped children than among non-disturbed children. Similar findings resulted from a study with behavioral problem children reported by Rogers, Lilienfield, and Pasamanick (1954). Woody (1968) found that "well behaved" boys scored significantly higher than "behavioral problem" boys on all three of the Verbal, Performance, and Full Scale I.Q. measures of the Wechsler Intelligence Scale for Children. Vane, Weitzman, and Applebaum (1966), however, found that "problem" and "non-problem" children had essentially the same mean scores on the Stanford-Binet. In a summary of much of the related research done to determine specific characteristics of behavioral problem children on intelligence tests (e.g., verbal versus non-verbal strengths and weaknesses), Woody (1969) concludes that few definitive diagnostic patterns can be found.

Are emotionally disturbed children *less* intelligent than children without emotional and behavior problems? If we return to our *capacity* and *experience* considerations, we see that whatever

ED

actual intellectual potential the emotionally disturbed child possesses, his selective and often faulty experience and relationships and the functioning problems he may display in the actual test situation (inattention, resistance, withdrawal) can greatly influence his test performance and result in a lowered I.Q. score. With such children (as with others to be discussed in this section) we must strive to remain open-minded regarding so-called innate capacity. We must also use test data to gain an understanding of how the child is functioning at any time in relation to normal expectations and of what he needs to learn; we should not use the test data as a basis for rigid classification.

Woody (1969), in a review of the research literature related to the academic functioning level of children with emotional and behavioral problems, concludes that there is consistent evidence indicating that such children do not perform in line with their intelligence (Fitzsimons, M. J., 1958; Tamkin, 1960; Stone & Rowley, 1964; Woody, 1964, 1968). Bower (1960) found that emotionally disturbed children functioned significantly below other children in their classrooms in reading and arithmetic. Differences were greater in arithmetic than in reading and increased in the higher grades.

Missing from such studies is a clear understanding of whether the emotional disturbance or the behavior problem caused the poor academic functioning, or whether failure to learn to read and progress in schoolwork created the emotional or behavioral difficulties. In all probability, the problems were multi-determined. Bower's finding that differences in academic functioning level increased in the higher grades suggests an accumulation of academic deficits and negative attitudes toward school and learning. Whatever starts the chain of events related to failure to meet expectations in school (falling behind, poor teaching, lack of experience, or functioning problems related to emotional disturbance), a vicious circle is likely to emerge. The more the child fails, the poorer he performs; and his poor performance only increases his chances of continued failure.

Taylor (1964) has described a number of factors related to a child's level of academic achievement: the ability to handle or cope with anxiety, feelings of self-worth, conformity to the demands and requirements of authority figures, social acceptance by members of his peer group, the degree of conflict due to needs for independence and dependence, involvement in activities related to academic goals, and the realism of goals. From our discussion of flexibility and sociality, we can predict some of the problems that emotionally disturbed children are apt to have in relation to several of these factors. Kessler (1966) adds that a major differentiating characteristic of underachievers is that they are predominantly males.

Children with learning disabilities are not mentally retarded; according to McCarthy and McCarthy (1969), they typically range from low-average to average on individual intelligence tests. The discrepancy between their normal intelligence and their academic achievement as measured by standardized achievement tests thus becomes the benchmark of learning disabilities. Individual intelligence tests, such as the Wechsler Intelligence Scale for Children (WISC) and the Wechsler Preschool and Primary Scale of Intelligence (WPPSI), are constructed so that a variety of individual subtests are included. Some subtests are designed to assess verbal functioning and others to test performance skills, such as hand-eye coordination and conceptualization. The differential functioning of many children with learning disabilities on verbal as related to performance subtests has stimulated interest in discerning unique patterns of abilities that might serve as a basis for the diagnosis of a learning disability and thus prove useful in remediation efforts.

LD

Clements and Peters (1962) suggest that the most frequently found pattern is unevenness (scatter) among scores obtained on verbal and performance subtests. The next most frequent pattern consists of verbal subtest scores that are significantly higher than performance scores. The third pattern, the reverse of the second, is considered typical of children with reading disabilities. These authors conclude that such patterns indicate the presence of minimal brain dysfunction. Myers and Hammill (1969), however, have found that children with demonstrable learning disabilities do not always display such patterns; they thus consider the use of patterns in differential diagnosis with respect to the presence of brain dysfunction highly questionable. McCarthy and McCarthy (1969) agree with this position, since subtest scatter alone often will not distinguish between the child with a learning disability and one who is mentally retarded.

Linguistic ability, or the ability to communicate and think in language symbols, is often affected in the child with learning disabilities (McCarthy & McCarthy, 1969). Tests such as the Peabody Picture Vocabulary Test (Dunn, 1959) and the Illinois Test of Psycholinguistic Abilities (Kirk, McCarthy, & Kirk, 1968) reveal that children with learning disabilities tend to score lower than do normal children and that they are often quite variable in terms of various language abilities.

Myers and Hammill (1969) describe four areas associated with adequacy in language or symbolization in which children with learning disabilities are apt to have problems:

1. Receptive-auditory — the understanding of spoken words
2. Receptive-visual — the understanding of printed words

3. Expressive-vocal — the formulation of thought for speech
4. Expressive-motor — the formulation of thought for writing

Perceptual adequacy, discussed earlier in relation to learning disabilities, is associated with these receptive areas and becomes the base upon which symbolic behavior is built. Cruickshank (1967a) considers perceptual difficulties as having the same origin as conceptual difficulties, and Rappaport (1964) combines the two under the heading of "inadequate integrative functions."

Overall, the child with a learning disability may function within the average range in terms of an individual intelligence test, yet certain specific disorders in areas of perception and conceptualization may markedly interfere with his learning.

The dimension of intelligence is perhaps the most crucial one in considering the traditional concept of mental retardation. The mentally retarded child has been described as "not able to keep pace intellectually in a world that places ever greater stress on intellectual accomplishments" (Robinson & Robinson, 1965). Although in many respects the retarded child can be considered as a functionally normal child at a younger age level, he also has been considered as inevitably learning at a slower rate and retaining less than the normal child. This latter view leads to the assumption that he is an inferior learner and lacks intelligence. Such an assumption has unfortunately determined much of what is "special" about special education — that is, assigning such children essentially the same material in the same manner as for the normal child but in lesser amounts and at a slower rate of learning (Baumeister, 1967).

However, research findings suggest something different. Mild and moderate mental retardation is not a global, general disability but may be task specific or related to only certain aspects of the learning situation. For example, comparison of the rate at which learning progresses in both retarded and normal children suggests that differences in learning discriminations are mainly in the early stages of a task or in learning how to learn (Zeaman & House, 1963). The retarded child takes longer at this stage than normal, but once he has learned the relevant cues and has overcome his tendency to attend to extraneous ones, he may learn nearly as quickly as normal children. This may apply to some types of tasks yet not to others. Retardates tend to do better in associative tasks (learning pairs of items and then naming one of the items when shown its partner) than in learning a series of items (Baumeister, 1967). Some studies using such paired-associate tasks show the retardate performing at a lower level than much younger children of his own mental age, yet others show no difference even when the retarded child is compared with his own age mates (Jensen, 1970).

Once the retarded child has learned a task he is likely to remember it about as readily as normal children over long periods of time, particularly if he has "overlearned" the task to begin with (Belmont, 1966). It has been shown that when meaningful and familiar learning materials are used, retardates recall about as well as normals after intervals of one week and one month (Eisman, 1958). There is a deficit, however, in the short-term memory of the retardate, i.e., when the retardate has to repeat back or use information within seconds after hearing it (Ellis, 1963). The retarded child is at a disadvantage here since he possibly cannot process the information as quickly as normal children or does not spontaneously use rehearsal strategies which normals do, such as grouping information into clusters and silently repeating them for easier recall (Ellis, 1970).

It is difficult to generalize on the intelligence of the retardate since, as we have indicated, many retarded children who serve as subjects for such studies are institutionalized. Comparison with normal children who may have had a wider range of experience, success in previous learning, and supportive environments tends to put even the non-institutional retardate at a disadvantage. Numerous other variables, both motivational and situational, determine how the retardate will use what "intelligence" he has (Bortner & Birch, 1970; MacMillan, 1971a; Zigler, 1966).

It is generally accepted that intelligence in the group of children whose mental retardation is a clear symptom of some underlying organic pathology is generally less amenable to change through motivational or situational variables. Those children tend to be "different" in the sense that their lowered performance is more likely the result of a limited neurological capacity, though it should be noted that biomedical research has yet to demonstrate cause and effect relationships except in a very generalized fashion. Yet there is a further issue, relative to the mildly retarded, which bears mentioning and is generally referred to as the "developmental vs. difference" issue (Zigler, 1969). "Developmental" theorists hold that the retarded child passes through essentially the same cognitive levels of development but at a later age than normals. The difference between a retarded child and a normal child is not markedly dissimilar from the difference between a normal and a gifted child. It is a matter of the level each has attained. When matched with younger normal children of the same mental age, but normal I.Q., the retarded will perform essentially the same on cognitive tasks, all other things being equal. The "difference" theorists, on the other hand, posit low I.Q. as something more than an indication of a retarded child's stage of mental development and suggest that it must further be a measure of neurological integrity, rate of information processing, or some other measure of cognitive functioning. The central cognitive processes are therefore said to be somewhat different than those of a younger child of the same mental age, and these differences are viewed as relatively independent of the child's background or experience.

The authors obviously favor the former view since it allows for more consideration of motivational and situational variables when dealing with the concept of mental retardation, and this is particularly critical in special education. Understanding the relationship between mental retardation and intelligence is thus far more complex than merely assuming that the retarded are "slow" or "stupid" or that they are invariably limited to functioning on a level commensurate with I.Q. alone. As we learn more about the unique characteristics of the learning situation and the specific tasks which determine a retarded child's functioning, we will hopefully be able to improve our educational efforts with him.

If we consider the experiential deficits suffered by many socially and economically disadvantaged children as well as their difficulties in attaining success in the largely middle-class school, it should come as no surprise that such children in general score more poorly on intelligence tests, particularly those with high verbal content, than do non-disadvantaged children. Cronbach (1960) found the mean I.Q. of lower-class children in urban and rural areas to be 90, whereas middle-class children in these areas had a mean I.Q. of 115. Siller (1957) reports that children from higher socio-economic level homes were superior to those from the lower levels on all verbal tests of conceptual ability but that the reverse was true when his subjects were matched on non-verbal concept tests dealing with the same level of conceptualization as the verbal tests.

Deutsch and Brown (1964), in a study of 543 urban public school children classified according to race, grade level, and social class, found that at each class level black children scored lower than white children and that I.Q. scores did not differ significantly from first to fifth grade. Dreger and Miller (1960), in a review of studies comparing intellectual functioning of blacks and whites published between 1943 and 1958, concluded that blacks score lower on both traditional and "culturally fair" tests. They also noted, however, that blacks averaged well within the normal I.Q. range for whites. Goldberg (1963) has called attention to the overlap existing in such group comparison studies that may be masked by the pooling of data. In any group, there are individuals who resemble the other group more than their own. A number of lower-class children actually score high on I.Q. tests and do well in school while a number of middle-class children do very poorly. This is a most important point to bear in mind before drawing conclusions and making general statements regarding the innate intellectual potential of any group — white or black, lower or middle class.

Ausubel (1967) rejects the notion that all intelligence tests are categorically unfair to disadvantaged children because of the inadequacy of such children's environment. He states that the social order that has permitted these children to develop under such conditions is unfair. He acknowledges, however, the functioning requirement in relation to traditional intelligence tests as unfair, since disadvantaged children, in comparison to their middle-class counterparts, often have fewer test-taking skills, are less responsive to speed pressure, are less motivated in taking a test, have poorer rapport with the test examiner, and may be less familiar with the specific vocabulary and types of tasks included. With regard to group intelligence tests, Burton (1967) claims the most important question to ask is not how unfair intelligence tests are to disadvantaged children but rather, "What information can be obtained from this test that will help in teaching and reaching this child that could not be obtained in other ways?" Despite continued research and conjecture regarding the relationship between heredity, environment, and intelligence with respect to children who are socially and economically disadvantaged (Jensen, 1969), Burton's question is probably the critical one for the special educator.

Visually handicapped children who are blind do not differ markedly from children with normal vision in terms of measured intelligence. We are, of course, referring to children whose visual impairment is not accompanied by mental retardation or other major disabilities. Samuel Hayes adapted the Stanford-Binet Intelligence test for use with the blind and administered it to 2,372 pupils in seventeen residential schools for the blind in the 1930's. According to his report (Hayes, 1941) the mean I.Q. obtained was 98.8, as compared with the mean I.Q. among the schools, which ranged from 108.1 to 92.

Subsequent studies using the Hayes-Binet and the verbal portion of the Wechsler Intelligence Scale for Children have reported similar findings (Hayes, 1950, 1952). Hayes also found that children who were born blind or who suffered visual impairment during the childhood years did not differ in intelligence level from those who became blind during later years. Also, there was no correlation between general intelligence and age at which sight was lost and no differentiation between the two groups in terms of functioning in various school subject areas. Hayes concludes that even though the "mental constitution" of those born blind may be different from others who suffer blindness later in their lives, their mental functioning as measured by standardized tests does not reveal a difference.

With respect to the partially seeing in special class programs in the public school, Bateman (1963) reports a mean I.Q. on the Stanford-Binet for 131 such children. When this group was evaluated according to severity of defect, those with a mild defect had a mean I.Q. of 95, those with a moderate defect a mean I.Q. of 101, and those with a severe defect a mean I.Q. of 106. These results are in agreement with the Hayes' conclusion that intelligence decreases as degree of vision increases among visually handicapped children selected for special education services.

In terms of overall cognitive development, Bateman (1967) has hypothesized that the visually handicapped individual does not have a decreased ability to process information but that he has limitations imposed on him by the sensory data available for such processing. In cases where sensory data were seriously limited due to the nature or range of experience, visually handicapped children could fall behind sighted children in cognitive development.

In the area of abstract thinking, Zweibelson and Barg (1967) found the visually handicapped inferior to sighted individuals in abstract concepts. Singer and Steiner (1966) reported that seeing children showed significantly higher imagination in play, spontaneous fantasy, and dreams, whereas the visually handicapped demonstrated more concreteness and lack of flexibility. Kenmore (1965) found visually handicapped children also inferior in mastering random shapes and distorted objects.

In discussing intelligence in relation to the hearing handicapped child, we must first consider his problems in language development. As stated earlier, one major definition of intelligence focuses on the ability to carry on abstract thinking, and abstract thinking assumes the presence of language symbols. Language symbols are learned with relative ease by hearing children from birth as they continually listen to people in the environment talk about objects, events, and feelings at the moment those experiences are happening. The child with a hearing impairment cannot begin to listen and learn in any manner approaching this until his problem is detected and some measure initiated to compensate for it.   This delayed start, plus the fact that no other sense or combination of senses can truly substitute for hearing, puts the child at a serious disadvantage in terms of acquiring language.   As he grows and matures with this often sizeable language handicap, a number of questions arise with regard to his intelligence.

Levine (1956), in a consideration of fundamental issues underlying all psychological investigations of the deaf, poses questions relating to intelligence:

1. Does a serious language handicap involve the inability to develop abstract intelligence?
2. Does the highest form of abstract intelligence always rely on language or other symbols?
3. Does a lack of hearing preclude the development of a symbolic structure, which is considered the basis of abstract intelligence?

The ultimate answers to these questions are yet to be provided (Myklebust, 1963), yet it *does not* appear that deafness, with its restriction on language development, has a generalized effect on intellectual functioning (Avery, 1967).   Rather, deafness appears to have a qualitative effect in such areas as memory and conceptualization (Myklebust, 1960).   In reviewing research with deaf individuals from 1964 through 1969, Furth (1971) draws the conclusion that deaf children do not differ significantly in their thinking processes as compared with hearing children. He, therefore, states that the thinking process of the deaf should be explained without consideration of verbal processes.   Furth's review provides strong support for Piaget's theory that language is not a basic element of logical thinking (Inhelder & Piaget, 1964).   Our previous discussion of capacity and experience is relevant at this point.   Whatever the capacity for intelligence of a deaf child, his lack of capacity for hearing greatly alters his experience, and thus definitive statements regarding the intelligence of the deaf are difficult to make.

In actual practice, we do the best we can by relying on tests that are as free as possible from reliance on language experience and verbal concepts.   Such performance-type tests do not measure language deficiency due to hearing loss but estimate problem-solving ability and adaptive potential in non-verbal areas.   Vernon and

Brown (1964) have summarized the basic considerations important in the intelligence testing of deaf and hard of hearing children that have emerged from research:

1. Intelligence scores obtained at the preschool or early school level are more likely to be inaccurate for deaf than hearing children
2. A low I.Q. estimate is more apt to be wrong than a high I.Q. estimate
3. There is greater probability that psychologists who have not had experience working with deaf and hard of hearing children will commit more testing errors
4. Tests with rigid time limits are probably less valid than tests which do not impose such limits
5. Administration of group tests to deaf and hard of hearing children is a questionable procedure

     Pintner, Eisenson, and Stanton (1945) questioned the Stanford-Binet Intelligence Test for use with deaf children because of its language emphasis; they suggested the use of non-language or performance tests such as the Porteus Maze, the Grace Arthur Performance Test, the Goodenough Draw-A-Man Test, the Ontario School Ability Test, and the Pitner-Patterson Non-Language Group Test. It was found that the average I.Q. of deaf children on such tests approached 90, as compared to 100 for hearing individuals.

     The investigators found no difference in intelligence on the basis of age of onset of hearing loss, no difference related to type of deafness, higher intelligence among day school rather than residential school children, very little difference in intelligence between children taught orally and those taught by a combined method of the spoken word and finger spelling, and lower intelligence for those taught exclusively by the manual method. The last finding, however, was attributed to the selection of students in the survey. For hard of hearing students, verbal intelligence measures revealed slightly but significantly lower scores as compared with hearing individuals; non-language tests showed little, if any, difference between the two groups (Wooden, 1963).

     Vernon (1968), in reviewing fifty years of research on the intelligence of the deaf and hard of hearing, reported that no major relationship appears to exist between type of deafness and I.Q., degree of hearing loss and I.Q., or age of onset and I.Q. In studying the relationship of I.Q. scores and later academic achievement, Brill (1962) found the correlation for 499 deaf children to be similar to a random sample of hearing children.

Since language proficiency is positively related to measured intelligence level, it is not surprising that speech handicapped children do not perform as well on intelligence tests (Everhart, 1953; Garrison & Force, 1965). Research, however, has shown that from eight to seventy-nine percent of children who are mentally retarded (depending on the intellectual level of the children studied) may have defective speech (Smith, 1962). We therefore must separate these children when discussing the relationship between speech defects and intelligence. Speech defective children, when taken as a group, score lower in average intelligence than does the general population (Carrell, 1936). They also appear to be retarded scholastically and they fail to take advantage of opportunities for higher education to a greater extent than would be expected in terms of their actual measured intelligence (American Speech and Hearing Association's Committee on the Mid-Century White House Conference, 1952).

MR

        Eisenson (1963) points out that, although they are not unanimous, research findings do suggest a relationship between speech and reading problems. Weaver, Furbee, and Everhart (1960) found that as problems of articulation increased, reading readiness decreased among first graders. Jackson (1944) found that whereas ten percent of a group of accelerated readers exhibited speech problems, twenty-three percent of a group of retarded readers had defective speech. In addition to the possibility that both reading and speech defects have a common cause, such as a neurological lesion of the language centers in the brain (Eames, 1950), speech defects can play a large part in causing reading problems. As the child with a speech defect makes errors in pronunciation or is affected by the rate and rhythm of his oral reading, he may not comprehend or interpret correctly what he has read. Also, the anxiety and concern generated by a speech defect can cause the child to avoid all forms of oral expression.

SH

PH

Efforts to determine accurately the intelligence level of physically handicapped children must consider capacity to participate in the testing situation and previous experience before an estimate of actual intellectual capacity can be made. Luszki (1966) compared fifteen children with cerebral palsy of the spastic type with fifteen normal controls matched on race, sex, age, and I.Q. in regard to verbal and performance items passed on the Stanford-Binet Intelligence Scale. He found that the cerebral palsied children did not differ in verbal ability, but that they were inferior on performance items requiring visual-motor coordination. Thus, the non-mentally retarded child with cerebral palsy may be primarily limited due to lack of capacity to perform certain hand-eye coordination tasks.

Excluding children with cerebral palsy, the measured intelligence of children in classes for the crippled in New York City was found to be similar to the general school population (Wrightstone, Justman, & Moskowitz, 1954). Heilman (1952) has reported that fifty-nine percent of all cerebral palsied children fall into the mentally retarded range; other studies, however, vary with respect to percentages: Phelps and Turner (1945) — twenty-five percent, Wrightstone, Justman, and Moskowitz (1954) — twenty-seven percent, and Greenbaum and Buehler (1960) — forty-five to fifty-five percent. Apparent in these figures is the selection factor operating in the public schools from which the children were drawn. The more selective the school, the fewer the mentally retarded among those with cerebral palsy.

According to Lennox and Lennox (1960), children afflicted with epilepsy display a wide range of intelligence, from low borderline to high superiority with the average level corresponding to the normal population. Bagley (1970) administered the Wechsler Intelligence Scale for Children to 118 epileptic children who were free from other handicapping conditions and found a mean I.Q. of 99.2. The distribution of intelligence levels, however, was significantly skewed from normal, with a larger number of children falling into the lower ranges and a smaller number achieving higher levels. Since a teacher's questionnaire relating to emotional adjustment of these children suggested that forty percent had serious psychiatric problems, the unevenness of these children's functioning may be explained on an experiential rather than a capacity basis.

Children with cardiac conditions in New York City were found to fall into low average categories on both group and individual intelligence tests (Wrightstone, Justman, & Moskowitz, 1953). In explaining their findings, the authors advanced the hypothesis that restriction of activity for such children had limited social, cultural, and intellectual stimulation, and this in turn had depressed their intellectual attainment.

Thus we see that there is no one-to-one relationship between crippling conditions or chronic health problems and intelligence, but rather that differences in capacity (the neurological disability associated with some cases of cerebral palsy) and experience (limited opportunities for the chronically ill to become involved with the environment, or faulty experiences of the epileptic) may be influential in determining measured intelligence.

Although we have tended to talk about gifted children as a homogeneous group, they do in actuality represent a wide range of differences. Three categories of gifted children can be defined: the high I.Q. child, the very high I.Q. child, and the underachieving gifted child.

The high I.Q. child, as described by Dunlap (1967), enters school from one to four or more years more advanced in learning ability than his peers. Unevenness may exist in his actual achievement, but he will know and understand a good part of the subject matter presented for the first three elementary grades. Before kindergarten, he may be able to count, do simple addition and subtraction, draw, paint, print his name, cut with scissors, paste, engage in block construction, and readily connect a series of pictures into a logical sequence and story. Some such children will have learned to read at home, and of these a few will have essentially taught themselves at age three or four. Those who are not ready will progress rapidly after the first few periods of instruction. Throughout the early school years, they will score well above grade level on standardized achievement tests and be quick and eager to learn. Concerns such as the meaning of life, religion, and the nature of the universe will develop by the age of seven or eight. They will grasp complex concepts readily and recognize relationships easily, sometimes before an explanation is completed. Speaking and writing vocabularies are often particularly advanced. Dunlap suggests that children attaining an I.Q. of 140 and above can learn the regular subjects in half the usual time and remember what they have learned.

The very high I.Q. child (170 or 180) will appear once among every 100,000 children (De Haan & Havighurst, 1957) and those with an I.Q. above 180 only once among every million children (Hollingsworth, 1942). We have discussed their tendency to be poor mixers and rather isolated; but Gallagher (1964) states that if such children are grouped with other children of high abilities (I.Q. range of 130–150), their tendency to become social outcasts is lessened. When the very high I.Q. child associates with many bright children, the resultant intellectual companionship can help draw him out socially. The need of the very high I.Q. child for special tutoring sessions and a highly individualized program is underscored by Dunlap (1967), who suggests that children with I.Q.'s of 170 or above are capable of learning and mastering the required school curriculum in one-fourth the time normally allowed.

Children with superior ability who function below their intellectual aptitude have been studied in relation to high achievers. The underachiever may have difficulty in his family relationships, particularly with a hostile and rejecting father, and may demonstrate significantly poorer creativity and social adjustment (Karnes, McCoy, Zehrbach, Wollersheim, & Clarizio, 1962). Parents who are highly authoritarian and low in acceptance appear to contribute greatly to poor academic performance in boys. High achieving girls, however, seem to have more dominant mothers (Pierce & Bowman, 1960). Gallagher (1964) has reviewed studies relating to the self-attitudes of underachievers; underachievers reject many of society's values, including those associated with the school and teacher, and have lowered levels of aspiration.

The Terman study (Terman & Oden, 1947) identified the 150 men who had maintained the poorest level of achievement over the course of the study and compared them with 150 of the men who were markedly successful. Self-ratings and ratings by wives and parents regarding personality traits were obtained. Four major characteristics separated the underachieving individuals from those who had achieved effectively: lack of self-confidence, inability to persevere, lack of integration of goals, and presence of inferiority feelings. When the early school records of members in both groups were considered, these same differences were found to exist even at the pre-adolescent level. The importance of early experience in determining the effective use of potential is clearly illustrated here. Also, the importance of early recognition and intervention in relation to behavioral and personality difficulties is underscored. Thus we see that superior intellectual capacity is a definite asset for most children but that attention must be given to experiential factors in the cases of children with very high I.Q.s and of gifted underachievers.

Conclusions

In the summary discussion of our exceptional learners across the dimension of intelligence, it is well to review some points made early in this chapter regarding the nature of intelligence and its measurement. When we give one of the commonly used individual intelligence tests such as the Stanford-Binet to an exceptional child, we are engaging in an indirect assessment of his innate ability by means of a man-made test instrument. This instrument has attempted to define the critical aspects of intellectual behavior in our society and then to sample these aspects by means of a selection of test items that do not demand excessive amounts of time, space, or elaborate materials for administration. The knowledge, skill, and experience required by these items is assumed to exist among the majority of individuals within the age range covered by the test and, in relation to our standard intelligence tests, no allowances are made for those who have never seen or who have only partial vision, those who have never heard or who have partial hearing, those who cannot use their limbs, those who have spent much of their lives in bed, those with problems with speech and language, and those whose experience has been limited or faulty due to emotional problems or lack of opportunity. Once enough items that cover the range of behaviors identified as related to intelligence have been assembled, the test is given to large numbers of essentially non-exceptional children to establish norms. These children become the standardization group; eventual comparison of other children who will be given the test is made with reference to the range of functioning demonstrated by this standardization group. Persons giving the test will follow strict rules for administering and scoring it based on procedures followed during the standardization. What does all this mean in terms of the intellectual ability of exceptional children? It relates to the functioning level they will display on measures of intelligence. In our summary discussion, we will consider the following four issues:

1. Differences in intellectual capacity
2. Differences in experience due to sensory, perceptual, and motor problems
3. Differences in experience due to social and emotional problems
4. Differences in functioning level in the test situation

Differences in Intellectual Capacity. The mentally retarded and the gifted tend to occupy the extremes on the intellectual capacity dimension. Severe retardation produces obvious limitations on the individual's ability to learn and function independently. As we move up the dimension toward mild and moderate retardation, we find that such retardation is not a global disability but that it may be task specific or related to certain aspects of the learning situation. Learning *how* to learn and short-term memory constitute two problem areas associated with the intellectual level of retarded persons.

Intellectual giftedness, on the other hand, can place the child one to four years ahead of his age mates on entrance into school. The high I.Q. child will grasp complex concepts readily, be quick to recognize relationships, and can progress through the regular school curriculum in half the usual time. The children in our other seven categories fall somewhere along this dimension, the majority of them in the middle range, as is the case with the population at large.

Differences in Experience Due to Sensory, Perceptual, and Motor Problems. The particular problems of some exceptional learners can influence their environmental experience and, hence, their opportunity to develop and utilize their intellectual capacity. The deaf child may be limited in areas such as memory and conceptualization due to the restriction on language development imposed by severe hearing loss. On non-language tests, the deaf child has been found to fall toward the lower limits of the average range of intelligence, as compared with hearing individuals; and the hard of hearing child shows little, if any, difference from the normal child on such tests. Blindness does not appear to affect measured intelligence negatively, and compensation for visual deficits can be provided to a considerable extent by environmental experience.

Children with crippling conditions such as cerebral palsy have been found to demonstrate normal verbal abilities on intelligence tests but inferior performance on tasks requiring motor and coordination skills for which they lack the capacity. Children with epilepsy display a wide range of intellectual abilities, with a greater number falling in the lower range and a smaller number achieving higher levels. However, problems related to emotional adjustment appear reflected here. The child with a learning disability typically ranges from low average to average on intelligence tests. Despite continuing interest in unique patterning related to his functioning on such tests, there is no unanimous agreement that such patterning is useful in diagnosis.

Differences in Experience Due to Social and Emotional Problems. Some exceptional learners are not adversely affected by problems of capacity in either intellectual or sensory and motor areas, yet function poorly in terms of learning and test performance. Emotionally disturbed children, in general, score lower on intelligence tests than do non-disturbed children. Selective and often faulty previous experiences may be major determiners of low scores. The underachieving gifted child may function poorly in learning due to similar determiners. When taken as a group, speech handicapped children score lower in average intelligence than does the general population. This may relate to problems in language proficiency and/or to disturbed environmental relationships.

The socially and economically disadvantaged child also scores lower on tests with high verbal content than does the non-disadvantaged child but he may be equal or superior to such a child on non-verbal measures. Blacks score lower on both traditional and so-called "culturally fair" tests of intelligence yet average well within the normal I.Q. range for whites.

It is difficult not to emphasize such factors as experiential deprivation and lack of intellectual stimulation in accounting for the disadvantaged child's lower measured intelligence as well as for his limited test taking skills and lack of familiarity with specific vocabulary and types of tasks presented. Chronically ill children, such as those with cardiac conditions, also score lower on group and individual intelligence tests than do normals. Activity restriction and limited social, cultural, and intellectual stimulation are probably the major determiners of these lower scores.

Differences in Functioning Level in the Test Situation. Once the exceptional learner arrives in the actual test taking situation, after the problems of capacity and experience have been considered, he still may not function in line with his true potential due to problems of attention, rapport with the examiner, response to speed pressure, and general motivation to do well on the test. These problems appear most often with the emotionally disturbed and the disadvantaged, although emotional and motivational problems that interfere with test functioning can be found in combination with any primary handicapping conditions, such as deafness, and even with the gifted. Deviations from standardized test administration practices used by an examiner to adapt the test to the special needs of an exceptional child can reduce or totally negate the validity of the test if standardized scoring procedures are used.

Earlier, we described specialized efforts that have been made to adapt and develop intelligence tests for use with exceptional children. The Stanford-Binet has been revised for the blind, tests minimizing language proficiency have been developed for the deaf and others, and instruments aiming at culture-free content that will not penalize individuals for lack of experience have appeared. These revised tests are an effort to help us better define the exceptional individual in terms of an I.Q. score. Is it all really worth it? Yes, if we can obtain a meaningful picture of where the individual stands in relation to others with whom he must grow, learn, relate, and work. Maybe not, if it becomes an indelible stamp that alters our expectations and restricts his opportunities.

At best, an I.Q. test creates a miniature arena into which an exceptional child can be placed and briefly observed in terms of his intellectual functioning. The restrictions of time, place, selection of items, and eventual evaluation in terms of a standardized population that may not include anyone like him can greatly limit its actual meaning.

Ideally, if we could actually live with and observe any child for, say, six months, we would be in a better position to speculate on his adaptive potential — his innate intellectual capacity — but such an elaborate assessment is unrealistic and impractical for many children. Even if such an arrangement were possible, it would still leave us with problems of organizing and reporting what we saw so that some meaningful statement could actually be made about the child in relation to other children.

Such total-environment observations were used during World War II by the Office of Strategic Services in an effort to assess the personality and leadership characteristics of men under stress. In place of the interview, the paper and pencil questionnaire, the projective test, or other indirect measures, actual real life situations were created in which an individual was observed under stress. The individual to be assessed might be assigned the job of taking a group of men to a remote and rugged forest area to supervise the building of a pontoon bridge across a river. As far as he knew, this was a regular training assignment; he did not know that the men assigned to him were psychologists with a carefully worked out plan to engage in varying degrees of sabotage directed toward placing the candidate in a series of frustrating and stressful decision-making situations. Fights among the group broke out, orders were disregarded, and clumsy, inept efforts were demonstrated by the work crew as they attempted to build the bridge. Through careful observation and record keeping, an assessment of the individual's ability to function under such conditions was made.

We can see how difficult such a procedure would be to standardize so that the evaluation criteria applied were identical for all individuals being assessed. But in terms of a single individual, this situation might provide more meaningful information than any current psychological testing approaches.

The classroom teacher who carefully observes children with learning problems, making note of their strengths and weaknesses, trying out various approaches to increase their successes and decrease their failures, is actually engaging in a similar kind of ongoing environmental intelligence and learning evaluation. Far from sabotage and stress, however, the teacher is concerned with supporting and understanding the child as he moves through, relates to, and works in the real world of the school. Formal intelligence testing, despite all its sobering limitations and questionable meaning with exceptional learners, will undoubtedly continue to be relied on. As Burton (1967) points out, such testing should not be judged on the basis of how unfair it is to the exceptional child but rather in terms of the help it provides in "teaching and reaching the child that could not be obtained in other ways." But more effort must go into making classrooms and learning situations real world evaluation settings, and observations must be made and data gathered that will help us find answers to questions such as, "What is it this child is ready to learn?" and "How can I go about teaching it to him?" This is the essence of "building the bridge from the other side" and will receive more of our attention in Part III of this text.

We will complete the collective portrait of exceptional learners across our four psycho-social dimensions with consideration of the dimension of individualization.

INDIVIDUALIZATION

Individualization is the unique characteristic of man that refers to his multiple potentiality for almost unlimited variation in the outcome of growth and development and for achieving career and vocational goals. Such potentiality is present at birth and may be ultimately expressed in a wide variety of ways. Some individuals will become physicians, others stockbrokers or college professors. Others may become artists, tradesmen, or professional athletes. The multiple potentiality of children that is present at birth is primarily determined by innate capacity; but as they grow and mature, it is shaped by countless interactions with the environment. Thus, experience plays an increasingly important role in its ultimate expression.

What happens to the emotionally disturbed child as he matures and grows up? A long-range study traced the adult social and psychiatric outcomes of 524 child guidance clinic patients after a thirty-year interval and compared them with 100 normal school children who were initially of the same age, sex, neighborhood, race, and I.Q. (Robins, 1966). The patients were separated into "anti-social" and "neurotic" categories; overall findings suggest that the anti-social group is more in need of help in adult life, whereas the neurotic group more resembles the controls in later years.

The anti-social children were found to have experienced more arrests and imprisonment, to be more mobile geographically, to have more mental difficulties, to have poorer occupational and economic histories, to have impoverished social and organizational

ED

relationships and poorer armed service records, to use alcohol more frequently in excess, and in many respects to be in poorer health. Anti-social behavior in childhood was not found to predict specific deviance but rather to be a generalized inability to conform and perform in society in many areas.

The neurotic group was found to have more difficulty in adult life than did the anti-social group in several areas. For example, more men never married, more men were deferred by draft boards for physical disability, more women earned less than eighty dollars per week, and more men and women reported nervous symptoms in one or more of their children. This group, however, also was rated as more favorable than the controls in some areas of later adjustment. There were fewer single women, fewer women married before age twenty-one, and fewer women sought medical help. Among the men, fewer received medical discharges in the armed services.

In selecting the control group for this study, three criteria were set: the control children had not been referred to a psychiatric clinic, had not repeated one full year of elementary school, and had not left elementary school due to expulsion or transfer to a correctional institution. Only two percent of these children were ever seen by a juvenile court. The author reports that the control children from working class backgrounds with predominantly average I.Q.'s actually achieved as good or better an adjustment as did the gifted children from upper-middle-class backgrounds in the Terman and Oden (1959) study, which we have discussed at various points.

The absence of serious problems in school is seen by Robins as an efficient predictor of successful adjustment in adult life. Whereas Terman and Oden's children enjoyed spectacular school success and the control subjects in Robins' study experienced only a lack of serious school problems, there was virtually no difference between the two groups in rates of deviant behavior in adult life. Thus, success in school appears correlated with adequacy of later adjustment. Only fifteen percent of the highly anti-social children ever entered high school, whereas more than half the children in the study with little anti-social behavior went on to high school. More than two-thirds of the highly anti-social children did not even complete the eighth grade.

G

This study emphasizes the critical role of the school in relation to success in later life. Although forces outside the control of the teacher and the school were probably primarily responsible for the poor performance by the anti-social group, it stands to reason that, had provisions been made for early intervention in the school with regard to increasing their chances of success, both school functioning and later adjustment might have been greatly improved. Whatever the limitations of our educational system, it exists as a miniature socialization arena within which many of society's demands for adjustment are made. Individuals who will eventually take their place in this society perhaps gain their most crucial training in this arena.

In considering what happens to children with learning disabilities as they grow and mature, we are again faced with problems of definition. We have already discussed the dilemma of verifying the presence of neurological impairment and have admitted that many of the problems associated with learning disabilities, such as underachievement, hyperactivity, and distractibility, are commonly found among children considered emotionally disturbed, mentally retarded, and socially and economically disadvantaged. Agreement as to when certainty of diagnosis allows us to exclude other primary causal factors and to settle on learning disability is not now universal in special education. Therefore, our discussion of individualization and the child with a learning disability will focus on the characteristic of hyperactivity and follow-up studies of hyperactive children. This focus appears justifiable since the characteristic of hyperactivity has been reported as the single most often observed characteristic of children with learning disabilities (Clements, 1966).

In general, the clinical literature suggests that hyperactivity diminishes with age (Bradley, 1957). Laufer and Denhoff (1957) have noted that hyperactivity tends to disappear somewhere between the ages of twelve and eighteen. However, serious educational and emotional problems have been found to persist (Laufer, 1962; Anderson & Plymate, 1962). The only criterion common to all is poor school performance despite average or above intelligence. Menkes, Rowe, and Menkes (1967) conducted a twenty-five-year retrospective follow-up of eighteen hyperactive children with I.Q.'s above 70. They found that, as adults, four were institutionalized as psychotic, two were totally dependent on their families, and only eight were completely self-supporting. In addition, hyperactivity was seen as still present in three of the subjects between ages twenty-two and twenty-three, although it had disappeared between ages eight and twenty-one in most of the others. These findings are limited by the fact the data were obtained retrospectively and by the possibility that the observed hyperactivity was a reflection of some primary problem other than a learning disability.

LD

Weiss, Minde, Werry, Douglas, and Nemeth (1969) did a five-year follow-up study of sixty-four chronically and severely hyperactive children who were between the ages of six and thirteen years at the initiation of the study, who had an I.Q. as measured by the Weschler Intelligence Scale for Children above 84, who evidenced no major brain damage or dysfunction such as associated with epilepsy or cerebral palsy, and who were living at home with at least one parent. There were sixty boys and four girls in the sample.

At the time of the follow-up evaluation, they ranged in age from ten to eighteen. The most striking finding was that, whereas restlessness had been the main problem for each child five years before, it was no longer the chief complaint for any child. Classroom observation of the children revealed more restlessness than normals but it was much more subdued and less disturbing (e.g., playing with a pencil) than it was five years earlier (e.g., walking around the room). Distractibility was still evident but less so than at the onset of the study. A significant decrease was also seen in aggressiveness and excitability. The most common behavioral problem was emotional immaturity, which was reported by seventy percent of the parents. The second most common trait was described as a lack of ambition and a severe lack of ability to maintain goals. Thirty percent of the children had no steady friends, and twenty-five percent had a history of acting out and anti-social behavior. Ten of these latter children had difficulties with the law. Eighty percent of the children were doing poorly in school. As in earlier studies, poor academic functioning was the feature most clearly distinguishing the group as a whole. The authors concluded that even though hyperactivity diminishes with age, other major handicaps such as underachievement and emotional immaturity persist.

Although these children had not reached adulthood, we can speculate, partly on the basis of the data on older individuals provided by Menkes, Rowe, and Menkes (1967), that many would be poorly prepared for advanced schooling or vocational training due to academic deficiencies, and as a result would have difficulty supporting themselves. Traits such as lack of ambition and inability to maintain goals may be strengthened by the adult years because of continuing failure and frustration and might thus further diminish the individual's chances for success in the adult world. It may be that the minimal neurological impairment that possibly was present in some of these children and contributed to their early childhood hyperactivity had been outgrown; but that what really limits the child with a learning disability in pursuing a happy and successful adult life are the secondary problems of accumulated school failure and his maladaptive behavior. Thus, capacity may be far less a determiner of individualization than is experience. Again, the importance of early intervention and provision for the kind of education that helps children with learning disabilities to learn and succeed is vividly illustrated.

LD

MR

What happens to the mentally retarded individual when he reaches adult life? A longitudinal follow-up study of persons who had been enrolled in public school classes for the retarded in Lincoln, Nebraska, was begun by Baller (1936) and continued by Charles (1953). Of the 206 in the original sample, the mortality rate was slightly higher than that of the general population, but only eleven were in institutions. More than half of the males had been prosecuted for some violation of the law but seldom for serious crimes and often for minor offenses such as traffic violations. About eighty percent had married, but roughly one-fifth of these were divorced — a rate equal at that time to the general population, although continuing follow-up (Baller, Charles, & Miller, 1967) showed a higher divorce rate in later years. The majority of their children were making satisfactory progress in school without evidence of retardation. A surprising number (fifty-five percent) owned their own homes and although these were often shacks, some were expensive new houses. Over eighty percent had been self-supporting for some time, though jobs seemed to cluster in the semi-skilled and unskilled range.

The average I.Q. of the group on follow-up was 81 as compared with a mean I.Q. of 58 when the group was originally tested. Fisher and Zeaman (1970) have indicated that the MA of higher-level retardates continues to grow even into their late thirties. Holt (1964) has suggested that perhaps if the retardate stayed in school till he was twenty-five or thirty, he might approach the educational accomplishments that he failed to reach at the time of high school graduation.

These studies reveal that retarded individuals may progress in their level of adjustment as they move through adult life. Also, many myths regarding the tendency of retarded individuals to produce large families including retarded offspring or to become chronic law violators, moral deviates, or welfare roll liabilities were dispelled. Channing (1952) found less optimistic follow-up results for retarded individuals paroled from institutions and, as also might be expected with normal persons with disturbed personalities or histories of social maladjustment, the severity of these problems determined later success outside the institution. Favorable economic conditions were also a factor in the adjustment of mentally retarded adults. It should also be noted that the more severely retarded, such as those who have attended TMR classes, are less apt to have a favorable adjustment in later life. Though very few long-term studies have been done on this group (Kirk, 1964), the results seem to indicate that nearly half will eventually be institutionalized and those living at home will seldom hold meaningful employment.

MR

Normative follow-up studies, however, may mask the true picture of the retardates' potential for individualization. Edgerton (1967) has presented an informative and moving account of the day-to-day life of forty-eight retardates paroled from a state hospital for the retarded near Los Angeles. They had a mean I.Q. somewhat comparable to Charles' subjects. Few achieved an adjustment that could be called successful by middle-class standards, and most could not have achieved their present marginal adjustment without the help of a normal "benefactor" upon whom they depended for assistance. The paucity of leisure time activities was especially striking. Riding a city bus to the end of the line and a preoccupation with television were characteristic of how they spent their time. One should keep in mind that a more favorable outlook might have been expected had these retarded adults not been institutionalized at one time. Edgerton describes their attempts to pass as non-retarded or to weave for themselves a "cloak of competence." Tattered as these attempts may have been, they did enable them to achieve some level of individualization.

Doll (1941) considers social incompetence or the basic incapacity for self-management beyond a marginal level as the only criterion for mental retardation that society can justly impose. He thus views the essential problem of the retarded as getting along in their environment, rather than adequacy in intelligence. Although opportunities for personal development and achievement in later life are certainly more limited for the retarded adult, current evidence reveals a more optimistic picture regarding individualization than might be assumed from the layman's traditional concept of mental retardation. Most incidence figures seem to show a marked decline of retarded persons so identified after the formal school years. After the ordeal of school and its particular demand on the mentally retarded is over, many of these people seem to blend back into the fabric of society and achieve, however marginal, a measure of individualization.

The potential for individualization of the disadvantaged child will reflect his motivation to succeed and his commitment to prepare himself for the future. Miller and Swanson (1960) found marked differences between lower and middle-class children with respect to such motivation and commitment. The middle-class children believed they could improve their economic position through effort and sacrifice. They expressed willingness to postpone immediate gratification for future rewards and saw a reputation for honesty, responsibility, and respectability as important. Individual advancement was seen as based on self-denial, competent performance, formal education, rationality, hard work, and above all mastery of self through a rational approach as a requirement for mastering the world.

SD

Lower-class children view success and security as uncertain and are more concerned with the present than the future. Formal education may be desirable but not essential for getting a job and holding it. Physical strength and manual skill are more highly valued. The lower-class child does not see self-control and responsibility as overly important and tends to seek pleasure now rather than to take any chance on an uncertain reward in the future.

Goldstein (1967) concludes that most American children, regardless of class, aspire to achieve a work career beyond the level of their parents. He acknowledges that lower-class youth may be less likely to move toward the professions and the higher education necessary to attain them and that they may not be as optimistic as higher-placed youth but that most of them are aware that "getting ahead" is expected of them.

Elder (1962) reported on a large-scale study done with 25,000 junior and senior high school students in North Carolina to determine, among other variables, effect of social class, parents' education, and pressure exerted by parents for achievement on adolescent motivation and achievement in schools. Among the findings were:

1. Social class and parental education are positively related to academic motivation and achievement
2. Low achievers are more apt to report strong achievement demands from parents than are high achievers with middle- and lower-class parents who were equally likely to put pressure on high achievers

Middle-class parents are much more likely to pressure low achievers. The author concludes that incorporation of middle-class values in either lower- or middle-class families is more likely a determiner of student motivation and achievement than is social class status alone.

SD

VH

The visually handicapped individual faces certain unique problems as he matures and moves toward adult life. Cholden (1958) suggests that three special preoccupations of the blind during adolescence are found among most normally seeing young men and women, but are complicated by the fact of blindness. One preoccupation has to do with the importance of bodily attractiveness to the female and masculine strength and independence to the male. The desire to impress the opposite sex and the anxiety surrounding sexual relationships are typical of adolescence but are made more difficult in the visually handicapped. The second preoccupation concerns independence and the dilemma of the blind adolescent who cannot achieve a position free from dependence on parents and others around him. The third common problem of all adolescents centers around achieving a certain degree of exhibitionism while preserving the desire for anonymity, both of which are more difficult for the blind. In terms of sexual curiosity, dating, mobility, and concern for the future, Lowenfeld (1971) sees that the difficulties encountered by the blind adolescent can possibly affect his self-concept and his attitudes toward interpersonal relationships but that perhaps they are no more severe than the process of adjustment that goes on in all adolescents.

Among the special needs of the blind adolescent is expert instruction in independent modes of travel (Abel, 1961). Finestone, Lukoff, and Whiteman (1960) found that many blind adults lacked the ability to travel alone, were dissatisfied with their level of performance, lacked a systematic or purposeful mode of travel, had had only limited travel training, and did not have active plans for improving their travel ability. Emphasis on mobility training for the blind has recently been stressed by the Veteran's Administration, state vocational rehabilitation programs, and the American Foundation for the Blind.

In preparing the blind for adult vocational adjustment, the sheltered workshop has played an important role. In these workshops, skills associated with the manufacturing of such items as rugs, brooms, and hand-woven ties are taught and employment provided for blind individuals. Such limited vocational opportunities were more typical of the past than they are of the present. The influence of organizations for the blind, the expansion of the United States Office of Vocational Rehabilitation, and an increased emphasis on integration of minority and handicapped group members in all walks of life have provided greater vocational and employment opportunities. Blind individuals can and do successfully undertake many types of jobs, such as farming, chemistry, teaching at all levels, osteopathy, and law. The critical fact seems to be society's acceptance of the blind in competitive employment. As societal acceptance of the blind increases and job opportunities for them become more available, the number of successfully employed blind individuals should greatly exceed that traditionally associated with sheltered workshops.

Over the past few decades, opportunities for continued educational achievement have increased for the deaf individual. The New York State Deaf Population Research Program revealed that 99.2 percent had attended school at one time, twenty-six percent left school after age sixteen, and 3.7 percent attended or graduated from college. Individuals who became deaf after age four had a greater chance of graduating from a grade school or school for the deaf. This fact has been attributed to the advantage of greater development of language before onset of deafness (Altshuler & Baroff, 1969). Seventy-six percent of those in the study reported they had liked school and teachers.

In the vocational area, eighty-seven percent were performing some kind of manual labor, with one-half of this group falling in the skilled labor category. Deaf individuals appeared to be excellent employment risks, with ninety-three percent of the men and sixty-nine percent of the women holding jobs for more than three years. Included in the study were a group of deaf persons of outstanding achievement in the fields of art, architecture, engineering, chemistry, dentistry, and accounting (Jarvik, Salzberger, & Falek, 1969). The authors concluded that unusual achievement among the deaf is associated with factors that are similar to high achievement by hearing individuals. Far more effort, endowment, and opportunity, however, were required for such equivalent accomplishment on the part of the deaf. The average deaf man is seen as holding a job, owning a home, marrying, raising a family of reasonably normal children, and participating in the social life of the community (Telford & Sawrey, 1967). However, only five percent of some 10,000 married deaf individuals had married hearing people (Brill, 1961).

According to McConnell (1973), data on the vocational

status of the partially hearing are not available. The increased ability in language and communication skills among the partially hearing probably causes them to become absorbed in the hearing world, and for some their hearing impairment will be acquired well after the establishment of a vocational career. However, if hearing problems interfered with communication, language, and educational levels in childhood and adolescence, we might expect that many of these individuals would fail to reach their full potential in the adult world.

In our previous discussion, we found a tendency for speech handicapped individuals to have limitations in motor proficiency, intellectual functioning, and educational achievement. We also found a tendency toward maladjustment, which, according to Berry and Eisenson (1956), seems to increase as the speech defective grows older. Duncan (1949) investigated the home adjustment of a group of college students with stuttering problems and found that as a group they felt they were not understood by their parents, that their maturity was underestimated, that they had strong desires to leave home, and that their parents were disappointed with them. Sheehan (1958), in his review of studies on the personality characteristics of stutterers, found little evidence to suggest that stutterers "are different from anybody else" but did conclude that their levels of aspiration were lower.

　　　　With respect to entrance into adult life and achieving success, it appears that many individuals with speech defects continue to deal with earlier, unresolved problems. The frustration and failure associated with social and educational experiences may dictate against full realization of their potential in later life.

The child who is physically handicapped often faces a difficult adjustment as he moves toward adult life. The personal aspiration level of crippled children was studied by Cruickshank (1952) by means of a sentence completion device. It allowed the child to project his attitudes and feelings in selecting endings to such incomplete sentences as, "I could be happy if _____," or "I'm afraid of _____." In response to the incomplete sentence, "If I weren't blocked by _____," more than twenty-five percent of the secondary students studied chose "my handicap" as the ending. Similarly some eighteen percent finished, "I could be happy if _____" with

"I weren't handicapped." An analysis of the total responses of the group to the items presented revealed:

1. A wish to compensate for the limited scope of behavior imposed on them by their disabilities
2. A marked drive for acceptance of a minimal nature, in contrast to the normal child's striving for something better than minimal acceptance
3. A realization that their handicap is a significant barrier to success, regardless of the basis of evaluation

A study of cerebral palsied students who entered college (Muthard & Hutchison, 1969) shows that they generally experienced more difficulty academically than did non-impaired students and that they required more time to complete undergraduate and graduate study. More handicapped students chose counseling as a career than did non-handicapped individuals. Only four percent of students with cerebral palsy who completed college were found to be unemployed, whereas about seventy percent of cerebral palsied adults are unemployed.

Schonell (1956) lists a number of occupations open to the individual with cerebral palsy whose handicap is largely confined to the legs. These include watch repairing, optical or dental mechanics, developing and printing film, clerical work, statistical and research work, assembling parts of small machinery or equipment, art, and pottery making. The chief obstacle found in gaining employment in one of these areas may be getting to and from the place of employment. Fewer opportunities for employment exist for the cerebral palsied adult with severe hand disabilities. For this reason, Schonell stresses the importance of therapeutic treatment for hand coordination over treatment for the legs. If the individual can gain some level of proficiency even in one hand, his chances for development of a skill in a craft are greatly increased.

Moed and Litwin (1963) reported two studies that attempted to determine the employability of persons with cerebral palsy. The first study was conducted with ambulatory individuals for the purpose of establishing methods of work evaluation. Three basic movements in manual dexterity were found to be the most related to employability. Other highly related factors were (1) verbal I.Q., (2) handwriting, (3) vocational adjustment, (4) severity of gait deficit, (5) ability to travel independently, and (6) performance I.Q. and speech intelligibility. The second study evaluated young cerebral palsied adults from vocational centers. It was found that sixty to seventy percent of the cerebral palsied individuals in their sample were marginal workers without the capacity for regular employment.

The major handicap confronting individuals with epilepsy in later life appears related to personality disorders rather than to the presence of seizures or mental retardation. The epileptic is placed in a very difficult situation in relation to occupation. Crowther (1967) estimates that some sixty percent of all employers in the country will not employ individuals with epilepsy under any circumstances. Dennerll, Rodin, Gonzales, Schwartz, and Lin (1966) consider social adaptation abilities to be as important as seizure control in retaining a job, but they do not believe drug therapy and changing employers' attitudes have significantly altered the employment problems of the individual with epilepsy. Bridge (1949) has described the occupational dilemma of the epileptic. On the one hand, he wants a job with a good salary and opportunity for advancement; he lives with the hope that he has had his last seizure. On the other, he knows a single seizure can cause him to lose his job or to suffer embarrassment or danger. Once his disease is known, employment and insurance laws can block any future employment.

Individuals with crippling conditions and chronic health problems can enter occupations that are commensurate with their abilities. When adequate measures are taken to protect them and those they work with from possible hazards arising from their handicaps, they can contribute productively.

PH

G

In considering the eventual attainment of the gifted individual as he moves toward mid-adult life, the Terman study (Terman & Oden, 1959) has provided us with information in regard to education, career achievement, and mental status.

The individuals in the Terman study undertook most of their college work in the decade 1930–40, a period of widespread economic depression in which less than eight percent of the general population of comparable age graduated from college. Within the Terman group, however, some seventy percent of the men and sixty-seven percent of the women completed their college work. Of these men and women, two-thirds of the men and almost three-fifths of the women entered graduate school; fifty-six percent of the men and thirty-three percent of the women completed one or more advanced degrees. Of the approximately thirty percent of the group that did not graduate from college, financial problems and lack of parental encouragement were frequently cited as responsible.

But the authors of the study conclude that the real cause usually was the failure of the high school to recognize the gifted individual's potentialities and to give him the needed encouragement and stimulation.

Occupationally, more than forty-five percent of the men in the Terman study entered professional fields, with law, university teaching, and engineering, in that order, being selected. An additional forty percent entered managerial ranks in business and industry, public or private administration, or semi-professional occupations. Among the women, one-half were housewives with no outside employment and forty-two percent held full time jobs. Schoolteaching, including elementary and secondary administration and supervisory positions, was the most frequent occupation of the women, accounting for almost one-fourth of the group. When career satisfaction and interest was examined, half the men expressed "deep satisfaction" and another thirty-seven percent stated they were "fairly content." Over fifty-five percent of the women placed themselves in the deeply satisfied category.

With respect to incidence of marriage, ninety-three percent of the men and almost ninety percent of the women were married by the time the average age of the subjects was forty-four years. This was approximately the expectant rate for the total national population of comparable age. Slightly more than one-fifth of those who married had a history of divorce. Although direct comparison with the national population at large was not possible, the authors concluded this incidence was probably somewhat less than for the generality.

A total of 1,525 children (786 boys and 739 girls) who were offsprings of the Terman study group were given individual intelligence tests. Both boys and girls attained a mean I.Q. of 132. Approximately one-third of the children had I.Q.'s over 140 and only two percent below 100.

The authors concluded that the longitudinal study of the group of gifted individuals over three and one-half decades has shown that the superior child, with few exceptions, becomes the able adult who is superior to the generality in nearly every aspect.

Conclusions

The socialization goal of success is basic to American society (Martin & Stendler, 1959). In many respects, individualization represents the degree of attainment of this goal by the individual in relation to his unique potential and to the societal definition of success. Exceptional learners may be limited in such attainment by problems in basic capacity. Yet continuing social experiences that tend to restrict acceptance and opportunities for individualization may constitute a greater limitation than does the capacity problem itself. Some exceptional learners have great difficulty overcoming problems of early experience in achieving success and individualization. Our summary discussion will consider:

1. Effects of capacity-based problems
2. Effects of experienced-based problems

Effects of Capacity-based Problems. In categorically listing the levels of individualization totally outside the realm of possible accomplishment for the handicapped, we are not confronted by an easy task. Even though the blind individual is not a good candidate for becoming an airplane pilot, the deaf person a symphonic conductor, the crippled individual a track athlete, the severely speech impaired a Shakespearean actor, or the retarded a computer scientist, on an individual basis some remarkable accomplishments have been demonstrated by exceptional people who might easily have been considered poor candidates for success. The story of Helen Keller is one of the most dramatic in this regard. Her superior intelligence had to overcome handicaps of both blindness and deafness for expression. Yet with excellent tutelage she achieved amazingly well in scholarly endeavors.

In describing deaf individuals who had achieved unusual prominence in such fields as art, engineering, and dentistry, Jarvik, Salzberger, and Falek (1969) concluded that far more effort, endowment, and opportunity was required than would have been necessary for equivalent accomplishment on the part of the non-handicapped. Blind individuals who succeed in such fields as teaching and law probably represent a similar case in point. Increased effort can make undergraduate and graduate study possible for the cerebral palsied and thus greatly increase their chances of successful employment. Yet effort and endowment must still be matched by opportunity for achievement and success. Specialized educational facilities may be necessary, unique materials such as textbooks in braille or tape recordings are essential, and above all, encouragement, support, and guidance from others are important. The individual with epilepsy may be denied opportunity for the success he is capable of because of societal attitudes toward his condition. We have come a long way in recognizing the effort and endowment of the handicapped and in offering them opportunities for individualization, but unquestionably we have a considerable distance to go.

Studies of the mentally retarded from childhood to adult life have revealed that many societal beliefs about the retarded are untrue. To begin with, the intellectual ability of the higher level retardate can continue to increase well into the adult years. This indicates that so-called intellectual capacity measured during the childhood years may be far from fixed. Retarded individuals do not have large families and a majority of retarded offspring. They do not become chronic law violators, moral deviates, or social welfare liabilities. That some, particularly those with institutional backgrounds, require continuing assistance from a normal "benefactor" and actually achieve only a "cloak of competence" points up the importance of encouragement, support, and guidance from others.

Effects of Experience-based Problems. Whatever capacity some exceptional learners possess in early life for eventual success, the effects of faulty experiences may ultimately determine their level of individualization. Many exceptional learners in our nine categories live with frustration and failure during much, if not all, of their lives. Such negative experiences can leave their mark in terms of lowered aspiration level and self-esteem, or personality patterns covering a range from hostility and aggression to fearfulness and withdrawal. The disadvantaged child is often present-oriented and not concerned with planning and preparing for the future due to the uncertainty of success and security in his world. The values of hard work, self-denial, and responsibility, which appear basic to the American socialization goal of success, may be lacking in his experience and thus limit his eventual level of accomplishment.

The child with a speech handicap and the child with a learning disability can carry the effects of their failure to gain social approval and success into the adult years. Even though the latter child may overcome the neurological immaturity related to problems in his early life, the fact that he was "out of step" during the critical periods of basic schooling can greatly limit his motivation and restrict his future scholastic attainment. Many emotionally disturbed children also outgrow their adjustment problems to some extent, particularly those who are not severely anti-social. But the long-range effects of fearfulness and anxiety can markedly interfere with satisfactory personal, marital, and occupational adjustment in later years.

As in previous discussions, the gifted child must receive separate consideration. Superior in capacity, he tends to achieve a superior level of individualization. However, as experience and opportunity do not support and enhance his capacity, we may find him functioning far below his actual potential in adult life.

ED

LD

MR

SD

SH

G

The attainment of success and true individualization in American society is predicated on endowment or capacity, effort, and opportunity or necessary experience. Exceptional learners are sometimes limited in regard to capacity, sometimes superior; they are sometimes limited by faulty experience in regard to effort, sometimes driven by the challenge and frustration of their handicap to achieve success; sometimes denied opportunities for attaining the individualization of which they are actually capable, sometimes given the support, encouragement, and guidance necessary to enable them to realize their potential.

In many ways, every individual in the society can be included in this description of the problems of the exceptional learner. We are all different in regard to capacity, different in terms of the experiences that we have that move us toward occupational and career objectives, and different in terms of the opportunities that are afforded us. What we have described with reference to the exceptional individual are problems of differing magnitude and degree, not of kind.

SUMMARY

This chapter concludes Part II, which has aimed at a psycho-social overview of exceptionality in the context of flexibility, sociality, intelligence, and individualization. What does it mean to be different in American society? Excluding the gifted individual for the moment, it means that one may be limited in terms of mastery of the physical environment. One may have major sensory deficits that restrict his experience and learning (blind and deaf), major problems of mobility in moving through the environment (blind, crippled, chronic health problems), behavior problems that interfere with adequate and active participation (emotionally disturbed, mentally retarded, learning disability), or restricted opportunity for experiencing and learning about the environment (disadvantaged). Thus adjustment in a flexible and independent manner to the environment can be difficult due to capacity, experience, or functioning problems.

The parameter of the physical environment is not as critical as that of the social environment in relation to the meaning of being different. Perhaps the most unifying aspect of all our nine categories is the role of social experience in affecting the lives of handicapped children. The categories themselves only partly determine the reaction of others toward exceptional individuals. In every category we find children who are accepted or rejected, guided or neglected, protected or overprotected, and free or dominated. The actual reaction of others reflects an almost endless variety of family, community, and school patterns. In some cases, the reaction and treatment of others is a primary determiner of the problem (emotionally disturbed, speech handicapped, disadvantaged). In others, it supports or aggravates basic capacity (blind, deaf, crippled, chronic health impaired, learning disability, mentally retarded, gifted).

The dimension of intelligence is truly distinguishing for the mentally retarded and the gifted. Here differences in capacity clearly contribute to functioning level. But we are not able to make definitive statements about the limitations imposed by lack of capacity and experience on the intellectual functioning of the blind, deaf, crippled, and chronic health impaired or the faulty or limited experience of the disturbed, disadvantaged, or speech handicapped. Once we understand the indirect, man-made, test-based provisions for estimating intelligence, the individuals in these seven categories may not differ significantly from normals.

The social environment again looms as a basic determiner in relation to individualization. It can restrict an individual's eventual attainment because of faulty early experience (emotionally disturbed, disadvantaged, mentally retarded, speech handicapped, learning disability, gifted) or it can greatly limit the realization of effort and endowment on the part of some (blind, deaf, crippled, chronic health impaired) by denying them opportunity for fulfilling their actual potential. Realistically, however, problems in basic capacity set limits of their own.

In Part III, the exceptional learners in our nine categories will be brought together for a discussion of their similarities and differences on dimensions specifically related to learning and education. Hopefully, our collective portrait of the exceptional learner will assume a clearer and more detailed character in relation to special education as we move from the general to the specific.

ED

LD

MR

SD

VH

HH

SH

PH

G

PART III

Learning Dimensions

CHAPTER 6

Levels of Learning Competence

From the broad psycho-social dimensions of flexibility, sociality, intelligence, and individualization, we turn to consideration of dimensions related to learning in the classroom — *attention, response, exploratory, social,* and *mastery.* These dimensions describe levels of learning competence that are essential for success in school. They are derived from a developmental sequence of educational goals established earlier by the author (Hewett, 1964b, 1968) as a guideline for assessment and educational programming with emotionally disturbed children.

Despite etiological complexity, the disturbed child is viewed as basically an educational problem when he walks through the classroom door and fails to pay attention, fails to participate, fails to follow directions, fails adequately to explore the environment around him, fails to get along with others, and fails to learn to read and acquire other basic academic skills. This simple sequence of educational goals aids in the translation of the problems of disturbed children so that they can be directly dealt with by the teacher. It also provides a means for "building the bridge from the other side," or formulating a distinctly educational definition for disturbance in contrast to traditional psychiatric approaches.

Such a behavioral statement can be applied to all children when considering their competence as learners. The normal child succeeds in school because he looks and listens, readily tries, follows established routines, has learned about the physical properties of the environment, gains the approval of others, and acquires knowledge and skill. The exceptional child assumes his educational uniqueness because he falters along one or more of these behavioral dimensions. Such faltering may be due primarily to capacity or to experience or to their interaction. In the case of the gifted, we are not concerned with limitations but rather with superiority in functioning along these dimensions.

The developmental sequence directly relates to the psychosocial dimensions of flexibility, sociality, intelligence, and individualization presented in Part II. Our capacity and experience equation thus can be extended to include the developmental sequence as follows:

$$\text{capacity} \times \text{experience} = \text{functioning level} = \text{flexibility} = \genfrac{}{}{0pt}{}{\text{attention}}{\genfrac{}{}{0pt}{}{\text{response}}{\genfrac{}{}{0pt}{}{\text{order}}{\text{exploratory}}}}$$

$$\text{sociality} = \text{social}$$

$$\frac{\text{intelligence}}{\text{individualization}} = \text{mastery}$$

From concern with the broader functioning levels of the exceptional learner as he moves through the physical and social environment and develops and utilizes his intellectual potential, we now turn to consideration of more specific functioning levels in the classroom. The concept of flexibility narrows to focus on paying attention and responding to stimuli related to learning and gaining knowledge of the physical environment on which language and academic proficiency depend. Sociality is re-defined as gaining the approval and avoiding the disapproval of teachers and peers in school. Intelligence and individualization become concerned with language development and with the academic curriculum of the school program.

In our discussion of exceptional learners across these classroom-specific dimensions of attention, response, order, exploratory, social, and mastery, we shall draw upon research contributions in the field of special education and describe a variety of instructional practices that are utilized to help the child improve his functioning level. Our discussion will be organized around three major environmental variables under the direct control of the teacher in the classroom:

1. Curriculum: the selection of educational tasks
2. Conditions: the specification and arrangement of expectations associated with curriculum tasks
3. Consequences: the selection and provision of reinforcement

We shall not maintain the sequential categorical approach of the earlier chapters, but shall adopt an issues orientation, illustrating our remarks with references from work done with specific types of handicapped children as they are relevant. The index-band system will continue to be used so that such categorical references are readily available to the reader.

Before introducing each level of learning competence and describing in more detail the curriculum, conditions, and consequences framework for our discussion, we will briefly review attempts that have been made to re-define the problems of exceptional learners in educational and learning contexts. Dunn (1968) and Blackman (1967) are among special educators calling for school relevant taxonomies of the psycho-educational characteristics of exceptional learners. Efforts in this direction have previously been made by Iscoe (1962) and Quay (1968).

Iscoe has proposed a functional classification based on four domains: visibility, locomotion, communication, and psychological acceptance. The domain of visibility (V) concerns itself with "How apparent on immediate or limited contact is the child's exceptionality?" Our exceptional learners differ markedly with respect to their characteristics. The blind or crippled child is easier to recognize on initial contact than is the disturbed, gifted, or disadvantaged child. Locomotion (L) relates to the ease with which the child can move about the environment without assistance. Communication (C) refers to verbal fluency. Psychological acceptance (P) is concerned with the child's relationship with his peers and the judgments they make about his problem. Iscoe suggests rating the exceptional child on a five-point scale in each domain, with the rating "1" used for a mild problem and the rating "5" for a very severe problem. Thus, the descriptive unit $\underset{1\ \ 3\ \ 2\ \ 4}{V\ L\ C\ P}$ presented in association with a mentally retarded child conveys the information that the child has no physical stigmata, has some difficulty in moving through the environment, exhibits a mild speech problem, and experiences considerable rejection by his peers. Iscoe conceives of his system as an aid in supplementing more traditional descriptive approaches and as a means of calling attention to critical areas of concern in the exceptional child's school experience.

Quay has developed a conceptual framework for assessment, grouping, and instruction that cuts across categorical boundaries and presents a model made up of variables related to the learning process that can be manipulated in the classroom. He has selected the parameters of input, response, and reinforcement. Within each parameter, he has defined certain functions that he further relates

MR

SD

VH

PH

to modalities. The exceptional learner is viewed in terms of his characteristics within the three parameters. The input parameter is defined by functions of acuity, orientation, perception, and storage. Response functions include dexterity, orientation, organization, and delay. Within the reinforcement parameter, Quay places the functions of acuity, orientation, effect, delay, amount, and ratio. Input functions relate to visual, auditory, and tactile modalities; response functions relate to motor and verbal modalities; and reinforcement functions relate to primary, social, and information modalities. Quay has illustrated the use of his conceptual model across exceptionalities. Thus, the mentally retarded child may exhibit input problems of orientation, perception, and storage in all sensory modalities, may have difficulty with all response functions in motor and verbal areas, and may prove a problem in terms of delivery of reinforcement in the learning situation because he has difficulty orienting toward certain reinforcers and tolerating periods of delay. These problems would be the critical concerns for a special educational program rather than the diagnostic designation of I.Q. 65 — educable mentally retarded. Quay argues for just such intervention-oriented assessment procedures. He conceives of a classroom technology emerging from his descriptive scheme in which specific remedial procedures are directly linked to diagnosis.

The Quay model relates to the developmental sequence or levels of learning competence model employed in this part of the text. The "attention" level of competence is clearly an "input" parameter. The "response" and "order" levels of competence are part of the "response" parameter. Our model, however, moves beyond these basic parameters associated with the fundamentals of the learning process to parameters concerned with content — exploratory, social, and mastery. We shall discuss all six levels of learning competence later in this chapter. Even though they do not contribute as formal and comprehensive a statement about the learning process proposed by Quay, the intent of the two models is similar — to describe and discuss the child in such a way that what you *say* directly relates to what you *do*.

LEVELS OF LEARNING COMPETENCE

At this point we will introduce the levels of learning competence to be used in our collective discussion in Part III. The definition for learning competence derives from the definition of learner presented in Part II. A learner is an individual in the process of acquiring knowledge and skill. Thus, learning competence is the child's knowledge and skill related to success in school.

Attention

The learning process is underway once the child notices "something." Basic to our flexibility discussion in Chapter 4 was the child making contact with the environment through his sensory modalities. Paying attention to relevant stimuli is essential for all children. Gagné (1970) has discussed attention as the most basic precondition within the area of readiness for learning. For purposes of definition in this text, attention is defined as the *level of competence associated with receiving and perceiving sensory stimuli (visual, auditory, and tactual) and with retention.*

Suppose Mrs. Jordon is attempting to teach a group of first grade children that includes exceptional learners from each of the nine categories. Although a hypothetical situation, this will serve to illustrate the similarities and differences existing among these various learners. Bruce is visually handicapped and Ann is hearing handicapped. Carl has a severe articulation problem, Tommy is emotionally disturbed, and Mary suffers from the crippling condition of cerebral palsy. Jack has a learning disability, Virgil is a mentally retarded child, Sally is intellectually gifted, and Wayne is from a disadvantaged background. Not all these children will be necessarily handicapped in each phase of Mrs. Jordon's lesson or in the school program in general. Therefore, we shall only refer to those children who will help us illustrate the level of competence under discussion.

Mrs. Jordon is holding up a word-picture card with bold, lower case letters "*b-e-d*" alongside a typical picture of a neatly made bed. At this moment our exceptional learners fall into various states of readiness to profit from such an introductory reading lesson. Their individual functioning levels will differentially reflect effects of capacity and previous experience.

Bruce, who is visually handicapped, will not see the card, and until Mrs. Jordon speaks he will for all practical purposes be absent from the lesson. At that time his listening attention will involve him. The reverse will be true for Ann. She will see the word-picture card through visual attention but will be eliminated when Mrs. Jordon speaks. Bruce's and Ann's attention problems are clearly and simply capacity based. Virgil, who is mentally retarded, may need more repetitions of the lesson before he retains it, and Jack, with a learning disability, may inaccurately perceive

ED

LD

MR

SD

VH

HH

SH

PH

G

the "*b*" and "*d*." They, too, may have capacity-based problems interfering with receiving, perceiving, and retaining sensory stimuli.

On the other hand, Tommy, our disturbed child, may not look
or listen because he is preoccupied with daydreaming. Wayne
may show little interest or understanding in paying attention or
retaining what is being presented because no such bed as the one
in the picture exists in his home. These two individuals have adequate hearing and vision and an intact central nervous system, but
fail to profit from the lesson because of problems associated with the
nature or lack of previous experience. As in so many of our previous
examples in the text, intellectually gifted Sally will be all eyes and
ears as she eagerly waits for Mrs. Jordon to get on with the lesson.

Even though Mrs. Jordon or any other teacher would not
attempt to conduct a beginning reading lesson for such diverse
types of learners with such a singular approach, this example has
gotten us underway in terms of looking at the first level of learning
competence and at how both capacity and experience operate as
determiners. Keeping in mind the interaction of both factors, which
ultimately determine functioning level, we could carry this example
on, discussing how environmental experience might compensate for
or aggravate the capacity-based problems of Bruce, Ann, Jack, and
Virgil.

Response-Order

Once the child notices a relevant something in a learning situation,
he is usually required to do something. That is, he must make a
response. In addition, most responding requires a sequence of acts.
The teacher asks the child to carry his chair from the center of the
room to his desk. The chair must be picked up, moved in the general direction of the desk, set down, and slid under it. Response
and order behavior are combined in our discussion here, although
they have been considered separately in earlier presentations of the
developmental sequence of educational goals. Flexibility was
largely concerned with responding.

Man's potential for responding in many different settings and
in a great variety of ways is one of his most distinguishing characteristics. Our definition of response-order behavior is the *level of
competence associated with initiating, maintaining, and organizing
motor and verbal behavior.* With respect to verbal behavior, we
are concerned with elicitation of speech rather than language competence which is included at the mastery level.

Because learning involves a continuous sequence of noticing

and doing, it is difficult to separate the attention and response-order levels. Gagné (1970), in fact, in a review of the developmental sequence of educational goals, considers these levels all part of what he designates attentional sets. He considers these sets a part of a much larger group of intellectual strategies such as "self-manage-ment behaviors" (Skinner, 1968). Even though it is true that atten-tion, response, and order behaviors are difficult to isolate in the analysis of most learning acts, we will consider them separately for purposes of organization and emphasis in our discussion of the sim-ilarities and differences of exceptional learners. Since the initial presentation of this framework as a "hierarchy" (Hewett, 1964b), however, the author has come to recognize the great degree of over-lap existing among all levels of the developmental sequence of edu-cational goals and the artificiality of separating out any one level. Thus, from "hierarchy," the framework has moved to "developmental sequence" (Hewett, 1968) and is further broadened to "levels of learning competence" in the present text. Such changes in the cur-rent "functioning level" of a special educator's thinking most surely reflect continuing interaction between capacity and experience!

Once the listening attention of Bruce, our visually handi-capped learner, was elicited ("How many letters are there in 'bed' — b-e-d?), he may give us the correct verbal answer. Motor responding, such as walking to the front of the class, will pose a more difficult problem. With Ann, our hearing handicapped child, lip reading skills or use of a hearing aid may make it possible for her to come to the front of the room and point out the letter "b" at the teacher's request, although problems with speech development may preclude adequate verbal responding. The capacity for motor and verbal responding may be present in both children, but visual and audi-tory capacity limitations plus experiential deficits will be deter-miners here.

If the task is understood, Virgil, the mentally retarded child, may have few problems in responding. Jack, with a learning dis-ability, may be awkward and poorly coordinated in his motor responding. Verbal responding may be a critical problem area for speech handicapped Carl on the basis of either capacity or experi-ence or a combination of both. Mary, who is afflicted with cerebral palsy, may be greatly limited by capacity to respond efficiently either on a motor or verbal level.

The problem of emotionally disturbed Tommy, stemming largely from the nature and range of previous experience, may cause him to "clam up" when asked to respond verbally, or to shy away from carrying out a set of directions motorically. Wayne, from a disadvantaged background, may be a ready responder but may prefer to do what he does and the way he does it in his own fashion. Verbal responding may be a problem for him in that he may have a limited speech repertoire or may experience difficulty in understanding spoken directions. This type of problem will receive more complete attention in our discussion of the mastery level, where language competence will be considered.

Exploratory

Competence at the attention and response-order levels enables the child to learn rapidly about his environment. The exploratory level, which we will now consider, is concerned with the *level of competence in relation to accurate and thorough knowledge of the physical properties of the environment.* This level is essentially one of content, in contrast to the process or skill levels of attention and response-order. It is closely linked to the dimension of flexibility, since knowledge of the physical environment is the logical result of interaction with it.

From an educational viewpoint, at the exploratory level we are concerned with the outcomes of sensory experience, perception, and retention, and motor and verbal responding. The attributes of objects and events in the environment that are discernible to the senses (color, texture, spatial, and temporal relationships), and discriminations associated with size and shape, and familiarity with the nature and identity of objects and events constitute the essential content at this level of competence.

Leaving Mrs. Jordon's reading lesson for a moment, let us speculate in a general fashion on the problems likely to exist among our group of exceptional learners at the exploratory level. Bruce will have restricted knowledge of the visual properties of objects and events in his environment, as will Ann in terms of auditory properties. Limitations due to capacity will be apparent here. Their significance in actual classroom learning will be elaborated on in Chapter 7. Bruce also will suffer from a limited range of experience due to his difficulty in moving freely through the environment. The motor response difficulties of physically handicapped Mary also will restrict her on a capacity basis in moving through, interacting with, and learning about the environment.

Jack's learning disability may prove to be more of a problem when it comes to spatial and temporal learning related to capacity. Tommy's preoccupation with fantasy or his reticence to move into unfamiliar situations may restrict his knowledge of objects and events in his environment due to an experiential deficit. Disadvantaged Wayne may have the most obvious experiential deficit of all if he lacks familiarity with the objects and events typically expected of children in the American public school because of his restricted early environment. Sally, on the other hand, may have sought out experiences in breadth and depth far beyond such expectations.

Social

As we stated in Chapter 4, in our discussion of the dimension of sociality, the exceptional child's experiences in the world of people are probably the most critical determiners of his overall functioning level. The problems of some exceptional learners derive directly from faulty social interaction. When the handicapped child is at home playing alone or interacting with his siblings or a few understanding neighborhood friends, he may get along fairly well; but when he enters the highly variable, interpersonal arena of the school and the classroom, he may encounter serious difficulties. The social level is defined as the *level of competence associated with meeting the social expectations of the school and gaining the approval and avoiding the disapproval of others.*

During Mrs. Jordon's reading lesson, we may see a wide range of reactions from the regular children toward our exceptional learners, and in turn the exceptional children themselves may vary in their reactions toward the teacher and others. Bruce, who is visually handicapped, may be the center of continuing interest as the children quickly and consistently seek to help him move about the room. Hearing handicapped Ann's difficulty with spoken language may make her somewhat of an isolate since the other children have difficulty communicating with her or understanding what she says. Mary's crippling condition may bring about a variety of reactions from the children, from curiosity and helpfulness to fear and avoidance. Carl may experience ridicule when called on to recite and his articulation problem becomes highly noticeable to the others. As a result, he may dread any such visibility and resist verbal participation in class lessons. Tommy may also be teased or rejected by the other children because of his babyish behavior and frequent episodes of crying when he is frightened or frustrated. Virgil may be hardly distinguishable from the other children since his retardation largely affects participation in formal academic lessons rather than in general classroom activities. Sally's

ED

MR

SD

VH

HH

SH

PH

G

ED

LD

MR

SD

VH

HH

G

brightness and alertness in class may make her a valued friend for many of the children and a particular source of satisfaction for Mrs. Jordon.

Mrs. Jordon may exhibit a variety of reactions to the presence of exceptional learners in her classroom. Our example, of course, is so atypical in terms of actual teaching situations that we cannot use it meaningfully to describe her behavior. But children who are socially isolated are often a real source of concern to regular classroom teachers, although children with behavior problems who are disruptive in the classroom may quickly generate disapproval. In addition, children who require excessive amounts of time because of their failure to understand directions, their slowness to grasp concepts and material presented, or their need for completely individualized lessons may not be readily accepted.

Mastery

From concern with sensory, perceptual, motor, and verbal skills, and exploratory and social experience, we turn to the mastery level of competence. Eventually, component skills of attention and response-order and fundamental knowledge and skill at the exploratory and social levels lead the child to involvement with the major enterprise of the American school — development of intellectual skills. The mastery level is *the level of competence associated with language facility and comprehension, with academic skills, and with subject matter.*

Mrs. Jordon will encounter unique problems teaching basic academic skills to Bruce and will have to rely on compensatory approaches such as braille to introduce the actual reading process. Once such approaches are mastered by Bruce, his reading achievement may equal that of sighted children. Ann's hearing handicap can greatly influence her reading comprehension and, despite good intelligence, will necessitate a special approach to ensure her understanding of the language concepts presented. Here, capacity-based problems outside the intellectual realm will interfere with academic learning in reading and in other areas. We may find Virgil's retardation and Jack's learning disability also interfering on a capacity basis in terms of academic learning. Tommy's emotional problems described in relation to the more basic levels of learning competence will cumulatively affect his school achievement, as will Wayne's disadvantaged background. Experience will loom as the major determiner here. Of course, Sally will probably excel if she is given stimulating materials and the proper motivation.

Motivation has special relevance to the learning and behavior problems of exceptional learners. Indeed, it is one of the most overworked words used by both regular or special educators to describe the problems they face getting children to pay attention, respond, follow directions, improve their social relationships, and acquire knowledge and skill:

"Johnny is poorly motivated and could learn if he tried."

"I wish I could increase Kathy's motivation to read at home."

"Darryl's poor grades reflect his negative motivation toward school and not his real ability."

"Frank could be the real leader of the class, but he simply isn't motivated to assume responsibility or cooperate."

What exactly is being talked about in these examples? The children being discussed seem to lack a force or direction in their behavior which, if present, would greatly improve their functioning level. Human motivation has long been studied by psychologists, who have pondered the variety of motives that may exist, how they originate and develop, and how they determine behavior.

For our purposes, we are interested in exceptional learners' motivation to pay attention, respond, follow directions, explore their environment, improve social relationships, and master academic skills and subject matter. When the child does not readily engage in one or more of these behaviors, we say he is "poorly motivated," but what we really mean is that the conditions of learning have not been arranged properly so that his active participation, involvement, and mastery all occur. Therefore, the real burden of responsibility for the existence of motivation among children in a learning situation rests with the environment; instead of worrying about the internal readiness of the child to learn, we should worry more about the external readiness of the environment to teach. Such an approach in relation to motivation has been taken by Skinner (1968).

ENVIRONMENTAL DETERMINERS

As stated earlier, curriculum, conditions, and consequences will be considered as we discuss special educational practices for increasing the exceptional child's learning competence. These are the educational, environmental determiners of motivation under the control of the teacher. The child who is pursuing a learning task, meeting the expectations associated with that task, and responding to the reinforcers provided may be said, operationally, to be a "motivated" learner.

Another term frequently encountered in descriptions of exceptional learners is "negative self-concept." We have used the term in Chapters 4 and 5 to describe the effects of frustration, failure, ridicule, and rejection often experienced by children who differ from the expected norms of the society. All of us depend on the reaction of others for the "picture" or "image" we actually come to hold of how worthwhile or valued we are. This dependency begins in early life. Our individual self-concept largely results from an accumulation of verbal and non-verbal reactions of others who state or imply that our status is good or bad, smart or stupid, adequate or inadequate, a joy or a disappointment, a winner or a loser. As they grow and mature, most of our exceptional learners do not fare too well in terms of such reactions. A faulty or negative self-concept constitutes a major unifying problem often common to them all. Such a problem relates to previous experience with parents and family members and later with the school and community. Edgerton (1967) has commented on the painful awareness of the real meaning of the word "stupid," among even severely retarded individuals, and on how they avoid reference to it for explaining their institutionalization or their problems of adaptation in the community.

What is the significance of such a problem in our present discussion of learning competence? We can readily see that the child who considers himself bad, stupid, inadequate, a disappointment, and a loser can be greatly affected in terms of attention and response-order skills and in acquiring knowledge and skill at the exploratory, social, and mastery levels. We shall treat this problem much the same as the one previously discussed in relation to motivation. That is, we shall consider the learning environment as being primarily responsible for improving the child's self-concept, whatever the negative determiners may have been in the past. The child who is successfully undertaking an educational task, meeting expectations associated with it, and who is susceptible to the reinforcing consequences provided in the learning situation may therefore be said to be both a motivated learner and one developing a more positive self-concept.

We will briefly discuss curriculum, conditions, and consequences. They will receive our attention as we discuss the characteristics of exceptional learners across levels of learning competence in the next three chapters.

Curriculum (Selection of Learning Tasks)

A learning task is any activity, lesson, or assignment that is directed toward increasing the child's level of learning competence. It is the "what," or the raw material of the learning situation. The selection of a suitable learning task for normal children may be made on a group or grade basis; for the exceptional learner, however, it often must be made on an individualized level. The content of curriculum tasks given both types of learners may be similar, with the most significant difference relative to the conditions under which such tasks are presented. These conditions will be discussed shortly. It also should be pointed out that learning tasks for exceptional children often reflect more concern for basic competence at the attention and response-order levels than is necessary for the normal learner.

By the time normal children enter school, they are usually reasonably accurate and consistent in attending to stimuli and are adequate motoric and verbal responders. In addition, they have learned to follow directions. The job of the school is to aid them in acquiring knowledge and skill at the exploratory, social, and mastery levels.

It is at the basic levels of learning competence, however, that many of our exceptional learners function poorly. Therefore, tasks selected will often emphasize component aspects of larger educational goals. Jack, our young man with a learning disability in Mrs. Jordon's class, may need help in establishing laterality, or a consistent left-to-right orientation, in reading before becoming an efficient beginning reader. Certain educational tasks focusing his attention on moving from left-to-right, which are not needed for most children, may have to be introduced. Virgil, who is mentally retarded, may need special help in understanding the directions associated with tasks presented in a beginning reading workbook, although they are quickly understood by the normal child. Once he understands the format and exactly what he is supposed to do, he will be more effective in working with the materials. Disadvantaged Wayne may profit from beginning word-picture matching exercises that reflect elements of his own environment. A neatly landscaped suburban home paired with the word "home" makes less sense than a two-story flat on a busy street front. Shy, withdrawn Tommy may be excluded from active participation in an oral reading lesson and only be expected to watch and listen until Mrs. Jordon considers him ready to engage actively in verbal

ED

LD

MR

SD

responding.   In the case of visually handicapped Bruce and hearing handicapped Ann, the content and the level of the task may not be as important as the mode of presentation.   For Bruce, tactual and auditory presentation will be necessary, and the visual mode will be emphasized for Ann.

The possibilities for varying educational tasks is almost endless. As we suggested earlier, variation in content may be less significant in the education of exceptional learners than variation in the conditions under which such content is presented.

Conditions (Selection and Arrangement of Expectations)

No matter what the nature of the educational task, certain conditions and expectations must be met before it can be said the child has successfully undertaken it.   Consider this assignment: "Beverly, come to the front of the room and read to the class the sentence I have just written on the chalkboard."   At first glance, this is a simple task; but on further analysis we are impressed with the conditions and expectations that are stated and implied in relation to it.

VH

HH

When.   The teacher has selected a given time for Beverly to be assigned this task.   It may be 9:00 A.M. or 2:00 P.M.   It may be following a fight Beverly just had on the playground during recess before coming into class.   It may be the day after Beverly stayed up until 3:00 A.M. watching a late night television movie.   Nevertheless, Beverly is expected to respond *now*, and this condition must be met if she is to be successful.

Where.   Beverly is expected to come to the front of the class — not remain at her desk or attempt the assignment privately in a study booth or with a small group of children seated around a work table.   At this moment, *where* she is to undertake the task is specifically defined.

How.   In addition, Beverly is expected to read out loud.   She is not expected to point to a particular word, push the button on an automated teaching device, or circle the correct answer with her pencil on a worksheet.   She is to walk to the front of the room, approach the chalkboard, and read orally what is written there.

How Much.   If Beverly successfully fulfilled the previous conditions associated with this task, there is still more to come.   She is expected to read the entire sentence, not just the first word or two. It is the sentence as a unit that constitutes the task, and Beverly must attempt it all to fulfill expectations.

How Long.   Next, Beverly will be expected to successfully complete the task within certain time limits.   She cannot stand in front of the chalkboard and remain mute for ten minutes.   In addition, she will only be given so many opportunities to attempt to read the sentence.   Following a certain number of repetitions, the teacher will probably ask Beverly to return to her seat, and another child will be assigned to take her place.   In that event, Beverly will not have been successful because she was unable to meet the condition of *how long*.

How Well.   Finally, Beverly will be expected to achieve a certain level of correctness in her reading.   Despite the meeting of all the conditions of when, where, how, how much, and how long, the ultimate determiner of success will be how well she performs. Stumbling on too many words, skipping over a word here and there, or totally mispronouncing a given word will all be weighed against her as the teacher makes the final judgment as to Beverly's competence in the assignment.

Importance of Conditions.   The world of school and learning is filled with expectations that must be met if the child is to be considered successful.   Perhaps nothing better distinguishes the approaches of regular and special education than the attention paid to individualizing such expectations.   We can briefly touch on the significance of some of these conditions for the exceptional learners in Mrs. Jordon's classroom.   The "how" condition will be of particular concern with respect to verbalization for hearing handicapped Ann and speech handicapped Carl.   Bruce, who is visually handicapped, will have more difficulty in motor responding, as will Mary due to cerebral palsy.   The condition of "how much" may be critical to consider for Virgil, who is mentally retarded, as well as of "how long" he is given to learn.   The "when" and "where" variables may be particularly important in the case of emotionally disturbed Tommy.   Depending on the content of the lesson, all the conditions may also be crucial to disadvantaged Wayne.   The "how well" condition will perhaps be the one single condition with the most common significance to all the children. We would expect gifted Sally to be relatively unaffected by these conditions, provided the selection of the educational task interested and challenged her.

The importance of conditions will come up repeatedly in the next three chapters as we describe approaches that are utilized in teaching exceptional learners. The special educator more than the regular educator must constantly exhibit flexibility in balancing environmentally determined demands with those determined by the child, his problems, and his functioning level of the moment. Thus, as stated earlier, the conditions imposed on the child in relation to a learning task may be more crucial determiners of his success or lack of it than is the content of the task itself.

A major issue relating to imposing conditions on children in the learning situation concerns *structure* and *permissiveness*. This issue has long been debated by both regular and special educators. A structured school program imposes demands and limits on the child, whereas a permissive program may allow the child considerable freedom in selecting and meeting such conditions on his own.

The teacher who adheres to a rigid classroom schedule with each activity to be done exactly when it is assigned, where it is assigned, in the manner prescribed, for as long as specified, and to exacting criteria of correctness with no exceptions, is a very structured teacher. Her permissive counterpart may allow the student to decide what to do when, where to do it, how much to do, how long to work, and may de-emphasize the importance of the quality of the work. Even though stereotypic representatives of either approach are probably rare, teachers of both normal and exceptional children do vary in terms of degree of structure and permissiveness reflected in their programs.

Consequences (Selection and Provision of Reinforcement)

Rewards and punishments, positive and negative reinforcement, constitute the final critical variables in the learning act that determine our success as teachers and the child's success as a learner. Once the child has attempted and undertaken the task, something usually happens. Perhaps the nature of the task itself has been rewarding because of the child's interest or sense of accomplishment, or unpleasant and frustrating because of its level of difficulty. Perhaps a grade is given, and this determines the positive or negative consequences. Or perhaps the child's teacher offers the consequences by means of a smile or frown, or comments such as "Good work!" or "This is not acceptable." Consequences may also be delivered by others in the class through looks of admiration or envy or devaluating giggles and ridiculing remarks.

Normal children do not cause the teacher to worry exces-

sively about the presence or absence of positive or negative consequences as determiners of her teaching effectiveness.   Exceptional
children, however, often present problems in this area.   Many of
them have experienced more than their share of negative consequences in school.   As a result, the special educator is particularly
concerned with selecting educational tasks that the child is ready
for and can be successful doing.   He tries to set reasonable expectations with respect to the task, and to guarantee, if possible, that
rewarding consequences will accompany the child's effort.   It is
rewarding consequences and their relation to learning success that
will primarily occupy our attention in this text; the effect of negative consequences will be discussed in Chapter 7.   At this point,
we will review seven types of positive consequences that may
relate to the success of our efforts with both normal and exceptional
learners.

Joy.   At the Mount Everest level of positive reinforcement in education is the joy of learning — truly intrinsic satisfaction from involvement in a task.   Although existing in a somewhat rarified
realm, it is the ultimate positive consequence that teachers would
like to be able to rely on with all children.   That it exists, no one
can deny.   But counting on its presence among the majority of
learners is somewhat naive.

Acquisition of Knowledge and Skill.   Coming down the slope from
the pinnacle of joy, we encounter the consequence of acquiring
knowledge and skill.   The child who finds himself able to read the
labels on the boxes in mother's pantry or the brand names in com-
mercials on television is being positively reinforced for his reading
efforts.   Additional examples are learning a new arithmetic skill
that can be put into practice in such real world activity as figuring
your favorite baseball player's batting average, or coming up with
the name of the state capital of Maine at just the right moment to
impress the family at the dinner table.   Of course, the latter examples also contain elements of gaining social approval, which we
will discuss shortly.

Knowledge of Results.   Somewhere around the same level on our
slope of reinforcement we find the positive consequence of knowing how you stand in relation to some criterion, such as grades.
Some children work hard to get a B rather than a C, 80 percent
correct rather than 50 percent, inclusion on the Dean's Honors List,
or a high standing in their class academic ranking.   The American
school has relied heavily on grading systems to reinforce children

both positively and negatively, yet the true value of such reliance has been increasingly questioned.

Social Approval.   Perhaps no other type of reinforcement dominates the classroom scene as much as social consequences.   In a society where the reaction of others toward us controls so much of our behavior, it is not surprising to find that teachers depend heavily on social control to manage their students and to provide an incentive to learn.

> I like the way row one is ready for dismissal and the way Michael has his hands folded.   Row two would be ready if Martin had his desk cleared.   If you continue talking to Ruth, Mary Ann, I'll have to ask you both to stay after class.

And so it goes.   In a study with several hundred upper elementary-age children (Dunn-Rankin, 1967), adult approval by the teacher was chosen as the most preferred positive consequence; it was more valued than peer approval, competition, independence, or consumables such as candy.

Multi-sensory Stimulation and Activity.   Recognition that children find looking, listening, touching, and moving enjoyable has been with us for a long time, yet, in general, it has not been systematically used in the classroom.   Such planned use of multi-sensory and activity rewards to strengthen and accelerate behaviors that normally occur at a low frequency derives from the Premack principle (Premack, 1959).   The teacher observes a given child for a period of time to determine his interests as expressed through behavior that occurs at a high frequency (e.g., model building, playing with a caged rabbit).   By setting up a plan whereby a certain amount of low frequency behavior, such as reading, must be accomplished before the child may engage in the more desired activity, considerable increase in the low frequency behavior can occur.   Use of the Premack principle is discussed in detail in Chapter 8.

Task Completion.   The child who completes a story writing assignment or a page of arithmetic problems may experience real satisfaction from the simple act of completion.   Task completion alone, however, is seldom enough in a regular classroom program to fulfill teacher expectations.   Stanley, who has written his version of the class story assignment on "My Pet," may sit beaming because he has completed the task until the teacher approaches, acknowledges that he has finished his story, then adds, *"You forgot to draw a margin on your paper, Stanley, and to indent the first word of your opening sentence. There are also six misspelled words in the story and your handwriting is not acceptable."* Allowing children to make errors may not be desirable, but it may be extremely important to reduce the condition of "how well" so that a measure of task completion reinforcement can occur with exceptional learners who otherwise seldom are candidates for higher level reinforcers. We will discuss task completion further in Chapter 7.

Tangible Rewards. We come at last to the bottom of our Mount Everest slope of reinforcement and enter the deep valley of M & M's! The use of candy, food, trinkets, and other tangible rewards to in-crease management and instructional effectiveness with various ex-ceptional learners has achieved an increased respectability during the 1960's. Although unnecessary to consider with most normal children (the Dunn-Rankin study cited earlier found regular class children ranked such tangible rewards as least appropriate and preferred), they often serve as ideal "launching fuel" for children who have come to know little joy in learning, acquired only limited knowledge and skill, received poor grades, experienced more social disapproval than approval in school, and who have found classrooms generally non-stimulating and unrewarding.

Despite the reluctance of some educators to enter into a realm considered by some to be one of compromise or bribery, studies have shown that so-called extrinsic rewards are usually only necessary on a temporary basis and that once the child begins to experience success in school, he becomes susceptible to other higher level reinforcers (Haring & Phillips, 1972). The logic behind their use is simple: the teacher who discovers that a child cannot add the numbers $2 + 2$ because he does not understand their numerical value or the concept of addition may quickly reduce the task to a concrete level and, by means of counters, demonstrate that two things added to two things equal four things. In a similar fashion, when it is discovered that a child is simply not rewarded by grades, praise, or more symbolic abstract reinforcers, the temporary use of concrete rewards is good educational sense. The child given the concrete arithmetic lesson will not have to carry around a large sack of counters to solve problems in addition for the rest of his life because he will soon learn to deal with numbers symbolically. The child given candy or tangible reinforcers will not become per-manently dependent on them but will come under the control of more traditional incentives in the classroom. As in our discussion of the selection and arrangement of conditions and expectations in learning, the flexible, open-minded extension of reinforcement prac-tices becomes one of the distinguishing characteristics of the special educator as compared with many regular class teachers.   In the three chapters to follow, we will present examples of how such flexibility has been used with success in managing and instructing exceptional learners.

This concludes our introduction to Part III of the text. As can be seen we are moving into the classroom and will devote Chapter 7 to consideration of exceptional learners at the attention and response-order levels of competence.   Chapter 8 will cover a similar discussion at the exploratory and social levels, and Chapter 9 presents the mastery level of competence.

CHAPTER 7

Attention and Response-
Order Levels

The classroom door opens and one by one our exceptional learners enter. The moment of truth is at hand. We must mobilize all our knowledge, competence, and experience and make every effort to see that these children receive the benefits of an education. What are they like as we survey the scene before us? How are they similar and how are they different in terms of management and instructional problems? What can we do to select curriculum, arrange conditions, and provide consequences that will increase our teaching effectiveness?

A variety of possible answers to these questions will be considered as we review the five levels of learning competence, beginning in this chapter with the attention and response-order levels.

Most of our exceptional learners have the capacity to receive and perceive sensory stimuli accurately and to respond motorically and verbally in an organized manner. Children with sensory and physical handicaps are the clear exceptions here. When our other learners are not paying attention or responding, we must look to the range and nature of their previous experience and to the curriculum, conditions, and consequences operating in the learning situation for an explanation. In this way, they are like many normal children, ready to be reached by incoming stimuli but handicapped because of a lack of interest or understanding. Problems in learning competence are by no means restricted to the exceptional learner. Most normal children are not as competent or efficient in learning as they could be. What separates them from our exceptional learners is that their problems are less serious in degree, less frequent in occurrence, and less apt to be patterned into clusters of learning problems.

In a like manner, we shall see that what is done to gain the exceptional learner's attention and to involve him in responding is often similar to what would be done with inattentive, non-responding, normal children. One surprise waiting for the reader who is being introduced to special education through this text is the plain, good, educational practice inherent in most of what special educators do. The author, in fact, has often defined special education as those aspects of good education that regular educators do not have to worry as much about or that can be overlooked in the typical classroom. There is no question that large numbers of so-called normal children would greatly profit from many of the practices that are being described in Part III of this text.

It may also come as a surprise that special educators do not use mutually exclusive approaches with children who fall into separate categories. We shall attempt to draw attention to the overlap that exists. One purpose of this text is to bring much of the current knowledge and practice in the field together for general, rather than categorical, consideration.

We now begin a review of major issues that relate to the attention and response-order levels. These issues will involve us in a look at the learning characteristics of many exceptional learners. Curriculum and conditions will constitute our major focus, with discussion of the role of consequences occupying a final section in the chapter.

ATTENTION: THE LEVEL OF COMPETENCE ASSOCIATED WITH RECEIVING AND PERCEIVING SENSORY STIMULI (VISUAL, AUDITORY, AND TACTUAL) AND WITH RETENTION

In attempting to gain the exceptional learner's attention, we are concerned with a number of questions relating to curriculum and conditions. These questions can be summarized as follows:

Curriculum
1. How important is it to emphasize attention in a special educational program?
2. What types of tasks are useful in improving visual and auditory perception?

Conditions
1. How can tasks best be presented to facilitate attention?
2. How is the condition of where the child works related to attention?
3. How can tasks best be presented to facilitate retention?

We shall now consider research findings and educational practices that relate to these questions.

Curriculum — How Important Is It to Emphasize Attention?

As stated in Chapter 6, getting the child to pay attention to relevant stimuli is the most basic precondition within the area of readiness for learning (Gagné, 1970). Thus it is a primary goal with all of our exceptional learners. With the disturbed child, however, the orientation of the teacher may affect the importance given this goal. Disturbed children have been focused on by special educators from two major points of view:

1. Concern with the inner-life of the child and understanding his psychological conflicts
2. Concern with his overt behavior and bringing it into line with standards required for learning

From the first point of view, the child may be allowed to pay attention to whatever he pleases whenever he pleases, for as long as he pleases. From the second approach, a careful plan may be devised to train eye contact and listening skills as a basis for more effective formal learning.

Berkowitz and Rothman (1966) state that concern with skill and discipline should give way to a new concept of teaching focused on the education of the emotions and complete acceptance of the child. The Summerhill program (Neill, 1960) for both disturbed and normal children includes a "child centered" classroom where pupils may sit on the floor or stand. They may also receive their instruction in or out of the classroom. In his description of the Orthogenic School at the University of Chicago, Bettelheim (1955) emphasizes a home-like atmosphere with much freedom for individual exploration and opportunities for academic learning if the child desires to pursue it. In these approaches, systematic concern with developing attentional skills appears secondary to allowing the child to get ready for learning on his own terms.

Approaches that see the disturbed child's problems as pri-

ED

marily emanating from his lack of adaptive behavior strive to create learning environments in which these behaviors may be
acquired. One such learning environment, the engineered classroom, has been developed by the author in the Santa Monica,
California, schools (Hewett, 1968; Hewett, Taylor, & Artuso,
1968). This classroom is designed to aid the child on all six levels
of learning competence. The room consists of four major centers,
each devoted to one or more levels. A floorplan of the engineered
classroom is presented in Figure 9.

The Mastery Center is the academic learning area and consists of individual student work tables and two study booths. The
Communication Center provides activities for two or more children
and emphasizes cooperative behavior and the social level of competence. The Exploratory Center features arts and crafts activities
and opportunities for engaging in simple science experiments.
Here, the child is involved in interesting, multi-sensory tasks de-

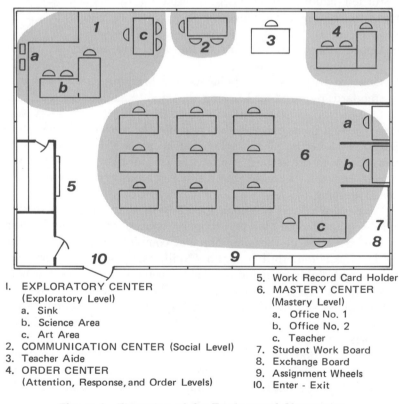

I. EXPLORATORY CENTER
    (Exploratory Level)
    a. Sink
    b. Science Area
    c. Art Area
2. COMMUNICATION CENTER (Social Level)
3. Teacher Aide
4. ORDER CENTER
    (Attention, Response, and Order Levels)

5. Work Record Card Holder
6. MASTERY CENTER
    (Mastery Level)
    a. Office No. 1
    b. Office No. 2
    c. Teacher
7. Student Work Board
8. Exchange Board
9. Assignment Wheels
10. Enter - Exit

Figure 9: Floorplan of the Engineered Classroom

signed to increase competence at the exploratory level. The Order Center is particularly relevant to our discussion here; it contains exercises, puzzles, and intriguing construction materials to promote paying attention, responding, and direction following. We shall discuss the engineered classroom design periodically throughout Part III as it relates to each level of learning competence.

Effective use has been made of operant conditioning techniques for teaching pre-academic skills, such as visual and auditory attention to autistic children (Hewett, 1964a, 1965; Lovaas, Berberich, Perloff, & Schaeffer, 1966). Autistic children often manifest extreme attention problems, seemingly looking through, over, under, or around, rather than at stimuli presented to them. The operant conditioning paradigm selects a discrete target behavior (e.g., eye contact between child and teacher), either waits for the child spontaneously to emit the behavior, or cues him ("Look at me"), sets an expectation or contingency that must be met (direct eye contact for a specified period of time), and provides a positive reinforcement (e.g., food, verbal praise) when such an expectation is met. The child's behavior is then shaped toward more complex levels by gradually increasing expectations. The framework of curriculum, conditions, and consequences chosen for discussion in this part of the text is based on the operant conditioning paradigm.

Curriculum — What Types of Tasks Are Useful in Improving Visual and Auditory Perception?

Learning disability children often have difficulty at the attention level of competence because of perceptual problems; disorders of attention (e.g., short attention span and distractibility) also rank high on lists of identifying characteristics. A number of special educators have designed specific materials to increase the child's visual perceptual competence. Getman and Kane (1968) have developed training procedures to improve eye-movement patterns, eye-teaming skills, eye-hand coordination, and visual-form perception. A visual-perceptual program intended to be both corrective and preventive has been devised by Frostig and Horne (1964). The Frostig Developmental Test of Visual Perception and the Program Work Sheets focus on five visual perceptual abilities: perception of position in space, perception of spatial relationships, perceptual constancy, visual-motor coordination, and figure-ground perception. The Fitzhugh Plus Program (Fitzhugh & Fitzhugh, 1966) consists of a series of eight workbooks similar in intent to the Frostig program. Spatial organization is one major aspect of the program. Exercises attempt to improve the child's ability to perceive, comprehend, and manipulate shapes or objects in space and time.

The listening attention of the visually handicapped child is a crucial competence at this level. This applies to both the partially seeing and the blind. As these children progress through school, reading requirements constantly increase while the availability of materials in large type and braille decreases. Thus, because these individuals will begin to depend on recordings or on the help of sighted readers, it is essential that they derive maximum benefit from listening. Bishop (1971) has described a variety of activities that have been found useful in increasing the visually handicapped learner's listening skills. From simple sound identification games, the child may be engaged in discriminating between tone and volume, reproducing sounds through imitation, and learning about the similarities between sounds through rhyming. In an effort to lengthen attention span, the teacher may repeat a sentence twice with a word or two changed during the second presentation. The child is asked to listen carefully and to note the exact changes that have been made in the second sentence.

Harley (1973) reports that development of listening skills among school-age, visually handicapped children and youth has gained increased recognition because of the superior learning efficiency of listening over large type and braille reading material. Nolan (1959) found partially seeing children in grades four to twelve read at a rate of approximately 100 words per minute with large print, less than half the rate of their seeing peers. Talking books and other recorded material for the visually handicapped can produce listening speeds of about 180 to 200 words per minute. A comparison of learning through listening with learning through braille, reading with children and adolescents who could read braille in grades six to ten, was made by Nolan (1963). The results revealed that information could be learned through listening in one-third of the braille reading time without loss of comprehension. Morris (1966) found that learning through listening appeared some 155 to 360 percent more efficient than learning through reading in braille or large type.

According to Harley (1973), conventional listening materials with their approximate speed of 175 words a minute still convey information at a relatively slow rate when compared to the speed of reading attained by high school and college students. As a result, accelerated or compressed speech approaches have been increasingly utilized to speed up the rate of presentation. Such approaches may include speaking rapidly, increasing the playback speed of tape or record, or sampling segments of the speech signal.

Speaking rapidly is only useful to a limited degree since a speaker cannot increase his rate of articulation beyond a moderate level. Increasing playback speed results in a higher pitch, which affects intelligibility at high speeds. By means of a speech compressor, pitch can be controlled within the original range. Such a device selectively shortens pauses and vowel sounds while retaining consonant sounds in their true duration. In studying the effectiveness of accelerated speech approaches, listener comprehension has been found to be dependent on the difficulty of the selection and the vocal characteristics of the reader. Harley concludes that as far as listener variables are concerned, many individual differences appear to exist with respect to the ability for comprehending accelerated speech and that more efficient training methods are needed to improve listener comprehension. However, overall evidence indicates that listening efficiency can be improved through training and that learning through listening is more efficient for visually handicapped children than learning from braille or enlarged type.

Auditory training for hard of hearing children attempts to develop systematically the child's discrimination of:

1. Gross sounds — including environmental noises
2. Rhythm patterns of speech and music
3. Easy speech sounds in words — the vowels
4. Difficult speech sounds in words — the consonants
5. Speech in noisy situations (Avery, 1967)

Since fully utilizing the child's residual hearing is critical in getting him to pay attention and learn, a hearing aid may be extremely important. The hearing handicapped child's acceptance of a hearing aid will be determined partly by the increased listening skill it fosters and partly by the enthusiasm and support that his family, teachers, and classmates show toward his wearing an aid.

In recognizing the verbal deficits of disadvantaged preschool children and their limited listening attention, Bereiter and Engelmann (1966) advocate the method of "verbal bombardment," in which teachers talk loudly and directly at the children continuously, whether the children talk back or not. All other activities are subordinate to verbalization.

Conditions — How Can Tasks Best Be Presented to Facilitate Attention?

When we present the exceptional learner with a task to which we hope he will pay attention, we are concerned with increasing the vividness or impact of the stimuli, emphasizing concrete aspects of the task (how much we give him to do), and the use of repetition.

The work of Strauss (Strauss & Lehtinen, 1947; Strauss & Kephart, 1955) and Cruickshank (1967) has focused on the adaptation of curriculum materials for exceptional learners, particularly those with learning disabilities. In terms of curriculum tasks, these authors emphasize increasing the stimulus value of the element to which the child's attention is to be directed. For example, a word recognition lesson will not be prepared with black crayon on white paper, but rather a bright color such as red will be used on colored paper. Perhaps a different color will be used for each letter written on the paper, and each letter may be of a different shape or size. As success is achieved in getting the child to attend to and learn under conditions presented in this manner, more traditional approaches are utilized.

Regarding the learning abilities of the retarded, Zeaman and House (1963) suggest an approach similar to that just described. They have investigated discrimination learning, since the ability to discriminate between two or more stimuli is basic to nearly every school learning task. A child, for example, has to learn to discriminate one letter from another before he can begin to read, and he must be able to tell one number from the next before he can learn to add. Discrimination learning has two components. First, the child must attend to the similarities or differences between two or more choices; and next, he must make the correct response, i.e., choose the right one. Zeaman and House have found that the mentally retarded tend to have considerable difficulty in the first area, attending; but that once they have learned to attend to relevant cues, they can acquire a response almost as well as normal children.

As a result, during the initial stages of a learning task, the teacher must increase the likelihood that the retarded child will attend to the relevant cues associated with each stimulus. In fostering development of this discrimination, a teacher should use a variety of different cue dimensions, such as color, form, size, and texture. Once correct discriminations are established, the teacher can begin to reduce emphasis on these cues. This easy-to-hard sequencing will ensure that the child moves gradually toward the final discrimination (such as between letters and words on a printed page) without undue failure or stress that might interfere with learning. The teacher also should try to establish a "set" in the retarded child to notice relevant cues and to attend to as many of the stimulus dimensions as possible before making a response. Zeaman and House also cite the work of Montessori (1912) as supporting the importance of increased emphasis on relevant details and avoiding emphasis on irrelevant cues.

The Fernald Method (Fernald, 1943) has likewise been used with children with a variety of learning difficulties. It is directly concerned with focusing the child's attention on the task. In the beginning stage, words to be learned are written in large letters in crayon on newsprint paper; then the child traces the letter with his index finger while saying the word aloud. Thus visual and auditory attention is heightened in relation to learning the word.

Zeaman and House also suggest novelty as an attention-getting aspect. They report that success with retarded children was increased dramatically when a candy unit was placed on top of a stimulus pattern to be learned. Another study done with very young, normal children suggests how important attention factors can become in a learning situation. Mehler and Bever (1967) used a task in which clay pellets were arranged in two rows with the shorter row containing the larger number of pellets. Children were asked to point to the row which had more pellets. In general, the children tended to pick the longer row even though it had fewer pellets. When the same task was presented using M & M candies instead of pellets, the children more often picked the correct row — the shorter one with more candies. Changing one aspect of the task, i.e., heightening the attention value or novelty of the objects, increased the probability of correct responding.

With disadvantaged children, Taba and Elkins (1966) emphasize the importance of operational and concrete approaches rather than verbal presentations to gain attention. In addition, materials and teaching methods clearly aligned with the psychological realities of the child's world are seen as most effective. These authors conclude that the essential learning processes of the disadvantaged do not differ from those of children in general, but that the particulars for generating these processes do.

Philip was a six-year-old blind boy with whom the author worked in the public school. He was bright and curious but presented extreme attention problems in the classroom. The resource teacher assigned to work with him in a braille readiness program became greatly frustrated as Philip rocked incessantly in his chair, made strange noises, and continuously asked irrelevant questions. In addition, when given a simple task such as tactually discriminating objects by size, shape, or texture, he merely played with the materials and failed to follow directions. The author observed Philip on several occasions and agreed to assist the teacher with the boy's serious attention problem. An electric horn

LD

MR

SD

VH

was procured that could be activated so that it sounded a constant "beep-beep" signal. This was introduced to Philip as the work horn and he was told that as long as the beeping continued he was to work on the task assigned to him. Following a ten-minute period during which he kept "on task," Philip was to be allowed a five-minute period to engage in his favorite playground activity — swinging on the swings. The immediate effect of the work horn was dramatic. Philip took the whole thing very seriously. His functioning on simple discrimination and matching tasks was impressive. Gradually, the length of assigned tasks was increased, as was the complexity of the tasks, and soon Philip was working for twenty minutes at a time with two short swing breaks each hour. The ingredients of this simple alerting program with Philip will be discussed in detail in Chapter 8 as we consider the Premack principle.

How much the child is given to do may be an important condition to consider for many of our exceptional learners. Cruickshank (1967a) points out the confusion that can ensue if the brain-injured child is given a single page with ten arithmetic problems on it. In the matrix of angles, problems, lines, and figures presented on the sheet, he can become lost. Cruickshank suggests placing one problem on a page and presenting ten successive pages to avoid such confusion. Such an approach may have direct relevance to the problems of other exceptional learners such as the disturbed, disadvantaged, and mentally retarded.

Beilin and Gotlein (1967) recommend smaller units of instruction for children with learning problems, including the disadvantaged. They refer to the problem of "overloading" the communication system between teacher and child and breaking it down with the condition of demanding "too much" at once.

In the engineered classroom design, the condition of "how long" is taken into consideration by limiting most of the work periods in the program to fifteen minutes. For example, longer arithmetic assignments that might normally be given to a child for a forty-five-minute period are presented as three fifteen-minute assignments. In addition, when it appears that the child is not attending or working on a given lesson, the teacher may implement an intervention such as tearing a worksheet of problems in half and asking the child to do only the remaining problems or reducing the length of a textbook assignment. Three problems of ten presented in a workbook might be circled and the child instructed to ignore the others and consider his assignment completed when the three problems were done.

In acknowledging the greater distractibility and more limited attention span of the lower as compared with the middle-class child, Beilin and Gotlein (1967) emphasize the importance of repetition and variety in presenting concepts. However, they caution against "ad nauseum redundance" because of the danger of boredom and frustration and suggest presenting multiple examples. They refer to the work of Gibson (1963), stating that the crucial determinant in learning is the "education of attention" and that this occurs when the child increasingly focuses on critically differentiating details and progressively eliminates concern for the irrelevant.

Conditions — How Is the Condition of "Where" the Child Works Related to Attention?

One major issue bearing on conditions related to attention and having applicability to several categories of exceptional learners has to do with controlling stimuli in the learning environment where we are attempting to teach. As we discussed in Chapter 1, the issue has an interesting historical basis when we refer to the methods of treatment advocated by Soranus in the second century with the emotionally disturbed:

> Maniacs must be placed in a moderately lighted room which is of moderate temperature and where tranquility is not disturbed by any noise. No paintings should adorn the walls. . . .

On a contemporary level, support for a non-stimulating environment with exceptional learners comes from the work of Strauss and Cruickshank on the brain injured child. Many of these children have recently been categorized as children with learning disabilities. Since the hyperactivity and distractibility common among them is also seen in emotionally disturbed, mentally retarded, and disadvantaged children, the role of a non-stimulating environment in relation to learning is of general interest in special education. According to Cruickshank (1967a), all visually and auditorily distracting stimuli in the classroom should be removed or reduced as much as possible. Walls, furniture, and woodwork should be painted the same color, bulletin boards removed, windows replaced with translucent glass, and cupboards equipped with solid wooden doors. Carpeting and acoustical treatment of ceilings is suggested. Even the pencil sharpener should be removed from the room because of the extraneous auditory stimuli it produces. The rationale for these adaptations is that a child who is unable to refrain from reacting to stimuli must have such stimuli removed so that he can

ED

LD

MR

SD

direct his energy toward those stimuli that are important in his learning and adjustment and through which he can achieve success. In addition, reduction of space is seen as important, and rooms smaller than the standardized classroom are specified. Within these rooms, small cubicles (each approximately 2¼ × 3¼ feet in size) with partitions between them are seen as useful for individual children since they further limit visual distraction.

Cruickshank, Bentzen, Ratzeberg, and Tannhauser (1961) conducted a study with hyperactive, distractible, brain injured children over a two-year period. Four small classes of children were included. Two of them rigidly adhered to an experimental condition of reduced stimulation and space as well as to a carefully planned routine. The teachers in the other classes had knowledge of the experimental condition but were free to maintain a more traditional program. At the end of the study, there were no significant differences between the experimental and control classrooms, but children in all four classes were reported as having significant gains in achievement, visual perception, and social behavior.

In their work with emotionally disturbed children, Haring and Phillips (1962) utilized aspects of the experimental condition in the previous study along with a behaviorally oriented approach that provided rewarding consequences for appropriate behavior and academic accomplishment. A comparison of children placed in such a classroom environment with others in a less structured learning environment favored the experimental group in terms of academic achievement.

The effect of cubicles on brain injured children's performance on a reaction time test was studied by Cruse (1962). Results indicated that children working under stimulus control conditions in a cubicle did not perform better than those working in cubicles with such extraneous stimuli as toys, moving balloons, and mirrors. The efficacy of assigning emotionally disturbed children to cubicles was investigated by Shores and Haubrick (1969), who found significant increases in attention span as a result of such assignments. Academic progress in reading, however, was not significantly related to working in a cubicle.

The engineered classroom mentioned earlier (Hewett, 1968), although initially devised for emotionally disturbed children, has been successful with children with learning disabilities, mentally retarded children, and the disadvantaged. One aspect of the design is reliance on a series of interventions that the teacher considers in an effort to keep the child paying attention and working in the classroom. The interventions would be utilized if a given child began to dawdle, looked away from his work, or became impatient or frustrated with an assignment. They will be discussed in detail in the "Consequences" section of Chapter 8.

In a study of six classes of disturbed and learning disability children (Hewett, Taylor, & Artuso, 1968), in which four classes maintained adherence to the engineered classroom design and two had knowledge of it but utilized more traditional procedures, the experimental classroom maintained significantly higher task attention among students than did the controls. Task attention was measured by observers sitting in the front of the classroom clocking the minutes a child's eyes were on the assigned task. Each child was sampled for five-minute periods on a rotating basis, and data were collected over a one-year school period. Where eye contact was not essential to the task (e.g., listening to a tape recorder), head attention or body posture were credited as task attention. Other aspects of the engineered classroom design that were undoubtedly reflected in the task-attention superiority of the experimental group will be discussed in more detail throughout this part of the text.

A study by Fassler (1969) examined the effect of reduced auditory input on the performance of cerebral palsied children with normal hearing acuity. Compared to a normal control group, the children with cerebral palsy demonstrated greater change in performance on a test of attention but no significant differences on other tasks. Fassler recommended that more experiments be conducted to determine if quieter classrooms would encourage greater attention and concentration in pupils with cerebral palsy.

Conditions — How Can Tasks Best Be Presented to Facilitate Retention?

A considerable amount of research related to retention has been done with mentally retarded children, since short-term memory problems are often found among them. Ellis (1963) has demonstrated that in situations in which information is presented and the child is asked to retain it over a short period of time (less than a minute), the retarded child does not retain the information as well as do normal children. Ellis reasons that the neural mechanisms of the retarded child are more apt to be deficient either through lack of experience or neuropathology or both. It thus takes more to activate the neural mechanisms of the retarded child so that a "trace" of the stimulus to be learned can be consolidated in the

ED

LD

MR

PH

child's memory system. This is the reason for the short-term memory deficit. The information was never really "learned" in the first place.

Even though such theoretical speculation seems, at first glance, of little significance to the teacher, it is a useful principle to keep in mind. The teacher must realize that the material should be presented in ways that make up for the retarded child's inferior trace. It should be remembered that it takes more to stimulate the child's neural mechanisms and thus activate a memory trace. For example, merely saying a vocabulary word to be learned may be enough for a normal child; but with the retarded child, the teacher may have to show him the printed word at the same time or show him a picture illustrating the word while saying it aloud and having him repeat it himself.

Suggestions for bolstering short-term memory (Smith, 1968) are reminiscent of the approaches already suggested for attention: control of irrelevant stimuli, heightening of relevant cues, and tasks that move from the simple to the complex. Also important is the notion of having the child verbally *label* the object to be remembered. The retarded child, in effect, needs to *overlearn* so that the memory trace can be firmly established. Merely repeating the word, however, is probably not sufficient since boredom can affect the retarded as well as the normal child. It is important to repeat the concept to be learned but to vary the presentation on each repetition, e.g., say the word, show him the picture illustrating the word, and then have him point to the picture while repeating the word again.

Summary

How can we go about aiding exceptional learners in paying attention and in improving perception and retention? In general, we have encountered few category-specific approaches. Those we have discussed relate more to capacity-based than to experiential problems. The blind and partially seeing will need particular help in profiting from listening; the hard of hearing will need to learn to discriminate general environmental and speech sounds. The deaf child will be a candidate for many of the visual training approaches suggested for other handicapped children. Learning disability children may need perceptual training, and a variety of special programs are available. Such children, along with the retarded, often profit from having the stimulus value of the relevant cues in the learning task increased and the focus on irrelevant cues decreased.   Inattentive, disturbed, and disadvantaged students also will profit from such heightening of cues as well as from a concrete rather than an abstract presentation of materials and novel, highly motivating approaches.   Aiding the retarded child in increasing short-term retention involves many of these considerations.   In addition, verbally labeling objects to be re-membered and overlearning material is important with retarded children.   Such approaches also will aid disturbed and disad-vantaged children who do not remember because they are not paying attention.

All exceptional learners can be greatly aided in sustaining attention if we consider "how much" they are assigned or "how long" they are expected to work.   Boredom, confusion, and frus-tration from "too much" to do for "too long" a time often results in distractibility and inattention.   The issue of stimulus control has been debated and studied, but we have no clear-cut evidence that any one group of exceptional learners is always better off when assigned to a classroom without bulletin boards and other distracting stimuli or placed in individual study booths.   No doubt some children in almost every category could profit from such an assignment at certain times, but it probably has to do more with individual children and the nature of the task assigned than with the learning characteristics of a category of exceptional learners *per se*.

Although special educators search long and hard for abso-lute answers to the questions that are raised in this section and that will be raised in the remaining portions of Part III, when all is said and done, what we really know is relative to time, place, task, and the individual child.   This is the underlying problem in translating basic research evidence into classroom practice.   We must ultimately rely on teacher experience, patience, understand-ing, dedication, and ingenuity for such translation with a given child at a given time.   But as we narrow the range of possibilities through research and study, we are, hopefully, aiding the teacher in increasing her efficiency.

ED

MR

SD

RESPONSE-ORDER: THE LEVEL OF COMPETENCE ASSOCIATED WITH INITIATING, MAINTAINING, AND ORGANIZING MOTOR AND VERBAL BEHAVIOR

At the response-order level, we are concerned with several major questions relating to curriculum and conditions.   They can be stated as follows:

Curriculum

1. How important is it to get the child actively participating in learning?
2. What types of tasks facilitate active participation and direction following?
3. What types of tasks will help the child improve motoric responding?
4. What types of tasks will help the child improve verbal responding?

Conditions

1. How can tasks best be presented to facilitate active participation?
2. How can tasks best be presented to facilitate direction-following and transfer of learning?

Let us review research evidence and educational practices that aim at answering these questions.

Curriculum — How Important Is It to Get the Child Actively Participating in Learning?

Smith (1968) stresses the importance of gaining the active response or participation of mentally retarded children if learning is to occur. He cites the advantages of such participation as:

1. Helping to focus the child's attention on the task at hand
2. Alerting the child to *his* importance in the teaching-learning process
3. Fostering greater efficiency in learning
4. Providing a more dramatic source of feedback
5. Serving as a more accurate means of diagnosing the extent of learning that has taken place as well as any unusual weaknesses

Such advantages definitely apply to our full range of exceptional learners and emphasize the importance of our making an active doer of any child we wish to teach.

According to Eisenberg (1963–1964), active participation is a critical factor to consider when attempting to teach the disadvantaged child. Having such children act out the part of storekeeper or customer will probably result in more understanding of a lesson on marketing than will be gained from listening to the teacher describe in detail "A Trip to the Grocery Store."

No matter how intense our efforts to present children with appropriate and interesting tasks, we have no indication of whether the instructional process is really underway until the child makes a move — either motorically or verbally.

Curriculum — What Types of Tasks Facilitate Active Participation and Direction Following?

In the initial stages of an educational program, non-responding, emotionally disturbed, and other problem learners may engage more readily in non-academic units such as creative arts (Hay, 1953; Cohen, 1965). Morse (1967) views "fun" as a subject of equal importance to emotionally disturbed children as arithmetic. The author has found that simple, factual, information worksheets asking for the names of several friends, several phone numbers often called, or favorite television performers or programs are effective "warm-up" assignments. However, the success of introducing academic assignments may not revolve around content as much as around the conditions and consequences associated with their presentation. We shall discuss these further in later sections.

Thematic content in reading material can greatly influence responding among children. With the emotionally disturbed, contrasting positions have been taken, depending on the special educator's point of view. Berkowitz and Rothman (1966) have suggested the use of projective language arts techniques in which the child freely expresses his feelings in story writing and talking games. Fairy tales and myths are recommended as reading material because they disguise obvious realistic situations that the child might find emotionally upsetting. On the other hand, Jacobson and Faegre (1959) caution against introducing subject matter that may stimulate conflictual and distracting fantasies; they describe a technique of "neutralization" in selecting reality-oriented curriculum materials for disturbed children. Newman (1959) views themes concerning happy family life, naughty pranks, and tender emotional themes as often too stimulating and conflictual for disturbed children.

In the author's experience, it is difficult to make generalizations regarding appropriate content for emotionally disturbed children that will readily engage them in responding and participating in learning and not prove upsetting or conflictual. For the most part, such children are drawn to topics and themes that are interesting and exciting to all children. Of course, exceptions

ED

exist; the author has worked with disturbed children who were preoccupied with bizarre subjects such as tatooing or medieval torture, or who demonstrated unusual interest in anatomy.   Others would work for hours on Civil War history, trigonometry, and physics to the exclusion of any other subject matter.   For such children, viewing ready responding as an end in itself and encouraging pursuit of narrow interests and activities is just poor teaching.   Each child has to be taken as an individual and helped as much as possible to become knowledgeable regarding the world around him.   An attempt to motivate a group of severely disturbed children in an institutional school by means of the dissection of a frog ended abruptly when several students became extremely upset; the dissection of a stillborn calf, however, by a teacher in a rural class for children with severe emotional problems was extremely successful in gaining the children's interest and participation. These examples illustrate the limitations in making generalizations regarding appropriate content for any child — exceptional or normal.

The Order Center in the engineered classroom has been successful in helping many children with problems at the response-order level.   This center is modeled after one originally developed by Birnbrauer, Bijou, Wolf, and Kidder (1965) for use with institutionalized retardates.   The following are a few of the activities that have been used over several years in Order Centers within engineered classrooms in the Santa Monica schools:

1. Direction boxes: a series of boxes filled with miniature toy animals, soldiers, cars, airplanes, and the like are available. Accompanying each box is a 6 × 16 inch card with three 4 × 4 inch squares on it.   Depending on the type of objects, the squares are labeled "cages," "forts," "lots," or "airports." A series of cards, graduated in difficulty, instruct the child to put so many objects in square 1, so many in square 2, and so many in square 3.   More difficult instructions include rearranging the number in each of the squares in order to arrive at a final number in each.   The instructions can be presented pictorially (for children who cannot read) or tape recorded.
2. Code deciphering: an alphabet-geometric symbol code is presented and coded messages are given to the child for deciphering. Actual words and messages can also be translated into code. The international Flag Code System or Morse Code also can be used.
3. Sorting: objects such as skeins of yarn and commercial paint chips are sorted on the basis of color.   Sorting on the basis of size, shape, and similarity also can be used with a variety

of materials. Various types and sizes of nuts and bolts can be presented mixed together, and the task assigned to separate them into common piles.

4. Matching: peg boards, different colored blocks, and simple wooden and metal construction kits can be utilized in such a fashion that the child is given a sample picture of a completed design or model and the materials to copy it.

Figure 10 presents several specific examples of order task assignments that can be illustrated on cards and kept at the Order Center.*

In addition to manipulative materials utilized in the Order Center, the engineered classroom uses direction-following worksheets for a "warm-up" activity at the beginning of the school day. Examples of some of these worksheets appear in Figure 11.

As can be seen, the child may be asked to complete numerical or alphabetical sequences, connect dots to match a sample pattern, locate differences between a numerical or alphabetical model and a similar example presented alongside, locate hidden geometric forms, and follow directions for color matching. These types of activities, often used in visual-perceptual training programs with learning disability children, also have been found to be useful as tasks for getting the child to pay attention, actively participate, and follow a specific routine.

Curriculum — What Types of Tasks Will Help the Child Improve Motoric Responding?

Response problems in the motoric area are of central concern when working with physically handicapped children. Interference in learning will be caused by slow, inaccurate movements of the hands and eyes in activities requiring coordinated motion. Physical difficulty in handwriting and unusual expenditures of energy in relation to routine tasks such as turning pages or changing body position can also be limiting factors. Teachers of children with motor handicaps work cooperatively with medical staff to assess the amounts and kinds of suitable physical activity to provide for their students. They must know the limitations necessary for the child's well-being. The objectives of the physical and occupational therapist will be adapted to the classroom environment, and

*The author is indebted to Frank D. Taylor of the Santa Monica Schools for permission to reproduce these order tasks (Figs. 10 and 11), which he developed.

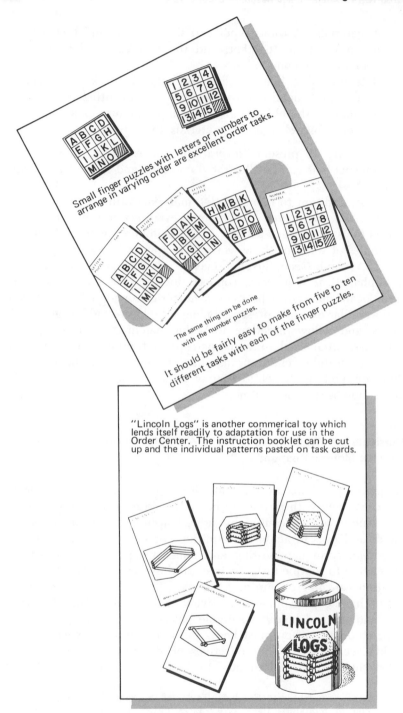

Figure 10: Manipulative Order Tasks

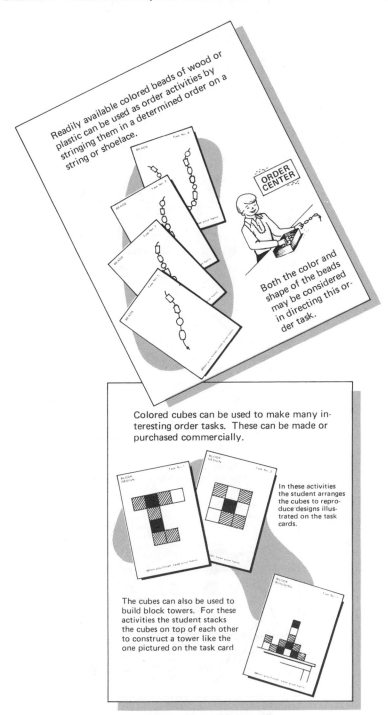

Figure 10 — Continued

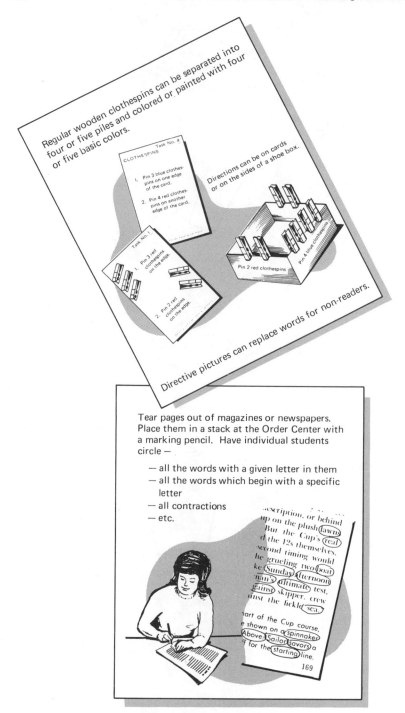

Regular wooden clothespins can be separated into four or five piles and colored or painted with four or five basic colors.

Task No. 4

CLOTHESPINS

1. Pin 3 blue clothes-
    pins on one edge
    of the card.

2. Pin 4 red clothes-
    pins on another
    edge of the card.

Directions can be on cards or on the sides of a shoe box.

Task No. 1

1. Pin 3 red
    clothespins
    on the edge.

2. Pin 2 red
    clothespins
    on the edge.

Pin 2 red clothespins

Pin 4 blue clothespins

Directive pictures can replace words for non-readers.

Tear pages out of magazines or newspapers. Place them in a stack at the Order Center with a marking pencil. Have individual students circle —

— all the words with a given letter in them
— all the words which begin with a specific letter
— all contractions
— etc.

Figure 10 — Continued

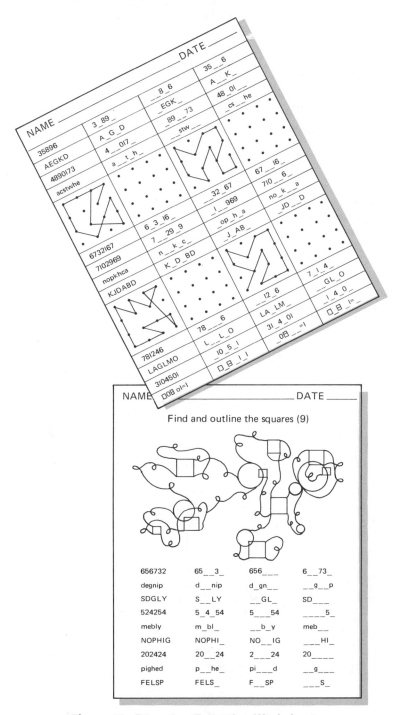

Figure 11: Direction-Following Worksheets

NAME_____ DATE_____

Which ones are different in each row? Circle them.

		100111	1001111	10011111
1001111	1001111			
		423423	423423	423433
423432	423423			
		noonili	nooneli	noonele
nooneli	nooneli			
		CDCDD	CDCDD	CCDCC
DCDCC	CDCDD			
		24568	24568	24569
24685	24568			

Place toothpicks on lines.

_____ _____
_____   _____   _____
_____   _____
_____   _____

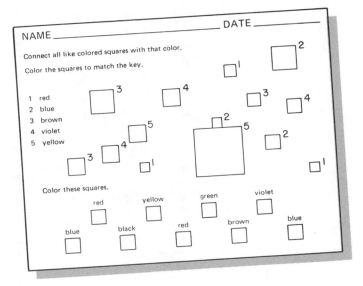

NAME_____ DATE_____

Connect all like colored squares with that color.

Color the squares to match the key.

1 red
2 blue
3 brown
4 violet
5 yellow

Color these squares.

Figure 11 — Continued

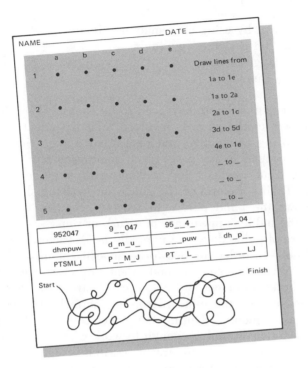

Figure 11 — Continued

the teacher will aid the child in functional use of his body in school activities.

Visually handicapped children, including both the partially seeing and the blind, tend to be deficient in physical skills and general physical coordination (Buell, 1950). This deficiency is not the direct result of visual impairment but rather of a variety of environmental influences. Not able to learn by imitation, greatly limited in terms of experiences during phases of creeping and crawling and later large muscle activities of normal childhood, the visually handicapped child often needs a specially designed program of physical education.

In Chapter 2, we briefly discussed the critical area of mobility in relation to the visually impaired. According to Scholl (1967), mobility refers to the individual's capacity for moving through the environment with relative ease and hence is directly related to the response-order level of competence in the motoric realm. There are four major possibilities for travel open to the visually handicapped person:

1. On his own by using his remaining vision
2. Reliance on a sighted guide
3. Use of a guide dog
4. Use of a cane

Partially seeing children may need to be counseled by the teacher with respect to the hazards involved in independent travel, such as fast moving automotive and pedestrian traffic. Since all visually handicapped individuals will at some time rely on a sighted guide, efficient methods for walking with a guide need to be taught. Taking the arm of the guide and walking slightly behind him allows the blind person to react to changes in the terrain such as the sudden appearance of a curb or step.

Use of guide dogs will normally be restricted to adolescents and adults. In order for this to be an efficient method of travel, the individual must have a good orientation or awareness of position in the environment so that he can instruct the dog where to go. The dog and the blind person are normally trained together for at least a month. During that time, certain individuals who are not emotionally stable enough to work with a dog may be discouraged from selecting this travel possibility.

The cane has long been a travel device for aiding the blind individual in moving through the environment. Since World War II, the method of use has changed from tapping to swinging the cane in an arc as wide as the body in front. Such a procedure involves the cane swinging to the right just before the right foot takes a step, then to the left before the left foot moves forward. Instruction in this technique can be given as early as the fourth grade and requires the services of a skilled instructor.

Myers and Hammill (1969) consider four disorders of motor activity often associated with learning disabilities: hyperactivity, hypoactivity, incoordination, and perseveration. They view these motor disorders as contributing to the severity of the learning disability but seldom as directly relating to problems in academic learning. We have discussed hyperactivity at some length in Parts II and III; it refers to the frequent restlessness, random activity, and erratic motor behavior often seen among children with learning disabilities. The hypoactive child is the reverse of the hyperactive individual; he is lethargic, inactive, and quiet. We considered the non-responding problems of emotionally disturbed children earlier; in the author's experience, passive, withholding children are often more difficult to successfully engage in learning than are their more active counterparts.   The problem with the hypoactive child is mobilizing and drawing him out, whereas with the hyperactive child, it is primarily one of controlling and directing.   Since responding is the raw material of the learning act from the learner's point of view, its presence, even though in the extreme, establishes an important starting point.

Myklebust (1954) has offered a comparison of motor activity characteristics among hearing impaired, learning disability, and emotionally disturbed children.   He describes the hearing impaired child as having heightened motor activity that is usually goal directed.   The learning disability child is often hyperactive, fidgety, and with little goal directedness in his behavior; the disturbed child may exhibit bizarre postures and movements and be preoccupied with stereotyped play with his fingers and other parts of his body.

Incoordination is the major problem for our concern at the response-order level; we shall shortly discuss several remedial approaches.   Perseveration, or persistent and seemingly involuntary continuation of a motor or verbal act, is another motor activity disorder sometimes associated with learning disabilities as well as with other exceptionalities.

Kephart (1971) has long been concerned with perceptual-motor development.   His approach emphasizes remedying underlying basic skills rather than attacking coordination problems on a direct basis.   Thus the child who cannot adequately draw a square is seen as a candidate for training in eye-hand coordination, laterality, directionality, ocular control, dexterity, temporal-spatial translation, and form perception rather than for repeated drill in square drawing.   The Perceptual Motor Rating Scale developed by Kephart aids in evaluating areas of sensori-motor dysfunction, and specific training procedures are suggested for increasing the child's response-order effectiveness:

1. Chalkboard training
2. Sensori-motor training
3. Training ocular control

Chalkboard training involves the child in visual-motor activities that move from random scribbling on a chalkboard to exercises that teach left-right orientation, form reproduction first on a direct copying basis and later from memory, and variations of such exercises with respect to size, speed, and direction.

Large muscle activity is central to Kephart's sensori-motor

LD

training.   Teaching the child bilateral, unilateral, and cross-lateral movements through activities such as angels-in-the-snow is included, as are stunts and games like duck walk, rabbit hop, crab walk, measuring worm, and elephant walk.   Bilateral and unilateral rhythmical activities are also part of the training.   In addition, the trampoline and walking and balance boards are used in this training phase.

Ocular control training moves through several stages.   At stage one, the child is taught to follow an object such as a small pen-shaped flashlight with his eyes as it is moved first laterally and then vertically, diagonally, and in a rotary fashion.   The intensity of the visual stimulus is increased in stage two.   During stage three, the child follows the penlight through the same exercises using his finger as well as his eyes.   Stage four involves the child actually placing his finger on the light from the penlight so that kinesthetic and tactile stimulation is increased.   At stage five, various sizes of balls are utilized, with the teacher holding one side of the ball, the child the other.   As the teacher moves the ball in various patterns, the child's hands are carried along, and he is instructed to keep the ball in sight as it is moved.   Kephart's procedures have wide application among exceptional learners since it is not the classification or label that is crucial but the developmental level of the child in sensory-perceptual-motor areas.

The work of Barsch (1965) has produced an experimental curriculum, designated "movigenics," which aims at studying and developing the movement patterns related to learning efficiency. The curriculum contains twelve dimensions; it includes specific exercises for increasing muscular strength, balance, and spatial awareness and for improving visual, auditory, and tactual functioning.   The work of Kephart and Barsch does not separate the attention and response-order levels; it includes combined emphasis on perceptual-motor learning.   Verbal responding receives secondary emphasis.

Curriculum — What Types of Tasks Will Help the Child Improve Verbal Responding?

Myklebust (1954, 1955, 1960) has written about the speech and language problems of children with learning disabilities based on his extensive study of diagnosis and remediation of children who are hearing handicapped and/or neurologically impaired.   Speech and language are closely associated but not synonymous.   Speech constitutes the observable verbal response.   It reflects the symbolic behavior of language, which is defined by Myklebust as the ability to abstract, to attach meaning to words, and to use these words as symbols for thought and for the expression of ideas, objects, and feelings. Man's language system is conceived within a framework of a developmental hierarchy consisting of five related levels of verbal behavior that move from experience to acquisition of verbal, symbolic behavior. The first level involves acquisition of meaning, of inner language. On the second level, auditory symbols and experience are associated, spoken words are comprehended, and auditory receptive language develops. Next, auditory expressive language appears as evidenced in speech. The fourth level involves comprehension of printed words and reading as visual receptive language develops and on level five the ability to express printed words in writing is established.

Myklebust attempts to establish a clear link between brain dysfunction and learning disabilities. He refers to problems in this area as "psychoneurological learning disabilities." Johnson and Myklebust (1967) conceived of five general groups of such disorders: disorders of auditory language, disorders of reading, disorders of written language, disorders of arithmetic, and non-verbal disorders of learning. These disorders reflect a failure to master one or more levels on the developmental hierarchy of language development.

In the remediation of auditory language disorders, the child may need training in generalized, receptive, or expressive areas. Generalized auditory language deficits are approached by training the child to understand the meaning of environmental sounds and of speech. Sound localization, discrimination, and auditory memory exercises can include identifying the position of a whistle blown in the room while blindfolded, matching noisemaking toys in terms of the type of sound each makes, and imitating hand clapping patterns.

Auditory receptive language disorders relate to problems in understanding speech rather than in comprehending non-verbal-social sounds. Training involves meaningful association of spoken words and experience, and the gradual building of an understanding vocabulary of the parts of speech beginning with sounds, then nouns, verbs, adjectives, and prepositions.

The child with an auditory expressive language disorder understands speech but has difficulty using spoken words. Three common forms of such disorders are: reauditorization, auditory-motor integration, and syntax. Reauditorization problems center on difficulty in recalling words or finding the correct word; training can involve sentence completion exercises or word-associations such as bread and butter. Auditory-motor integration problems reflect the inability to say words; the goal of training is to develop voluntary repetition and meaningful oral communication. Problems in syntax are experienced by children who have difficulty in formulating sentences. Exercises with scrambled sentences requiring correct sequencing and incomplete sentences calling for appropriate endings may be used. Additional discussion of problems of language usage and understanding in relation to the disadvantaged child will be presented in Chapter 9 on the mastery level of competence.

LD

An instrument that aims at assessing an individual's competence in receptive, associative, and expressive aspects of the communication process is the Illinois Test of Psycholinguistic Abilities (ITPA) (Kirk, McCarthy, & Kirk, 1968). With respect to the response-order level of our discussion, two subtests of this instrument, verbal expression and manual expression, are of interest. Verbal expression involves the ability to express concepts verbally; manual expression is the ability to express ideas motorically. In the area of verbal expression, the child may lack basic vocal skills, have an inadequate vocabulary, not be able to express ideas spontaneously, lack automatic grammatic skills, or lack adequate interpersonal communication. Manual expression difficulties may reflect a lack of prerequisite perceptual-motor skills, a lack of ideas leading to motor expression, or an inability in making ideas operational. Bateman (1963) found that visually handicapped children do not differ significantly from normals on auditory-vocal subtests of the ITPA but that they did significantly less well on visual subtests and those associated with motor expression. Kirk and Kirk (1971) have prepared a set of specific guidelines to remedy problems in these areas covered by the ITPA. In general, many of these are similar to some of the techniques suggested for improving the child's verbal and motoric functioning by authors previously discussed.

VH

SH

Verbal responding is the central problem area with speech handicapped children. Ainsworth (1967) has discussed the role of the classroom teacher in relation to this area. First, a gross analysis of the type of speech problem should be attempted. Most classroom teachers can identify disorders of articulation, voice, stuttering, or developmental delay. A second step involves a detailed analysis of the disorder. With respect to articulation, it is important to find out exactly what sounds are in error. Evaluation of voice problems often requires more training on the part of the teacher, as the variables of loudness, pitch, rate, and quality must all be considered. The child who stutters in class is best helped by the teacher if the situations causing the most trouble are identified and avoided.

In an effort to help speech handicapped children, the teacher will usually go beyond efforts in the classroom itself and refer the child to specialists qualified to conduct speech and hearing examinations and provide therapy if necessary. However, Ainsworth describes a number of corrective procedures that many teachers can implement on their own. With articulation problems, the first step is to teach the child to hear differences. This is done by focusing his attention on the difference between the word as he is pronouncing it and as it is actually spoken correctly. He must learn where the problem in articulation is located, whether it occurs due to a substitution of an incorrect letter sound or an omission of a correct sound. The second step involves teaching him to make the correct sounds. This can be done by having him imitate the teacher. General instructions such as asking him to open or close his mouth, or raise his tongue may be added; elaborate attempts at instructing him in methods to produce letter sounds are unwise for the teacher, however, and require the assistance of a skilled speech therapist who is thoroughly familiar with the study of phonetics and the limitations of such methods.

Next, an effort is made to teach the child to use the correct sound. Once he is able to produce the sound, practice is needed in using it in words in isolation and in phrases. Such words and phrases should be meaningful and chosen from the child's own vocabulary. When he is able to use correct sounds with a high degree of consistency and to check his own errors, he is ready to go on to the last stage, which involves carrying over the correct sound into conversational speech. Beginning with controlled conversation as provided in discussion of a picture, practice is extended into general conversation. Very specific assignments should be given the child. He may be instructed to concentrate on using new sounds for a short time in specific situations, such as in an oral reading lesson or during mealtimes. Gradually, attempts are made to get the child to systematically transfer these assignments into everyday conversation.

What can the classroom teacher do to aid the child who stutters? Since stuttering is related to the child's attitudes and emotions about speech and speaking as well as to his feelings about himself and his relationship to others, it is often a complex problem. A few general suggestions, however, may enable the teacher to create a less conflictual situation in the classroom and lessen the probability that the child will stutter. First, there are certain things to be avoided. Offering instructions designed to stop stutter-

SH

ing such as "Talk slowly" or "Think about what you want to say" will not help most children who stutter. Also, providing praise for fluency may constitute an implied criticism of stuttering and reinforce the child's notion that stuttering is wrong or bad. Five positive things that the classroom teacher can do are:

1. Give the child the opportunity to enjoy oral communication
2. Do not ignore the child's stuttering but emotionally help him recognize that the teacher accepts his speech problem
3. Help him understand that even though many individual differences in speech exist, they are not necessarily a cause for rejection
4. Find out when or where he happens to be able to talk most easily and provide him opportunities to speak at these times and in these places
5. Make every effort to improve his general emotional adjustment in the classroom

Adequate verbal responding in the classroom is extremely important for all children — normal and exceptional. Problems in speech are found across all our categories, and aiding the child in improving his verbal functioning will be a basic concern for both regular and special education. Egland (1970) has authored a text specifically aimed at providing classroom teachers with a guide for dealing with speech and language problems.

Speech training constitutes one of the most important areas of specialized curriculum for the child who is deaf. Kirk (1972) has summarized five approaches aimed at aiding the deaf child in speech development. The first is speech training through vibration and the sense of touch. With eyes closed, the child feels speech vibration by placing his hands on the teacher's face and he begins to discriminate between sounds, words, and sentences. He feels the teacher's voice with his hand in front of her mouth as she speaks consonants such as b and p. With his hands on his own cheek, nose, or throat he tries to reproduce the same vibration and gradually to pronounce sounds and words correctly. Another approach involves the use of visual aids. The child learns to read other people's speech; by watching the teacher's face and his own in a mirror, he attempts to reproduce what he sees as well as what he feels. Speechreading is related to this approach. It is usually emphasized from an early age with deaf children.

Kinesthetic or proprioceptive cues are involved in a third approach. The child attempts to control his speech by sensing the muscular movements in his mouth, jaw, tongue, lips, and larynx.

Internally felt cues thus become an aid in controlling articulation and voice.   Auditory stimulation is an approach directed toward taking advantage of the child's residual hearing.   Powerful hearing aids can help the child learn rhythm patterns and discriminate differences in sounds.   A final approach utilizes visible speech developed on an electronic device called an oscilloscope.   This device has a small screen across which wave-like patterns of light move.   These patterns correspond to various sound vibrations made into a microphone and monitor the child's speech utterances.

Brieland (1950) has studied the speech characteristics of the blind which have been reported in the literature.   Although the blind tend to show less vocal variety, tend to talk louder than the sighted, speak at a slower rate, use gestures and bodily actions less effectively, and use less lip movement in the articulation of sounds, they do not, in general, exhibit serious problems in verbal responding.

Conditions — How Can Tasks Best Be Presented to Facilitate Active Participation?

At the response-order level we are particularly concerned with getting the child to "do" something.   As mentioned earlier, doing and learning cannot be separated.   Our discussion here will definitely bear a relationship to the acquisition of knowledge and skill concerns of the exploratory and mastery levels.   It is important, however, to emphasize strategies for initiating participation since all too often the criterion for success with a given task from the teacher's point of view is, "Did he learn what he was supposed to?" rather than, "I am very pleased he made an effort to try." The latter is the name of the game with many of our exceptional learners, particularly in the early stages of our work with them.

In this section, we will find that guaranteeing success is perhaps the unifying concept that cuts across all our categories with respect to getting children involved in learning.   Indeed, it applies equally well to children without special learning and behavior problems who do not readily respond or follow directions.   It is a beautiful concept, but although admired in principle, it may be overlooked or even resisted in practice.

The author is reminded of two severely disturbed boys with whom he worked who were successfully launched into learning by a program designed to guarantee success.   Louis was institutionalized in the UCLA Neuropsychiatric Institute (NPI) suffering from a condition officially labeled "catatonic schizophrenic stupor with severe psychomotor retardation." The boy was totally immobilized, would not respond at all, would not walk, talk, eat, or care for himself. He was eleven years old, had been a good student in school, and had a superior I.Q. Louis was carried into the NPI School and presented to the author and a classroom teacher as a new student. The official label was overwhelming. What could mere educators do to contribute to the remedying of such a condition? In recounting this event to others, the author has facetiously reported that both he and the teacher immediately went to the school's special education curriculum library and looked on the shelf under the section "Catatonic Schizophrenic Stupor with Severe Psychomotor Retardation." But someone had checked out the curriculum guide before us! What to do?

Seriously, the educational problem was clear cut. We had to get Louis *doing something*. He was perhaps the most classic example of a severe response-order problem ever to be faced by a teacher. The program designed for Louis has been described in detail elsewhere (Hewett, 1968) and only the basic elements will be described here. We found out that Louis was interested in prehistoric animals, namely dinosaurs. A series of colored slides of such creatures were obtained along with a slide projector, a frosted glass screen, and a box with a large lever on it that turned the projector on and off. Louis was seated at a table, the projector set up at the opposite end, and the frosted glass screen in the middle. The lever box was put on Louis' lap and his right hand placed on the lever. After a few trials during which the author moved the lever to activate the projector and demonstrated to Louis how everything worked, the boy was told he could turn the projector on and off himself by slight movements of the lever. If he did, a series of different slides would be inserted in the projector for him to view. There was a considerable delay when control of the lever was turned over to Louis, but he eventually responded and became an active participant once again in his environment.

It was a victorious moment for both the author and the teacher, but a regular elementary classroom teacher who happened to be visiting the NPI School had some reservations.

"I understand Louis is eleven years old and would normally be in a sixth grade class," she said. "I don't know of any sixth grade science curriculum that includes the study of dinosaurs."

Louis had made it up the learning ladder to the response-order level because of the minimal expectations and guarantee of success built into the initial program. This particular teacher appeared to find it most difficult to settle for such a first step.

Malcolm was a nine-year-old severely disturbed boy who

had been out of public school since the early third grade. His basic problem was that he would not stay on the school grounds. He ran away constantly and even when taken into the classroom and supervised, he refused to do anything but sit and daydream. The author assisted the teacher of an engineered class for emotionally disturbed children in setting up a response-order program for him. Initially, the goal was to get him on the school playground before the morning bell and playing on the swings in an apparatus area next to the classroom door. If he was in this area when the bell rang, the teacher called him to the door and awarded him ten check marks on a Work Record Card identical to that carried by all of the members of the class during the day. (The specifics of the check mark system will be presented within the "Consequences" section of this chapter.) When a Work Record Card is filled with check marks, it can be exchanged for food, candy, simple trinkets, or a period of free-choice activity time.

After receiving his first check marks, Malcolm returned to playing on the swings for another fifteen minutes. At the end of this time, the teacher again called him to the door, awarded him check marks, and invited him into the classroom for a fifteen-minute order assignment. As described earlier, the engineered classroom has a special area called the Order Center specifically devoted to getting children paying attention, responding, and following directions. Jigsaw puzzles are one type of activity utilized in this center. Malcolm liked to put puzzles together and often spent his first fifteen-minute classroom period assembling a portion of a puzzle at the Order Center. The teacher would award him check marks at the close of the period and reassign him to the playground area outside. Gradually, over a period of several weeks, Malcolm could be kept longer in the classroom. The plan was to work toward making him a full-time student by first introducing simple academic tasks at his desk, and increasing these both in length and complexity day by day. All was going fine until the teacher approached the author shortly after Malcolm began almost full-time class participation. It was obvious she was upset. She explained she really felt Malcolm had been "getting away with a lot" by only having to do simple response and order activities while the other children were expected to work at higher levels. "He could do so much more arithmetic if I really pushed him," she said, thereby revealing her discomfort at settling for the thimbleful goal initially set and moving toward greater demands at such a slow pace that the boy's success in school was guaranteed.

One essential requirement for a special educator is the thim-

ED

MR

bleful philosophy.   All around us in education we find a bucket-ful orientation, partly because there is so much for children to learn in a relatively short period of time and partly because the majority of learners do not present serious problems at the basic levels of learning competence.   The initial settling for thimbleful may be a distinguishing characteristic between the special and regular educator.   That thimbleful eventually can fill a bucketful is evidenced in the outcomes of the program for both Louis and Malcolm.   Louis slowly began to enter into more complex tasks that required using a pencil and holding a book.   Speech returned only after many months, but several years later he was maintaining an adequate, if somewhat borderline, educational and social adjustment in a small private school.   Malcolm was working on a par with other members of the special class by the close of the school semester and within a year went on to enter a regular classroom where his social and academic progress was reported as "satisfactory."   No miracles involved in either case — just a temporary extension of good educational practice so that both boys achieved some level of a winner's status rather than maintaining a loser's role in school.

Even though we emphasized that the primary concern at the response-order level of competence was with getting the child doing something rather than learning something, we cannot overlook those aspects of responding that have been found to be qualitatively related to learning efficiency.   Again, studies with the retarded shed more light on these aspects than does work done with other exceptional learners.   Speed of responding may be related to the overall effectiveness of a learning experience.   There is almost unanimous agreement in the literature that the mentally retarded are slower than normals in reaction time.   Behavioral traits such as perceptual problems and attention difficulties appear to slow reaction time further.   In light of our discussion at the attention level, it should not come as a surprise that evidence exists that heightening stimulus intensity will often result in a more favorable reaction time among the retarded (Baumeister, Urquhart, Beedle, & Smith, 1964).

Although speed of responding may be an asset in some learning situations, Smith (1968) stresses the importance of accuracy over speed.   Impulsive, uncritical responding often results in a marked increase in errors.   This occurs particularly with emotionally disturbed individuals, and also exists as a problem with any of our exceptional learners.   Smith advocates concern with accuracy, particularly in the early stages of learning when new and basic concepts that will form the basis for subsequent learnings are being formulated.   The more that speed of responding is emphasized through imposition of rigid time limits or competition between children, the greater the chance that accuracy will be sacrificed.

Conditions — How Can Tasks Best Be Presented to Facilitate Direction-Following and Transfer of Learning?

The order component of the response-order level of competence involves the skill of associating or organizing concepts or facts so that logical, complete units of learning are mastered.   Smith (1968), writing with reference to the retarded but pointing out important aspects of order or association training for all exceptional learners, suggests: (1) Focus initially on the criterion of likeness among objects related to everyday life, such as things to ride in, eat for dinner, or wear to school. (2) Emphasize the fact that some events naturally precede others. A story describing a boy arising in the morning, eating breakfast, walking to school, attending school, returning home, eating dinner, and going to bed might be pictorially presented with the sequence mixed up.   Having the child re-order the logical sequence is a useful association training task. (3) On a higher level, the relation between cause and effect should be stressed. Learning to cross the street by careful watching of the traffic lights avoids accidents. Frequent use of the word "Why?" in relation to rules and expected behavior also aids the child in learning the component aspects of cause-and-effect situations.

     Baumeister (1967) summarizes much of the literature suggesting that meaningfulness of material to be learned is an important consideration for the retarded in terms of learning efficiency. The retarded learner is more adversely affected by abstract non-meaningful material than is the normal individual; this is linked to the difficulty that retardates have in applying verbal labels to stimuli to be learned.   In facilitating transfer of response patterns from one problem situation to another, educable mentally retarded children profit most when the instructional presentation is concrete, the materials can be manipulated, and the tasks involved require little need for abstraction (Orton, McKay, & Rainy, 1964). This is in contrast to practices best suited for bright and gifted students, who often transfer response patterns best when they are first taught the use of rules, principles, and generalizations.

     Mentally retarded learners also show a definite tendency to transfer negative rather than positive learning (Bryant, 1965);

MR

the reverse is true for intellectually normal children. The concerns expressed earlier for stressing accuracy in instructional approaches with the retarded are particularly relevant when this tendency is considered. Thus, in attempting to teach a retarded child the skills to be applied in assembling a mechanical device, a trial and error approach would best be avoided. In the eventual final assembly stage, an accumulation of previous mistakes might be recalled more readily than the correct procedures.

Smith (1968) calls the teacher's attention to the following considerations in order to promote more effective transfer with retarded children:

MR

1. Logical sequencing of instruction, making liberal use of materials and concrete examples before a principle or rule is considered
2. Placing the child in situations that will be successful, thereby encouraging positive transfer
3. Providing a variety of rewards for correct responses
4. Early identification of retarded individuals and potential retardates
5. Stressing relationships between situations and problems by focusing on commonalities that exist

In addition, improvement in learning, retention, transfer, and relearning is facilitated with retardates if overlearning has taken place (Gilbert, 1957; Postman, 1962; Mandler & Heinemann, 1956). Overlearning is achieved when the child practices a task well beyond the point of initial mastery. Such practice reduces the possibility of eliciting random responses at future times. A related consideration has to do with distributing the practice of tasks, in contrast to asking the retarded child to practice for a longer period during a single sitting. Madsen (1963) has found that spacing or sequencing practice sessions over time is of considerably greater benefit to retarded children than to bright or average learners.

The thimbleful approach suggested earlier in relation to guaranteeing success is particularly applicable in the teaching of the retarded. Small, discrete shifts in demand are more apt to result in learning than are larger, abrupt expectations. The Hegge, Kirk, and Kirk (1936) remedial reading series follows this principle. When introducing a new series of drill words, the new list will only differ in a minimal way from a previously presented list. Thus, following presentation of words such as sat, mat, and rat the new series may include sap, map, and rap, involving only a change in final letters.

Summary

In this section, we have discussed the importance of making exceptional learners active participants in learning and of increasing the quality and organization of their motor and verbal responding.   Capacity-based problems, such as found with the physically handicapped, may set fixed limits on the range of motor responses possible.   Such problems also will tend to restrict the level of verbal responding among the deaf.   With most of our exceptional learners, however, we can alter the learning environment to aid them in improving their response-order competence.   The blind individual often needs special help in improving physical skills and coordination.   Particular emphasis must be made on increasing his mobility, or free and easy movement, through the environment. The child with problems in motor coordination, regardless of the traditional category in which he falls, may profit from a number of training approaches defined in programs by Kephart and others. Basic language disorders also can cut across categories; the work of Myklebust and the Kirks specifies corrective procedures.   Speech problems, again common to many types of exceptional learners, often require the assistance of a trained speech therapist, although the classroom teacher can be of considerable assistance to children with disorders of articulation and stuttering.

Capturing the child's interest with meaningful instructional material becomes a critical factor in getting him involved.   The concepts of guaranteeing success and thimblesful of learning, which are of general significance in all of our work with exceptional learners, are particularly relevant in terms of making them active participants in learning.   With the retarded, overlearning and careful sequencing of task difficulty to avoid errors are response-order considerations that relate to transfer of learning.

CONSEQUENCES

In Chapter 6, we introduced the role of consequences as a major area of concern in the effective teaching of all learners.   It was pointed out that special educators working with exceptional children often must pay more critical attention to this variable than must regular educators. We shall consider a number of general principles underlying the use of positive consequences, or reinforcement, in this section along with examples of such consequences on the tangible, token, and task completion levels. We also shall briefly discuss the problems associated with the use of negative consequences, or punishment.

The basic principle of positive consequences, or positive reinforcement, is that presentation of a pleasant event after the child has responded will increase the probability that such a response will be repeated. Thorndike (1913) summarized such a principle in his Law of Effect: "An act may be altered in its strength by its consequences." The use of the word "reinforcement" rather than "consequences" has emanated from the work of Skinner (1953); it more directly and precisely implies the strengthening or weakening effect of consequences on behavior. However, we shall continue to use the latter, broader term consequences in our discussions in order to emphasize the overall relationship between the task (curriculum), the expectations associated with successful undertaking of the task (conditions), and the environmental reaction to the child's task efforts (consequences).

Four considerations are crucial to the effective use of positive consequences in the classroom: timing, targeting, shaping, and learner susceptibility. With respect to timing, it is critical that the consequence follows as closely as possible to the child's response that it is intended to strengthen. Consequences that are delayed too long can be greatly weakened in terms of their effect on performance. Thus, teacher social approval ("Good job, Tommy!") intended to strengthen Tommy's promptness in returning his paints and brushes to the art cabinet is better given immediately following placement of the materials on the shelf rather than at the end of the day ("I was happy you returned your paints and brushes after our art work this morning, Tommy").

We cannot overlook, however, the individual differences found among children. Many American school children learn to live with the delayed promise of positive consequences (e.g., test score returned one week after the test, grades given at the end of the semester, selection by teacher as "Good Citizen of the Week"). The entire socialization process involves learning to delay gratification related to current efforts for often long periods of time (e.g., accumulation of enough money in a savings account to purchase a home or begin a family or years of apprenticeship at a beginning job position for possible consideration as an executive). But exceptional learners are often distinguished by their lack of ability to postpone rewards. Indeed, the frustration and failure that many of them encounter on a day-to-day basis may preclude long-term hopefulness or positive expectations that their efforts will pay off. For this reason, immediacy of reward becomes crucial, particularly in relation to pre-academic behaviors such as paying attention, starting, working, and following directions. These behaviors are also of critical concern in relation to the second consideration in our discussion, targeting.

Once we have established the importance of immediacy in providing rewarding consequences in the teaching situation, we must look closely at exactly what it is we are to reward. Targeting involves the selection of a particular behavior for strengthening. In the typical regular classroom, this may be determined largely on a class activity and group basis; that is, the activities in the program call for certain appropriate behaviors from the group that will be singled out for approval by the teacher:

"Jim is the first student in his row to have his reading book out and ready to go"

"Mary, you may take your place at the head of the line for recess since you have cleared your desk"

"I'm giving you an 'A' on this arithmetic assignment, Bill, since all the problems are correct"

In addition to alert and cooperative Jim and Mary and academically capable Bill, however, the classroom will include others who do not measure up to the teacher's expectations:

"Why do I always have to remind you several times to get out your reading book, Mark?"

"Victor, you can just stay in your seat during recess because you haven't done anything I asked all morning"

"This arithmetic worksheet is unacceptable, Henry. The problems are all wrong, and you evidently weren't listening during yesterday's lesson on 'carrying' "

Of course, there will be great variability among teachers with respect to what is seen, what is singled out as important, and what is actually reacted to. We cannot enter into a discussion of "traditional" versus "open" classrooms, "teacher-determined" versus "child-determined" limits, and "structure" versus "permissiveness," all of which are issues related to classroom climate and teacher style and that have much to do with targeting or the lack of it. But we can discuss some principles that have wide application across many types of classroom climates and teacher styles. One of these principles harkens back to the thimbleful philosophy. Global goals for children, such as good citizenship and better reading ability, may have to be broken down into seat sitting and eye contact with the printed page.

Thimbleful targeting recognizes small increments of larger desired objectives and makes a big deal out of these smaller units. Thus, rewarding consequences (e.g., an approving look or remark) would be immediately given when the child is demonstrating some appropriate aspect of a larger goal. It is easy to overlook these smaller units since we take them for granted with most children. But exceptional learners are often particularly unique because we find them at various levels of competence in relation to behaviors we do not have to worry about with normal children. No doubt that Mark, in our earlier example, did something deserving of positive consequences during the day. Victor's behavior must have been in line with the teacher's expectations at some time, and despite Henry's poor paper, he at least tried to do the problems. All three boys showed up for school and were sitting in the classroom, if little else. The point we are trying to make is simple: make every child a candidate for some positive consequence by targeting in on thimbleful levels of accomplishment rather than overlooking these or only judging the child in terms of bucketful expectations.

Now let us take a closer look at the examples of Mark, Victor, and Henry and the possible effects of the teacher's negative remarks on them. When we criticize children or disapprove in some way of their behavior, it may be that our intentions are positive. We may hope that by alerting Mark to his slowness in getting ready he will improve. Keeping Victor in from recess might bring him in line the next day, and rejecting Henry's work could result in better attention during subsequent lessons. If these changes occurred, then the negative consequences given to the three boys would have had positive effects. That is, we would have diminished their problem behavior. But, unfortunately, with children who have behavior or learning problems, things are not always so predictable and simple. Besides the ideal of bringing about improved behavior by means of negative consequences, at least three other effects may occur.

First, the teacher may simply be tuned out and the message inherent in the consequences will not be heard or understood. With many of our exceptional learners, verbal chastisement and lecturing have occurred with such frequency in their interactions with the environment that they have acquired a broken record quality that renders them totally ineffective. Examples of this can readily be found with the disturbed, retarded, and disadvantaged. Words are abstract and may be essentially meaningless to many children. What may be more effective, particularly in the initial stages of a program to help them with behavior and learning problems, is a more concrete means of feedback. We shall describe several examples of this shortly.

A second effect of the teacher's remarks to Mark, Victor, and Henry may be merely to establish them more firmly as losers. Exceptional learners seldom need to be reminded of the fact that they do not measure up or that they are deficient. In school and outside of school many of them have received more than their share of criticism, ridicule, rejection, and disapproval, and as a result have come to view themselves in an essentially negative light. As clearly established losers, they accept the role and make little effort to try to win when the odds appear so overwhelming. Problem behavior should not always be overlooked, but in our efforts to help children who are having difficulties we should be concerned that what we do has a reasonable chance of accomplishing something positive and of improving the situation, not merely contributing to an already existing problem or ending up a waste of time.

Finally, it is possible that Mark may make no more of an effort to be ready for tomorrow's reading lesson, that Victor will not cooperate any better the next day, or that Henry will not try harder to profit from the next arithmetic lesson; in fact, things may get worse. Even though the teacher's remarks were clearly negative (with a possible long-range positive effect expected as discussed earlier), they may actually have served on an immediate basis to reward the problem behavior evidenced by the three boys. Incongruous and illogical as it may seem, an often unexpected effect of teacher attention to or verbal criticism of problem behavior is the increase of that behavior. Consider Mark for a moment. If he does little that gains him positive consequences of any kind in the classroom, and if the teacher only pays attention to him when he is slow in getting ready or misbehaving, why not at least be noticed rather than ignored?

Targeting on misbehavior with children who are consistent losers may provide the only means of being noticed available and, as negative and critical as the teacher's remarks are, they may be better than no attention at all. Inadvertently strengthening problem behavior through rewarding it by teacher attention can thus establish the teacher as a loser. This possible effect can best be handled by providing such attention at moments when the child is at least approximating desirable behavior. Catch John, who is constantly leaning back in his chair against classroom rules, when the four legs are at least momentarily on the floor ("I like the way your chair is in place and you are working, John"). Chatterbox

ED

Susan might be best helped to lessen her talking by calling attention to her quiet working periods ("You are really working hard, Susan; keep it up"). These examples relate to our earlier remarks regarding thimbleful targeting.

The emphasis in this text is on an individualized, creative, and flexible provision of positive consequences with exceptional learners. Even though we have reviewed several problems associated with negative consequences, their use with children is not likely to disappear from the classroom scene. Indeed, they are effective with some children. It is our intention, however, to focus on the positive. In this regard, Lindsley (1970) has called attention to the relevance of the lyrics from a popular song of some years back, "Accentuate the positive and eliminate the negative." Although reality does not permit total "elimination of the negative," special education should be committed to assigning "accentuating the positive" top priority in our work. We shall not consider the use of extremely negative consequences or punishment in our discussion. Strongly aversive consequences are likely to have unpredictable effects on behavior (Haring & Lovitt, 1967). They may only temporarily suppress undesirable behavior and may increase such maladaptive behaviors as escape and avoidance (Whelan, 1966). The use of such consequences appears to have most justification when applied to problems of extremely disturbed children with self-destructive behavior that may endanger their lives (Lovaas, 1965).

In the process of helping children improve in their behavior and learning, the principle of successive approximation, or shaping, is important to recognize. Once we have selected a target behavior as a starting point, we gradually increase demands until the desired goal is achieved.

For purposes of illustration, let us take Henry, the poor learner in class lessons on arithmetic who turns in papers with every problem wrong. The desired goal is to get him to learn arithmetic and to be able to demonstrate what he knows in written assignments. But we must back up and look at certain component aspects of this goal that might be set as behavioral milestones along the way. First, we would have to be certain that Henry actually had the understanding of basic arithmetic concepts (e.g., addition) before introducing him to more complex steps (e.g., carrying). If he has no idea what the class lesson in carrying is all about, then we have lost before we have begun. This will necessitate individual work at his level; but for purposes of our illustration, let us suppose he is a candidate for the lesson. Looking and listening in line with the attention level of competence are of initial importance now.   Having Henry sit nearer the chalk-board, asking him frequent questions, and rewarding him for such attention and responding will get us on our way.   The standard class follow-up assignment may be reduced in size for him.   That is, one row instead of four rows of problems may be given.   If he gets at least one problem correct, a big deal is made out of this and the incorrect problems given less attention.   Here we are emphasizing the response-order level of functioning.

Gradually, we may see a change in his ability to profit from class lessons.   If not, we might back up again, perhaps eliminate independent written work as a follow-up assignment and have him work with the teacher or another child on a problem-by-problem basis.   There is nothing spectacularly new about what is being suggested here.   Most teachers would handle Henry in this way based on their experience and knowledge of how children learn. What we are attempting to do is emphasize good teaching:

1. Select component aspects of desired educational goals and focus sequentially on these with the child
2. Reward each aspect and carefully note progress
3. Be prepared to back up and re-select or re-emphasize certain component aspects and, if necessary, start over again
4. Gradually increase demands until the child has attained the desired goal

More definitive and dramatic examples of the use of shaping tech-niques, or the principle of successive approximation, are found in behavior modification literature.

Through the use of behavior modification, Ayllon and Haugh-ton (1962) improved the functioning level of a group of institu-tionalized psychotic adults.   These patients presented serious eating problems; much staff time was spent coaxing and support-ing them during mealtimes.   A program was instituted that re-quired all patients to enter the dining room in order to eat.   With the receipt of food as the reward, increasingly complex demands were made.

The first step involved telling the patient when it was time to eat and allowing an hour for him to get to the dining room. Step two required entrance into the dining room during shorter and shorter periods of time following the nurse's announcement — a half hour, then fifteen minutes, and finally five-minute inter-vals were imposed.   Step three required the patient to stop by the nurse's office and pick up a penny to deposit in a can at the dining room door in order to gain admittance.   And in the final step, each

ED

patient had to get the assistance of a fellow patient in order to obtain a penny. The patients quickly adapted to these increased demands, and the degree of interaction among them increased considerably.

Another application of behavior principles to the problems of an autistic boy was demonstrated by Wolf, Risley, and Mills (1964). Dicky was an institutionalized three-and-one-half-year-old who refused to wear glasses even though he had a serious visual problem that made wearing them essential. Much time and effort had gone into attempting to force him to wear them with little success. In fact, the glasses had become so aversive to Dicky that he became increasingly upset when they were given to him. In an experimental program designed to shape glasses-wearing behavior, several empty glasses frames were placed about his room and Dicky was reinforced with bites of candy, fruit, or ice cream for first picking them up, then holding them, then carrying them around, and later for bringing the frames closer to his eyes in successive stages. There were two or three twenty-minute sessions each day for six weeks.

During the sixth week, the full prescription lenses were placed in the frames. Once wearing the glasses was established in the training sessions, it was easily maintained during the rest of the day by contingency management — Dicky was required to wear the glasses during meals, snacks, automobile rides, walks, outdoor play, and so forth. If he took the glasses off, he was withdrawn from the activity. At the time of his release from the hospital, Dicky was wearing the glasses for about twelve hours a day.

A final consideration in our present discussion was introduced in the last chapter — learner susceptibility. What truly constitutes a positive consequence for an exceptional learner in school? We pointed out the major categories of possible positive somethings that teachers can rely on in order to make it worth the child's while to work and learn. These were joy, acquisition of knowledge and skill, knowledge of results, social approval, multisensory stimulation and activity, task completion, and tangibles. We also stated that our exceptional learners may vary in their susceptibility to any of these. For example, emotionally disturbed children who were engaged in a simple response-order task (dropping marbles in a box) were found to work more efficiently when given food rewards than they did when verbal praise was provided by an adult. Their task performance was also superior when food rewards were given alone as compared with the effects of pairing such rewards with social praise (Levin & Simmons, 1962).

Even though this simple study does not approximate the complex classroom learning situation, it suggests that verbal, social praise may have limitations as an effective incentive with disturbed children.

ED

The author doubts whether exceptional learners actually are unique in terms of susceptibility to positive consequences in general, but has observed the following:

1. Incentives of joy, acquisition of knowledge and skill, good grades, and social approval are normally provided in school for success in meeting academic and behavioral expectations. Where such success has largely not been achieved, the child has failed to receive these positive consequences, and, hence, he may not have learned to value them as incentives.
2. The above incentives are part of the traditional system of schooling and may not be as amenable to flexible and individualized provision as less traditionally relied on incentives, such as multi-sensory stimulation and activity, task completion, and tangibles and tokens.   The novelty effect of the latter rewards is also an important consideration.
3. Special concern for selection and provision of positive consequences is probably most critical in the initial stages of a special educational program.   Once the curriculum and conditions variables are operating at the child's level, the importance of individualizing incentives and consequences diminishes.

In the following sections and in Chapters 8 and 9, we shall continue our discussion of the use of positive consequences with exceptional learners. Our focus will first be on tangible and token incentives, then will shift to multi-sensory experiences and activities and social approval in the next chapter. Chapter 9 will consider knowledge of results and acquisition of knowledge and skill. In summarizing at this point, we can echo the goals made earlier: accentuating the positive through immediacy, targeting on critical basic behavioral goals, systematically increasing expectations by means of successive approximation, and individualizing the types of positive consequences provided.

Patterson (1965) developed a unique procedure for increasing the attention of a hyperactive, disturbed nine-year-old boy, maintaining him for longer periods of work and reducing his disruptive behavior. The boy was first trained outside the classroom. A small box, six-by-eight-by-five inches, was mounted on a desk and a small flashlight bulb installed on the top of the box. The dial of an electrical counting device was also visible on top of the

ED

box. During the pre-training sessions, the boy was given a book to look at. For each ten second interval during which he was attending to the book, the light flashed on, the counter clicked, and the experimenter placed a candy unit on the desk. It was explained that each time the light went on it meant he had earned a piece of candy or a penny and that he could collect his earnings at the end of the lesson.

Once the pre-training sessions were concluded, the experiment moved to the boy's regular classroom where the involvement of the entire class was enlisted. In the boy's presence, the class was told that the box on his desk was a magic teaching machine that was going to help him to sit still and learn like the other children. The light flashes and counter were explained and the news announced that each lesson's worth of candy or pennies would be divided equally among the entire class. It was pointed out that the class could help the boy by not paying any attention to him while he was working. The classroom situation used during the training program included silent reading, art work at the desk, reading or arithmetic in small groups, and class recitation. A significant decrease occurred in the boy's non-attending and non-working behavior in a relatively brief period of time. Follow-up information from teachers four months after the study indicated that he was much quieter and learning more effectively.

The most visible consequences that were responsible for aiding in increasing this boy's attending and working behavior were the tangible rewards. The experimenter points out how the peer group also functioned as a source of positive reinforcement. At the end of each training session, when the boy's score was announced to the entire class, they would typically applaud him for his efforts. The other children also walked by his desk to check the counter during work periods, and at recess they frequently sought him out and made such comments as, "You sure are doing good; you get better every day." Although it may be difficult accurately to pin down the exact component in the boy's training program that exerted the most influence, the consequences for his efforts played a major part in establishing him as a classroom winner rather than as a perpetual loser.

Quay (1966) has used a similar method on a group basis to increase the listening attention of children with behavior problems. The author (Hewett, 1964a) developed a program designed to teach a non-verbal, twelve-year-old autistic boy to read and write. Before any actual reading instruction could begin, the boy had to be trained to pay attention and sit in a chair. Although he typically avoided attempts to confine him in any way, the learn-

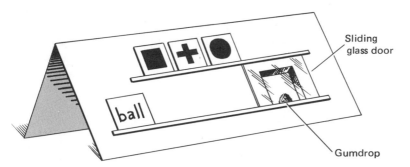

Figure 12: Word Board Used with Autistic Boy

ing device or word board illustrated in Figure 12 was effective almost immediately in gaining his cooperation. A candy gumdrop was deposited behind the sliding glass door to the right, in plain view. The door was held shut by the teacher until the boy was sitting still and had his eyes on the teacher. At the moment of eye contact, the door was opened and the candy was made readily available. Once the rules of this candy game were understood, the boy became highly cooperative and attentive, and reading instruction began.

A similar approach was taken with severely emotionally disturbed, deaf children at the California School for the Deaf in Riverside, California. Some of these children had to be actually physically restrained and carried into the classroom by aides because their behavior was so bizarre and assaultive. They would be held in a chair by the aide while the teacher placed a candy unit on the desk in front of them and covered it with a clear plastic cup. Despite all their struggling to get the candy, the cup was held firm until they relaxed and sat quietly for a brief moment. Once this occurred, the cup was lifted and the child was given access to the candy. After a few trials, all physical restraint could be removed and the child quickly took his place at the desk and waited attentively until the cup was lifted. Following such an attention breakthrough, these severely disturbed children were engaged in simple direction-following tasks, such as making pegboard designs or puzzles, and eventually were led into basic academic activities.

On a group basis, teachers of severely disturbed deaf children found the use of an attention mask effective in establishing eye contact with a small class. On arrival in the morning, each child put on a rectangular mask of black plastic that framed his

ED

MR

SD

eyes. The teacher also put on a similar mask. With the directions, "Now, all of you look at me," given by means of finger spelling, the teacher walked slowly back and forth in front of the group looking directly at the mask on each child's face. Those children who were looking attentively at the teacher's mask were given a piece of candy on their desk for every five-second interval of looking. This warm-up activity soon had a generalized effect at other times during the day; even though the children did not put on their attention masks, they readily established eye contact when so directed by the teacher. In this example, curriculum, conditions, and consequences all worked together to produce the desired behavior.

On a classroom basis, the direct use of tangible rewards such as candy may be cumbersome and unnecessary. Less severely disturbed children, the mentally retarded, and the disadvantaged often can be reached with a token reward system involving accumulation of points or check marks with later exchange value for some tangible reward or valued activity.

One of the first efforts to develop such a token reward system for classroom use with mentally retarded children in an institutional setting was made by Birnbrauer, Bijou, Wolf, and Kidder (1965) at the Ranier School in the state of Washington. The school program for these children included a small teacher-pupil ratio, careful programming of reading, written language, and number concepts, and the use of a token system for acknowledging pupil accomplishment in academic and behavioral areas. Throughout the class day, each child carried a sheet ruled with small boxes on it. As he completed assignments, he was given marks in the boxes as immediate rewards for his work. Once the sheet was filled with marks, it could be exchanged for small trinkets or edibles, or several sheets could be accumulated and later exchanged for participation in special activities such as field trips or visits to a nearby shopping center.

The Ranier School project demonstrated that in a well-planned, educational program in which curriculum, conditions, and consequences receive maximal attention, retarded individuals can make gains in academic and behavior areas considerably above what would be expected on the basis of their tested intelligence level. One exciting aspect of this and other work done with the retarded in recent years is that it indicates that we really do not know how much the mentally retarded child is capable of learning when optimal conditions for learning are provided. This attitude is in marked contrast to earlier beliefs discussed in Chapter 1 that such-and-such an I.Q. level meant such-and-such a level

**Figure 13: Work Record Card
Used in Engineered
Classroom**

of possible learning with certainty and finality. The learner first
and disability second orientation of this text hopefully reflects this
current open-mindedness and optimism.

The engineered classroom utilizes an adaptation of the
token system introduced in the Ranier School program. Each
child is given a Work Record Card such as the one shown in
Figure 13. These cards are kept in holders at the front of the
class and are picked up by the child as he enters the classroom.
Throughout the day, the child is given check marks on the card
acknowledging his accomplishments in relation to assigned tasks
and behavioral expectations. The original engineered class design
awarded a possible ten check marks each fifteen minutes. Two
were given for starting, three for working, and a possible five
bonuses for being a student. In this way, the primary focus was
on attention, response, and order levels of competence. Check
marks were withheld to alert the child to a problem area, but an
effort was made to be as liberal as possible in giving them as a
means of continuously providing positive consequences in the
classroom. Once a Work Record Card was filled with check
marks, it could be exchanged for tangible items in line with the
Ranier School approach. This check mark system has been described in detail elsewhere (Hewett, 1968). In Chapter 11, we
will present a modified version of this system utilized in the Madison School Plan, which is an extension of the original engineered
classroom design.

Task completion is an important reward that largely involves guaranteeing success through reducing the criterion of how well the child must do in order to be rewarded. An example of this in a story writing activity was given in Chapter 6. In general, task completion emphasizes starting, working, and finishing rather than quality of effort or being correct. It is a controversial issue to reward a child when words in the lesson are misread or misspelled, or when arithmetic problems are incorrect. In so doing, we are essentially rewarding such errors and might well expect them to occur with increased frequency in subsequent lessons. From our earlier discussion of the tendency of retarded children to recall errors more frequently than do normals, we might be particularly concerned with allowing errors made by the retarded to go unchecked. In addition, impulsive, uncritical children may race through a page of subtraction problems, add all the numbers and hand in the assignment as complete. Should we reward this behavior? The answer is certainly not a clear-cut yes, but let us look at what we are talking about in terms of task completion rewards:

1. Task completion can best be utilized with tasks that do not require skills the child does not possess (e.g., reading). The Order Center materials in the engineered classroom presented earlier are examples of these.
2. Task completion can be used as a reward in relation to tasks that the child has done incorrectly if the teacher calls attention to some aspect of the task the child has done well. Even writing his name on the paper or making an effort to try can be acknowledged with positive consequences. The incorrect work can be (a) ignored (without telling the child he is right), or (b) examined and a small portion pointed out as incorrect and discussed. Future assignments should be made in line with the child's functioning, and no child should be continuously given impossible work for the sake of task completion rewards.

What is to be avoided is a wholesale rejection of all the child's efforts. Help him feel good about responding and carefully move into a discussion of improving the quality of his work. We are not talking about every exceptional learner. Some are more than ready for imposition of the "how well" condition. We are talking about the real losers who are seldom candidates for positive consequences in the classroom. Task completion can be a meaningful starting point for accentuating the positive with them.

An interesting area of study relating to task completion rewards and guaranteeing success is found in errorless training. This is a form of teaching that literally makes it impossible for the child to fail. Some additional principles derived from programmed instruction and learning theory are involved, namely prompting and fading. Acker (1966) attempted to teach color and letter form discrimination to young normal and autistic children who could not correctly pick a given color or letter from two choices when directed. By initially presenting the correct choice as the smaller of the two choices and telling the child that the small one was always right, he soon had them responding in an error-free manner. Thus, the dimension of size served as a prompter to aid the child in his selection. Gradually, the size differences were reduced between the two choices until both were exactly the same. This gradual reduction of the prompting dimension is an example of fading. Acker demonstrated that such errorless training resulted in effective learning of the color and letter form discrimination so that in the final stage the children could make the correct choice on the basis of color and form alone.

Application of errorless training principles to reading instruction has been attempted by the author (Hewett, Mayhew, & Rabb, 1967) with severely emotionally disturbed, neurologically impaired, and mentally retarded children. In Phase I of the experimental program, two words, "Tom" and "ride," were presented with prompts of both color and geometric form. That is, the word "Tom" always appeared in a red box, and the word "ride" in a blue ball. Presentation of the words to the child was made on a teaching machine with the instructions: "Find the word 'Tom' in the red box" or "find the word 'ride' in the blue ball." Thus, the child was given the answer while he was given the question; if he could discriminate between "red" and "blue" and a box and a ball, he did not have to be able to read the words correctly. As in the Acker study, the color and form prompts were gradually faded; and most children who had failed to learn any beginning reading skills from more traditional approaches were able to read the words when presented alone. One autistic child took seven months to learn to discriminate correctly and to read three basic words that were presented with the prompts of color and form. Once she had mastered these three words, however, she went on to learn six new words each week without such prompting and rapidly acquired a first-grade reading ability.

These examples demonstrate the effectiveness of the task-completion reward in the preliminary stages of an instructional program. Settling initially for the simplest of criteria for success (e.g., picking the smallest, picking the red one) with inattentive and resistant learners does not mean that they will require such special consideration forever. On the contrary, an innovative, creative, and flexible introduction to learning often results in a breakthrough and the launching of the child as a candidate for learning under more traditional circumstances.

In this chapter, we have begun our look through the classroom door at exceptional learners in the process of learning. Few of the considerations at the attention of response-order levels of competence are category-specific, and most highlight a logical extension of good teaching practices with all children. Chapter 8 will focus on the content that children learn in the physical and social world through which they move as attentive and active participants.

CHAPTER 8

Exploratory and Social Levels

Noticing and doing are the essential processes that launch children into learning. In Chapter 7, we reviewed the differences and similarities among our exceptional learners with respect to the attention and response-order levels of competence. As they encounter difficulty in receiving and perceiving sensory stimuli, in retaining what they experience, and in freely and accurately responding motorically and verbally, they are handicapped in terms of acquiring the amount of knowledge and degree of skill considered necessary for effective functioning in the school and society. It is to this knowledge and skill that we now turn. As described in Chapter 6, our levels of learning competence emphasize both process and content in learning. The attention and response-order levels are process levels; they set the stage for acquisition of knowledge and skill on the exploratory, social, and mastery levels. These latter three levels are primarily concerned with content, which is learned by the child as a logical outcome of his attending and responding. Each level has its own unique area of content. The exploratory level gives the child knowledge about the physical properties of objects and events in the environment, such as color, texture, size, shape, and spatial and temporal relationships. Social level content includes knowledge and skill relating to gaining approval and avoiding disapproval from others. At the mastery level, we are concerned with language understanding and usage and with academic learning. This chapter will discuss research evidence and educational practices in the field of special education that focus on improving the exceptional learner's knowl-

ED

edge and skill at the exploratory and social levels.   Chapter 9 will be devoted to consideration of the mastery level.

EXPLORATORY: THE LEVEL OF COMPETENCE
IN RELATION TO ACCURATE AND THOROUGH KNOWLEDGE
OF THE PHYSICAL PROPERTIES OF THE ENVIRONMENT

We will begin our discussion of the exploratory level by posing several questions related to curriculum and conditions.   Consequences at the exploratory and social levels will be discussed in a final section in this chapter.

Curriculum
1. What general considerations are important in selecting tasks and experiences to improve the child's competence at the exploratory level?
2. What specific types of tasks and experiences will aid the child in learning about the physical properties of the environment?

Conditions
1. How can tasks and experiences best be presented to improve the child's competence at the exploratory level?

As in Chapter 7, we shall examine each question and relate it to the exceptional learner.

Curriculum — What General Considerations Are Important in
Selecting Tasks and Experiences to Improve the Child's Competence
at the Exploratory Level?

Due to a combination of capacity and experience-based deficits, it can be simply stated that many exceptional learners have had incomplete or inadequate interactions with the physical environment around them.   For this reason, we find special educators particularly concerned with broadening their range of experiences and with assisting them to compensate for deficits that limit such interaction.

The emotionally disturbed child is often an incomplete or faulty explorer of his environment due to withdrawal, fearfulness, and self-preoccupation.   It is important to involve him actively with as much of the real world around him as possible.   For this reason, an Exploratory Center is included in the engineered class-

room introduced earlier. The tasks and activities provided here
emphasize:

1. A wide range of multi-sensory experiences
2. A focus on reality
3. Predictable outcomes

LD

MR

SD

Simple experience-oriented science curriculum tasks are utilized
to accomplish these goals, along with arts and crafts activities,
Examples of these tasks will be presented shortly.

Basic to the school problems of many disadvantaged children is their narrow range of previous experience and their limited
understanding of the environment. Perhaps no other issue receives
as much attention from educators concerned with the problems of
the disadvantaged as that of compensating for such limitations.
Morlan (1968) points out the necessity of providing opportunities
for interaction with the people, places, and things that will promote the understanding needed for building concepts and abstrac-
tions required for effective development of language. Ramonda
(1968) stresses providing such experiences as early as possible.
The Headstart program is a national effort to promote such early
enrichment.

The mentally retarded child is also a candidate for a wide
range of experiences with the environment so that he can acquire
a more extensive and complex repertoire of information to use in
order to solve problems later in school (Smith, 1968). Limited
experience may actually account for some of the differences in
abilities found between retarded and normal children, according to Baumeister (1967). The problems retarded individuals
have in selecting relevant cues in learning tasks may be partially
explained by restricted previous experience. Thus, emphasis on
building the retardate's exploratory level of competence may positively affect his functioning at the attention and even the response
levels. With the trainable retarded child, exploratory activities
are particularly important, since knowledge of the environment is
essential for survival. Such children need systematically to learn
about their environment so that problems with safety (e.g., touching something hot) or health (e.g., eating the wrong substances)
can be avoided (Johnson & Blake, 1960).

Johnson and Myklebust (1967) have written about the
hierarchies of experience leading to language development and
related to types of learning disabilities. The most primitive level
of experience is sensation and the next is perception. Both were
considered in our discussion at the attention level of competence.

Johnson and Myklebust posit imagery as the next level of experience; this has direct relevance to our exploratory level. Perception concerns awareness relative to *ongoing* sensation; imagery pertains to sensation or information *already* received and perceived. Johnson and Myklebust view the concept of imagery as a way to describe processes covered by the term "memory." They point out that some learning disabled children cannot recall visual and auditory events associated with daily experiences. They report children who could not recall common features of their bedroom or whether there were trees along the streets as they walked to school. In their book, Johnson and Myklebust describe procedures for remedying non-verbal disorders of learning. Many of these remedies aim at improving the child's ability to learn from everyday experience and to recall such experiences in the form of imagery. Such objectives are clearly in line with exploratory level concerns with disadvantaged and retarded learners. The Johnson and Myklebust hierarchy of experience in relation to types of learning disabilities goes on to consider symbolization, inner language, receptive language, expressive language, and conceptualization. These are more clearly related to the mastery level of competence in this text.

The issue of compensatory experience for capacity-based deficits is critical at the exploratory level for children with visual and hearing impairments. In our discussion at the response-order level, we discussed the importance of mobility training to aid the blind child in moving efficiently and safely through the environment. At the exploratory level, we will briefly consider orientation as an aspect of mobility. Orientation refers to the awareness an individual has about his environment and his position in it. For the blind individual, this awareness must be learned largely through auditory and tactile media (Scholl, 1967). Hapeman (1967) says that for adequate orientation toward his environment, the blind person must acquire the concepts needed for:

1. Understanding the true nature of the environment: body image, nature of objects, nature of fixed, movable, and moving objects, nature of terrain, nature of sounds and odors
2. Achieving and maintaining orientation: path of moving objects, position of objects in space, direction, sound localization
3. Efficient mobility: distance and time, following a sequence of fixed objects, turning, detouring, moving with and against moving objects

Hearing handicapped children largely rely on visual stimuli for learning about their environment. Research by Gaeth (1963), however, stresses the importance of encouraging use of residual hearing, or visual cues will be utilized exclusively.

Curriculum — What Specific Type of Tasks and Experiences Will Aid the Child in Learning about the Physical Properties of the Environment?

In the literature related to the building of learning competence among exceptional learners, a recurrent theme is the emphasis on multi-sensory experience. Where contact with the environment is made simultaneously through looking, listening, touching, and even moving, we can expect a greater probability of learning to take place. Such increased stimulus impact may also aid in promoting attention, retention, and active participation. Hermelin and O'Connor (1963) stress that the mentally retarded child should anchor his experiences and explorations of the environment through physical, tactile, kinesthetic, olfactory, visual, and auditory modalities whenever possible. In addition, the effects of exploration are enhanced by the teacher's verbal labeling of experiences so that the child can immediately pin down what he is discovering and learning. The Fernald method of learning to spell and read, briefly described in Chapter 7, even though it is aimed at increased mastery level competence, is a multi-sensory approach to learning. The child actually traces large cursive forms of words on four-by-eight inch slips of paper or on the blackboard while studying the word visually and saying it aloud. Thus, through combined kinesthetic, visual, and auditory input, his focus on the word is maximized.

Multi-sensory stimulation has been stressed by Lord (1966) in teaching orientation skills to the blind. The more ways in which sensory inputs can be received and interpreted correctly, the more efficiently visually handicapped individuals will acquire functional concepts on which to build their knowledge of the environment. Preschool blind children need firsthand experiences in all aspects of the environment around them. Walks through city streets should call the child's attention to olfactory, tactile, and auditory cues to identify various types of stores (e.g., the smell of fresh baked bread in the bakery). The sounds of traffic can be utilized to determine the direction it is moving. Tactile cues will aid in discriminating differences in walking surfaces. The sounds, smells, and tactile experiences of nature can be learned through walks in the country.

Blind children will particularly be drawn to toys that are noisemakers or musical. Perhaps even more than sighted individuals, blind children also enjoy playing with and exploring materials that can be formed, such as damp sand, mud, dough, and snow. Water play activities offer many opportunities for exploration. Sorting and matching objects on the basis of size, shape, and texture also will aid in developing touch discrimination.

In an effort to provide experiences comparable in reality emphasis to those of seeing children, blind children are often given models of various physical objects to examine by touch. A model of a house, a tree, a car, or an animal can be held and explored thoroughly by the blind individual as a step in learning the concepts of houses, trees, cars, or animals. Just how relevant such concrete exploration is to later acquisition of abstract concepts continues to be debatable (Mandola, 1968). Lowenfeld (1971), however, considers use of touching models justified on a pragmatic basis until proof to the contrary is provided, so long as teachers make sure that the child does not develop misconceptions about the objects themselves in the process.

Some sighted disadvantaged children may share in common with the visually handicapped individual a need for impactful, multi-sensory experiences to compensate for his limited opportunities for learning. In this case, the problem is particularly related to development of adequate language usage and understanding. Teachers may use words such as heavier, smoother, or uneven with little awareness that some children do not understand what is meant. The actual experience of looking, touching, and lifting, linked with the verbal label, may be essential for instilling an understanding of such concepts in much the same way as has been suggested for the mentally retarded.

What is being stressed is building the abstract from the concrete, a notion that is turning up with remarkable predictability throughout our discussion. Exceptional learners may not only notice and respond to the concrete more readily, but they also may learn more when they are confronted with a real world experience. The author is reminded of two such learners who learned something about the concept of size from concrete experiences. Sammy was a six-year-old blind youngster who was highly verbal and socially outgoing. He spent much of his first grade year in a regular class with sighted children and received beginning braille instruction from a resource teacher in the school. Sammy's best friend in the class was Mike, who had a small metal file box for 3 × 5 cards on the desk. The box never ceased to intrigue Sammy who would hold it, flip open the lid, and finger the cards kept inside.   One day he announced to the teacher that he would like to crawl inside Mike's file box.   The teacher promptly took the box, removed the cards, and handed it to Sammy. "Put it on the floor, Sammy," she said, "and see if you can crawl inside it." Sammy set the box down and the teacher guided his foot toward the box. "See," she said, "not even your foot will go inside. Mike's file box is a box all right, but it is a very small box, far too small for a big boy like you to crawl into."

The teacher then led Sammy to a large cardboard packing box in the room and had him explore it with his hands. "This is a big box, Sammy," she told him.   "This box is big enough for you to crawl into." Sammy was helped to crawl inside the box and the small–big concept was emphasized in a most concrete manner for him.

The author was sitting in a class for ten-year-old, educable mentally retarded children during a lesson on volcanoes.   The teacher asked the class if anyone could describe a volcano.   Jeff, a boy always eager to respond, even though he sometimes volunteered before he understood the question, raised his hand. The teacher nodded in his direction, and Jeff spoke out, "A volcano is a big pile of rocks that has fire coming out of it." The author and the teacher were impressed.   Then Jeff went on.   "Why a volcano is so big it might even fill up this room!" Several children who knew how big volcanoes actually were snickered. The teacher praised Jeff's basic description of a volcano and went on with the lesson. Sometime later, she showed Jeff some pictures of volcanoes in relation to trees, houses, and even people.   The concept of "mountain" rather than "pile of rocks" was stressed, and Jeff was helped to link the concept of rocks, fire, and mountain together so that he had a more accurate understanding of volcanoes.

Examples such as these are endless and are commonplace in preschool, kindergarten, and the primary grades. Much of the uniqueness of special education stems from never considering any child too old for translation of an abstract concept down to the concrete level to ensure basic understanding.   In this way, the special educator must function as a composite of many regular educators across the school years and as a teacher who can never narrowly identify with chronological age or school grade expectations.   The individual child, rather than some normative reference, must always determine the educational practice undertaken.

The engineered classroom design described throughout this part of the text attempts to provide a wide range of concrete, manipulative experiences for exceptional learners in the various interest and activity centers in the room. Toys and teaching materials common to preschool and kindergarten programs can be included at the centers even through middle- and upper-aged elementary children are in the class. One example used at the Order Center is a nesting block activity often given to two- and three-year-olds to introduce the concept of size difference. Five or six hollow blocks can be fitted together sequentially so they are eventually all enclosed in the largest block. Most sixth grade boys would consider such an activity baby stuff if it was presented in its original toy box. But some of them might indeed profit from the hand-eye coordination and size difference training aspects of such a task. The author has taken nesting blocks and placed them in a plain cardboard box with a mechanical timer. Older students are then presented with a challenging task: to place the blocks individually on the table, start the timer, and see how long it takes them to reassemble all the blocks together. There is nothing babyish about this activity, and it can provide a valuable learning experience for the child. This is an example of camouflaging a task or activity so that it is acceptable to older children. In this way, we can capitalize on many primary-level activities that continue to have direct relevance to the problems of exceptional learners. The author has actually referred to the engineered classroom as a camouflaged kindergarten in that it seeks to include and make acceptable many types of tasks related to all levels of learning competence.

Kephart (1971) echoes the importance of encouraging all children to experiment with the objects in their environment — to feel them from angles, smell them, and tap them to produce sounds. By so doing, the child matches sensory information to motor information and acquires knowledge that will help him adapt his behavior to the varied demands of the changing environment. Learning the relationships between objects and how they fit together is also important. Kephart sees experimentation with some objects in the physical environment more difficult today than several decades ago. In the past, children might take a percolator apart and put it together again, deriving considerable knowledge and satisfaction in the process. Concepts like "up–down," "full–empty," and "inside–outside" might all be involved. But the sealed units of modern appliances and gadgets that often defy even Daddy's expertise as fix-it man can limit such free exploration.

The curriculum area of science has always appealed to the author as an excellent source of tasks and activities to aid all

exceptional learners in increasing their exploratory level of competence. The engineered classroom features an Exploratory Center
with science equipment, materials for performing simple experiments, microscopes for looking at tiny organisms, and small telescopes
for looking out classroom windows at birds and other objects
of interest. Window-box gardens can be kept and cared for,
and animals and fish maintained. The author has observed with
interest the kinds of classroom pets that lend themselves to successful exploratory activities. Over the years he has watched a
passing parade of turtles, rabbits, white rats, mice, hamsters,
guinea pigs, toads, frogs, snakes, lizards, chickens, parakeets, pi-
geons, and even owls serve in this capacity. A baby alligator
was one classroom favorite; but, unfortunately, he grew rapidly,
escaped from his tank one night, managed to find a small stream
that ran through the school playground, and provided a number
of unique if somewhat unexpected and harrowing exploratory experiences for children in the school until he was captured!

In general, it is difficult to rank animals, reptiles, insects,
and birds in terms of their suitability for being kept in the classroom. Much will depend on the ease and comfort with which
the teacher approaches them (e.g., snakes) and the durability of
the creature itself (e.g., large tortoise vs. tiny baby rabbit).
White rats have been very successful with many types of exceptional learners and are more adaptable than hamsters and guinea
pigs. The actual experience of picking up, handling, and observing at close range a small, tame animal is a constant source of
delight. Even though emotionally disturbed children may lack
understanding and control in playing with small, fragile animals, the author has been impressed with how readily they can
learn if clear-cut expectations are presented by the teacher and
if appropriate supervision is provided. In fact, just what constitutes a hazardous situation in the classroom is difficult to
define even when working with very disturbed youngsters. Allowing such children to use gas burners, delicate scientific instruments,
and sharp objects in science experiments under supervision
has seldom proven a problem in either institutional or public
school programs with which the author has been associated. One
exception is presenting excessive stimulation to disturbed, retarded,
or disadvantaged children who are easily overwhelmed with too
many choices or too much going on all at once. This relates more
directly to our conditions discussion and will be elaborated on
shortly.

An impressive and touching example of the extension of exploratory competence building to one of the most extreme group

of exceptional learners is provided by a program undertaken with the profoundly retarded at Sonoma State Hospital in California. As in many state institutions, certain cottages or wards are set aside to house children who fall at the very low end of the adaptive continuum and who are continuously dependent on the care and attention of others for survival. These children are characteristically kept in crib-type beds most of their lives, and the staff is primarily concerned with feeding, changing diapers, and maintaining hygienic standards. The profoundly retarded child may not be able to move and cannot speak. His life expectancy may be very limited. His world is confined to a small patch of bed linen and protective bed railings that shut off most outside visual stimulation. No one can deny that the situation is hopeless. What can anyone do to extend these children's range of exploratory experience? The staff of one such unit at Sonoma State decided something could be done. They introduced a more intensive program of physical rehabilitation with the assistance of trained staff. Body positions of the children were changed through the use of pillows, slight movements of fingers and toes were encouraged, and constant stimulation was provided.

As unlikely as it may seem, chickens were let loose in the ward to perch on the bed railings and catch the children's eyes. Large, live, furry rabbits were placed in the cribs next to the children for tactual stimulation. Some of the children were carried from the ward to the grounds outside. They were put down in tall, wet grass, given flowers to touch, and placed in strollers and wagons for rides through the woods. No miracles occurred. The situation was still hopeless, but an important effort had been made to extend these children's exploratory experience. And slight evidence was seen that the children were more attentive and responsive as a result. This is but one example of a seeming paradox often faced by the special educator: the situation is hopeless — but not hopeless; we cannot do anything — but we can do something. Reflected in this paradox is much of the spirit and dedication on which the field was founded and greatly depends at the present time.

Exploratory activities in the engineered classroom with mildly retarded and disturbed children include a series of science tasks that have been developed over several years (Taylor, Artuso, & Hewett, 1973b). Examples of these tasks are presented in condensed form in Figure 14.*

*From Taylor, F. D., Artuso, A. A., and Hewett, F. M. *Exploring Our Environment: Science Tasks.* Denver, Colorado: Love Publishing Company, 1973, tasks #12, 46, 59, 94. Reprinted by permission.

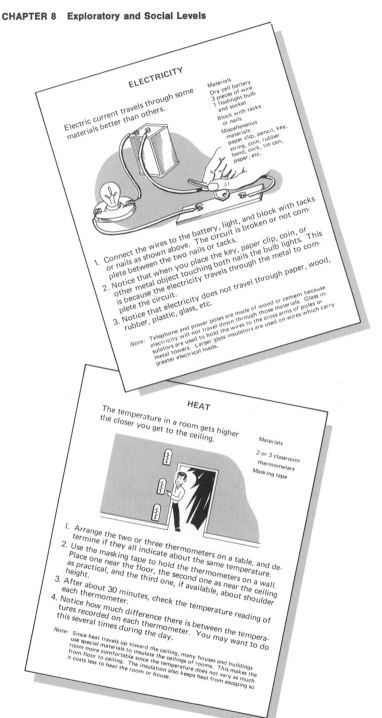

Figure 14: Exploratory Science Tasks

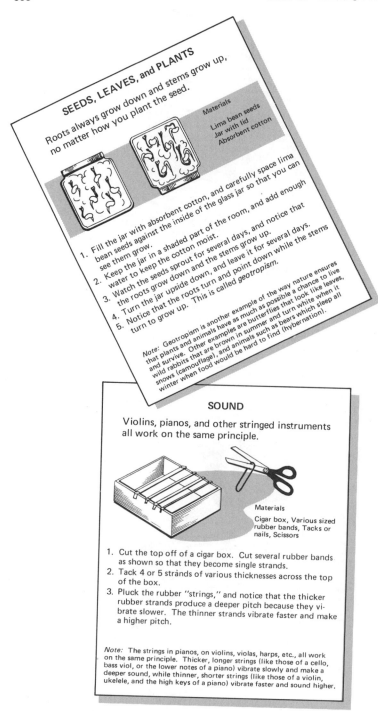

SEEDS, LEAVES, and PLANTS

Roots always grow down and stems grow up, no matter how you plant the seed.

Materials

Lima bean seeds
Jar with lid
Absorbent cotton

1. Fill the jar with absorbent cotton, and carefully space lima bean seeds against the inside of the glass jar so that you can see them grow.
2. Keep the jar in a shaded part of the room, and add enough water to keep the cotton moist.
3. Watch the seeds sprout for several days, and notice that the roots grow down and the stems grow up.
4. Turn the jar upside down, and leave it for several days.
5. Notice that the roots turn and point down while the stems turn to grow up. This is called *geotropism*.

Note: Geotropism is another example of the way nature ensures that plants and animals have as much as possible a chance to live and survive. Other examples are butterflies that look like leaves, wild rabbits that are brown in summer and turn white when it snows (camouflage), and animals such as bears which sleep all winter when food would be hard to find (hybernation).

SOUND

Violins, pianos, and other stringed instruments all work on the same principle.

Materials

Cigar box, Various sized rubber bands, Tacks or nails, Scissors

1. Cut the top off of a cigar box. Cut several rubber bands as shown so that they become single strands.
2. Tack 4 or 5 strands of various thicknesses across the top of the box.
3. Pluck the rubber "strings," and notice that the thicker rubber strands produce a deeper pitch because they vibrate slower. The thinner strands vibrate faster and make a higher pitch.

Note: The strings in pianos, on violins, violas, harps, etc., all work on the same principle. Thicker, longer strings (like those of a cello, bass viol, or the lower notes of a piano) vibrate slowly and make a deeper sound, while thinner, shorter strings (like those of a violin, ukelele, and the high keys of a piano) vibrate faster and sound higher.

Figure 14 — Continued

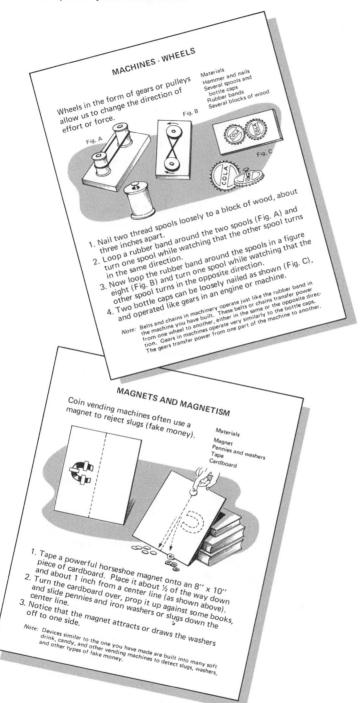

MACHINES - WHEELS

Wheels in the form of gears or pulleys allow us to change the direction of effort or force.

Materials
Hammer and nails
Several spools and bottle caps
Rubber bands
Several blocks of wood

Fig. A   Fig. B   Fig. C

1. Nail two thread spools loosely to a block of wood, about three inches apart.
2. Loop a rubber band around the two spools (Fig. A) and turn one spool while watching that the other spool turns in the same direction.
3. Now loop the rubber band around the spools in a figure eight (Fig. B) and turn one spool while watching that the other spool turns in the opposite direction.
4. Two bottle caps can be loosely nailed as shown (Fig. C), and operated like gears in an engine or machine.

Note: Belts and chains in machinery operate just like the rubber band in the machine you have built. These belts or chains transfer power from one wheel to another, either in the same or the opposite direction. Gears in machines operate very similarly to the bottle caps. The gears transfer power from one part of the machine to another.

MAGNETS AND MAGNETISM

Coin vending machines often use a magnet to reject slugs (fake money).

Materials
Magnet
Pennies and washers
Tape
Cardboard

1. Tape a powerful horseshoe magnet onto an 8'' x 10'' piece of cardboard. Place it about ½ of the way down and about 1 inch from a center line (as shown above).
2. Turn the cardboard over, prop it up against some books, and slide pennies and iron washers or slugs down the center line.
3. Notice that the magnet attracts or draws the washers off to one side.

Note: Devices similar to the one you have made are built into many soft drink, candy, and other vending machines to detect slugs, washers, and other types of fake money.

Figure 14 — Continued

Each task is printed on an 8½ × 11 inch card so that it can be set up on a small easel in the Exploratory Center. The tasks are usually introduced to the children by the teacher during a small group lesson. The directions for the tasks are read, and the simple experiment performed, with each child being given a turn. Subsequently, the task cards are placed at the Center so that the children themselves can return at a later time and undertake them singly or in pairs. Children with reading problems seldom encounter difficulties in doing the tasks because the illustrations are usually comprehensive enough to guide them.

As seen in Figure 14, an effort has been made to select simple but intriguing science tasks that relate more to Exploring Our Environment than to formal science curriculum units. The materials utilized are not expensive or difficult to find. This program grew out of five years of exploratory curriculum development in the engineered classroom. The authors were guided by the following objectives in selecting these tasks:

1. Engage the child in maximum contact with reality through as much multi-sensory involvement as possible
2. Select tasks that have predictable outcomes and that provide a high probability of "working" when the simple directions are followed
3. Utilize informal materials and tasks that are highly relevant to the child's outside environment and that can be replicated at home and shared with others

Parker (1968) supports the notion of developing an extensive elementary school science program for disadvantaged children. He calls attention to the fact that success in science activities can occur with children who are doing poorly in reading or other academic areas. This success may be a key for encouraging them to respond more readily in the classroom and to move toward success in other subject areas.

The lack of order in the general life of the disadvantaged child may make it difficult for him to see cause-and-effect relationships clearly. These limitations can be dealt with directly in a creative science program. In addition, disadvantaged children often lack an adequate orientation to the environment because they have not had the necessary experience or guidance to understand much of what they see going on around them. Children in some disadvantaged areas have been found to hold more superstition and mystical explanations for natural occurrences than do similar children living in middle-class neighborhoods. In this respect a meaningful science program can be of real value to them. Parker describes elements of such a program, which includes study of foods that are a part of the child's home environment and adaptation of units on air, water, insects, and weather so that they directly relate to his total life experience.

A series of woodworking tasks have been developed for use with retarded children in the UCLA Neuropsychiatric Institute School. These tasks involve the construction of simple ˙ trucks from pre-cut materials. The steps in the construction are clearly illustrated with a minimum of written directions, as shown in Figure 15.*

It has been found that with only limited supervision retarded children can assemble the trucks, and derive satisfaction from completion of their efforts and the object that they actually made. This approach can provide more success for children who are restricted in hand-eye coordination and motor skills than can tasks involving the child's sawing of each piece of wood or tasks using commercially available models that have many small components and complex directions. The Exploratory Center in the engineered classroom also includes an area devoted to arts and crafts activities. Several of the tasks that were developed for use in this area appear in Figure 16 (Taylor, Artuso, & Hewett, 1973a).†

One major goal of the Headstart programs for preschool disadvantaged children is to increase competence at the exploratory level by providing youngsters with sensory, perceptual, and conceptual experiences in a rich and multi-varied environment. The Los Angeles Urban League Headstart Project includes such goals as "extending the opportunities for children to ask questions, make their own choices, develop the ability to solve problems, challenge their environment, acquire an enthusiasm and zest for living and learning, and to develop an inquiring and curious wonder about themselves and their world."

Playground experiences directed toward gross motor activity in a typical Headstart program use such equipment as a jungle gym, steps, punching bags, bean bags, jumping boards, jumping ropes, hula hoops, crawl-through barrels, wheeled toys, and rock-

*The author is indebted to Robert L. Thornton of the UCLA Neuropsychiatric Institute School for permission to reprint these plans which he developed.

†From Taylor, F. D., Artuso, A. A., and Hewett, F. M. *Exploring our Environment: Art Tasks.* Denver, Colorado: Love Publishing Company, 1973, tasks #31, 43, 85, 90, 110, and 119. Reprinted by permission.

Step 1:

Motor compartment assembly

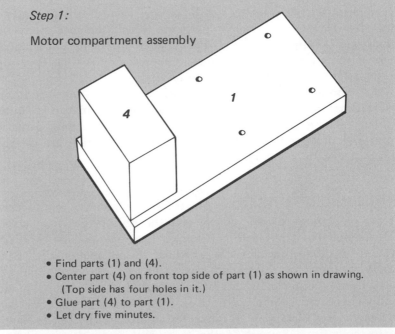

- Find parts (1) and (4).
- Center part (4) on front top side of part (1) as shown in drawing. (Top side has four holes in it.)
- Glue part (4) to part (1).
- Let dry five minutes.

Step 2:

Nailing motor compartment

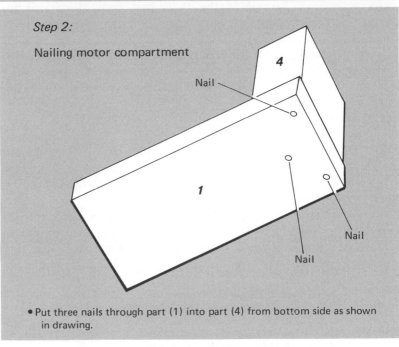

- Put three nails through part (1) into part (4) from bottom side as shown in drawing.

Figure 15: Log Truck Construction Task Plans

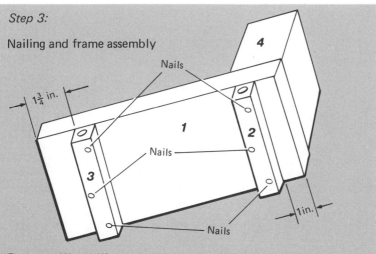

Step 3:

Nailing and frame assembly

- Find parts (2) and (3).
- See measurements on drawing.
- Measure 1 inch (blue line on ruler) and glue part (2) in place as shown in drawing.
- Measure 1 ¾ inch (red line on ruler) and glue part (3) in place as shown in drawing. Let dry five minutes.
- Now put three nails in part (2) and part (3) as shown in drawing.

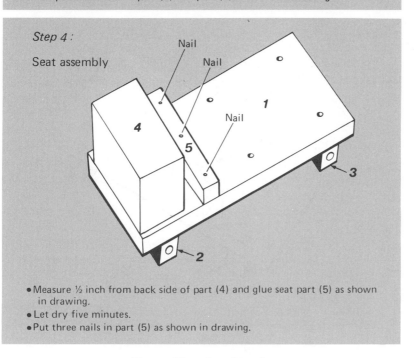

Step 4 :

Seat assembly

- Measure ½ inch from back side of part (4) and glue seat part (5) as shown in drawing.
- Let dry five minutes.
- Put three nails in part (5) as shown in drawing.

Figure 15 — Continued

Step 5:

Steering wheel assembly

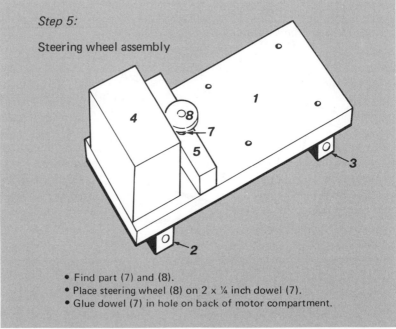

- Find part (7) and (8).
- Place steering wheel (8) on 2 x ¼ inch dowel (7).
- Glue dowel (7) in hole on back of motor compartment.

Step 6:

Cab assembly

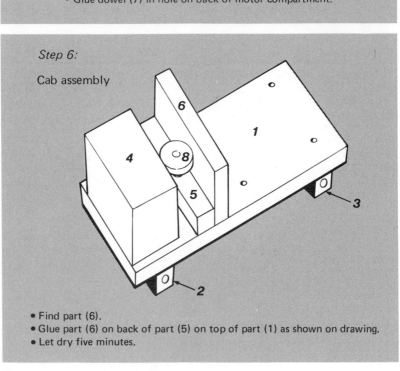

- Find part (6).
- Glue part (6) on back of part (5) on top of part (1) as shown on drawing.
- Let dry five minutes.

Figure 15 — Continued

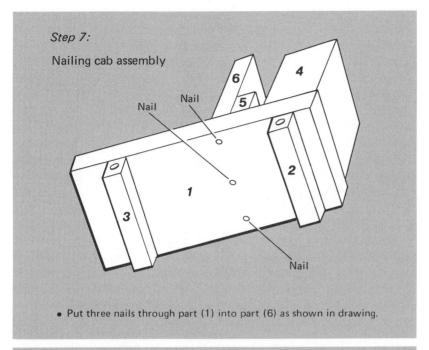

Step 7:

Nailing cab assembly

• Put three nails through part (1) into part (6) as shown in drawing.

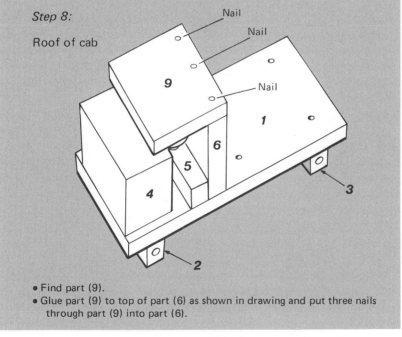

Step 8:

Roof of cab

• Find part (9).
• Glue part (9) to top of part (6) as shown in drawing and put three nails through part (9) into part (6).

Figure 15 — Continued

Step 9:

Log tie downs

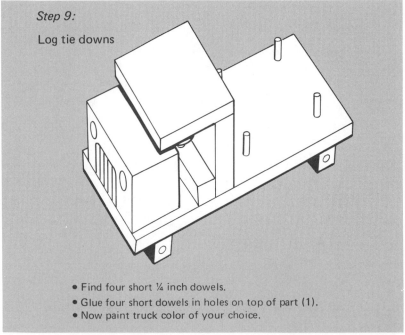

• Find four short ¼ inch dowels.
• Glue four short dowels in holes on top of part (1).
• Now paint truck color of your choice.

Step 10:

Wheel assembly

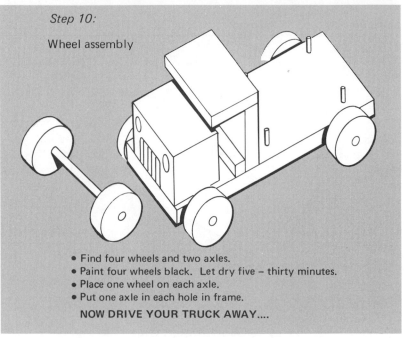

• Find four wheels and two axles.
• Paint four wheels black. Let dry five – thirty minutes.
• Place one wheel on each axle.
• Put one axle in each hole in frame.

NOW DRIVE YOUR TRUCK AWAY....

Figure 15 — Continued

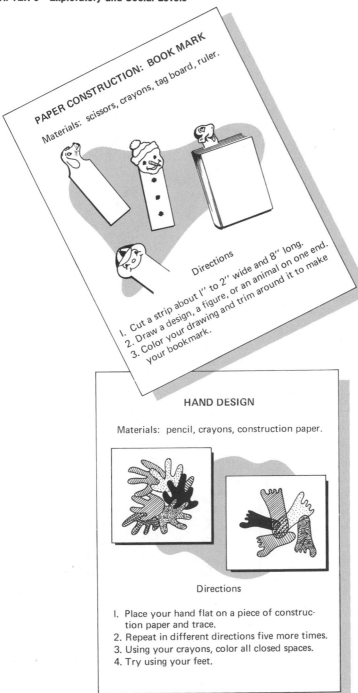

PAPER CONSTRUCTION: BOOK MARK

Materials: scissors, crayons, tag board, ruler.

Directions

1. Cut a strip about 1" to 2" wide and 8" long.
2. Draw a design, a figure, or an animal on one end.
3. Color your drawing and trim around it to make your bookmark.

HAND DESIGN

Materials: pencil, crayons, construction paper.

Directions

1. Place your hand flat on a piece of construction paper and trace.
2. Repeat in different directions five more times.
3. Using your crayons, color all closed spaces.
4. Try using your feet.

Figure 16: Exploratory Art Tasks

FIGURES AND FACES: YARN FACES

Materials: yarn, construction paper, white glue, felt tip pens.

Directions

1. Glue yarn to paper in the shape of a funny face.
2. Add yarn for hair, eyebrows, ties, etc.
3. Use felt tip pens to complete your picture. (Face may be first sketched in pencil.)

FIGURES AND FACES: FLOWER FACES

Materials: heavy cardboard box lid, crayons, scissors, sucker sticks or plastic straws, glue, old magazines, a nail, construction paper.

Directions

1. Color cardboard box lid to represent dirt or grass.
2. Use a nail to punch holes for flower stems.
3. Cut straws or sucker sticks to different lengths, glue into the holes.
4. Use bright construction paper to make flowers, leaves. Glue to stems.
5. Either cut faces from magazines or draw your own. Glue to center of each flower.

Figure 16 — Continued

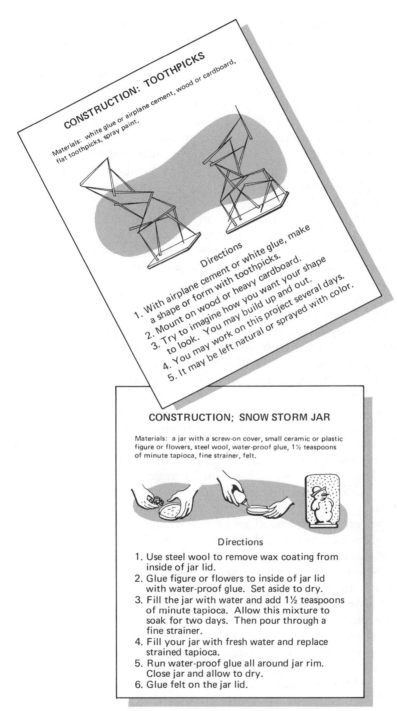

CONSTRUCTION: TOOTHPICKS

Materials: white glue or airplane cement, wood or cardboard, flat toothpicks, spray paint.

Directions

1. With airplane cement or white glue, make a shape or form with toothpicks.
2. Mount on wood or heavy cardboard.
3. Try to imagine how you want your shape to look. You may build up and out.
4. You may work on this project several days.
5. It may be left natural or sprayed with color.

CONSTRUCTION; SNOW STORM JAR

Materials: a jar with a screw-on cover, small ceramic or plastic figure or flowers, steel wool, water-proof glue, 1½ teaspoons of minute tapioca, fine strainer, felt.

Directions

1. Use steel wool to remove wax coating from inside of jar lid.
2. Glue figure or flowers to inside of jar lid with water-proof glue. Set aside to dry.
3. Fill the jar with water and add 1½ teaspoons of minute tapioca. Allow this mixture to soak for two days. Then pour through a fine strainer.
4. Fill your jar with fresh water and replace strained tapioca.
5. Run water-proof glue all around jar rim. Close jar and allow to dry.
6. Glue felt on the jar lid.

Figure 16 — Continued

ing boats. Small muscle activities center around putting on wraps, tying shoes, hanging up coats, using scissors, clothes pins, crayons, chalk, primary pencils, small blocks, brushes, puzzles, and manipulation toys. Much of the emphasis of the Headstart program is aimed at language development through building conceptual understanding at the exploratory level of competence. Cause-and-effect relationships are stressed. Basic forms, such as circles and squares, are presented until the child can reproduce them on request. Classification of objects in the environment, including wild and domestic animals, birds, food, fruits, and vegetables, is taught, and concepts of position in space (i.e., up-down, in-out, over-under) are stressed. By utilizing many of the approaches discussed in this and the previous chapter, an attempt is made by the Headstart program to help the disadvantaged child learn to learn by providing him with the experiential base that is commonly learned by most middle-class American children before they enter school.

As mentioned previously, Johnson and Myklebust (1967) place imagery at the critical step between sensation and perception and the beginning of symbolization and conceptualization in the hierarchy of experience leading to language development. The concept of imagery embodies consideration of perception and retention; it also implies acquisition and understanding of content, one of our major concerns at the exploratory level. Some children with learning disabilities need assistance in comprehending the significance of many aspects of their environment. They may be deficient in social perception in that they do not learn the basic non-verbal aspects of daily living even though their level of verbal intelligence may be better than average.

Educational procedures for improving the child's imagery utilize a variety of visual stimuli. Realistic pictures or photographs are recommended, and initial training can involve the actual matching of a real world object (e.g., comb or key) to its picture. The authors stress starting with a flat object, such as a comb or key, for matching to a two-dimensional picture so as not to complicate the task with emphasis on a third dimension. Activities such as matching objects to outline, filling in details in an incomplete picture (e.g., missing windows in a house), and assembling jig-saw cut-outs of familiar objects are also suggested. Non-verbal motor and body image training and procedures for improving spatial and right-left orientation involve many of the same basic approaches discussed earlier in our response-order section in Chapter 7.

Conditions — How Can Tasks and Experiences Best Be Presented to Improve the Child's Competence at the Exploratory Level?

Much of our discussion on curriculum has direct bearing on conditions. Enriched environmental stimulation, multi-sensory emphasis, and concrete experiences are all related to "how" tasks might best be presented.

It should come as no surprise that the condition of "where" is vital at the exploratory level. Efforts to extend the disadvantaged child's knowledge of his environment often include field trips to museums, theaters, factories, offices, newspaper plants, and department stores. We have already stressed the importance of giving the visually handicapped individual as much direct, real world experience as possible to increase his orientation and mobility skills. Sighted children are often valuable partners for the visually handicapped on field trips since they can describe activities in detail to him, answer questions, and share their own experiences (Pelone, 1957).

Children with borderline vision are unique in terms of colors they best perceive, lighting conditions best suited to maximize their residual vision, and contrasts between shading of objects to help them discriminate more adequately. Jones (1963), therefore, recommends that a careful analysis of such unique characteristics be undertaken in an effort to improve such children's efficiency in orientation and independent travel.

The use of centers in the classroom where interesting activities and displays are available for exploration by all exceptional learners has been discussed several times in this section of the text. Lowenfeld (1971) emphasizes the importance of leaving exploratory materials in the classroom for extended periods of time with visually handicapped children, since if they have access to them only during periods of instruction they may be confined to only cursory examination.

The condition of "how much" can be critical in aiding some exceptional learners to profit from use of classroom centers. Preschool programs for mentally retarded children are generally organized around numerous centers of interest to facilitate the child's interaction with his environment (Kirk, 1972). Downs (1971), however, cautions against offering too many alternatives at once to young retardates since they may run from one to the other and never really learn from any single experience. Decision-making skills can be limited with many of our exceptional learners. The impulsive, disturbed child given his choice between three games, two puzzles, and four construction kits may dump all nine out on the table, sift through the material aimlessly, and generally waste time. No hard and fast rules can be stated, however. For some withdrawn and shy children, creating a highly variable and stimulating center display area may more readily invite their participation. The author has observed that the Exploratory Center in the engineered classroom with middle elementary level emotionally disturbed, learning disability, and mildly retarded children can be successfully arranged with many stimulating displays and task materials. A fish tank, several animal cages, a microscope, an old disassembled telephone, several lengths of wire, a large bolt, a dry cell battery for making an electromagnet, and a series of science task cards like the ones described earlier combine to make the center attractive and to invite participation. In practice, children assigned to the Center are not told to "Go find something to do," but rather are assigned a specific task (e.g., "Wrap this wire around the bolt and attach it to the battery and make a magnet like the one you see in the drawing").

These specifications for an Exploratory Center have proved to be successful with many exceptional learners with whom the author has worked. They may, however, prove disastrous with certain children. One group of inner city, disadvantaged children with serious behavior problems literally went to pieces when a similar multi-stimulating Exploratory Center was set up in their room. On entering the class, they raced to the Center, plunged into all the activities at once, pocketed many of the materials, and engaged in wild bouts of shoving and pushing. It appeared that an invitation to explore can be overwhelming with youngsters who have very limited access to intriguing gadgets and materials in the outside environment. The teacher, recognizing the "how much" problem, wisely began to set out single exploratory tasks each day and allowed each student to explore them thoroughly. Gradually, as the students became familiar with the Center and the materials, it became possible to set out more than one activity without resultant chaos. Thus the teacher shaped the behavior of the class along the lines discussed in the last chapter.

The author was impressed with how well the students in the class eventually engaged in various exploratory activities utilizing tools such as hammers, saws, and screw drivers. Of course, these tools can be dangerous when used inappropriately; but careful planning, explanation, and supervision by the teacher, and consideration of the conditions of "when," "where," and "how much" can keep any serious problems from arising. The looks of satisfaction on the boys' faces as they completed simple two-piece tug boats (which involved nothing more than a pointed length of 2 × 4 wood with a smaller block nailed on it and a large nail mast) gave evidence of the significance of providing such exploratory activities as part of the classroom program.

Summary

We have encountered three major issues in our discussion of the exploratory level of competence. First, most exceptional learners can profit from enriched environmental experiences that broaden their exposure to objects and events and that help them become more familiar with the physical world around them. Such exposure is essential in building the experiential foundation on which symbolization, conceptualization, and language mastery can be built. The second and third issues are closely related. Concrete experiences with the real world teach more vividly than do abstract presentations by the teacher. No beautifully colored picture of an apple labeled "a-p-p-l-e" will ever convey "appleness" as will looking at, smelling, and holding a ripe, red apple and biting into it, savoring its special flavor, and saying aloud, "This is an apple." Trips to the zoo via teacher storytelling will never approach the learning that takes place when the sights, sounds, and smells of a wide assortment of animals and birds collectively impinge on the child during a real trip to a zoo. Multi-sensory experience provides vital confirmation and impact in the exploratory act. And if our exceptional learners lack the capacity to interact via one or more sensory modalities, we make every effort to involve them as totally as possible with their intact modalities.

SOCIAL: THE LEVEL OF COMPETENCE ASSOCIATED WITH MEETING THE SOCIAL EXPECTATIONS OF THE SCHOOL AND GAINING THE APPROVAL AND AVOIDING THE DISAPPROVAL OF OTHERS

In Chapter 3, we saw how critical the exceptional learner's environment was in terms of aggravating or lessening the problems associated with capacity-based handicaps, and in terms of actually creating the handicapping condition itself either on a persistent or transient basis. Learning how to gain approval and avoid disapproval is more complex than learning how to pay attention, participate actively, or acquire knowledge and skill regarding the physical properties of the environment. The subtleties associated with interpersonal relationships, the vast individual differences among those with whom the exceptional learner comes in contact, and the relationship between the child's self-image and the way he perceives and interacts with others make generalizations regarding building the social level of competence difficult to make. Kirk (1972) calls attention to the "intangible" type of development of social skill training with exceptional learners — such training cannot be taught in the same manner as chemistry. Perhaps the primary concern of special educators working with exceptional children is to help them become more competent in the world of people.

In this section, we shall be concerned with several questions related to curriculum and conditions at the social level.

Curriculum
1. What types of tasks and activities will aid the child in improving his general social skills?
2. What types of tasks and activities will aid the child in improving peer relationships?
3. What types of tasks and activities will encourage the development of more positive peer attitudes toward the child?

Conditions
1. How can tasks and activities best be assigned to improve the child's relationship with others?

Some of the educational practices relating to these questions will be discussed at this point.

Curriculum — What Types of Tasks and Activities Will Aid the Child in Improving His General Social Skills?

Social skill training has received considerable attention by special educators working with the retarded. Retarded children, particularly those in the educable range, may have the physical appearance of others of their chronological age but may be limited by a social awareness more typical of a younger child. Such children are often socially immature or insensitive about what is expected of them. In addition, they often do not learn social expectations "incidentally" as is the case with normals. In order to be effective in social interaction, an individual must understand the requirements of the environment and be responsive to appropriate ways of dealing with social demands. Edgerton (1967) has pointed out how retarded adults have particular problems in social interactions and how vitally important it is for them to appear competent in social situations in which they are indeed often not competent at all.

The educable mentally retarded child needs to have experiences with other children in numerous situations with differing degrees of supervision and direction. The trainable retardate, however, may need specific help with certain socialization skills to enable him to enter into group situations. He may need to learn to greet people by saying "hello," to offer his hand for a handshake, to learn to be quiet when someone else is talking, to develop acceptable table manners, and to help others who need assistance (Kirk, 1972).

In terms of the social level of competence, some retarded children may be overly concerned with obtaining adult approval and as a result rely more on outside sources than on their own ability in problem solving. This "outer-directedness" has been observed in a number of studies. Turnure (1970) and Turnure and Zigler (1964) found that retarded children involved in a learning task tended to glance more frequently than normals at the adult experimenter. In one study, retardates appeared more interested in watching an adult putting a puzzle together at a table across from them than they were in solving the puzzle that they had been assigned. Thus they did more poorly on solving this puzzle than did normal children in a similar situation. The retarded children were more "tuned" to the adult's puzzle than to their own; the reverse was true for the normal children. When the second puzzle was given to both groups, however, the retardates did better than the normals since they had been observing it being worked on in advance. Carlson and MacMillan (1970) further demonstrated that educable mentally retarded children would change their prediction of how an event would turn out more readily at an adult's suggestion than would normal children. This was seen as an indication that the retarded children trusted the adult's judgment more than their own.

Even though initially a degree of such outer-directedness may be helpful in learning situations, Zigler (1961) suggests that the retarded child must become more inner-directed if he is to move to higher levels of cognitive development. Independence training with increasing age should be characterized by a continuous reduction in the cues provided the child by adults in an effort to help the child rely as much as possible on his own basic abilities. Thus, one task for the teacher at the social level of competence is to help the retarded child to become less social in cer-

ED

MR

VH

tain situations and to form his own judgments independently of what others might be doing.

The blind child needs more social experiences than does the sighted child in order to overcome the environmental isolation brought on by his disability. He must learn the give and take of social contacts and be helped to avoid self-preoccupation or egocentricity. Facial expressions are important in social communication; early in life blind children need to be encouraged to make faces depicting happiness, sadness, joy, and other emotions and to use such facial expressions appropriate to their mood and conversation. The child should be instructed to look toward the person with whom he is speaking. Developing these habits early in life will aid the blind child in appearing more normal in later contacts.

One area of concern in relation to social competence with the blind has to do with the development of peculiar mannerisms called "blindisms," which may appear unpleasant or bizarre to others. These behaviors include body rocking, head rolling, waving the hands before the eyes, and poking the fingers in the eyes. Such mannerisms are not unique to blind children and can be seen in some mentally retarded and severely emotionally disturbed children. The cause appears to involve a lack of stimulation by the environment and an attempt on the child's part to compensate for this lack of self-stimulation. Even though blindisms tend to disappear as the child grows older, they are best dealt with by parents and teachers on a preventive level. Providing constant activities of interest and increasing environmental stimulation will prevent boredom from occurring and lessen the chances of the child seeking to stimulate himself (Scholl, 1967).

Modeling and role playing techniques have been found to be useful with several types of exceptional learners. Real life situations, such as eating out at a restaurant, introducing oneself to a prospective employer, or asking a girl to go on a date, can be acted out with the children themselves serving alternatively as actors and audience. The teacher assumes the role of director or discussion leader and attempts to help the children learn phrases and gestures appropriate to the social situation. In addition, it is important for the children to learn how to handle the varied types of reactions and expectations of others. Giving the waiter your order, gracefully withdrawing if your prospective date declines, and anticipating the types of personal questions likely to be asked by a job interviewer constitute valuable social learning experiences for many exceptional learners.

A comprehensive attempt at devising a Social Learning

Curriculum (SLC) has been made by Goldstein (1969) for the educable mentally retarded. It is unique in comparison to more traditional unit approaches, which are organized around specific categories of social skills. Goldstein's approach postulates a theoretical base for social training that incorporates research findings and is directly concerned with the learning characteristics of retarded children. This broader, more encompassing orientation conceives of an eventual adult-occupational role for the retarded individual building on experiences from day one in kindergarten.

The core of the theoretical model of the SLC is the self, which undergoes increasing interaction and modification as the child explores new environments and expands his experiences through social encounters with peers and adults. From an egocentric level of self-development, the child moves through interactions with the home and family, neighborhood, and community. Each phase includes three major aspects: social, psychological, and physical. According to Goldstein, the major goals of social competency are independent action and critical thought.

The curriculum tasks presented by the teacher emphasize each environmental level and relate the experiences of that level to the self. For example, the home and family environment is presented as a social institution having direct influence on the child's behavior. But beyond this, the child learns that his individual actions can have a disruptive influence on the family constellation. The child is not only taught the role his parents play in providing nourishment for him but also that this role is aided if he helps with the kitchen chores or is disrupted if he refuses to set the dining room table. Such reciprocal relationships are stressed by the SLC because they lead to higher level critical thought and independent action.

The comprehensiveness of the SLC approach is further exemplified by a brief review of some of the specific social goals in the area of study concerned with the self. The goal of understanding and dealing with dependence is fostered by sub-goals of:

Admission (recognizing dependence)
Assistance (identifying helpers)
Authority (accepting restrictions)
Cooperation (becoming independent and dependable)

Relating to others, or interaction, develops through:

Communication (conversing)
Companionship (being with others)

ED

Friendship (making friends)
Belonging (joining groups)

In the area of social adequacy, or coping with others, the child learns:

Basic skills (attaining social skills)
Understanding milieu (recognizing the environment)
Attitudes (adapting to the environment)

MR

The SLC has undergone field testing in various school districts across the nation. Its focus on translating the complex social environment and its requirements into sequential curriculum tasks clearly delineated for the teacher and child appear to be valuable and highly promising contributions to the field of special education.

As pointed out in Chapter 4, a major reason for referring emotionally disturbed children for evaluation by the school psychologist and possible special class placement is poor social relations. Emotional disturbance is primarily an experientially and environmentally determined disability. Thus, the child's relationships with his peers in school are of significant concern. For this reason, the engineered classroom discussed throughout this section provides for the social level of competence by including a Communication Center in its design. Here, simple games and tasks are stored. They involve two or more children and require appropriate communication and social skills, and that the child respect the rights of others, cooperate, and wait his turn. Some of the tasks used in the Center are shown in Figure 17.* The activities are presented on cards, as were the science tasks illustrated in the last section. The children are introduced to each activity by the teacher so that when they are paired together at the Center they know exactly what to do.

The game of "Battleship" is an example of a successful activity utilized at this center. In this game, the child draws a fleet of ships among printed coordinates on a paper without letting his partner see the position of his fleet. The children take turns calling out coordinates to see if they can score a "hit" on another child's ships. Simple games like this that are based largely on luck rather than skill are more apt to be successful with disturbed children than are complicated games with many directions, rules,

*The author is indebted to Frank D. Taylor of the Santa Monica Schools for permission to reproduce these communication tasks which he developed.

Figure 17: Communication Tasks

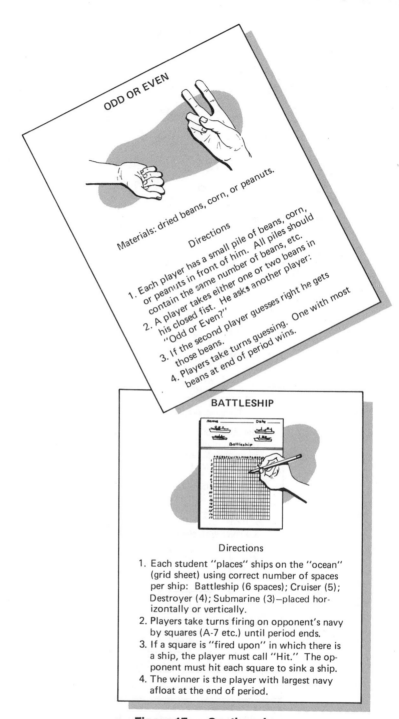

ODD OR EVEN

Materials: dried beans, corn, or peanuts.

Directions

1. Each player has a small pile of beans, corn, or peanuts in front of him. All piles should contain the same number of beans, etc.
2. A player takes either one or two beans in his closed fist. He asks another player: "Odd or Even?"
3. If the second player guesses right he gets those beans.
4. Players take turns guessing. One with most beans at end of period wins.

BATTLESHIP

Directions

1. Each student "places" ships on the "ocean" (grid sheet) using correct number of spaces per ship: Battleship (6 spaces); Cruiser (5); Destroyer (4); Submarine (3)—placed horizontally or vertically.
2. Players take turns firing on opponent's navy by squares (A-7 etc.) until period ends.
3. If a square is "fired upon" in which there is a ship, the player must call "Hit." The opponent must hit each square to sink a ship.
4. The winner is the player with largest navy afloat at the end of period.

Figure 17 — Continued

BUILDING FORTS

1 head – color in one brick marked 1
2 heads – color one brick marked 2
3 heads – color one marked 3
4 heads – color one marked 4
5 heads – color any one you choose
6 heads – color any one you choose
6 tails – color any one you choose

3		
5	2	
1	4	1
2		5

				3
5	1	1	1	3
4	2	1	3	1
3	1	2	3	
2				
4				

Directions

1. Each player is given a fort to "build" (blank).
2. Each player shakes a cup filled with six pennies, and rolls them on the table.
3. The player colors in the bricks of his fort, depending on how the pennies turn up.

Example: one player is x
          one player is o   Loser

X O O X X O X X X O O O X O O X X O O O X O O O X

_ _
_ _
_ _
_ _
_ _
_ _
_ _
_ _
_ _
_ _
_ _
_ _
_ _

Directions

1. Each player takes a turn filling in one, two, or three symbols.
2. The player who ends the line of 25 blank spaces is the loser.

Figure 17 — Continued

and possible outcomes, or games like checkers and chess in which the more skilled child predictably ends up the winner.

Curriculum — What Types of Tasks and Activities Will Aid the Child in Improving Peer Relationships?

A basic problem faced by many exceptional learners is learning to live with the stigma and labeling associated with their handicaps and with the name-calling, ridicule, and rejection that are often directed toward them by their peers. In a study of this problem area, Jones (1972) has reported on conclusions reached by teacher-led discussion with educable mentally retarded children that focused on negative peer experiences. In general, the retarded students concluded that they:

1. Should accept themselves, do the best they can, and develop a better outlook
2. Should ignore or tolerate negative comments
3. Should attempt to improve their own behavior and act intelligent as do regular students
4. Actually have some advantages and skills themselves and can learn and excel in some areas
5. Should consider other persons ignorant, immature, or inferior for calling them names

Smith (1968) has stressed the importance of working with older retarded children on personal grooming since peer pressure is such a basic part of the child's social life. The teacher should call the individual's attention to the possibilities of offending others by not maintaining appropriate grooming and the health reasons for cleanliness and good dress. This is seen as particularly important since it is easier to detect and "size-up" an untidy person at a glance than it is to identify an academic problem in the retarded.

The likelihood of remaining in a regular classroom rather than being labeled "mentally retarded" and referred out for special class placement has been found to be related to the social level of competence. Mercer (1971), investigating the differences between similar retardates, some of whom were functioning adequately in a regular class and some of whom were in special classes, found that the child who had a "friend" in the regular classroom was significantly less likely to be called retarded or to be given a special class assignment. Aiding the retarded child in improving his peer relationships and thus increasing his chances for forming friendships becomes particularly important in light of this finding.

The gifted child also needs a variety of friendships in order for adequate social adjustment to occur. Ideally, the gifted child should be given opportunities to work and play with children who share his superior intellectual potential. This will assure him of challenging and stimulating conversation and experiences. But opportunities to interact with children who function at more average levels is also important since their interests and activities will broaden the gifted child's social skills and will enable him to enjoy the company of many types of children and to become an acceptable member of varying social groups. Dunlap (1967) has pointed out that the lack of companionship, not the degree of intelligence, sometimes makes social adjustment for very bright children a problem area.

Curriculum — What Types of Tasks and Activities Can Be Utilized to Encourage the Development of More Positive Peer Attitudes toward the Child?

An example of the social environment's aggravation of a capacity-based problem is found in relation to the physically handicapped. The actual physical disability may not contribute to the overall functioning level of the disabled individual as much as does his interaction with the social milieu (Block, 1951). This interaction may be more favorable in the early years when normal children are less aware of developmental expectations, more inclined to be helpful to a less capable peer, and not repulsed by a handicap that is not yet seen as carrying a social stigma. Thus, providing the physically handicapped child with opportunities for associations with the non-handicapped in the preschool years can help him develop a more positive self-concept and establish a more adequate, early social adjustment.

PH

G

As the physically handicapped child matures, a significant increase in unfavorable attitudes toward him by his nondisabled peers occurs. Therefore, young elementary age handicapped individuals are subject to fewer negative attitudes than are disabled teenagers, and disabled college students encounter fewer such attitudinal problems than do graduates seeking employment.

Connor, Rusalem, and Cruickshank (1971) conclude that the most promising approach for improving the attitudes of others toward the disabled is planned interaction between the two groups under favorable conditions. Such conditions would no doubt include opportunities for the disabled to enter into activities commensurate with their actual abilities and to demonstrate to the nondisabled that they are not as restricted and handicapped as others may believe them to be. Favorable interaction between the two groups would also aid the disabled individuals in developing interests, social skills, and a more realistic and positive self-concept. Although authors cited earlier see such group encounters under adult leadership as requiring social and psychological sophistication and educational engineering, they view the stakes as significantly high enough for the adjustment of the handicapped child to warrant the careful planning that must take place. The group encounter approach is recognized by them as the most productive method for modifying the attitudes of nonhandicapped peers.

Realistic and positive interaction between disturbed, retarded, visually handicapped, hearing handicapped, and speech handicapped children and normal peers probably also holds promise for effective attitude change. The author recalls a community program for blind adolescents that included a weekly dance held with sighted teenagers. Discussion with the sighted young people after the dance often revealed their genuine surprise at the sense of humor, knowledge of adolescent interests, and good dancing ability of the blind teenagers. Yet the success of these dances relied at times on careful pairing of more mature, non-handicapped individuals with the more shy and less secure blind adolescents, as well as specially planned ice breaker games to acquaint the members of the groups with each other.

Steinzor (1966) studied the attitudes of school peers of visually handicapped children. On the elementary level, the lowest attitudes for cooperation and highest attitudes of rejection were found among those classmates who were having their initial experience with blind children in the classroom. Their attitudes improved as they had increased experience with blind individuals. At the junior high level, attitudes of independence on the part of sighed peers (respect for another person's needs without entering into cooperative activities) were modified by increased contact with blind teenagers and changed to attitudes of mutual cooperation.

Conditions — How Can Tasks and Activities Best Be Assigned to Improve the Child's Relationship with Others?

The condition of "where" the exceptional learner interacts with others can be critical for his social success or failure. One such aspect of this condition has to do with the regular versus the special class. Educable mentally retarded children have been found to be rejected significantly more often as playmates than are normals regardless of whether they were integrated in regular classrooms or separated in a special class (Goodman, Gottlieb, & Harrison, 1972; Gottlieb & Davis, 1971). Special class placement, however, appears to lower the self-esteem of retarded children. Some evidence suggests that such children may be played with less often in their home neighborhoods even though in these settings they are generally accepted as normal children. The earlier-cited findings of Mercer (1971) that retarded children with a friend in a regular classroom were less often labeled retarded or referred for special class placement leads to an interesting speculation in this context. On one hand, this may indicate the superior social skills of such retardates in the first place; but on the other hand, it may indicate that a friendship with a normal peer might develop more readily in the regular classroom and that this relationship puts the retarded child in a more favorable position to adapt to school and thus to gain the acceptance of others.

Integration of the educable mentally retarded child in a regular class may solve some of the problems associated with special class segregation but may create others. For example, if the child is perceived by normal peers as no different from themselves, they may subject him to the same standards of behavior. In a special class more excuses for poorer social and academic behavior may exist and, as a result, less is expected of the retarded child. Probably no ideal condition for increasing social competence can be postulated for all retarded children. The special class may lower self-esteem and increase the probability of rejection by peers, but it may also remove the child from expectations and stresses he cannot handle in the regular classroom. The regular classroom may exert such stresses and expectations but offer more opportunities for friendships and experiences with normal peers. The most appropriate match of child and setting must be determined by studying the individual child — a lesson we constantly encounter and will continue to encounter in matching the child to any educational approach.

For retarded children unable to participate in any group situation, Johnson (1967) suggests shaping the child's behavior according to development stages of normal children's play. Initially, the child should be placed in a parallel play situation where he plays in the vicinity of, but does not interact with, other children. Next, play experience with one other child should be provided. A second child and gradually several others may be added until appropriate play is undertaken with minimal teacher supervision.

Summary

Although our previous discussion about aiding the exceptional learner at the social level of competence drew heavily from studies and work done with the mentally retarded, almost every approach mentioned applied across all our categories.   Difficulties in critically evaluating social situations, understanding the implications involved, and selecting an appropriate strategy for dealing with them are apt to be encountered by many exceptional children.   The focus of Goldstein's Social Learning Curriculum, with its concern for the child in interactions with the ever-expanding social environment from home and neighborhood to the larger community, is actually an analytic organization of the socialization process applicable to all children — normal and exceptional.   Exceptional learners are unique in that their acquisition of these social skills is often uneven — interfered with by capacity or experience-based problems or a combination of both.   The incidental learning that marks the normal child's social development cannot be taken for granted with exceptional children, and we must target in on deficiencies and remedy them.   Personal grooming skills are important to emphasize with disturbed, disadvantaged, blind, deaf, and physically handicapped youngsters.   Social isolation can occur with any of them, and with it a lack of knowledge and skill regarding basic expectations of others.   Peculiar mannerisms such as rocking, thumbsucking, or nailbiting can add to many exceptional children's visibility and thus increase the probability of their rejection by others.   When it comes to changing the perception of peers toward exceptional learners, probably no single approach holds more promise than favorable interaction between the two groups.   Dispelling the distortions and myths associated with the handicapped through actual observation and experience has been found to be effective with regular classroom teachers as well.

The effects of regular or special class placement is of concern across all nine categories, including the gifted.   We shall examine the literature relating to this issue in more detail in Chapter 10.

CONSEQUENCES

In our discussion of various types of consequences that can be relied on in the classroom (see Chapter 6), we considered two that have relevance at the exploratory and social levels of learning competence — multi-sensory stimulation and activity, and social attention and approval.

Three major issues emerged in our section on exploratory curriculum and conditions. These issues had to do with providing experiences for the exceptional learner that offered enrichment, concrete involvement, and multi-sensory feedback. The rewarding consequence of multi-sensory stimulation and activity is directly built into each issue; hence, pursuit of tasks related to the three issues carries with it promise of its own reward. The materials used with Victor by Itard in the early 1800's and later training materials developed by Seguin relied on such rewards in their appeal to the learner. The carefully designed, intriguing, and colorful teaching materials in the Montessori classroom are further examples.

Special educators working with individuals in each of the nine categories have long recognized the value and importance of attractive curriculum materials that invite the child's looking, listening, touching, and moving; and as a result, multi-sensory stimulation and activity rewards are associated with many types of specialized curriculum materials.

A systematic use of exploratory level rewards to aid in the improvement of social and academic behavior is found in the application of the Premack principle, briefly introduced in Chapter 6. Essentially, the principle states a well-known technique used by all parents and teachers for influencing children's behavior. Two kinds of information are required:

1. What behaviors *do not* occur with the frequency and ease that the parent or teacher considers desirable (e.g., taking out the garbage, completing an arithmetic assignment)
2. What behaviors *do* occur with predictable frequency and ease when the child is left to his own resources (e.g., watching television, browsing through the Exploratory Center in the classroom)

The Premack principle simply states that low frequency behaviors can be increased or accelerated if they are followed by high frequency behaviors. Thus, the parent who states "Take the garbage out and then you may watch television" is utilizing the principle. We may expect garbage-taking-out behavior to occur more frequently if television watching is made contingent on its occurrence. In a like manner, the teacher who announces, "Once your arithmetic assignment is complete you may spend time at the Exploratory

Center," may expect assignments to be completed more frequently since time at the Exploratory Center depends on such completion.

Whelan (1966) has discussed the use of the Premack principle in programs for exceptional learners. Initially, the teacher observes the child and notes both high and low frequency behaviors. Then, task assignments such as reading and arithmetic are given to the child and presented with the "how much" condition specified (e.g., "Here is a page of six division problems"). When the six problems are done, the teacher specifies a "how long" condition for the high interest activity (e.g., "You may now spend five minutes at the Exploratory Center"). Over time, the "how much" condition for the task assignment can be increased. From six problems, such assignments can be lengthened to eight, ten, twelve, or more with each task assignment followed by a five-minute free-time period. Care must be taken not to increase the task assignment demand too abruptly (e.g., from six problems to three pages of problems in a workbook) or the approach will not work. The subtleties of the shaping techniques discussed in the Consequences section of the previous chapter are relevant here.

A study undertaken at the New Mexico School for the Deaf utilized exploratory rewards as a consequence for appropriate work behavior (Osborne, 1969). Six deaf girls, ages eleven to thirteen years, given to out-of-seat wandering and disruptive behavior were assigned fifteen-minute work periods followed by five minutes of free time if they remained in their seats during the work period. Free time was restricted to the inside of the classroom. The procedure was reported as highly effective, and work periods were gradually lengthened to twenty-five minutes with no increase in the five-minute free-time period. The study was replicated by Medland and Stachnik (1972).

Barrish, Saunders, and Wolf (1969) used an exploratory reward approach on a group basis with a fourth-grade class of twenty-four students. Seven students were identified who had problems of out-of-seat behavior, noisemaking, talking out, uncooperativeness, and general classroom disruption. The entire class was divided into two teams. Opportunities for privileges for each team, such as extra recess time, first in line for lunch, and time for special projects, were made contingent on the team's maintaining appropriate behavior. Whenever a child on either team was inappropriate, a mark was made on the chalk board, and his team's chances for such privileges were jeopardized. Thus the entire team shared loss of privileges when individual members demonstrated problem behavior. The approach significantly and reliably reduced the disruptive behavior of most of the problem

ED

students. Two of the students, however, had to be given marks on an individual basis since whenever they behaved inappropriately, they appeared to be positively reinforced by the negative comments of their team peers. We see here an example of the paradoxical effect of negative reinforcement on some children, which was discussed in the last chapter.

In the engineered classroom, the Premack principle is used in a less specific and individual manner. Check marks are given periodically throughout the day for appropriate task and social behavior. When a Work Record Card is completed, the child has the option of exchanging it for a small amount of food or candy, fifteen minutes of free-choice time at any of the classroom's interest centers (Order, Exploratory, or Communication), or an opportunity to draw from a Take-a-Chance deck of cards on the teacher's desk. The second option involves use of an Activity Card such as the one shown in Figure 18.* The teacher writes in the child's name and draws the hands of the clock showing the child when his fifteen minutes of activity time will be up. This third option in-

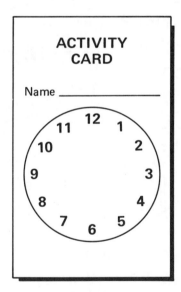

Figure 18: Free-Choice Time Activity Card

*The author is indebted to Frank D. Taylor of the Santa Monica Schools for permission to reproduce these materials (Figs. 18 and 19), which he developed.

volves gaining the privilege of participating in one of a number of desirable classroom events. Figure 19 depicts some of the privileges appearing on the cards, each of which is pictured and described on a card in the deck. Both the second and third options involve exploratory level rewards of multi-sensory stimulation and activity.

Although all three options are available, the author has observed that after five or six weeks in an engineered classroom program the majority of children choose free time or "take-a-chance." Those who decry the bribing or enticement they attribute to the giving of tangible rewards in the classroom and who feel children will become dependent on them to the exclusion of intrinsic incentives, such as joy, should take note. Exploratory rewards involving intriguing sensory and motor experiences are powerful consequences that are intimately woven into the acquisition of knowledge and skills related to the physical properties of the environment.

Social approval and disapproval may well constitute the most frequently relied-on consequences found in the classroom.

Figure 19: Take-a-Chance Examples

There are literally hundreds of social exchanges between teachers and children, children and children, and children and the principal, school clerks, librarian, custodian, playground coach, school bus driver, and crossing guards. Some of these exchanges are positive and some negative, but in the main all are directed toward helping the child understand and learn the rules and expectations of this community setting. That is not to say there is always a constructive, fair, sensitive, and consistent pattern to such exchanges. Unfortunately, the real world is a human world, the real people in it human beings, and as a result children on occasion experience hard knocks at the hands of others. Most learn to adjust and to handle unfair, insensitive, and inconsistent social experiences. Our exceptional learners, however, may be particularly vulnerable to these experiences. In the remaining section of this chapter, we shall examine social consequences.

The susceptibility of the retarded child to social consequences has been discussed at several points throughout the text. Some authors (Forness & MacMillan, 1972) suggest that such consequences are much more powerful than tangible or token forms of reinforcement and that relying on the latter unnecessarily may be an example of "reinforcement overkill." The point is made that the teacher should recognize the power of social attention, approval, and disapproval and use it carefully and wisely in improving the classroom performance of retarded children. The susceptibility of the retarded to social praise has been further illustrated in a study by McManis (1967). Educable mentally retarded children who were seated next to another retardate who was praised by the teacher actually increased in their performance even though they themselves were not the targets for such praise.

In Chapter 7, we mentioned the study by Levin and Simmons (1962), which compared the effectiveness of food rewards, social praise, and food and social praise combined during a simple marble-dropping task. The food rewards alone were more effective than were social praise or food and social praise combined. Despite the primitiveness of this study, the author has observed that some emotionally disturbed children are not responsive to positive social reinforcement given by the teacher, especially in the initial stages of a program. One severe behavior problem boy bit the teacher on the arm as she attempted to give him an approving pat on the shoulder. Another angrily shouted "shut up" when the teacher verbally praised him. An eleven-year-old disturbed boy would tear up his paper if the teacher made such comments as "Good work," and a withdrawn, anxious girl would run from the classroom if the teacher in any way spoke out to her. The under-

ED

lying reasons for these children's discomfort in such social situations were undoubtedly varied. But the fact remained that all the good intentions in the world on the teacher's part did not make social control or approval effective.

Although space does not permit a lengthy aside at this point in our discussion, it must be mentioned that teachers as well as children need positive consequences for their efforts. The children just described could hardly be said to have contributed to the teacher's job satisfaction and feelings of personal and professional worth. The author has talked with numerous teachers during the early stages of their work with disturbed children and has heard their frustration, sense of failure, and even anger when they told of children who seemed to go out of their way to reject them despite the teacher's genuine interest in relating to and working with them. Two considerations appear relevant in this regard:

1. Despite any exceptional learner's seeming rejection of attempts at contact or approval, his behavior may not reflect true feelings or the eventual importance such experiences may assume once a secure relationship is developed
2. Effective teaching with any exceptional learner requires a tolerance for failing gracefully in many areas

Thus, a patient and objective orientation is vital in working with children whose problems may well be rooted almost entirely in previous unsatisfactory interpersonal relationships. Bruno (1969) found teachers who stayed for a relatively short time in the field of teaching emotionally disturbed children were characterized by needs of "nurturance," whereas those who remained in the field demonstrated needs of "dominance" and "autonomy." Extremely dominating, aloof teachers are not desirable and teachers with excessive needs to nurture and develop emotionally satisfying relationships with their children may not be able to stand the real world ups and downs inherent in work with disturbed children. The author has never been able to sketch the profile of the ideal teacher for disturbed children with certainty and finality, but has come to recognize the importance of such teachers having not only a deep concern for the problems of children but also a personal life and adjustment of their own that was thoroughly satisfying and fulfilling once the classroom day was behind them.

Returning to our socially uncomfortable children, the author has found the check mark system used in the engineered classroom an effective shaping procedure. Initially, the check marks are administered in a strictly task and behavior oriented manner.

The checks are given "because you have earned them" or withheld because "you did not earn them." No mention is made of the teacher's pleasure or displeasure, approval or disapproval. Since the teacher is the agent giving the check marks, however, her involvement and presence in the process is undeniable. By emphasizing the positive aspects of the child's behavior with the check marks, by assigning tasks clearly at the child's level so that he can readily be successful and earn check marks, and finally, by having a completed card of check marks redeemable for tangible or exploratory rewards, the system becomes a positive interaction between teacher and child. The author has found that the interaction can become increasingly more social as the teacher adds comments such as, "I liked the way you raised your hand for help," or "This work is exactly as I wanted it," when it appears the children like the ones described earlier can tolerate and profit from this social emphasis. Thus, the check mark system can move from a more objective, neutral meeting ground for teacher and child to a highly social interaction. Initially, respecting some exceptional learner's preference for social distance from others and gradually shaping the environment so a positive, comfortable interaction occurs when they are ready for it is an important consideration for teachers at the social level.

A number of studies have appeared in the literature that have investigated the effect of teacher social consequences — both positive and negative — on the behavior of children with learning and behavior problems. Hall, Lund, and Jackson (1968) observed one first grade and five third grade students who were given to disruptive, dawdling behavior. The teacher gave these children social attention for appropriate behavior and ignored them when they were inattentive or disruptive. This procedure sharply increased the study rates of the children. A reversal stage, during which time the teacher paid attention to non-study behavior, produced low study rates. However, once the initial approach was reinstated, study rates again markedly increased and were maintained even after the experimental program terminated.

A study of the effects on classroom behavior of imposing rules, ignoring inappropriate behavior, and showing approval for appropriate behavior was conducted in two elementary classrooms by Madsen, Becker, and Thomas (1968). The findings indicated that rules alone had little effect on controlling classroom problem behavior and that ignoring inappropriate behavior and giving approval for appropriate behavior in combination was effective in reducing such behavior. The authors concluded that providing approval for appropriate behavior is probably the key to effective

ED

classroom management. Thus, accentuating the positive, as discussed earlier, is given support by this study.

An interesting aspect of social verbal control in the classroom was investigated by O'Leary, Kaufman, Kass, and Drabman (1970). Initial observation of several regular classrooms that included a number of problem children revealed that most teacher reprimands for inappropriate behavior were loud in nature and could be heard by many children in the class. When the teachers were asked to speak in private, in a soft voice audible only to the child in question, the frequency of disruptive behavior declined in most of the children. Reversal of the procedure produced an increase of disruptive behavior, and a later return to the private, soft voice condition caused such behavior to decline again.

Selective attention to appropriate behavior and de-emphasizing attention to or actually ignoring inappropriate behavior appear to be approaches that have utility for managing many types of children. As discussed earlier, however, the susceptibility of individual problem learners to social consequences can vary considerably. As a result, individual rather than universal conclusions regarding application must be drawn by the teacher.

Throughout this text, we have discussed how point of view toward the emotionally disturbed child can differentiate certain special educational procedures utilized by the teacher. The behavioral studies cited above focused on such children as learners whose behavior could be influenced by social consequences under the control of the teacher. This orientation is concerned with overt behavior and bringing it in line with standards required for learning.

A contrasting orientation that focuses on the inner life of the child and understanding his psychological conflicts might prefer an approach such as Life Space Interviewing, particularly in dealing with more "crisis" type behaviors than those of inattention, dawdling, or talking out in the classroom. The Life Space Interview technique is a form of therapeutic assistance that involves both the teacher and child in a discussion of the events associated with a problem in school. If a child becomes so frustrated following his unsuccessful efforts to complete an assignment that he tears up his worksheet, throws his book on the floor, and angrily strikes out at a classmate sitting nearby, he might be taken aside by the teacher, calmed down, and engaged in a therapeutic interview regarding what had happened. The teacher would focus on the actual environmental situation, what led up to the problem, and how such an upset might be avoided in the future. The psychodynamics of the child's problems over time would not be dealt with as they might during a more formal therapy session by a psychiatrist or psychologist. Rather, an attempt would be made to provide psychological first aid in the immediate real world setting in which the problem had occurred.

The Life Space Interview technique has evolved from the work of Redl (1959), Morse and Small (1959), and Morse (1963, 1965). It aims at strengthening the child's coping skills so that he can deal with a wide variety of environmental demands. The concept of social consequences is broadened by this approach to include a therapeutic relationship between teacher and child and a more complex interaction than is involved in teacher-controlled attention, approval, or disapproval as a management technique. Life Space Interviewing requires a high degree of training, supervision, and sophistication in order for a teacher to understand and utilize it effectively. In addition, it requires time to be spent with the child away from the classroom.

In the national study by Morse, Cutler, and Fink (1964) that investigated school programs for disturbed children, the Life Space Interview or some form of counseling on an individual or group basis was one of three overall ways in which teachers attempted to manage classroom behavior. A second was indirect; it consisted of attempts to maintain a good program and reasonable routine, thereby keeping management problems from arising in the first place. A third stressed the student's individual responsibility for behavior and included exclusion from the classroom until the student stated he was ready to return.

When a child is excluded by the teacher, he is technically being removed from the physical and social environment of the classroom and hence from opportunities to obtain exploratory or social rewards. In addition, the act of exclusion itself, with the teacher leading the child to the door and saying, "You'll have to stay out in the hall until you can be good," is a negative social reinforcement—underscoring the teacher's disapproval of the child and his behavior and bolstered by the child's peers witnessing the whole scene. That is the way it is supposed to work. But some children, bored and miserable in the classroom, are only too glad to escape and some may find the exploratory and social rewards of the hall or principal's office more exciting than those in the classroom.

However, a time-out period of isolation in a quiet, nonstimulating area or room may be effective in getting some children who are upset to settle down. It also serves to remove them from the class so that the effect of disruptive behavior on other children is limited. Whelan and Haring (1966) have reported suc-

ED

cess with such a time-out management technique. In the engineered classroom, a time-out period is utilized as one of a series of interventions designed to deal systematically with problems of disruptive behaviors. It is not employed, however, until after consideration of a series of alternatives available to the teacher for maintaining the child as a learner in the classroom. These interventions have been conceptualized in relation to the levels of learning competence utilized in this part of the text and will be briefly summarized.

If a given assignment is resisted or if inappropriate behavior occurs that cannot be ignored, the teacher may consider:

1. Keeping the assignment but reassigning the child to a study booth where he may change body position, engage in some motor activity, and work freer from distraction (mastery level)
2. Changing the assignment by making it easier, harder, or different (mastery level)
3. Verbally restructuring classroom expectations (social level)
4. Sending the child to the Exploratory Center where he may undertake a simple science or art task (exploratory level)
5. Sending the child to the Order Center for assignment to a direction following activity such as working on a puzzle, assembling a construction kit, or matching a peg-board design (order level)
6. Taking the child outside the classroom and assigning him a motor activity task, such as running around the playground, punching on a punching bag for several minutes, or turning somersaults on the grass (response level)
7. Providing individual tutoring at the child's desk (attention level)

All these interventions are considered student interventions; that is, each involves participating in an assigned classroom activity and maintaining the child as a candidate for receiving his full complement of check marks. An issue that immediately arises in light of our discussion of reinforcement principles is: isn't allowing a child to leave an assignment that upsets him or that is something he does not want to do (e.g., arithmetic worksheets) and then assigning him a possibly more desirable activity in the classroom (e.g., doing an order task) an example of actually rewarding inappropriate behavior? Wouldn't you then expect the child to actively seek such reassignment in the future and to increase his frequency of rejecting academic tasks?

According to certain principles of behavior theory, the answer to this question would be yes. Yet, over seven years of observing children with serious behavior and learning problems in engineered classrooms, the author has found that this occurs very infrequently. In most cases, the child settles down with the intervention task and can soon be brought back to his desk for continued academic work. On subsequent days, the teacher carefully selects academic tasks that appear to hold promise for success and selects conditions for presenting them (e.g., "how long," "how much") that also contribute to success. Most exceptional learners truly want to learn. The term learner used throughout the text is not a one-way designation conjured up by the special educator and imposed on the child. It is a two-way statement of the objectives of the teacher and the desires of the child. That not all exceptional children directly communicate such desires has largely to do with the nature of their previous experience. It is up to the teacher and learning environment to create conditions and experiences that counteract negative previous experiences and allow these desires to find expression.

Such counteraction is the aim of the intervention approaches just discussed. By removing the child from a conflictual situation, yet keeping him involved with an assigned student task, we are going beyond the simple operant conditioning paradigm that suggests that rewarding negative behavior will increase its frequency in the future. In actuality, we are desensitizing the child to some of the unpleasant, negative stimuli associated with the teacher, the classroom, and learning due to past experience. Making tasks in the classroom positive through instant change if necessary, establishing the teacher as an agent of such change directed toward keeping the child a winner, and engaging the child in learning activities that guarantee success are the critical elements of this desensitization and are in line with principles of respondent rather than operant conditioning. Space here will not permit a lengthy aside to consider the differences and similarities between these two types of learning; they have been discussed elsewhere (Forness, 1970; Hewett, 1968; Bijou & Baer, 1961).

Although we would like to close our discussion of intervention approaches with an air of certainty that they always work, we must again assume our position of relativism rather than absolutism. Often such efforts in a structured classroom in which all the children clearly understand the rules and know the program is systematically success-oriented are very effective in maintaining student behavior. But "often" is not "always," and additional measures may be necessary to use in the classroom management process. This brings us back to the time-out technique briefly

ED

mentioned earlier. In the engineered classroom, intervention number six in our list is a non-student intervention and involves removal of the child from the classroom for a time-out period according to the following considerations:

1. It should occur only after the child's behavior has exceeded the limits that have been clearly stated to him previously, and after consideration or trial has been made of one or more of the student interventions
2. It should occur matter-of-factly rather than as a result of teacher exasperation
3. It should be presented to the child as a constructive aid to learning rather than arbitrary punishment (e.g., "It seems as though you cannot function as a student right now in the classroom. I hope you will be able to after a time-out period")
4. It should involve a specific period of time rather than an open-ended exclusion (e.g., "You may come back when you think you can behave")
5. It should place the child in the best available setting where exploratory and social stimulation is limited
6. Once the time-out period has passed, the child should immediately return to the class without any lecturing or attempt to get him "to promise to be a good boy from now on"

What is implied is a systematic procedure, free from a punitive and arbitrary attitude on the part of the teacher. In the engineered classroom, the child cannot earn check marks during the time-out period, which is usually for five or ten minutes. Once he returns, the teacher again reconsiders the intervention possibilities and attempts to assign him to a task level where it appears he can be successful. The success for any time-out procedure hinges on a basic assumption that the positive aspects of the classroom program are so powerful that removal from the room is clearly a negative condition. The author has long advocated the creation of classroom learning environments that are so stimulating and rewarding that the child literally cannot afford to be away from them for any period of time. As idealistic as this may sound, it echoes the concern of many that education go on the offensive rather than remain on the defensive in terms of reaching and teaching children. How much more desirable to have the child actively seeking maximum time in the classroom because of the promise of stimulation and success rather than relying on coercion to get him to school.

The time-out procedure can be misused; the author has

ED

witnessed several examples of this in public schools. One district built a special classroom for emotionally disturbed children that included a so-called time-out room with a self-locking door. The room was small and had no windows. A single light bulb was in the ceiling. When serious behavior problems occurred with a child, he was instructed to go to the time-out room. If he refused, he was physically forced to go despite his kicking and screaming. Once he was inside, the door was locked, and he was left for a period of time to quiet down. The district claimed this technique worked with some children, but there was an occasional child who kicked and clawed at the door until his fingers bled and who became extremely upset by the procedure. One such boy was put in the room after the light bulb had been broken by a previous occupant and left for several hours in the dark.

Without speculating on the error in judgment involved in locking a child in a darkened room as a classroom management procedure, or even on the effects of such an experience on the child, the point should be made that physically dragging an upset child to a time-out room and locking the door after him is probably a losing proposition from the start. The message that "we want to help you be successful in the class but you must meet us· at least part or half way for this to occur" is simply overshadowed by the message, "We are bigger and stronger than you and will punish you if you are bad." Some readers of this text will undoubtedly recall experiences with aggressive, delinquent children and adolescents who seem to live by the "law of the alley" with its respect for physical force and violence. The author has witnessed teachers working with such children who periodically used force to keep their students in line. But at best, an uneasy truce seemed to be maintained as a result.

It is the author's contention that unless the time-out intervention is linked clearly and systematically to maintaining the child in an educational program oriented toward helping him succeed and learn, it will only increase anxiety toward the school and resentment toward the teacher. There is no way to conclude this discussion with cookbook finality with respect to all children with behavior problems and to all special education programs. The author's orientation toward time-out has been stated at length earlier.

What do you do if the child will not cooperate when he is assigned a time-out period? What do you do if he attacks another child or the teacher? By that time, there is no question but that we have lost and the issue becomes one of picking up the pieces. In the engineered classroom, if a systematic time-

ED

out procedure does not work or if the child becomes so unco-operative and disruptive that he must be removed from the classroom, he is often sent home immediately. This is by no means a simple matter because it depends on someone's being at home to receive him and on the understanding and cooperation of the parents. Also, physically getting him out of the room may be a problem. If it can be arranged, it is probably better to have someone other than the classroom teacher physically remove a child. The principal, vice-principal, custodian, or playground coach can assist in this regard. This keeps a physical power struggle from occurring in front of the other children, and it avoids drawing the teacher and child into a showdown in the classroom. Some teachers skilled in Life Space Interviewing techniques may be effective in circumventing both a time-out and send-home intervention, but, as was mentioned earlier, this involves training and supervision not available to a majority of teachers working with disturbed children.

At any rate, when we must utilize non-student interventions, something is wrong and, in terms of our orientation in this text, it is the learning environment rather than the psychopathology of the child that should receive attention. The curriculum-conditions-consequences triad probably holds the answer, and the creative, accountable teacher must ask: "How can I decrease my chances of losing next time by modifying the task assignment, altering the conditions under which it is presented, and utilizing more effective consequences in order to help the child and myself become winners instead of losers?"

SUMMARY

This brings our discussion of the exploratory and social levels of competence to a close. We have reviewed a multitude of content, much of it reflecting common sense rather than complicated, theoretical notions. As special educators, we are forced into playing catch-up in our efforts to help the exceptional learner learn about the physical and social environments. Not all of our learners will catch up quickly or equally well, but our goal with them all is to utilize educational experience to improve their functioning levels.

CHAPTER 9

Mastery Level

Our discussions in Chapters 7 and 8 on the attention, response-order, exploratory, and social levels of competence have been a prelude to our discussion of the mastery level in this chapter. In fact, the basic elements of language and academic skill that constitute our focus at this point have been building continuously as the child notices and interacts with stimuli and events in his environment. For this reason, our levels of learning do not represent a true hierarchy but rather a framework of overlapping competencies, all leading us to consideration of the cognitive domain.

In this chapter, we shall review research, observations, and educational practices concerned with the exceptional learner's understanding and mastery of language and his acquisition of basic academic skills of reading, written language, and arithmetic. Since most of the special considerations regarding conditions for learning at the mastery level have been discussed in the previous two chapters, we shall restrict our questions in this chapter to curriculum tasks and approaches. However, we shall devote a section at the end of the chapter to consequences.

MASTERY: THE LEVEL OF COMPETENCE ASSOCIATED WITH LANGUAGE FACILITY AND COMPREHENSION AND ACADEMIC SKILLS AND SUBJECT MATTER

Questions in the language and academic areas involving curriculum tasks and approaches can be stated as follows:

353

Curriculum

1. What types of tasks and approaches increase the child's language understanding and mastery?
2. What types of tasks and approaches can be utilized to teach the child reading skills?
3. What types of tasks and approaches can be utilized to teach the child written language skills?
4. What types of tasks and approaches can be utilized to teach the child arithmetic skills?
5. What types of tasks and approaches are useful in curriculum development for the gifted child?

Curriculum — What Types of Tasks and Approaches Increase the Child's Language Understanding and Mastery?

The area of language development received our attention briefly in Chapter 7, when we discussed verbal responding. The developmental hierarchy of language development proposed by Myklebust (1954, 1955, 1960) was reviewed with its five levels:

1. Aquisition of meaning, or inner language
2. Comprehension of spoken words, or auditory receptive language
3. Speech, or auditory expressive language
4. Reading, or visual receptive language
5. Writing, or visual expressive language

Disorders of auditory language as they occur in children with learning disabilities and corrective training procedures were also discussed. At the mastery level, disorders of reading, written language, and arithmetic are of concern with such children; we shall consider them under questions two and four. In our present discussion on language understanding and usage, it is the disadvantaged child, the child who is hearing handicapped, and the mentally retarded child who will receive major consideration.

In terms of Myklebust's hierarchy, the child from a deprived, lower-class background is in trouble from the start in developing inner language, in comprehending spoken words, and in learning to express himself adequately with speech. Englemann (1970) describes the language problems of the disadvantaged child as far more crippling than mere dialect problems. A four-year-old child from a disadvantaged background may not understand the meaning of such basic words as "first," "before," "or," "if," "all," and "'not." He may not be able to repeat a simple statement such as, "The bread is under the oven," or to identify pictures correctly on the basis of directions to "Find the one that is big" or "Find the one next to the chair."

Williams (1970) contrasts the two major approaches in the field that aim at explaining the language differences between lower and middle-class children and that suggest courses of action for the educator in order to attack the problem. The first approach he designates as the deficit argument. This approach views the disadvantaged home as a poor environment for learning language with its experiential limitations and limited models of language usage. With such a poor beginning, the child finds himself unable to keep pace with the complex language demands of the school. Such failure in turn leads to lack of employment opportunities and perpetuation of the economic disadvantaged cycle. The work of Bernstein (1970) is cited in relation to the deficit approach. After studying the language patterns of members of the working and middle classes in Great Britain, Bernstein conceptualizes a theory of "restricted" and "elaborated" language codes to explain the differences he found. Lower-class individuals were seen as restricted due to failure to develop a language system that has accurate grammatical order and logical modifiers and that is mediated through a grammatically complex sentence structure with frequent usage of prepositions, impersonal pronouns, and a discriminative selection of adjectives and adverbs.

Deutsch (1967) and Bereiter and Englemann (1966) also have contributed to the deficit argument. Deutsch views the most effective remedial approach as one following developmental stages and introducing curriculum change at the earliest possible time in the school in order to arrest the cumulative deficit in the language area. Bereiter and Englemann are more direct in their specifications. They see the problem as one of catch up and have designed a preschool language development program that specifically teaches language rather than assumes that such skills will be indirectly learned through a middle-class type nursery school experience. As minimum goals they propose fifteen competencies that are viewed as essential for success in the first grade. The competencies include the ability to:

1. Name the basic colors, plus white, black, and brown
2. Count objects correctly up to ten
3. Use both affirmative and "not" statements in reply to the question, "What is this?" "This is a ball. This is not a book."
4. Use the prepositions "on," "in," "under," "over," and "between"

in describing the arrangement of objects. "Where is the pencil?" "The pencil is under the book."

In teaching these competencies, the teacher concentrates on two strategies: verbal bombardment, which consists of including a great deal of teacher-directed verbal experience into each class period; and direct instruction, which involves carefully planned lessons with demonstrations, drills, exercises, and problems.

The Distar Instructional System (1971), which has grown out of the work of Bereiter and Englemann, consists of programmed instructional materials for preschool and primary grade children in areas of language, reading, and arithmetic. The language program has been successful with disadvantaged children but has applicability to any child who "for whatever reason" has failed to learn the basic language concepts that make up the language of instruction used in the school. Children are systematically taught to use complete sentences regarding identity, negatives, prepositions, multiple attributes, comparatives, and why and if–then relationships. The instructional objective is to teach the language of observation, the actual language utilized by teachers in explanations and demonstrations.

SD

The second approach discussed by Williams is designated as the "difference position." In contrast to the deficit position, with its focus on remediation to correct the disadvantaged child's apparent unreadiness for school, the difference position accuses the school of being unready for the child. The unique language pattern of the disadvantaged is not viewed as a deviation from standard English but as a linguistic system in itself. When the child encounters difficulty in the school, it is because he is being forced to perform in a linguistic system other than his primary one. Contributors to this position include Stewart (1970), Labov (1970), Shuy (1970), and Baratz (1970). Baratz advocates utilization of basal reading primers written in the black child's vernacular and then teaching him the pragmatic and expressive contrasts between his dialect and standard English. Such teaching is in line with the familiar "teaching-English-as-a-second-language" approach, but proponents of this position are arguing for more than a teaching technique. They are challenging the entire monocultural school system in America on the basis of the fact that the society is polycultural.

HH

The inability to hear words spoken by others creates a serious deficit for the deaf child in the process of gaining language understanding and mastery. Even though he may readily learn the concept of a ball or the meaning of "jump" through direct concrete experience, the complexities of language go far beyond such simple examples. Consider the concepts of "forever" or "perfection." These cannot be directly experienced and require a high level of abstraction for understanding.

Kirk (1972) summarizes the two major theoretical approaches to teaching language to deaf children. One approach assumes that all children learn grammatical forms of language through imitation. The deaf child, then, may acquire the syntax of language through speechreading or reading words and phrases that are repeated over and over again. The other approach has been proposed by psycholinguists and goes beyond imitation to the teaching of generalizations and rules for words that may not be encountered in the child's experiences.

The Fitzgerald Key (Fitzgerald, 1954) is the best known teaching system for language training of the deaf. Once the child has learned some language forms as a result of everyday experience, the teacher questions the child's expression by asking "Who?" "What?" "How many?" and "Where?" Such questioning leads to the child's gradual understanding of grammar, which can later become automatic in speech and writing.

The so-called natural method of teaching language to the deaf (Groht, 1958) initially uses language in informal, natural situations through speechreading and writing and encourages the child's spontaneous expression. Later, language principles are formally introduced. The teaching of language and reading is normally combined because the two skills are dependent on each other. Kirk states that deaf children who truly develop language of a complex nature acquire it primarily from reading and experience.

Two interesting studies comparing later language and academic functioning with early exposure to manual communication were done by Stuckless and Birch (1966) and Meadow (1968). Stuckless and Birch found that deaf children reared by deaf parents and given early training in manual communication were superior to a control group of children not provided with such training in reading, written language, and speechreading. The two groups were equal in speech intelligibility and in psycho-social development. Meadow's findings reported comparable superiority in self-concept, academic achievement, and written language with no difference in speechreading and speech ability.

Speech and language training, or development of the broad area of communication skills, is the primary goal of special educators working with mentally retarded children. Reviewers of the literature on language facility among the retarded indicate that such individuals are consistently inferior in both quality and quantity of language as compared with normals (Smith, 1962; Spradlin, 1963a; Schiefelbusch, 1963; Webb & Kinde, 1967). Problems generally center in the areas of language delay, shortened sentence length, and restricted vocabulary size.

We have already discussed the issue of enhancing the retardate's performance in learning tasks by insisting he verbally label each step. This is made more difficult by the fact that mentally retarded individuals not only have small vocabularies, but also are often reluctant to use what they possess (Hermelin & O'Connor, 1963).

MR

Studies with the Illinois Test of Psycholinguistic Abilities (ITPA) (McCarthy, 1964) indicate that the educable mentally retarded do better in vocally expressing ideas than they do in expressing them through gestures. This pattern reverses with the severely or trainable retarded, as such individuals are relatively better in gestural expression as compared with vocal. A partial explanation of the latter finding concerns the lack of emphasis on vocal expression found in many residential institutions for the retarded. Thus, optimal educational programs for trainable retarded children concentrate heavily on developing and encouraging vocal communication.

In addition to the ITPA, two other instruments are commonly used to assess the language functioning of the retarded: the Parson's Language Sample (Spradlin, 1963b), and the Peabody Picture Vocabulary Test (Dunn, 1959). The Parson's Language Sample covers ages 6-0 to 15-0. It assesses object and picture naming, digit and sentence repetition, question answering (verbal and gestural), imitation of motor acts, completion of motor task by vocal and gestural instruction, and question asking by the subject. The Peabody Picture Vocabulary test covers years 1-9 to 18-0. It consists of a series of pictures that are responded to by auditory word comprehension and association.

In addition to these more formalized procedures, Smith (1968) describes a number of informal procedures that teachers can use to assess the effectiveness of retarded children's language skills. For example, the teacher can compare the performance of each child with the general level of performance of the class in such activities as remembering the words of a song. Smith also cites a number of classroom tasks and activities that can be utilized to increase the child's language proficiency.

The Peabody Language Development Kit (Dunn & Smith, 1967, 1968, 1969) is a sequentially developed language program. It includes two hundred lessons that can be used on a regular basis in classes for mentally retarded children and other exceptional learners who need language training.

Curriculum — What Types of Tasks and Approaches Can Be Utilized to Teach the Child Reading Skills?

LD

MR

According to Myklebust, the acquisition of inner language, comprehension of spoken words, and meaningful speech lead to the next level of development in man's language system — reading. Reading skill, as is the case with spoken language, is a cognitive symbol system that develops as a result of a myriad of sensations, perceptions, and exploratory and social experiences. Reading constitutes the major task for all children as they begin their ascent up the academic ladder. Most learn by almost any method, some require temporary specialized approaches, and a few present such complex and puzzling problems that considerable effort and planning must go into their reading instruction program. The child who lags behind in learning to read during the first and second grades but who does not present any discernible emotional, intellectual, experiential, or physical abnormalities is not necessarily an exceptional learner. Some may eventually join the ranks of the disturbed as a result of prolonged failure and frustration at home and in school. Some may be found to have subtle but specific and persistent problems in visual or auditory perception that will place them in the category of the learning disabled.

Most of the techniques and approaches to be discussed are extensions or modifications of good reading instructional practices. Many will reflect considerations already presented in the sections of the text on the attention, response-order, and exploratory levels of competence.

A type of learning disability presumed to be the result of neurological dysfunction is dyslexia. It is a reading disorder that can involve difficulties in visual or auditory perception. Visual dyslexia includes such problems as confusion of similar words and letters, frequent letter reversals (b for d), and difficulty following and retaining visual sequences. Whole-word teaching approaches may be unsuccessful with this type of disorder. The child with auditory dyslexia may have visual strengths but encounter difficulty developing phonetic word attack and sound blending skills.

Johnson and Myklebust (1967) discuss remedial procedures for both types of dyslexia. The phonetic approach is recommended for the visual dyslexic. Isolated sounds are initially emphasized, and these eventually are blended into words. Several consonants, such as *m, t,* and *s,* markedly different in both sound and appearance, may be selected in the beginning stages of the reading program. After mastering the letter sounds, the child relates them to words he knows that begin with the same sounds. Next, the child may be asked to point to letters that correspond to consonant sounds the teacher voices. This leads to sound blendings, long vowels, and finally, simple sentences, paragraphs, and stories.

Whole-word emphasis can be effective with children who have auditory dyslexia. Initial words that differ in both visual and auditory form can be drawn exclusively from the child's speaking vocabulary. These words are then paired with both objects and experiences. The word "house" can be printed on the left-hand side of a flashcard with a picture of a house on the right. Verbs such as "hop" can be printed on a card and given to the child as he actually hops, thus facilitating the development of the association. Adjectives, prepositions, short phrases, and sentences then can be gradually introduced.

Myers and Hammill (1969) have summarized a number of instructional approaches that have been effective in teaching reading to children with learning disabilities. Some of these, such as the work of Strauss and Lehtinen, Cruickshank, and Fernald, we have alluded to in previous sections. The Gillingham method (Gillingham & Stillman, 1965) is a highly structured phonic system for teaching reading. It begins with teaching the sounds of the letters and builds these letter sounds systematically into words like "bricks in a wall." It is geared to children who have many of the characteristics of the visual dyslexic and who have been unable to learn to read by "sight word methods."

The Distar Instructional System (1971) introduced earlier as a language development program with preschool and primary grade children includes a program designed to teach the component subskills of reading. Letters are initially taught as sounds only. Before such sounds are sequenced into words, the child learns to sequence simple actions. Rhyming, blending, and "sound sliding" exercises precede actual reading instruction. The reading program then moves to systematically developing word attack, sight vocabulary, and comprehension skills.

The performance of visually handicapped children in relation to reading skills has received considerable attention. Bateman (1963) examined ninety-six partially seeing children in the public school in grades two to four and found the reading achievement level of this sample similar to the level of achievement of sighted children. However, Birch, Tisdall, Peabody, and Sterrett (1966) in a study of school achievement of 903 fifth and sixth grade partially seeing children found that despite average intelligence for the group, they were some two and one-half years retarded in academic achievement.   Since Bateman found that the most educationally retarded in her study were also those with the most minor visual handicaps, Kirk (1972) concludes the children in the Birch sample may have been referred to classes for the visually handicapped primarily because of educational retardation and only secondarily because they had a minor visual disability.   In the Birch study it was also found that no one type size could be considered superior for teaching reading to the partially sighted.

With respect to the level of reading achievement attained by the blind through the medium of braille, Lowenfeld, Abel, and Hatlen (1967) found fourth grade blind children equal to seeing children who read print in reading comprehension, although the reading tests in braille allowed considerably more time for the blind children.   They also found by means of a questionnaire circulated nationally to residential and day school programs for the blind that braille reading is introduced in the first grade, that eighty-five percent of the teachers try to teach the child to use both hands in learning braille, and that most teachers teach braille writing through reading utilizing a braille writer.

A recent technological advance is the development of the Optacon, a portable electronic device that includes a camera for converting print to vibrating letter images.   This is accomplished by means of a photochemical to mechanical energy conversion process. By sliding a small probe with photocells across the printed page with one hand, the visually handicapped individual "reads" the vibrating reed letters with a finger on the other hand.   Although reading speed is a major problem, the Optacon holds promise for reducing dependence on sighted readers and the transcription of special materials from print into braille.

In addition to concern with the structure of the reading process with its visual and auditory components, the content of reading material given to the child has received increasing attention. Despite the proficiency in word attack skills that the child acquires, and despite the size of his sight vocabulary, we can hardly expect him to become a motivated reader if he is presented with dull, confusing, or unfamiliar reading content.   In this regard, the appropriateness of traditional basal reader content for use with disadvantaged children has been increasingly questioned.   The Detroit Project (Whipple, 1967) included a study of pre-primers commonly used in beginning reading instructional programs.   The study found that even though many pre-primers were well conceived and structurally sound, they were largely designed for middle-class children.   As a result, a number of recommendations for more relevant pre-primers for the disadvantaged child were

ED

SD

made.   In general, such beginning books should include fewer pages so that the immediate rewards of task completion are enjoyed.   The content should not ignore the values of middle-class America, but it should focus initially on the world of the disadvantaged child and then gradually introduce such values.   The characters in the stories should represent different races.   Blacks presented in the text in illustrations should be shown in as favorable a light as are white characters.   It is important for all children to have characters in the stories they read with whom they can positively identify.   The illustrations used in the pre-primer should be easy to interpret.   The characters should be as large as possible, with only enough background detail to support the theme of the story.   The stories themselves should be suspenseful with an exciting climax.   They should not assume that the child has had a wider and richer experience than he actually has had before coming to school, and the vocabulary should be drawn from the child's own speaking vocabulary.   Finally, the teacher's manual should present a great variety of activities to stimulate the child's attention, to reinforce words and sentences used in the stories, and to build language understanding and usage.

Disadvantaged children, however, have not been the only victims of boring and meaningless content in basal reading series used in the elementary school grades.   Many children with reading problems, particularly boys, who outnumber girls three or four to one, have found little to interest them in the animal stories, fairy tales, and stories of family life traditionally a part of such series.   Stanchfield (1961) studied the reading preferences of boys from grades four to eight and found a diminishing interest in traditional content and an increasing motivation to read stories containing unusual experiences, suspense, action, and surprise.

The author studied the types of subject matter that appealed to young, adolescent boys with learning and behavior problems. Over a several year period, the following topics were very successful in getting the students to ask questions, engage in discussion, and do follow-up reading and writing assignments:

1. Deep sea diving and study of marine life
2. History of the development of the submarine
3. Knighthood
4. History of the development of communication techniques
5. Tunnel building and famous tunnels built around the world
6. History of the development of kites and balloon aircraft

In recent years, more attention has been paid to providing suspense and excitement in reading materials for all children, particularly those with reading difficulties. Some examples are the Deep Sea Adventure Series (Berres, Coleman, Briscoe, & Hewett, 1959–1971), Morgan Bay Mystery Series (Rambeau & Rambeau, 1962), Checkered Flag Series (Bauman & Bauman, 1969), the Cowboy Sam Series (Chandler, 1959), the Dan Frontier Series (Hurley, 1959–1964), the New Practice Readers (Stone, Grover, & Anderson, 1962), and Teenage Tales (Strang & Roberts, 1964).

The use of basal reading texts with mentally retarded children has been questioned by Jordan (1963), who views the experiential and inferential story approach as superior. The experiential story is written in the classroom and can be based on personal experiences of students or classroom activities, such as field trips or outings. The children themselves create the story, which directly relates to people and events around them. Jordan summarizes the value of the experiential story as compared to the basal reader in teaching reading to retarded children as follows:

MR

1. Real life stories adapt more easily to the characteristics of slow learners
2. Real life stories by or about children hold their interest
3. Success in reading can be ensured by controlling story content
4. The reading experience is more functional

The inferential story approach is based on the experiential story. It involves asking questions and making inferences about the people, things, or events in the story.

The attribute of meaningfulness in learning is a central issue in the use of experiential stories to teach reading. Again and agan we have encountered this issue in Part III of the text, beginning with approaches to get the child to pay attention and respond, and continuing with respect to learning about the physical properties of the environment, and improving social behavior. The issue is far from a contemporary one. In the 1800's, Seguin reflected on the limitations of rote learning with the retarded:

> Exclusive memory exercises do not improve idiots; they impede them — better one thing understood than a hundred remembered. We must never confine to automatic memory what can be learned by comparison, nor teach a thing without its natural relations and generalizations — what enters the mind alone, remains alone.

Elliott (1970) systematically studied the effect of meaningfulness on learning and retention with nine-year-old educable mentally retarded children. He found that a learning unit composed of meaningful proper nouns or familiar associations was learned and retained significantly better than was the same unit composed of impersonal and unfamiliar proper nouns or associations.

The Fernald approach to reading and spelling is based on experiential story writing. Initially, all reading and spelling activities are derived from stories the child writes on a daily basis. In Stage One of the Fernald method, each word the child needs to learn to put in his story is manually traced on a tracing slip, as described in Chapter 7. The completed stories are typed by the teacher and later returned to the child, who reads them aloud over a several day period until he can successfully recognize initially unfamiliar words both in and out of the story context.

MR

Kirk (1933) compared the Fernald kinesthetic word tracing technique with the traditional look-and-say approach with six retarded boys, each of whom served as his own control. The boys learned five words a day for thirty days and alternated between the methods in terms of number of trials in learning; retention of the words over a twenty-four-hour period significantly favored the tracing method.

Dunn (1963b) has suggested that the whole-word sight method is the least efficient way to teach the mentally retarded. He advocates the following sequence in building a sight reading vocabulary:

1. Listening comprehensiveness for instruction and stories
2. Auditory discrimination of familiar sounds and then speech sounds
3. Sound blending ability
4. Visual discrimination for individual letters
5. Direct word attack skills

However, no single approach to reading instruction is generally recognized as always best with retarded any more than it is with normal children.

Woodcock and Dunn (1967) undertook a systematic two-year study of six approaches to reading instruction with 360 educable mentally retarded children with a mean chronological age of eight years and eight months and a mental age of five years and six months. The six approaches studied were: (1) the experiential story, (2) basal reader, (3) programmed reading material, (4) the experiential story with the Initial Teaching Alphabet (a unique system of forty-four characters, each of which represents only one English phoneme (Downing, 1965), (5) basal reader with the Initial Teaching Alphabet, and (6) basal reader with a rebus symbol word learning technique. Using seven dependent variables, the study found no significant differences among any of the six instructional approaches utilized.

The search for more effective instructional programs to teach all children to read will continue in both regular and special education. We will probably never uncover the one superior approach but will develop and refine a range of approaches and improve our diagnostic skill in analyzing a given child's uniqueness and matching it to the most appropriate type of instruction.

LD

Curriculum — What Types of Tasks and Approaches Can Be Utilized to Teach the Child Written Language Skills?

According to Myklebust, written language is the highest form of verbal achievement on the developmental hierarchy of language. Johnson and Myklebust (1967) have delineated three major disorders of written language. The first is a disorder in visual-motor integration. The child can speak and read but cannot coordinate the motor pattern for writing letters, numbers, or words. A disorder in revisualization constitutes the second problem area. Children with deficits in this area can read but cannot revisualize the words or their letter components so that they can write them from memory or dictation. Finally, disorders in formulation and syntax prevent some children from organizing their thoughts into the proper form for written communication although they can communicate orally, can read, can copy, and can spell words correctly.

In terms of remediation, a series of training exercises and activities are directed to aid the child with any of these written language disorders. The child with problems in visual-motor integration may initially watch the teacher draw vertical lines or other simple figures on the blackboard without attempts to reproduce the figures himself. Next, he may be blindfolded and his index finger guided repeatedly over the figures until he can follow the pattern on his own. The coordination of visual and motor tasks is next attempted with the child being encouraged to reproduce the figures on the board without the blindfold. Stencils, dot-to-dot figures, and tracing exercises are additional reinforcement techniques suggested. Manuscript printing is then introduced rather than cursive handwriting because of the greater consistency of letter forms.

Training visual memory involves techniques previously discussed in relation to heightening the vividness of visual stimuli. Words are printed in larger type than usual and color can be utilized to provide extra emphasis. A pocket flashlight used as a pointer

ED

LD

MR

will help the child focus more intently on words and their letter components.   Remediation of disorders of formulation and syntax may begin by making the child aware of his errors in writing. The teacher reads aloud what the child has written and the errors in content and sentence structure are pointed out.   The child is then encouraged to analyze his own sentences as he reads them aloud.   Additional work involves presenting the child with sentences and paragraphs that contain a variety of mistakes and asking him to locate as many errors as possible.

In these techniques, we see attempts to gain the child's attention, to get him to respond and participate in a learning act, and to follow a sequence of directions as basic considerations. In addition, emphasis on thimbleful accomplishments and on a gradual increase in task difficulty is demonstrated.   Finally, in line with much of our previous discussion, an effort is made to guarantee the child's success by careful provision of curriculum and condition.

The Ranier School project with institutionalized retarded children was introduced earlier (Birnbrauer, Bijou, Wolf, & Kidder, 1965).   Bijou (1965) has described the written language portion of the reading program developed in the project.   First, the child is given separate printed letters and instructed to put these in the correct sequence to match a printed word example.   When he can do this task, he is trained to spell from the spoken word or study of a textual representation of the word.   Cursive handwriting is taught by means of an illuminated tracing box.   A handwritten word is placed under a frosted glass screen, which is illuminated by a light underneath.   The child traces the word repeatedly with a pencil on a paper placed over the screen.   The light can be gradually dimmed so that eventually the child is asked to write the word with no visual tracing cue from the word under the screen. Additional stages include assigning the child the task of copying a word model alongside his paper, then copying longer items, and finally writing from dictation and completing sentences to describe pictures.

The author has used a similar approach in developing story writing skills with emotionally disturbed children and children with learning disabilities.   The first level involves having the child draw a picture and write a title for it.   If this is too difficult, he may dictate the title and have the teacher write it for him or have the teacher write the title on a separate piece of paper and have the child copy it under the picture.   Next, the child may copy sentences or short stories from the chalkboard or from a model on his own desk. Finally, he may dictate his story to the teacher, who first writes it for him, but who later encourages the child to participate in a cooperative effort and write an occasional word or complete sentence by himself. It is the author's contention that free and easy communication is initially more desirable than emphasis on handwriting perfection or spelling correctness and, hence, would much rather have the child excited and involved in expressing himself in writing no matter how much support is required. Such an orientation is clearly in line with building basic skills at the attention and response-order levels before focus on the mastery level.

LD

MR

Curriculum — What Types of Tasks and Approaches Can Be Utilized to Teach the Child Arithmetic?

Johnson and Myklebust (1967) view disorders in arithmetic as stemming from two basic problems: (1) problems in other language areas and (2) disturbances in quantitative thinking. Children with auditory receptive language problems may do poorly in arithmetic in school, not because they fail to understand the principles involved in calculation, but because they fail to profit from the teacher's verbal presentation of these principles; they fail to understand word problem context utilized in the teacher's spoken instruction. Children with reading difficulties will be at a severe disadvantage in interpreting word problems and children with disorders in visual-motor integration may be unable to write down answers correctly. Disturbances in quantitative thinking involve problems in comprehending mathematical principles themselves.

Remediation of problems associated with other language areas would follow the approaches previously discussed. Helping a child to acquire a skill in understanding and using quantitative relations must often begin at a basic, non-verbal level, and the principles of quantity, order, size, space, and distance must be taught. Visual perception exercises utilizing puzzles, pegboards, and formboards can be a first step. Counting aloud while stringing beads or touching pegs will help the child learn the concepts of quantity, and gradually the number symbols associated with concrete units are introduced. The work of Piaget and his ideas regarding the assessment of conservation of quantity provide guidelines for creating tasks to assist children with problems in quantitative thinking. In addition, concrete materials associated with the Montessori approach have proven valuable with such children.

The curriculum area of arithmetic has not been as completely researched with retarded children as has reading; but studies indicate the retardate achieves in this area at a level consistent with his mental age (Bensberg, 1953; Dunn & Capobianco, 1956). Cruickshank (1946, 1948a, b) found that educable mentally retarded children did not differ from normals matched for mental age in computational skills but that they were inferior in arithmetic vocabulary and in separating computative facts from extraneous material. They also were less able to solve word problems, relied more on counting on their fingers, and were more careless and less able to name the process involved in solving a problem. Thus the retarded child may do fairly well in straight computation (e.g., $2 + 2 = ?$) but when this problem is presented as a word problem, is given verbally, is presented with extraneous numbers, or requires abstract reasoning, he is apt to be less successful than is the normal child. Since drill on computational facts is easier to present and more frequently assigned in the classroom than are lessons designed to improve understanding of quantitative concepts, some of the retarded child's limitations may reflect overemphasis on such drill.

Finely (1962) compared arithmetic test performances between a group of educable mentally retarded adolescents and a group of younger children who were matched on the basis of mental age. Three types of tests were employed: concrete, pictorial, and symbolic. The concrete tests used actual objects (e.g., a real nickel or dime) fastened to a board to illustrate the problem. The pictorial test presented drawings of the objects related to the problems (e.g., pictures of a real nickel or dime), and the symbolic test used actual number symbols (e.g., 5¢ or 10¢). The three tests involved basic processes of addition, subtraction, multiplication, and division. The results of the comparison of test performances revealed that the retarded individual did better on the symbolic tests than did the normals but less well on the concrete tests. This finding may reflect the fact that the retardates were older and had been exposed to a longer period of formal academic drill, whereas the younger normals were still in programs utilizing concrete examples and emphasizing understanding of quantitative concepts. Such formal drill may actually put the retardate at a severe disadvantage when it comes to translating arithmetic concepts to real-life situations. Training in the symbolic manipulation of number symbols without the understanding of the concrete objects such as money they represent becomes a useless exercise. Hence, emphasis on adaptation to the real world stressed in our discussion at the exploratory and social levels of competence is underscored.

The author once observed a class for high school retardates involved in an hour-long lesson on percentage. The teacher focused on the placement of decimal points and correct computation of symbolic problems. Not one word was spoken about the meaning of percentage and how the concept is involved in many of our transactions in the real world. When the seat work was corrected by the class, the teacher collected the papers and passed out a duplicate copy of the assignment "to see if you can all get a perfect paper this time." It is difficult to see how these children really profited from this lesson or how they could be motivated to work in subsequent lessons when the pay off for their efforts was merely a chance to do the assignment over again.

Smith (1968) has written extensively about methods for teaching arithmetic to retarded children. He stresses practical application in areas such as measurement. Beginning instruction with money must start with manipulation of the real thing. The fundamental operation of changing a coin into an equivalent sum using other coins, making purchases, making change, recording the amount of a purchase, or calculating the amount of money to be returned, and understanding the reasons for saving money should be practiced in a variety of ways in any instructional program.

The concept of time is abstract and must be taught to retarded children with considerable patience and repetition. The relationship between hours and minutes can be demonstrated by the teacher rigidly adhering to a time schedule each day. The child will eventually come to see the relationship between the position of the hands on the clock and the activities of a particular time period in the day. The subject of weight can be introduced by having each child weigh himself and maintain a weekly record. Special attention must be given to helping the child learn to convert ounces to pounds and vice versa. There are many possibilities for activities in relation to weight measurement using such materials as flour, sand, sugar, and wood and a kitchen scale.

In the past, the visually handicapped individual frequently encountered difficulty learning arithmetic skills because he could not profit from visual demonstration on the chalkboard. Traditional approaches to arithmetic instruction have relied heavily on such visual demonstration. However, the so-called new math, with its emphasis on reasoning and use of concrete materials, appears to make the subject easier to present to children with visual problems. The abacus also has become a widely accepted teaching aid for use in arithmetic instruction with the blind, and the Nemeth Code of Braille Mathematics has enabled blind students to study higher mathematics more easily.

As we have discussed, deaf children have difficulty in developing abstraction and in learning vocabulary and language construction. Hence, arithmetic concepts will not be easily mastered. Techniques involving manipulation and visualization should be emphasized in the teaching of arithmetic. The teacher must

MR

VH

HH

continually test the child's understanding of underlying concepts to be certain that they have been grasped by the child. As with the retarded, arithmetic concepts should be reinforced throughout the school day in problem situations that provide meaningful practice.

Curriculum — What Types of Tasks and Approaches are Useful in Curriculum Development for the Gifted Child?

Curriculum development for the gifted child does not necessarily entail the preparation of new materials but does involve the creation of novel conditions, teaching styles, and types of learning activities. According to Martinson (1973), some of the current curriculum planning and approaches for the gifted are the following:

1. Flexible, multiple, and changing administrative organization
2. Emphasis on conceptually advanced learning for the gifted
3. Less reliance on exercises and workbooks and on artificially contrived curriculums
4. Providing wide opportunities for creativity in the curriculum

Martinson notes that educators are providing gifted students with increasing access to diverse course offerings as compared to classes related to specific grade levels. She also states that transition between school levels is increasing to the extent that students who need or wish to take courses from higher level institutions can do so. In addition, increasing opportunities for independent study and seminars are available at both elementary and secondary levels.

Flexible organization is also in evidence in the matching of student-teacher as well as student-student competencies and interests. In this type of program children individually or in small groups are paired with adults or older students with whom they can share interests and from whom they can learn. For example, a high school student who has a great deal of interest and background in mathematics may tutor other high school students.

Currently in the education of the gifted is also a trend toward providing the gifted child with curriculum content which is topical in nature and which concerns the identification of central concepts and ideas. Mere acceleration of standardized grade content is quickly losing favor as a means of disseminating advanced information to the gifted. Findlay (1965) describes a program

G

devised by the Physical Science Study Committee to provide children with the structure or basic principles and theories underlying the physical sciences. The content of the course of the Physical Science Study Committee is divided into four parts (White, 1960). Part I is an introduction to matter, time, and space. The course begins with a consideration of the dimensions of time and space and how they are sensed. Through laboratory work the student sees how his senses can be extended by instrumentation and he begins to develop a perception of the role, nature, and limitations of measurement. In Part II the student begins the process of observation of, and abstraction from, a family of physical phenomena, for example, light. The natural development of the subject leads to an examination of the theories of light. This section of the course illustrates how models are abstracted from experimental observation, how they open up further investigation, and how they are established, modified, or rejected. Part III discusses the concept of motion, again depending heavily on laboratory work and extensively reinforced with films. The course moves through the relation between form and motion, the story of the discovery of universal gravitation; and the conservation of momentum and energy. Part IV develops the nature of electrical forms and energy, begins to bind together dynamics, electricity, and waves in a consideration of electromagnetic radiation, and returns with all these tools to an exploration of the structure of matter — atoms.

In the area of reading, Terman (1925) reported that approximately half of the gifted children in his study could read at the kindergarten level, and nearly all were reading at the beginning of the first grade. Thus, the usual reading readiness programs are irrelevant for approximately ninety percent of the gifted. Martinson (1968) suggests that the gifted be given many opportunities for independent reading. A library is a valuable resource in the development of a child's diverse research interests. If a school library is available, all children who read should be given freedom to use it. Very young children should be given the opportunity to go to the library as frequently as those who are older.

To extend the reading interests of students, teachers may use several approaches. Reading to the children to arouse their interest in a book is one means; another is having students read freely from a given group of books, after which the teacher may ask them to discuss the books and stories they found to be the best and present the best sections.

Wilson (1958) has listed a number of suggestions for the development of creative thinking in children, including: (1) brainstorming, (2) stimulating sensitivity to problems, (3) encouraging ideational fluency, (4) encouraging originality.

The purpose of "brainstorming" is to obtain as many ideas as possible in relation to a given problem. Wilson proposed four rules to follow when the teacher uses brainstorming:

1. Judgment is ruled out — criticism of ideas must be withheld until after the session
2. "Freewheeling" is welcomed — the wilder the idea, the better. Wilson believes it is easier to tame down ideas than to think them up
3. Quantity is wanted. Wilson contends that the greater the number of ideas, the greater likelihood there may be some excellent ones
4. Combination and improvement are sought. In addition to contributing ideas of their own, participants should suggest how ideas of others could be synthesized into still another idea

To solve a problem one must be sensitive that a problem exists. Wilson states that we may become aware of problems by closely observing the world around us and by questioning assumptions that had previously been taken for granted. He states that students may be encouraged to increase their awareness of the world through greater use of observation trips. Wilson also suggests that students may be encouraged to question some of the things they have taken for granted by asking questions of the "What would happen if _____?" or "What would it be like if __?" variety. An example of this type of question may be, "What would happen if there were no longer any wars?"

Encouraging ideational fluency entails providing individual students with an opportunity to increase their flow of ideas. The following are some suggestions to assist the student:

1. List on a piece of paper all the uses you can think of for a brick. You will have five minutes.
2. Write as many things as you can think of that are rectangular in shape.
3. Write down all the things you would need if you were to climb Mt. Everest.

In the area of encouraging originality, activities should encourage a deliberate effort to give uncommon or unusual responses, to look for a different or new way of doing something other than the usual or common way. For example, in presenting social studies reports, pupils are told that they may use any method other than reading or talking directly to the class. As a result pupils individually or in groups may decide to use dramatizations, quiz sessions, opaque projectors, tape recorders, or interview techniques, to cite a few examples.

ED

LD

CONSEQUENCES

In Chapters 7 and 8, we discussed tangible, task completion, exploratory, and social rewards as types of consequences possible to provide in the classroom to give the child an incentive to improve his level of learning competence. We come now to consideration of knowledge of results and acquisition of knowledge and skill as reinforcing consequences.

SD

Knowledge of results is typically provided in the classroom by a system of letter grades. Children learn early in their school careers that an A means their efforts are excellent, a B — good, and a C — average. Although systems vary, with some using numbers instead of letters, the ranking is very similar. Receipt of a D or F is clearly undesirable and communicates near-failure or failure. Children in regular classrooms learn to live with the system and are affected to varying degrees by it. Some strive for A's and B's, others settle for C's and avoid failing grades because of their stigma or because they may have to repeat subjects in which such grades are given.

Special educators, particularly those working with exceptional learners in self-contained classrooms, are faced with a real dilemma when it comes to giving or not giving grades. Three problems immediately arise. First, if no grades are given, both the child's parents and the child himself may feel the educational program was inadequate in comparison to work given children in regular classrooms. This may be particularly true of disturbed children, children with learning disabilities, and disadvantaged children who often have spent time in regular class programs. Second, if a wholly unique and individualized grading criterion is established in the special program and children get inflated grades of A and B for performance levels below what would be expected in a regular program, then an unrealistic expectation is set up that may be hard to live with if and when the child returns to a regular classroom. The author has observed programs in which A-triple-pluses were commonly given for individualized efforts by exceptional learners. Such super grades appealed to the children, but the false expectations they created in relation to the real world

G

made the practice questionable. Finally, adhering to a traditional grading system and actually giving the exceptional learner the grade he would likely receive according to regular class standards is also a losing proposition, since it would all too often result in a devaluating D or F.

There is no easy solution to the problem if some version of the letter grade system is seen as necessary to maintain. The best solution is to set up a different system that gives the child knowledge of how he is doing and that does not conflict with traditional grading practices. Such a system was illustrated in Chapter 7, when the check mark system used in the engineered classroom was introduced. The child receives a possible ten check marks on a Work Record Card each fifteen minutes as an acknowledgment of what he has earned in task and classroom behavior areas. An attempt was made to give the child as many check marks as possible, but when his behavior clearly fell below standards understood by him and most reasonable to expect, some might be withheld to alert him to the problem. At the end of each class day the children total up their entire number of earned check marks and graph them on the histogram Work Report, illustrated in Figure 20. The author has observed how the totaling of the check marks, graphing procedures, and comparison of the day's

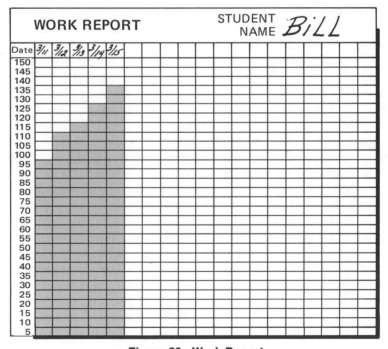

Figure 20: Work Report

totals with previous levels was highly motivating to the disturbed and learning disability children in the program. There appeared a concreteness and vividness to the record keeping that was reinforcing, notwithstanding the fact that the check marks eventually led to tangible and free-time exchanges.

Similar findings are discussed by Haring and Phillips (1972) in their work in the Experimental Education Unit at the University of Washington in Seattle. In this school, a careful record of certain pre-academic and academic responses is maintained for each child. The children in the unit are not classified by traditional categories but represent individuals who might be called disturbed, retarded, learning disabled, or disadvantaged. Initially, the teacher may keep a record of the number of correct and incorrect responses made by the child. The number of times a child talks out inappropriately, leaves his seat, looks up from his paper, or leans back in his chair are all pre-academic behaviors that lend themselves to response counting. By setting a fixed time period during which the observation will take place, the teacher can determine a response rate (i.e., total number of responses divided by time in minutes). Similar recordings can be made during academic work periods relating to number of problems done correctly or incorrectly. Haring and Phillips have found that even children in the very early grades can take over the responsibility for counting their own correct and incorrect responses if the procedures utilized are not too complicated. They can then make a chart or graph of the number of correct or incorrect things that they did over a period of time and compare their records day by day. Teachers at the Experimental Education Unit report that the children are often reinforced by merely plotting their response rates. In addition, as self-management skills increase and the child becomes aware of the problem areas in which he needs help, he is moving toward re-entry into a regular class.

Lovitt and Curtis (1969) found that the correct academic response rate of children with behavior problems increased when the children took charge of keeping their own records and deciding what criteria they would have to meet in order to obtain free time privilege. These privileges were delivered in line with the Premack Principle discussed in Chapter 8. The author reported that academic improvement was not determined by how much reinforcement was possible to obtain and concluded that the children were reinforced by the opportunities for self-management that were provided. Thus, knowing where you stand and deciding on the value of your efforts yourself can be rewarding consequences.

Wolf, Giles, and Hall (1968) conducted an after school and Saturday morning remedial academic program for sixteen low achievers who attended regular classrooms during school hours.

ED

LD

MR

SD

A point system was developed that first gave points for the correct completion of one problem and later required several correct problems before points were awarded. Pages of points were redeemable for various reinforcers, including field trips, daily snacks, money, and store items. For each reinforcer, a specific number of completed pages of points was required. Points also were given correct answers in remedial assignments and homework completed in the after school setting. They were also provided for grades awarded in the regular classroom during the school day. An A earned 100 points; B — 75 points; C — 50 points; and D — 25 points. Report card grades given by the regular teacher also were converted to points: A — 1600 points, B — 800 points; C — 400 points; and D — 200 points. And for several children who had serious records of academic failure, the point totals were doubled for all letter grades associated with the regular classroom.

The results of the study indicate that the points were highly valued and definitely influenced the children's performances. The procedures followed (i.e., giving to letter grades in regular class work a token reinforcer exchange value) demonstrate how approaches such as the check mark system in the engineered classroom can be utilized to give letter grades concrete value and meaning. Such value and meaning can be extremely important to emphasize with children who have little incentive to work for traditional letter grades.

CONCLUSION

This brings Chapter 9 and Part III of the text to a close. We have reviewed six levels of learning competence and presented examples of curriculum tasks, conditions, and consequences that relate to improving the exceptional learner's learning effectiveness. Even though we have dealt with a melting pot of content, it is hoped that our discussions have demonstrated that special education is essentially concerned with good education. Special education gains its uniqueness from extending sound educational practices that are applicable to all children to children who are basically different because they are less competent across our six levels. Capacity-based differences require the most dramatic extension of such practices; and children whose problems stem from the nature or range of previous experiences are often candidates for changes in degree rather than kind in the educational program. Part IV will deal with critical issues facing the field of special education and the world of the public school.

PART IV

Future Dimensions

CHAPTER 10

Current Issues in Special Education

Chapter 1, "Historical Origins," ended with the early 1960's and President Kennedy's mandate for furthering the cause of the mentally retarded through training, research, and service. The impetus created by this mandate launched a remarkable period of growth for the entire field of special education. Growth and growing pains are inseparable, and special education has not been spared. As the field has grown, it has become increasingly self-critical and aware of unresolved problems. It has also become increasingly accountable for resolving these problems on a nationwide basis.

In this chapter, we will review three major problems or issues currently being examined by people in special education and by others, including parents and allied professionals, who are concerned with exceptional learners. The first problem relates to labeling and categorization and has been a focal issue for discussion throughout this text. The second problem is directly related and concerns special class placement versus regular class integration for exceptional learners. Finally, the third problem focuses on the impact that changes occurring in the field of special education have on regular education.

By way of introduction to this discussion, we will first examine a phenomenon with special relevance to both historical and current problems in the field. The phenomenon is dissonance; it occurs when our experience in the real world does not match up with our previously held beliefs and expectations. The beauty queen aspirant who considers herself a sure-winner over all other contestants because of her self-perceived superior beauty and who does not even gain a place among the finalists experiences dissonance. The intellectually oriented student who dismisses a written exam as a snap, writes his answers quickly, and hands in his paper long before his classmates, fully expecting an A, and who later finds he has failed the test also faces an experience of dissonance.

Historically, special educators have experienced dissonance as they have developed expectations and had to face the reality of what followed. Recall the bitter disappointment experienced by Itard described in Chapter 1. His efforts with Victor were predicated on the belief that he could cure the wild boy; but when it became apparent that Victor would never be normal in all areas of development, Itard was thrown into a state of dissonance in relation to his original expectations. Recall Seguin's much heralded move to the United States from France and the belief held by some American special educators that he would close down our hospitals for the retarded as custodial placements and convert them to training centers that would literally eliminate mental retardation as a societal liability. When this failed to occur, a dissonant state followed, resulting in a generalized pessimism in relation to the value of educational and training efforts with the retarded.

Dissonance often leads to extreme reactions; under its effect, the pendulum may move full arc rather than undergo a partial swing. Itard gave up, and Seguin's followers experienced great disenchantment. This is unfortunate, for both efforts were highly successful when viewed in the light of more realistic expectations. No cure for Victor, but many extremely important changes were brought about by Itard's training. No elimination of the social problems of mental retardation due to the training methods of Seguin, but a most significant beginning of special educational approaches with the retarded took place.

Dissonance continued in the field on into the twentieth century. Consider the development of the I.Q. test discussed in Chapter 1 and the range of qualifications regarding intellectual measurement covered in Chapter 5. An approach to assessing intellectual capacity, initially viewed by some with a sense of certainty and finality, has become highly suspect and subject to continued questioning. Once again the field of special education experienced dissonance and was forced to live with reality by re-examining original assumptions and expectations.

This historical overview of dissonance in special education is a prelude to consideration of the three contemporary problem areas cited earlier. Each area carries with it the probability, if not the inevitability, of dissonance as solutions are formulated and implemented.

LABELING AND CATEGORIZATION

The question of pinning diagnostic labels on exceptional learners and assigning them to categories is one of the most overworked issues in special education. We discussed it in the introduction and referred to a number of the clichés that have emanated from it: "medical rather than educational-model based," "self-fulfilling prophecies," and "hardening of the categories." Even though the issue is an old one and "Down with labeling and categorization" is a familiar battle cry of special educators, complete elimination of labeling practices is apt to create dissonance in the field.

Although it has become increasingly apparent that such practices do a disservice to our exceptional learners in many ways, let us look at two major pitfalls that may await us if traditional labeling is abandoned totally. First, we have the communication problem in building the bridge from the other side. Our earlier position in Chapter 3 was that special education should consider turning the tables on the disability labeling practices of extra-educational disciplines that often assume primary responsibility for diagnosis and evaluation and that we should describe learning and behavior problems first in educationally relevant terms. This would support abandonment of traditional labeling and categorizing.

Yet bridge-building is a two-way enterprise, and even though the most pressing need may be for special education to take a long overdue initiative, we must still recognize the importance of maintaining meaningful communication and interaction with the physicians, neurologists, pediatricians, psychologists, social workers, and other professionals standing by to contribute to the welfare and understanding of the exceptional learner. These individuals will continue, at least for a while, to translate their efforts into diagnostic labels, particularly with those children who manifest physical and sensory-based problems. A complete refusal on the part of the special educator to continue to communicate in terms of such labels might seriously disrupt our important interdisciplinary working relationships. Here we have dissonance reflected. We would like to free all exceptional learners from the negative effects of labels, but in the process we could create a problem that might limit our overall effectiveness to help them.

ED

LD

The author has observed, however, an interesting trend away from traditional psychiatric labeling in the Neuropsychiatric Institute on the campus of the University of California, Los Angeles. Here, children and adolescents with serious emotional and behavior problems are hospitalized for limited periods of time for intensive study and evaluation. In the early 1960's, it was not uncommon for complex labels such as childhood schizophrenia or neurotic depressive reaction to be given these individuals during the course of their stay in the hospital. In 1971, such labels had all but disappeared; the majority of diagnoses fell into the broad categories, adjustment reaction of childhood or adjustment reaction of adolescence. Thus, in other disciplines concerned with exceptional individuals, the labeling practices of the past are also currently undergoing scrutiny and alteration.

The second problem area is related and has to do with communication and maintenance of traditional working relationships with others outside the field of special education. Programs to educate exceptional learners cost money, and this money comes from federal, state, and local community support. In the past, we have presented our case to legislators utilizing the concept of handicapping conditions among school-age children to obtain funds. Utilization of this concept inevitably relies on reference to traditional labels and categories. Whether we like to admit it or not, such an approach facilitates a simple, direct, and meaningful communication with these individuals and carries with it an emotional appeal. Some people may deplore advocating emotionality in gaining support for educational programs for exceptional learners; but the author contends it can be a valuable means of calling attention to the needs of these children and that in actuality it represents a fact of life.

In this regard, the author recalls a situation in which a legislative body was to be approached regarding the allocation of funds to help children with serious reading disabilities. On the one hand, the special educators who were formulating the request could describe the children as having difficulty in learning to read and as needing special help to catch up. If this were done, there was a good chance the officials representing a layman's point of view regarding education might shift focus to the educational system that had failed to teach these children to read and negatively react to continued demands by the field of education for help with its problems. On the other hand, these special educators could describe the children as victims of specific developmental dyslexia, an affliction with a suspected neurological basis suffered by two to five percent of school-age children in the United States. Now the focus is clearly on a handicapped child who is designated by a specific label and category; the impact and emotional appeal vary considerably. It was the latter plan that was followed in this case, and the request for special funds was readily granted. Here we have another example of dissonance. The category of dyslexia may adversely affect the teacher's expectations in working with a child and constitute one of the most questionable labels we ever apply to a child, yet it serves its purpose well in obtaining support for special education.

This example illustrates the complexities involved in any such "out with the old, in with the new" maneuver in special education. Labels and categories are not desirable, yet they may be inevitable for certain communication and funding purposes. The way out of this dissonant situation is clear-cut: learn to live with traditional labels in the extra-educational domain but replace them with educationally useful and relevant descriptive terms once the child crosses the classroom threshold. This has been a theme throughout this text; little more needs to be said here regarding the author's position. In the next chapter, a public school model for dealing with the three dissonant issues described here will further illustrate alternatives to the traditional labeling and categorization approach.

Despite the current hue and cry about labeling (much of it centered on the mentally retarded and emotionally disturbed), special education has some examples to its credit of building the bridge from the other side, or replacing reliance on medically based labels with a functional educational approach. One of the most notable examples began in the 1930's and concerns the visually handicapped. In 1935, the Social Security Act required a legal definition of blindness so that eligibility for federal aid could be determined. For this reason, a definition based on visual acuity was adopted for both the blind and partially seeing. This definition was presented in Chapter 2 and individuals were classified according to it as a result of ophthalmic measurement.

Those children who functioned according to the definition as "legally blind" were candidates for braille instruction and those functioning as "partially seeing" children as being able to learn to read print. But the classification based on ophthalmic measurement did not hold up in practice. When viewed in purely educational terms, that is in terms of actual ability to read print, large numbers of so-called legally blind children were found to have residual vision that enabled them to read print. Therefore, the ophthalmic measurement utilized as a basis for assigning legal labels of blind and partially seeing was not wholly adequate for educational purposes.

ED

MR

VH

A far more useful classification reflecting an operational educational approach has emerged. Partially seeing children are those who can learn to read print, and blind children are those who cannot learn print but who need instruction in braille. Thus, the shift from a medical measurement to an educational operation has resulted in a major step forward in resolving the labeling dilemma with the visually handicapped. In a somewhat similar fashion the label learning disabilities has replaced earlier categories of brain damage and neurological impairment, moving us a bit closer to relating what we call a child to do what we do with him in the classroom. We still have a long way to go with such categories as emotionally disturbed, mentally retarded, and socially and economically disadvantaged, but we have made a beginning.

Of particular note is a project which has grown out of a concern of the United States Department of Health, Education, and Welfare. The Project on Classification of Exceptional Children (Hobbs, 1973) is being guided by a distinguished group of physicians, psychiatrists, special educators, sociologists, lawyers, administrators of national, state, and community agencies and programs for the handicapped, and parents of exceptional children. The project will culminate in a report to the Secretary of Health, Education, and Welfare covering (1) theoretical issues of classification and labeling, (2) the adequacy of classification systems, (3) labeling in institutions, (4) consumer perspectives on labeling, (5) public policy issues, and (6) recommendations for policies. On the basis of this comprehensive look at the entire labeling process, it is hoped positive action will occur on the part of government agencies and professional associations to correct inequalities in our present classification system across all areas of the handicapped.

SPECIAL CLASS PLACEMENT VERSUS REGULAR CLASS INTEGRATION

Historically, as exceptional learners were identified and schools were assigned responsibility for educating them, the special school or class model was seen as the logical approach to follow. Children with physical and sensory handicaps were among the first to receive special school assignment; by the late 1800's, unruly boys and mentally retarded children were assigned to special day classes in a few large cities. The only alternative for most of these children was exclusion from school, since their learning and behavior problems markedly interfered with meeting the expectations of a regular class program.

Even though the issue of special class placement versus regular class integration concerns each type of exceptional learner, more current attention has been directed toward the mildly retarded and the emotionally disturbed and the child with a learning disability. Simply stated, the issue is concerned with the optimal instructional setting for helping exceptional learners receive the maximum benefits of an education. Should they be isolated and taught full time as special children? Or should they be placed in the mainstream of the regular classroom and educated there? For some of our exceptional learners, the issue has been dealt with for a longer period of time, and in many cases a workable solution involving both special and regular education has been found. The visually handicapped child may spend long periods in a regular class and receive outside resource help with assignments and instruction in braille. The hearing handicapped child who is provided with amplification by means of a hearing aid may also be a candidate for regular class programs for much of his school day, although outside resource help in language and speech training may be provided. Many physically handicapped children can work well in regular class programs if physical facilities are conducive to their moving about (e.g., ramps instead of stairs for wheelchairs). Speech handicapped children who receive speech therapy on a scheduled basis are usually assigned full time to a regular classroom. Educational provisions for gifted children often involve participation in a combination enrichment and regular class program. The disadvantaged child presents a separate problem in relation to this issue. Many so-called regular classes in large urban cities are filled with children with learning and behavior problems who need special educational approaches, and as such the regular class *is* the special class. In other situations, these children may be classified as emotionally disturbed, learning disabled, or even mentally retarded and assigned special class placement according to these categories.

Most research that focuses on the special class versus regular class integration issue concerns the mildly retarded, and questions regarding efficacy of either placement have centered on social adjustment, problems in level of self-esteem, and academic achievement. Bruininks and Rynders (1971) have examined the positions that have emerged from such research studies and have provided an interesting if dissonance-producing picture of where things stand. To begin with, the controversy surrounding the special class for retarded children is not new. In 1896, when the first

ED

LD

MR

SD

VH

HH

SH

PH

special class for the retarded opened in Providence, Rhode Island, a newspaper columnist in that city composed a sarcastic report entitled, "The Fool Class" (Kanner, 1964). Binet and Simon, who developed the first widely accepted intelligence test, challenged special class placement in 1905 by stating, "To be a member of a special class can never be a mark of distinction, and such as do not merit it, must be spared the record" (Binet & Simon, 1961, p. 82).

The 1960's brought forth a number of research studies and position papers also challenging the use of the special class with the mentally retarded. MacMillan (1971b), in reviewing many of the studies, concluded "the child can't win," since some evidence has been presented suggesting he suffers in a special class and other evidence reported that he suffers in a regular class, thus setting the stage for dissonance in the field. The validity of these research efforts is a major consideration since sampling bias, lack of control of preplacement experiences, and questionable criterion measures were frequently found to be limitations. The predicament of the "child who can't win" is highlighted by the conclusion of a number of special educators who have written regarding this issue. Perhaps most notable was the position paper of Dunn (1968), which indicted special education for imposing special class placement on the mildly retarded with minimal justification, for including large numbers of disadvantaged children in such classes, and for failure to develop viable options. Other writers who have expressed viewpoints related to this issue are Johnson (1962), Christophos and Renz (1969), Kidd (1970), and Lilly (1970). Bruininks and Rynders (1971) have summarized some of the positions taken by these authors, and Forness (1972) has illustrated how even regular education must share the blame for the problems in special class placement.

To begin, we can conclude from some research studies that mentally retarded children placed in regular classrooms are rejected by their more able peers, thus supporting special class placement. But evidence also exists that the special class isolates the retarded child from normal social experiences, thereby restricting his opportunities for learning interpersonal skills. The mentally retarded child placed in a regular classroom may suffer from loss of self-esteem because of his inability to cope with demands and expectations that are a part of that program. The same child in a special class, however, is apt to suffer loss of self-esteem because of the stigma of being isolated and rejected by other children. Even though we may support special class placement for the retarded on the basis that homogeneous grouping by ability level leads to more effective learning, there is little evidence to support such grouping as providing the optimal learning situation for either normal or retarded children. We may also assume that a special class designed to deal specifically with the major learning problems of the retarded will constitute a superior educational setting for him, but we also must face the fact that such settings clearly place the responsibility for academic failure on the child rather than on schools and teachers. A smaller class offering individualized instruction would seem to guarantee that better academic learning would take place, but studies show the retarded often make as much or more academic progress in the regular classroom as they do in the special classroom. In defense of the special class, we can take the position that such classes should not be held responsible for mistakes in diagnosis and placement. The mere existence of the special class, however, encourages misplacement of many children, particularly those from minority groups.

The theme of dissonance is evident throughout the statements made in the preceding paragraph. Once again we are faced with the unenviable position of not being able to deal directly with the issue on an either-or basis. The solutions must lie somewhere in the middle, for it is highly improbable that a full swing of the pendulum and total abandonment of the special class concept will serve the cause of education of the exceptional learner.

There are some children with special learning and behavior problems who can never be in school if they are not separated from the regular class program. Certain severely disturbed and retarded children are a case in point here. There are other children with learning and behavior problems who are not candidates for full-time placement in the regular classroom and if that is the only option, they will fail to receive the education appropriate for them. Among these groups would be representatives from every category of exceptional learners. Then there are children with learning and behavior problems who may well profit most from full-time placement in the regular classroom, provided there is an individualized curriculum and a teacher knowledgeable and understanding in relation to their problems and willing to accommodate their uniqueness in the program.

Forness (in press) has stated that the special versus regular class issue may lapse into irrelevance for two reasons. First, class action lawsuits initiated on behalf of plaintiffs from low income or minority backgrounds who allegedly have been placed in special classes for the retarded in inordinate numbers have forced discontinuation of special class placement as a single option in a number of instances.   Thus, the courts have had and probably will continue to have a direct influence in modifying special education practices.   Cohen and De Young (1973) have prepared a comprehensive report on the role of litigation in affecting educational programs for exceptional learners.   Under such influences, special education will never be able to wait until all the evidence is in regarding the efficacy of special versus regular class placement.   We must act now and create a range of placement options that more adequately meet the educational needs of exceptional children in the nation.   Secondly, Forness challenges the notion that the mildly retarded constitute a homogeneous group.   He sees the singular option of the special class as creating an either-or situation for retarded children, one that falsely assumes that mental retardation is an all or none phenomenon.   Such a situation, in fact, places the burden of proof for retardation squarely on the child in that he must prove to us by repeated failures that he is retarded enough to be eligible for special class placement.

In dealing with the special class placement versus regular class integration issue, we must plan for all types of children, and indeed movement in this direction is occurring in the field.   Bruininks and Rynders summarize some of the options in personnel roles, instructional resources, and administrative placements that are emerging.   The range in personnel roles to aid the mildly retarded is being extended to include paraprofessionals to support the regular class teacher, resource learning specialists to provide consultation, special education resource teachers offering part-time help, and full-time special class teachers for some children.   Administrative placements may range from nongraded, open school plans through regular class placement with various supporting outside services to the special class part or full time to homebound instruction, and residual school placement.   Thus, the solution to the dissonant special versus regular class issue is to be found in extending the range of resources available in the school and community on both a creative and practical level.   The logic of this approach is obvious and sound; yet such an extension of resources makes many demands on both special and regular educators that will take time to meet effectively.   In the next chapter, we will examine in detail an administrative arrangement for delivering instruction to exceptional learners from several categories that aims at dealing directly with the special versus regular class issue.

IMPACT OF CHANGES IN SPECIAL EDUCATION
ON REGULAR EDUCATION

Discussions of opening the door of the special class and integrating some exceptional learners into the regular classroom often fail to consider how open the regular classroom door might be and just how ready, willing, and able the regular classroom teacher is to include such children.   Regardless of how intensive the individualized work with children with learning and behavior problems is in a special class setting or how it is focused on preparing the child for survival and success in the regular classroom, if there is a lack of understanding or acceptance on the part of the regular teacher once the child arrives, we have hardly improved the present state of affairs.

Hewett, Quay, Taylor, and Watson (1973) have explored the opinions of regular classroom teachers regarding the effects of having mildly retarded, emotionally disturbed, and learning disabled children integrated in their classrooms.   An "Information Survey" was developed, which asked regular teachers to respond on a five point scale (from "strongly agree" to "strongly disagree") to statements related to placement of these exceptional learners in their program.   The statements focused on behavior and learning problems that might be presented by the children themselves (e.g., "The behavior of an emotionally disturbed child will be disruptive in a regular classroom"); the effect of these problems on the rest of the class (e.g., "The presence of an educable mentally retarded child will adversely affect the motivation to learn of normal children in the regular classroom"); the academic learning potential of the exceptional learners (e.g., "If properly taught, an emotionally disturbed child will learn reading as well as the normal child"); and the additional problems that might be faced by the teacher if such children were integrated (e.g., "Teaching the educable mentally retarded child will require at least weekly consultation with the school psychologist").   Three hundred regular elementary teachers were given the survey.   An extensive range of responses was obtained.   A comparison of the top twenty-five percent of the most knowledgeable and positive responses with the bottom twenty-five percent of the least knowledgeable and positive responses revealed that many of the statements significantly differentiated the teachers in the sample. Even though this survey was developed as a means of measuring changes in regular class teachers' opinions after actually working with exceptional learners in their classrooms and participating in in-service training programs, this standardization data provided interesting evidence regarding the widely discrepant positions that regular class teachers hold regarding the inclusion of exceptional learners in the regular classroom. This is an important problem area that must be dealt with if we are effectively to resolve the special versus regular class issue.

In the author's experience, regular classroom teachers do vary in terms of their range of tolerance for behavioral and academic differences among children in their classrooms. There is no way of describing the typical regular classroom into which we may be placing an exceptional learner. Each classroom will be unique as each teacher is unique. If we are going to move toward increased integration we will have to help regular teachers broaden their ranges of tolerance for behavioral and academic differences, increase their effectiveness with individualized instruction, and effect an appropriate teacher-child match-up with respect to placing a given exceptional learner in a classroom so that he falls within the existing ranges of tolerance of a given teacher.

One approach to accomplishing the first task might be increased emphasis and course work in teacher preparation programs on individual differences among children in general and among exceptional learners specifically. Such programs leading to certification seldom stress these areas, although some exceptions can be found across the country. A major increase in this regard would probably be difficult to implement because of the slowness with which curricular change occurs in college and university programs. The author is reminded of a survey of the credentialing standards of the fifty states with respect to courses in reading instruction required for an elementary teaching certificate. Until the early 1960's, more states required course work in music and art areas than in basic reading instruction. If our teacher preparation programs have been that slow in incorporating required coursework in such a critical and basic area as reading instruction, it is highly doubtful that we can effect an overnight increase in required study in areas related to the problems of exceptional learners.

The more realistic approach is probably on an in-service level. That is, we may not have the time to wait until major changes are brought about in teacher training programs; we need to consider ways to communicate directly with the regular teacher working in the field at the present time.

To bring about more direct communication between special and regular education, special educators must work as hard to decrease the specialness and separatist orientation as regular education must work to increase its ranges of tolerance for behavior and learning differences and effectiveness in individualizing instruction.   During the 1960's, when the field of special education was rapidly going through infancy, childhood, adolescence, and moving toward maturity, we may have overemphasized a specialized identity.   Reliance on labels and categories played a large part in shaping such an identity.   The point was reached at which teachers with specialized credentials in one area of exceptionality often were reluctant to include children with problems falling outside their specialized area of preparation in their classrooms. Assigning a blind child to a teacher of the blind in a school district was fine, but if this child was also mentally retarded or emotionally disturbed, serious questions might be raised about the appropriateness of such a placement with the teacher.   Obviously, special educators have become far too special when categorical boundaries are rigidly established for programs.   Such boundaries are also a serious deterrent to establishing more meaningful and direct communication with regular educators.   Part III of this text was devoted to an attempt to re-orient special education away from specialized, categorical boundaries for communication and practice and toward generalized areas of learning competence that cut across these boundaries.   Hopefully, this re-orientation will positively contribute to improving communication between special and regular educators.

Despite in-service training and improved communication efforts, can we really hope to enlist the regular class teacher's support and increased acceptance of exceptional learners in regular classrooms?   A positive answer appears doubtful when we consider some provisions often included in contracts drawn up by teacher organizations for negotiation with school districts.   Such provisions may call for complete control to be given regular teachers over who is kept in or who is referred out of the classroom.   Children whose behavior falls outside the teacher's range of tolerance can be referred out to the principal on a permanent basis.   Although such teacher organization demands do not exist on a nationwide basis, they suggest that many regular teachers are more ready to remove problem children from their classrooms than they are to accept additional children with learning and behavior problems.

In this regard, it is the author's contention that two basic points must be stressed when communicating with regular educators about establishing a closer working relationship between special and regular education.   The first point is this: *no matter how many children with learning and behavior problems we remove from your classroom, when the state and district quotas are filled you are still going to find children with problems left for you*

ED

MR

VH

to teach. The second point is closely related: *most of what special education is all about concerns extending good teaching practices so that more children receive the benefit of an education. As special and regular education achieve a closer working relationship, we can anticipate better quality education for all children in our schools.*

The channels for communicating these points become an important consideration. In the next chapter, we will describe an in-service approach with regular classroom teachers that is aimed at such communication as well as implementation of an integration-oriented option to special class placement.

We have briefly examined three contemporary issues in the field of special education and the dissonant state each of them places us in. Labeling and categorization is undesirable but perhaps necessary at some levels in our total efforts to provide resources for exceptional learners. Special class placement as a single option is inadequate, but elimination of all special classes will deny educational opportunities for some children with serious learning and behavior problems. Special education has come of age building on its specialness, but the time has come to alter our identity somewhat if an effective working relationship is to be developed with regular education. The pendulum must swing from established positions, but not full arc.

As the field of special education contemplates the issues before it, we find legislative activity across the nation also reflecting major changes in provisions for the education of exceptional learners. Some of this activity has been brought about by lawsuits directed against state departments of education and local school districts by individual parents and organizations of parents of handicapped children. The State-Federal Information Clearinghouse for Exceptional Children, a project of the Council for Exceptional Children and part of a project supported by the Bureau of Education, United States Office of Education, has summarized five current trends in state legislation that are related to the education of exceptional learners. Briefly stated, these trends are:

1. Mandatory laws for guaranteeing that all handicapped children will receive the benefits of an education. In the past, a permissive structure in some states allowed considerable flexibility for local districts to operate within when it came to accepting responsibility for certain types of exceptional learners. About thirty-five states now have some form of mandation and others are considering it.
2. Consideration of cultural and ethnic differences in identifica-

tion and placement of children in special education programs. Keeping parents informed of identification and placement practices as well as state laws governing such practices is also receiving attention.

3. Creation of laws to provide early education programs for both handicapped and non-handicapped children.

4. Alteration of definitions of handicapping conditions so that certain types of children are not excluded.

5. Increase in comprehensive services such as transportation facilities for handicapped children. Also, laws have created regionally based programs in areas where local school districts alone cannot provide good programs for certain types of handicapped children.

In California an attempt is underway to translate these trends into a practical framework through which special education will be delivered to all children according to their needs. The *Master Plan for Special Education* (California State Department of Education, 1973) is a unique and comprehensive document that is being reviewed by educators at all levels. If approved, it will ultimately serve as a philosophical and practical framework for pertinent legislation. The plan calls for a series of options to serve every child "with exceptional needs" and affirms not only that regular education be more responsive to individual needs of exceptional children but also that special education must take the responsibility for showing how this can be done and for helping regular classroom teachers to do so.

This chapter has attempted to touch primarily on issues and to a lesser extent on actions that are part of the contemporary special education scene. In Chapter 11, we will examine actions as they are reflected in a comprehensive attempt to deal with issues in the field at the present time.

CHAPTER 11

*The Santa Monica Madison School Plan**

Throughout this text, we have utilized the theme of a transitional journey in the field of special education. Starting with a review of traditional approaches to describing and conceptualizing exceptionality, we moved through collective consideration of children in nine categories across dimensions of flexibility, sociality, intelligence, and individualization. In Part III, we narrowed our focus within these dimensions and discussed our exceptional learners in terms of their characteristics on five levels of learning competence — attention, response-order, exploratory, social, and mastery. We organized our discussion around the implications of these levels of competence for selection of curriculum tasks, arrangement of conditions, and provision of consequences in the actual learning situation. At this point, we had set the stage for approaching the education of the exceptional learner in a somewhat innovative,

* The program described in this chapter was developed with support from a Title VIb grant allocated by the California State Department of Education, Department of Special Education. The author is indebted to the following individuals in the Santa Monica Unified School District who were instrumental in the development of the Madison School Plan: Ron Merriman, principal, Madison Elementary School, and his entire faculty including the Learning Center Staff; Mary Jane Cheetham, Karen Clark, Bonnie Kramer, Bea Rethlake, and Linda Williamson; Alfred A. Artuso, Superintendent, Frank D. Taylor, Assistant Superintendent, Special Services, Robert J. Stillwell, Supervisor, Special Services, Kathleen Peterson, Special Assistant, Special Services, and the principals and many regular and special teachers throughout the District who have participated in the program.

contrasting manner as compared with traditional practices. But we still faced the task of converting this approach into programmatic action. This is what we will attempt in the present chapter and as we discuss an approach that has been both public-school conceived and implemented to *do something with* the conceptualization upon which this text has been based and to *do something about* the critical issues raised in Chapter 10. No matter how bold your intentions or how grand your plans, until action replaces armchair speculation and deeds replace discussion, we are not truly contributing to the exceptional learner in the schools today.

The Madison School Plan was developed in the Santa Monica Unified School District in California over a five-year period. It represents an extension and elaboration of the engineered classroom design that had been developed in the district sometime earlier (Hewett, 1968; Hewett, Taylor, & Artuso, 1968). The engineered classroom design sought to create a learning environment in which educationally handicapped children were assigned tasks they were ready for, needed, and could do successfully. It also maintained a flexible approach to conditions and readily altered "when" children were assigned certain tasks, "where" they worked, "how long" they worked, and "how much" they were expected to do. Consequences were provided largely through the check mark system. The details of the engineered classroom design were discussed at various points throughout Part III of this text. Even though it proved effective in many respects, the design was somewhat limited in that it was largely a self-contained program, did not emphasize social, interactional, and group learning skills, and did not systematically prepare the child for re-entry into a regular classroom. For these reasons, a broader plan was devised that would preserve the philosophy of the engineered classroom but that would follow a resource rather than self-contained model. Two basic assumptions were involved in the plan:

1. All exceptional children are first and foremost learners at varying, levels of learning competence and many can be combined, regardless of category, into a single special educational program
2. Most exceptional children can profit from some integration in a regular class program, provided they are properly scheduled and are provided with appropriate supportive services

With regard to the first assumption, it was decided to combine children traditionally placed in categories of emotionally disturbed, learning disabled, and educable mentally retarded into a single program. Blind and partially seeing children, and partially hearing children also were included from time to time, as were speech handicapped, disadvantaged, and gifted children. In fact, only the severely retarded child and the deaf child were not considered candidates for this modified plan. Had children with crippling conditions or chronic health problems been among those in the Santa Monica schools needing special educational assistance, they could have been included.

The second assumption dictated the major focus of the approach, which was later called the Madison School Plan after the elementary school in the Santa Monica district where it was developed. This focus was on preparing exceptional learners for integration and participation in the regular classroom by means of a special education program. Both of these assumptions can be debated. What exactly is the effect on children with one type of learning or behavior problem as a result of being combined with children with various other types of problems? What is it that is so good about the typical regular classroom with its emphasis on conformity and lack of individualization that justifies a special education program directed toward preparing children to fit into it? The author has had some interesting discussions with students and colleagues about these questions but will not discuss them in detail at this point. After five years of careful study, there has been no evidence to suggest to the author that heterogeneous grouping adversely affects any type of exceptional learner, although it is possible that this might occur with a particular child in a particular group. We have referred several times in this text to the high-risk nature of "always" statements, and here we have another good example. The issue is largely unresearched, although Bower and Messenger (1965) have debated it partially in the literature.

What's so good about the public school regular classroom? A brief anecdote about a patient receiving psychotherapy at the UCLA Neuropsychiatric Institute will reflect the author's position. The patient was having delusions about people tapping his telephone and hiding tape recorders in his room. The therapist continually called the patient's attention to the fact that these beliefs were unlikely to be true and that they were simply not reality. After many sessions during which he heard the term, reality, over and over again the patient angrily confronted the therapist with, "Tell me, Doc, what's so good about this reality?" The therapist looked him straight in the eye and calmly stated, "I never said it was good. I only said it was there." Whatever else the contemporary American public school regular classroom may be, it most certainly is "there." In the long run, as special education moves toward closer collaboration and involvement with regular education, many positive changes are likely to occur. In this way, the special education field has an important opportunity to make a significant contribution to the American school.

READINESS FOR REGULAR CLASSROOM FUNCTIONING

In utilizing the regular classroom as the major reference for the focus of the Madison School Plan, it was necessary to conceptualize the primary requisites for survival and success in such a classroom. This conceptualization reflects concern with the three major determiners associated with effective learning and instruction discussed at length in Part III — curriculum, conditions, and consequences. Readiness for regular classroom functioning is as follows:

Curriculum
  The child must have competence in pre-academic skills
  The child must have competence in academic skills
Conditions
  The child must be able to profit from instruction and learning in the varied instructional settings utilized in the regular classroom
Consequences
  The child must be susceptible to the various incentives provided by the regular classroom as a basis for his motivation to learn

Each of these areas of functioning can be utilized to describe an individual exceptional learner. That is, he may have primary problems in pre-academic skills, such as paying attention, or perceptual-motor adequacy. He may work better under the condition of a one-to-one teacher relationship and be particularly motivated by a check mark system backed up by tangible rewards or consequences. Or he may primarily be an academic curriculum problem, ready for work in remedial or grade-level material, needing experience in a highly interactional, teacher-small group setting, and very susceptible to consequences of social attention and praise. The Madison School Plan conceptualizes the exceptional learner in terms of his strengths and weaknesses within these three areas and provides an administrative and instructional framework on four levels for increasing his competence in functioning in a regular classroom. In presenting the specific design of this plan, we will begin with an elaboration of curriculum, conditions, and consequences as they apply to regular classroom functioning and discuss four levels of expectancy that might be associated with each one.

Curriculum

Once the normal child is underway in elementary school, the curriculum tasks that he is assigned follow an increasing grade level-based pattern and become more academically oriented.   Let us look at our two statements presented earlier about pre-academic and academic curriculum expectations in the regular classroom and conceive of four levels of emphasis.

Level Four.   We will consider level four the highest level of curriculum expectations and the one directly associated with the regular classroom.   Pre-academic skills, such as the attention, response-order, exploratory, and social levels of competence, are taken for granted.   Also, we expect the child to function adequately in the perceptual-motor area.   Our main order of business is on the mastery level.   Here, our task is to move the child along in basic skill areas of reading, arithmetic, and written language, and to introduce the content of subjects such as social studies and science.

Level Three.   Lowering our expectations slightly, we can conceive of a curriculum emphasis that is still largely academic in focus but that includes remedial instruction in basic skill areas and use of a wider range of materials in teaching subject matter.   Also, reference and study skills such as use of an index might be emphasized for children in the middle and upper grades who have not learned them effectively.   Learning to carry out homework assignments may also be an area of emphasis.

Level Two.   Here we shift emphasis from primary focus on the mastery level and introduce concern with pre-academic skills on the social and verbal response levels.   Helping the child learn to work and participate in a group setting in which he must share desk space, wait his turn, cooperate and interact with others, and communicate verbally is one of our goals.   On the academic level, we will emphasize basic tool skills in relation to subject matter content and utilize a wide range of remedial techniques and materials in this regard.

Level One.   On the most basic level of curriculum concern, we

shift primarily to the pre-academic area and many of the competencies discussed in Chapter 6. Paying attention, starting, working,
finishing assignments, following directions, and observing classroom rules are competencies we must bolster by means of tasks
we assign the child. Perceptual-motor skills will be given special
attention, as will increasing the child's exploratory level skills
and knowledge through provision of many multi-sensory activities.

As can be seen from our descending levels of expectancy,
which start with traditional academic emphasis in the regular classroom, we have gradually broadened the notion of curriculum to
include concern with basic pre-academic skills. The latter may
not receive major attention in the regular classroom as distinct
curriculum areas. But if we are attempting to help the exceptional
learner move toward some level of participation in the regular program, we must be prepared to start with some of them on an
almost exclusively pre-academic oriented level.

Conditions

In Chapter 6, we reviewed the importance of such conditions of
learning as "when," "where," "how," "how much," "how long," and
"how well." Most of these conditions are going to be task-specific
and can be varied continuously in both regular and special programs. However, the condition of "where," or the nature of the instructional setting and what the child is assigned, is apt to be
determined by the program itself. For example, regular classrooms
typically have twenty-five or thirty-five children in them with a
single teacher, whereas the traditional special class may have only
half that number and in some cases provides the supportive services
of a teacher's aide. Indeed, the condition of "where" the child
works has constituted one of the most visible and distinct contrasts
between the regular and special class. In our discussion of four
levels of expectancy under conditions, therefore, we will focus on
the nature of the instructional setting.

Level Four. Here is the regular classroom with the major instructional setting involving a teacher and a large group. Although the
author recognizes the many alternatives and options in this regard
that may be found in open classrooms and other innovative regular
classroom arrangements, we will use the more traditional setting
as typical. The child receives much of his instruction from the
teacher at the front of the room. He is expected to work independently at his desk. Teacher-small group or child-small peer group

settings will also be utilized from time to time. The individual teacher-child instructional settings will probably not be provided too often.

Level Three.   At this level, we will conceive of a teacher-group instructional setting in many ways like that at level four but involving perhaps only half as many children. In addition, there will be an increased emphasis on teacher-small group instruction and some provision for a one-to-one teaching situation. An activity center emphasizing academic tasks will also be found.

Level Two.   Now we shift to teacher-small group instruction exclusively, with our group size consisting of perhaps six to eight students. More one-to-one instruction will also be provided at this level. Activity centers emphasizing exploratory, social, and academic tasks will be available.

Level One.   Continuing our emphasis on more supportive and individualized instructional settings, we finally arrive at level one, where the teacher-child setting will be primarily utilized. In addition, interest and activity centers will be found at this level where instruction may be provided in relation to pre-academic competence at attention, response, order, exploratory, and social levels. Thus, we have covered the full range of instructional setting possibilities and hopefully have considered at lease one level at which any child — normal or exceptional — might learn effectively.

Consequences

Chapter 6 also presented a sequential framework for viewing the types of consequences possible to provide in the learning situation. We will also organize these according to four levels.

Level Four.   In the regular classroom, which has been our focus at this level in discussing curriculum and consequences, we will find consequences of acquisition of knowledge and skill, knowledge of results or grades and social attention, recognition, and praise frequently relied on to make it worth the child's while to participate and learn. Grades may be the most systematically provided consequence and given intermittently on a daily, weekly, mid-semester, or end of semester basis. Hence, a child at this level must be largely susceptible to these cognitive, academic, and social motivational approaches.

Level Three.   A variation on level four that is still in the academic and social domain might be a numerical grading system reflecting the child's classroom behavior and work accomplishment. This would be offered on an hourly basis throughout the school day, thus increasing considerably the child's awareness of how he was doing in the classroom as compared with level four grading approaches. Social consequences would be particularly emphasized by the teacher at this level.

Level Two. Here we shift from a grading approach on an hourly basis to the use of a check mark system implemented every twenty minutes. The check mark system would focus on both pre-academic and academic accomplishments and would provide the child with a free choice activity time period when he completed a full card of check marks. Social consequences would continue to be utilized with those children who demonstrated that these were meaningful and effective for them.

Level One. At this most basic level, we will utilize the check mark system at twenty-minute intervals, particularly with reference to pre-academic accomplishments, and will add tangible exchange items such as food and trinkets for completed cards. A free choice activity period will also be retained as an option.

The Madison School Plan is based on these four levels of expectancy across the determiners of curriculum, conditions, and consequences. It combines the expectancies at each of the four levels to conceptualize steps along the way to adequate functioning in a regular classroom. Thus, level four expectancies across curriculum, conditions, and consequences constitute the regular classroom in its traditional sense, whereas levels three, two, and one constitute transitional expectancies leading to this goal. For purposes of description, the plan refers to each level in the context of pre-academic or academic emphasis; thus, level four becomes Academic II (A-II), level three Academic I (A-I), level two Pre-Academic II (PA-II), and level one Pre-Academic I (PA-I). Placed along a continuum that might be considered readiness for regular classroom functioning, the relationship between these levels can be graphically depicted as in Figure 21.

With this conceptualization before us, the task becomes one

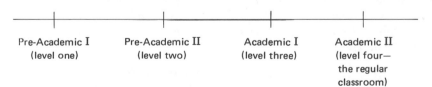

Figure 21: Readiness for Regular Classroom Functioning

of translating it into a workable plan to put into practice in the public school as an option to the self-contained class.   In the past, levels one, two, and three have included components combined together in special education classes for exceptional learners, with level four constituting a separate placement altogether.   Our goal will be to preserve the continuity between level one through level four and to create a continuous program for educating the exceptional learner, which systematically leads to integration in a regular classroom.   We will be utilizing, therefore, a type of resource room approach that will offer a full range of options for the exceptional learner, from the self-contained classroom to full-time integration in a regular classroom.   In doing this, we will need a three-level special education resource program, each level of which reflects the curriculum-condition-consequences provision assigned to these levels. The components of these levels are presented in Table 3.

As a final attempt to interrelate some of the conceptual components that have been the basis for our discussion in this text, we can expand our original capacity × experience equation as follows:

$$\text{capacity} \times \text{experience} = \text{functioning level} =$$

$$\text{flexibility} = \begin{array}{l} \text{attention} \\ \text{response} \\ \text{order} \\ \text{exploratory} \end{array} = \text{Pre-Academic}$$

$$\text{sociality} = \text{social} = \text{Pre-Academic II}$$

$$\begin{array}{c} \text{intelligence} \\ \text{individualization} \end{array} = \text{mastery} = \begin{array}{c} \text{Academic I} \\ \text{Academic II} \end{array}$$

Thus the Madison School Plan is conceptually organized on the administrative and instructional level to translate the orientation of this text into actual educational practice.

THE MADISON SCHOOL PLAN —
ORGANIZATIONAL FRAMEWORK

In the next section, we will examine the organization of the Madison School Plan. We will then review the implications of this approach for dealing with the three major issues confronting the field as presented in Chapter 10.

Table 3: Summary of Curriculum-Conditions-Consequences on Four Levels of the Madison School Plan

	Pre-Academic I	Pre-Academic II	Academic I	Academic II
Curriculum	Emphasis on pre-academic skills of attention, response, order, and exploratory levels. Deemphasize social and mastery levels.	Emphasis on pre-academic skills of verbal participation and social level. Emphasis on mastery level with intensive remedial work.	Emphasis on academic skills and mastery level. Regular class curriculum content with remedial work as necessary.	Emphasis on grade level curriculum and academic work.
Conditions	Primary use of teacher-child instructional setting with de-emphasis on group instruction. Interest and activity centers utilized.	Primary instructional setting — teacher-small group with provision of one-to-one instruction as needed.	Simulated regular classroom teacher-large group setting. Small group and individual instruction available as needed.	Teacher-large group setting with alternative settings as indicated or as possible to provide.
Consequences	Check mark system administered every twenty minutes backed up by tangible and free choice time exchange. Task completion and exploratory rewards appropriate.	Check mark system administered every twenty minutes and backed up by free choice time exchange only. Social praise also emphasized as appropriate.	Numerical grading system for work accomplishment and behavior administered hourly. Social praise, grades, acquisition of knowledge, and skill emphasized.	Regular school grading system with acquisition of knowledge and skill, social praise, and exploratory rewards available.

In any innovative approach designed for implementation in the public school, careful attention must be paid to the requirements for facilities, staff and equipment, and teaching materials. Should these requirements greatly exceed those required by the existing program, the innovative efforts may well be dismissed as impractical and unrealistic. For this reason, the Santa Monica Schools attempted to utilize resources for the Madison School Plan that were already in existence in the district's self-contained classroom program for emotionally disturbed, learning disabled, and educable mentally retarded children. The typical school offering a program for these children would provide two classrooms, two teachers, and two teacher-aides. In California, children with emotional disturbance and learning disabilities are combined under the category "educationally handicapped," and the educable mentally retarded are considered a separate group. Thus, these resources became the basis for the Madison School Plan.

Facilities

In our introductory overview of the philosophy and organization of the Madison School Plan, we ended by stating that the first three levels associated with curriculum, conditions, and consequences (Pre-Academic I, Pre-Academic II, and Academic I) would make up a special educational, resource-type program that would be set up outside the regular classroom (Academic II), but that would be oriented toward preparing the child toward participation in that setting. The facilities for these three levels are provided by two adjacent classrooms with a doorway cut between them. Thus, we have the floorspace formerly allotted to two self-contained classrooms available for PA I, PA II, and A I. One entire classroom was assigned to the PA I setting, and the other classroom was divided into areas for PA II and A I. Figure 22 presents the floorplan of the two-classroom facility, which was called the Learning Center.

The author and those who worked with him in the development of this plan can claim no originality for this designation as it has become a commonly used descriptive label for similar resource room facilities in many school districts across the nation. The term, Learning Center, does, however, clearly and directly state the intent of the resource facility. It is not an educational resource for the handicapped, disturbed, maladjusted, or retarded, but rather a place where, hopefully, any child in the school who needs some type of special help with learning can be assigned. We will discuss how such assignments might be provided in a later section.

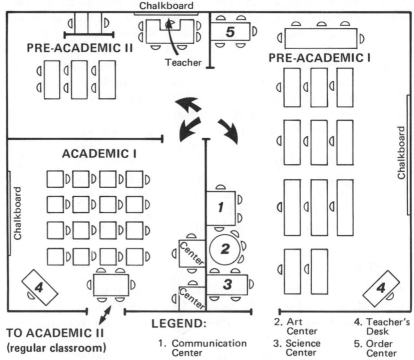

Figure 22: Learning Center Floorplan

LEGEND:

1. Communication Center	4. Teacher's Desk
2. Art Center	5. Order Center
3. Science Center	

TO ACADEMIC II (regular classroom)

As seen in the floorplan, PA I has been arranged with twelve double desks in the central area of the room. These are 2×4-foot tables that provide a large working area for each student and allow the teacher to work individually with the child in the one-to-one instructional setting that is utilized in this setting. (Three screened-off study cubicles are also available for children who may profit from a lessening of visual distraction.) Four centers surround the room, providing activities in science, art, communication, and order areas. The general floorplan of the PA I setting is identical with that of the engineered classroom developed earlier; but as can be seen, the connecting open doorway to PA II and A I allows easy access to higher level, transitional settings that move toward the regular classroom. Thus, the Madison School Plan not only builds on but also extends the original engineered classroom design.

The PA II setting is located in the adjoining classroom; it takes up approximately one-third the floorspace. The desk arrangement supports the type of instructional setting at this level. Several tables are clustered around a teacher's station, where group lessons are provided. Individual and shared desk space is provided nearby where independent and child-with-child assignments can be undertaken.

The A I setting takes up the major floorspace in the room. The intent here is to create a simulated regular classroom, with the desks arranged in a manner similar to what the child will encounter in a regular class in the school. Bulletin boards and activity centers that might be found in the regular classroom are also established here.

Staff

As stated earlier, it was our intent to utilize facilities and staff already available in the Santa Monica special education program for the Madison School Plan. Our staff potential, then, becomes two teachers and two teacher aides. Because of the highly individualized nature of the PA I setting, we will assign one teacher and one aide to work with the twelve children. PA II and A I next door will utilize the services of the other teacher and aide. For academic instruction, the teacher will alternate between the PA II and A I settings and the aide will work in these settings for follow-up and drill-type assignments. Six to eight children will be assigned to the PA II group and twelve to sixteen students will work in the A I setting.

The teachers in the program will be certificated elementary teachers who may also hold special teaching credentials for the educable mentally retarded. California, at the time of this writing, does not have a special credential for the educationally handicapped or for teaching children with emotional disturbance or learning disabilities. The teacher aides are usually individuals with bachelor degrees without special education training, although some very competent aides have not had any higher education. Ability to work with children with learning and behavior problems and to form an effective working partnership with the teacher appear the most important requisites for this role. When children who are visually or hearing handicapped have participated in the Madison School Plan, their special needs in areas of brailling instruction and language training have been handled by certificated teachers of the blind and deaf who functioned on an itinerant or resource basis.

Students

The typical exceptional learner population included in the traditional self-contained program in the Santa Monica schools had numbered approximately thirty students. Eighteen of these were usually classified as educable mentally retarded and twelve as educationally handicapped. However, recent education code changes in California have altered past practices for identifying and classifying the retarded; now, only children below I.Q. 70 are considered candidates for placement in classes for the mentally retarded. The others with I.Q. levels in the 70's have been integrated into regular classrooms and provided with various transitional programs. For these children, the Madison School Plan has had the potential of offering whatever supportive services may be necessary since the basic conceptualization of the plan, that all children are first and foremost learners rather than categorical problems, teaches to the learning needs of the child rather than to his label.

The California State Department of Education requirements for identification of both retarded and educationally handicapped are followed in placing most of the children in the Madison School Plan. These requirements include administration of an individual I.Q. test by the school psychologist, a medical examination, and evaluation of each case by a district Admissions Committee, which makes recommendations regarding special educational placement. The process usually starts with a regular classroom teacher calling the principal's attention to a child who is having learning or behavior problems in a given class that appear to require some special help, and the principal in turn calling on the district department of special services for assistance. In the event special program assignment is recommended by the Admissions Committee, the child's parents are contacted and must give written permission before such placement occurs. Once the Madison School Plan is underway, some other children who are never so classified but who need help, as well as some gifted students, become candidates for participation in the Learning Center program. We shall elaborate on this later.

Placement

Once the major groups of exceptional learners are identified in the school, the task of assigning them to one of the three levels in the Learning Center is of major concern. Before explaining how this is done, we need to review a unique procedure followed by the Santa Monica Schools at the beginning of each school year. Rather than set up a special education program for identified children that starts the first day of the fall semester, as many such children as possible are assigned full time in a regular classroom for what will constitute a two-week period of evaluation. This assignment is made by the school principal, who attempts to provide the best child-class-teacher match-up he can within the possibilities existing in the school. The purpose of this regular class placement at the start of the year is:

1. To establish the child as a member of an existing regular class group from the beginning of the year and the regular class teacher as "his" or "her" teacher in the school
2. To establish a desk or working area specifically for the child to which he may return during periods of eventual integration over the year; this desk is permanently assigned to the child
3. To allow the regular class teacher to become familiar with the child and his problems and to aid in his placement in one of the settings in the Learning Center
4. To allow the regular class teacher to assess the child's readiness for continued participation in various scheduled activities in the regular class program

Within any group of children who have serious learning and behavior problems there will be some who would become automatic losers if full-time placement in a regular class was attempted at the start of the school year. But over a five-year period, the Santa Monica School District has found the number of such youngsters to be small; perhaps no more than three or four of the thirty identified exceptional learners in a given school would fall in this category. These children would not start school until the third week or until the Learning Center program was underway. Undoubtedly they would be assigned to the Pre-Academic I setting, which, as we will detail later, offers a full time traditional self-contained placement for such children.

It becomes extremely important to maintain continuous and open communication with the regular class faculty when attempting to implement the initial two-week placement of exceptional learners and the ongoing Madison School Plan itself. One of our major issues for concern in Chapter 10 was the coming together of special and regular education; this approach forces us to deal directly with the problem. The school principal will spend some time before the start of the school year explaining the plan to his entire faculty. He will attempt to counteract the impression some of his teachers might have that the initial integration period constitues a dumping procedure and that they will be stuck with additional problem children for the entire school year. Let's face it, most regular classroom teachers have no shortage of certain children who require special attention among their students. The prospect of adding retarded or disturbed children to their classes is likely to be viewed with reluctance, if not outright anger. Thus, from the beginning, the concerns and questions that the regular teachers may have must be anticipated if possible and dealt with directly. It will not be enough merely to state that exceptional children who have traditionally been isolated and kept apart in special classes may be better off, at least part time, in a regular classroom. Even though such an approach may appeal to some teachers' concern with the education and welfare of *all* children, it may be seen by others as a threat to the effective learning of their normal students and an unwelcome, added burden to their already heavy load of teaching and management responsibilities.

In presenting the Madison School Plan to the regular faculty, the principal will stress the following:

1. The trend on both a state and national level is toward integration of exceptional learners in regular class programs. This is being both recommended and mandated as a result of court decisions and legislative action. Thus, what is being dealt with is a major change in public school education rather than a local level innovation.
2. The initial evaluation possible when the exceptional learner participates for a two-week period in a regular classroom provides information about the child's readiness to profit from such participation in a way that never can be matched by psychological testing or other evaluative procedures.
3. The child is not being abandoned in the regular class. At any time during the two-week period or thereafter, if the teacher does not consider him a candidate for participation for all or even part of the regular class day, he may be referred out to the Learning Center as required.
4. However, if the regular class teacher is able to maintain him for certain periods of the day once the two-week period is passed, another child in the classroom who has never been classified as retarded or disturbed but who needs special help with basic academic skills or in areas of behavioral improvement or motivation may be assigned to the Learning Center for help during such periods of integration.

With this orientation established, the Madison School Plan is underway. As any exceptional learner is referred out by the regular teacher, the Learning Center staff is ready to include him full or part time in the special education program. To aid in placement of the child in a particular setting within the Learning Center, the regular class teacher making the referral is asked to fill out a Placement Inventory. This inventory consists of a series of statements relating to the four levels of functioning in areas of curriculum, conditions, and consequences.

Name _____

Teacher _____

Date _____

Madison Plan Placement Inventory
Santa Monica Unified School District, Department of Special Services

Please answer the following questions based on your knowledge or observation of the child in either special or regular classroom settings:

	YES	NO	MAYBE
1. Can child spend time in a regular classroom during non-academic activity periods (e.g., music and art)?			
2. Can child spend time in a regular classroom during academic work periods (e.g., reading, arithmetic, social studies)?			
3. Do child's problems in paying attention, starting, working, doing what he is told, and getting along with others overshadow his problems in reading and arithmetic?			
4. Can child pay attention, start, work, and do what he is told in a group of 8 to 10 children?			
5. Can child work independently for 20-minute periods?			
6. Can child take part orally in discussion with 8 to 10 children?			

	YES	NO	MAYBE
7. Can child use and understand language correctly?			
8. Can child get along with other children in a group of 8 or 10?			
9. Can child share desk, working, and storage space with another child sitting close by?			
10. Can child function well behaviorally and work on assignments without immediate and frequent consequences in form of check marks and tangible rewards?			
11. Does child work for letter grades and are these meaningful to him?			
12. Does the child work for social approval from the teacher?			
13. Does the child work for social approval from his classmates?			
14. Can child pay attention and listen in a group of 11 to 18 children?			
15. Can child start and work in a group of 11 to 18 children?			
16. Can child understand and follow directions given by a teacher to a group of 11 to 18 children?			
17. Can child pay attention and listen in a regular classroom group of 30 children?			
18. Can child start and work independently in a regular classroom group of 30 children?			
19. Can child profit from instruction given to an entire regular classroom group of 30 children by the teacher in front of the room?			

	YES	NO	MAYBE
20. Is it likely that child will take part orally in a discussion held in a regular classroom group of 30 children?			
21. Can child follow classroom rules with respect to being out of seat, talking out, raising hand, etc., in a regular classroom group of 30 children?			
22. Can child get along with others in a regular classroom group of 30 children?			
23. Is the child functioning within two years of grade level in reading?			
24. Is the child functioning within two years of grade level in arithmetic?			

The inventory is scored with a differential weighting given items that reflect the four functioning level concerns of PA I, PA II, A I, and A II. What emerges is a total score that describes the child's overall functioning in relation both to the Learning Center settings and to the regular classroom that is utilized for making the initial placement. The Placement Inventory is only a rough screening instrument that makes no definitive statement about the child's academic or behavioral problems; rather, it summarizes his overall functioning in relation to the basic provisions of the Learning Center in areas of curriculum, conditions, and consequences. Continuing assessment and observations once the child is placed will determine the actual ingredients of the special education program given him and his readiness to profit from work in other settings.

As can be seen, the Madison School Plan aims at exchanging labels of mental retardation, emotional disturbance, and learning disabilities, as well as other traditional categories, for a description related to the type of special educational setting that the child appears to be ready to profit from most. It is not aimed at firmly categorizing a "PA I child" or an "A I child." This is an important point to stress; if we are to truly avoid the potential "dead-end" effect of labeling, then we must resist merely exchanging one set of labels for another. Once the child is placed according to the inventory, he is a continuing candidate for reassessment and reassignment across all three levels of the Learning Center.

In practice, however, this is easier said than done.   The fondness with which educators tag children with learning and behavior problems with labels is not a simple matter to overcome. The author is reminded of one school that set up the Madison School Plan program in a series of temporary buildings or bungalows adjacent to the school.   The regular school staff quickly shifted from calling the children handicapped, retarded, or disturbed, but on more than one occasion were heard to refer to the students receiving help in the Learning Center as the "bungalow kids."

Placement Inventories can be obtained from the previous year's special education teacher for those children who are not assigned the two-week integration period in the regular classroom. In addition, inventories for initially integrated children can also be filled out by teachers working with them the previous year, thus providing a more comprehensive picture of the child's functioning level.   Children do mature and change over the summer period, however, and relying exclusively on information from individuals who have not seen the child for several months may not be wholly meaningful or accurate.

Once the Placement Inventory is filled out for each child who will be considered for assignment to the Learning Center, an important decision must be made.   Figure 22 illustrated the allocation of space to the three settings, PA I, PA II, and A I.   This allocation was based on twelve children in PA I, six to eight in PA II, and twelve to sixteen in A I; it works well when the inventories suggest that the children needing the three placements fall neatly into those numerical groupings.   But what if, say, all thirty children appear functioning at the PA I level or twelve appear to be at the PA I level and eighteen at PA II?   There are numerous grouping combinations other than the one we used in our initial example. Although it has worked out many times that this example covers the needs of the exceptional learners to be placed, a flexible approach must be maintained so that settings fit children and not vice versa.   It may be that starting with two PA I settings will be necessary for certain groups of children.   Or perhaps keeping one-half of the Learning Center for a PA I group and providing two PA II settings in the other half will more closely meet the children's needs.   In any event, we can adjust our allocation of space and instructional emphasis to the types of children we meet; this appears a basic requisite for any viable resource room plan.   This flexibility in relation to the Madison School Plan has been described elsewhere (Taylor, Artuso, Soloway, Hewett, Quay, & Stillwell, 1972).

Program

Following the end of the two-week period of regular class integration and the completion of the Placement Inventories, the Learning Center program begins. The following considerations determine how each child will utilize the facilities:

1. If the child cannot participate during any regular classroom activity, he will be assigned full time to PA I, which will function as a self-contained class for him. In general, only children functioning at the PA II and A I levels spend time in the regular classroom.
2. All children who have been maintained for the two-week period or longer in the regular class before referral out for Learning Center assistance are initially assigned to the setting suggested by the Placement Inventory. However, an attempt is made to continue the child for some time in the regular classroom during opening exercises in the morning, physical education, or during art or music activities.
3. Even though the child initially starts his work in the Learning Center at one of these settings, he may be included for certain activities at other settings. Thus, the child may be assigned to PA I for the major part of the day but join the PA II group for an arithmetic lesson, since he may be ready to profit from group-oriented instruction in that subject.
4. Changes in setting and program assignment are made during frequent meetings of the two teachers and aides. No one type of formal evaluation or record keeping has been found effective as a basis of making such changes.
5. Changes in the scheduled time for the child in the regular classroom are based on informal contacts between the Learning Center staff and the regular classroom teachers. Again, no simple evaluation or record keeping system has proven effective in this regard. The school principal maintains close contact with all faculty concerned with an individual child and participates in any decision making.
6. While the child is integrated in the regular classroom, the management procedures utilized with all the children are followed in case of discipline problems. If behavior problems are typically handled by sending the child to the principal's office, then this is done. Under no circumstances does the teacher send the child back to the Learning Center because "you can't behave in the class."

The actual Learning Center program operates on a regular daily schedule offering instruction in basic skill and subject areas. Keeping in mind the curriculum, conditions, and consequences emphasis presented earlier in relation to each of the three settings, we will review the daily Learning Center schedule.

Curriculum.   In the Pre-Academic I setting, the day begins with an order task similar to the example presented in Chapter 7.   Reading activities are provided during the first hour.   These are divided into individual reading, word study, and skill reading.   Individual reading consists of oral reading by the child to the teacher in a book approximately at his reading level.   Basic vocabulary words that the child needs to learn are recorded and become the basis for word study activities.   These words may be printed on cards for word recognition drill, or a variety of remedial approaches may be utilized, depending on the child.   Skill reading may involve such programs as the Sullivan and Distar series introduced in Chapter 9.   These reading activities make up the general framework of the reading period; but considerable variations may occur due to the individualized focus of the PA I setting.

The second hour is devoted to a three-segment arithmetic period — drill on basic skills, instruction in new skills, and follow-up independent or group work.   Language skills are taught on an individual or small group basis for the remainder of the morning program.   Following lunch, an exploratory period is held, with the children rotating among the art, science, order, or communication centers.   Some children will leave at this point; others may remain an additional hour for individualized remedial instruction.

No attempt is made here to cover the many curricular possibilities in the PA I setting.   Perceptual-motor training may be introduced for some children and order or exploratory tasks freely utilized during the morning session as interventions or alternative assignments.   The intervention strategy relied on in the PA I setting is identical to that described in relation to the engineered classroom in Chapter 8.

The small group-teacher Pre-Academic II setting begins the morning session with story writing or remedial reading activities.   The first of these may be a group discussion centering around some topic of interest to the children that is designed to inform and motivate them so that they will be ready for story writing. This activity emphasizes the focus of PA II: verbal participation by the children and opportunities for improvement of social and language skills.   Individual reading, word study, and skill reading activities similar to those utilized in PA I also are a part of the initial hour, with group lessons and follow-up activities emphasized. Arithmetic instruction makes up the second hour and includes group experiences. The morning concludes with a language development period that may also include remedial work in spelling. Following lunch, the PA II students either join the PA I exploratory period with later remedial instruction or go to A I for a more formalized social studies program.

Since all of the students at the PA II and A I levels are participating for some time in the regular classroom, a given child may leave for physical education, art, music, or even academic periods throughout the school day. During such participation, a child with learning problems in the regular classroom who is not classified in any way but who needs help may take his place and join the Learning Center program for individualized or group work in any of the three settings.

The Academic I program begins with typical opening exercises similar to those followed in the regular classroom. Reading is the focus of the first hour; a combination of the reading approaches utilized in the other settings may be followed. However, the structure of the hour is more in line with a regular classroom reading period, and basal readers and other graded reading materials are included.

An issue of concern arises here regarding the grade-level range possible to include in this large group instructional setting that aims at emulating a regular class program. Since children may be assigned to the Learning Center from grades two to six, it is difficult to imagine a meaningful curriculum and class grouping at the A I level covering such a span. In practice, children who are assigned to the A I level are largely from grades four to six. Younger children may be returned to second and third grade classrooms for combined A I and A II level work since the class groupings and range of academic material provided often offer more opportunities for individualization and flexibility than in the upper grades.

As in the other settings, the second hour in A I is devoted to arithmetic, utilizing materials and instructional approaches resembling those in regular class programs. Spelling will be studied during the last period before lunch. Following lunch, the teacher typically reads to the entire class from a book of interest to them. This is usually done for 15 minutes; it has been found useful as a settling down and group listening experience in the other settings. Many of the A I students will spend their afternoon time in regular class activities of social studies, physical education, music, or art. However, a separate social studies and written language program is maintained for those who are not integrated, and as was stated earlier, some PA II students may join this program.

During the afternoon periods when a large number of Learning Center students are integrated and few regular class non-classified children with learning problems are referred out for reciprocal assistance, the Learning Center staff has devoted time to working with gifted young students from the primary grades. These children, identified by their regular teachers, will come to the Learning Center for enrichment in areas of arithmetic and science using some of the special materials designed for remedial work with older children. The children work in small groups in either the PA I or PA II–A I areas.

This extension of the Learning Center program to include work with gifted children as well as its reciprocal remedial offerings for non-classified regular class children with learning problems truly moves it toward a total school resource role as compared with traditional self-contained programs. This can be a vital component in bridge-building efforts between special and regular education. The children in the entire school population are conceived of as individuals who are functioning at varying levels of learning competence. What is special about special educational approaches is that they encompass the entire range of the differing levels of competence and offer assistance for everyone needing it. How much more total-educational-field-oriented this concept is in contrast to considering special education a field that is designed to aid the retarded, disturbed, or handicapped!

Conditions. The arrangement of the instructional setting in Pre-Academic I has been discussed at various points earlier. The teacher may work alongside the student at his desk. The child may work there independently or be assigned to a study booth for independent work. He may work with a small group at a work table or with one or two classmates at the Communication Center. The Exploratory and Order Centers offer pre-academic task areas where he may be assigned alone or with another child. Even though emphasis is on individual teacher-child instruction, it can be seen that the PA I setting is ready to go to work with the child with a variety of instructional approaches.

As has been stated, the instructional setting in Pre-Academic II is largely teacher-small group. However, independent and shared work space will be provided, as will activity centers to build pre-academic skills on the verbal response and social levels. In many respects, the determiners of curriculum, conditions, and consequences relate to concepts of instruction rather than to facts as they are utilized in the Madison School Plan. Children simply are not calibrated with respect to their absolute need for any version of the three determiners. Thus, PA I students get academic work if they are ready for it, work in small groups when appropriate, and may be given social reinforcement if it is effective. Students assigned to PA II may work on a one-to-one basis with the teacher, and those in A I may get the full range of provisions associated with our notion of curriculum, conditions, and consequences. The important point is emphasis with respect to approaches that are likely to be most effective with certain types of exceptional learners. The Madison School Plan aims at defining such emphasis with its multi-level framework, but flexibility and individual child-centeredness ultimately determine what is actually utilized in any of the three Learning Center settings.

In the Academic I setting, the teacher-large group setting is implemented whenever possible to help the child gain experience in looking, listening, verbally participating, and following directions as well as in obtaining information and developing skills in what is a traditionally relied-on means of instruction in the regular classroom. Social studies offers content and activities that fit well into this setting, as does presentation of fundamental arithmetic processes. Again, varied settings are available for purposes of individualizing the program.

Consequences. In Chapter 7, we introduced the check mark system developed in the engineered classroom design that became the prototype for the Pre-Academic I setting. A number of changes in that system were found to be advantageous as a means of more clearly providing feedback to the student regarding his work and behavior. We shall present this revised system in detail at this point in our discussion of the Pre-Academic I setting.

The check mark system focuses on two general aspects of the student's functioning in the class: task behavioral and setting behavioral. Task behavioral functioning relates to competencies associated with accomplishing the assigned task; setting behavioral functioning reflects how well the student followed the rules of conduct established in the class. Every twenty minutes, the teacher and aide assign a possible five check marks to every student in each of these two categories. Slash marks printed diagonally across the box on the Work Record Card comprised the system in the engineered classroom, but it was found useful to elaborate on this and use alphabet letters specifically related to the behaviors being reinforced. At the Pre-Academic I level, the following task behavioral categories are utilized, with the appropriate alphabet letter actually written in the boxes on the student's card:

A — Attention
S — Starting
W — Working
F — Following directions
R — Being right
N — Being neat

The setting behavioral categories utilized are:

B — Being a student
D — Doing what you are told

Thus, the teacher will select one category from the task behavioral group and one from the setting behavioral group when it is time to acknowledge how well the child functioned during a class work period. Even though twenty-minute periods are the general rule at the PA I level, longer work periods may be introduced, with the checks coming at half-hour intervals. In a like manner, shorter work periods may be more appropriate for some students, and checks administered every ten minutes. At the risk of redundancy let us emphasize again: the system must fit the child, not vice versa.

In practice, the teacher elects one of two options in giving the task behavioral check marks:

1. Select a behavior that the child exhibited during the work period that you wish to reinforce positively and assign him the full five checks using the appropriate letter and calling his attention to the fact, "You've earned all five W's because you worked so well." This is the bolstering-a-strength option.
2. Select a behavior that the child did not exhibit during the work period that you are concerned that he develop in the future and withhold one or more check marks: "You have only earned three of the possible five check marks for your assignment because you did not continue working during the period." This is the altering-to-a-weakness option.

With regard to the setting behavioral check marks, the teacher follows the same two options and either gives the student all five because his behavior was appropriate or withholds one or more to alert him to the fact that he needs to improve.

In relation to selection of task behavioral categories, it

should be stated that the teacher will use the categories "being right" and "being neat" for the altering to weakness option only when they serve a meaningful purpose with the child. Many children working in the PA I setting are not candidates for evaluation on these levels and may need the bolstering a strength option for such efforts as "starting" in order to give them success and to build their motivation. It should also be noted that in giving the check marks, the teacher uses the terms associated with the category being assigned (e.g., "starting") in order to communicate clearly with the child. In the author's experience, the children take pride in relating to others — "Look, I earned five S's for starting!"

When the child's Work Record Card is filled with check marks, he can exchange it for a small food item such as candy or cookies, for twenty minutes of free choice activity time at one of the centers in the room, or for an opportunity to select a classroom privilege from a Take-a-Chance deck of cards. From observations over time, the author has noted that following the first several weeks of the semester the vast majority of children in the PA I setting elect either the free time or chance exchange.

The check mark system appears a useful approach for providing a continuous interaction between teacher and child focused on the behaviors of the child that need strengthening if he is to move toward successful participation in the regular classroom. Teachers using the system report that it may do as much if not more for them as compared with their children since it assures that they will be continually monitoring each student's functioning and will have a series of planned moments of evaluation with him throughout the class day.

The check mark system is maintained in Pre-Academic II with all of the categories and two options for administration related to task and setting behavioral functioning retained. However, there are several important additions. In the task behavioral area we add:

T — Taking part orally

In the setting behavioral area, the following is emphasized:

G — Getting along with others

These additional categories zero in on the two major goals of the PA II setting — helping the child improve in the quality, ease, and frequency of verbal participation and aiding him in developing social interactional skills. The twenty-minute interval is usually followed in administering check marks; only the free-choice activity time to be taken at one of the centers is available as an exchange.   The teacher in the PA II setting makes liberal use of verbal social praise both in connection with the check mark system and during group and individual work.

In the more academically oriented program of the Academic I setting, we shift from a check mark system and back-up rewards to a straightforward numerical grading system.   This is organized in relation to task and setting behavioral functioning, but uses terms more in line with traditional grading criteria in the regular class-room.   Task behavioral criteria become effort and quality of work, and setting behavioral criteria are combined under citizenship. Each child has a grade sheet on his desk that provides for an hourly accounting of his work and behavior.   The sheet covers all class periods for an entire week.   At the top of the sheet is a five-point numerical continuum covering 1 — Poor, 2 — Needs to improve, 3 — Satisfactory, 4 — Good, 5 — Outstanding.   At the end of each hour, the teacher assigns a numerical grade in effort, quality of work, and citizenship in boxes opposite each class period.

SUMMARY

The Madison School Plan was conceptualized to deal with the three issues in the field of special education discussed in Chapter 10.   We will summarize it with reference to these issues as we bring this chapter to a close.

What does the Madison School Plan have to contribute to resolving the labeling dilemma in special education?   It does not completely erase the traditional categorization used for state funding and district identification.   On paper, the children in-cluded in the program were still called mentally retarded and edu-cationally handicapped.   As stated in Chapter 10, it is the author's contention that we will have to live with traditional categorization for some time to come for funding and administration purposes. However, as stated in Chapter 10, national concern about the label-ing issue, reflected in a comprehensive look at alternative approaches being taken by the Office of Education, eventually may have far-reaching effects on federal, state, and local levels (Hobbs, 1973).   Until such time as a total reorganization is implemented, those concerned with delivery services to exceptional learners should take the initiative and begin to conceptualize programs and imple-ment services with alternative approaches *now*.

Beginning with the global notions that every child is a learner and that some regular classroom integration is a positive goal for most, the Madison School Plan attempts to describe the exceptional child in terms of his level of learning competence in relation to curriculum, conditions, and consequences and to assign him an educational program that meets him where he is.   Karen, the educable mentally retarded child, becomes Karen, the learner who needs help in building pre-academic skills of responding and following directions, and academic skills in reading and written language.   She works best on a one-to-one basis and is highly susceptible to social attention and praise from the teacher.   Michael, the emotionally disturbed child, becomes Michael, the learner, who must learn to work cooperatively with other children and to improve in his oral participation and language skills.   He is ready to work in a small group instructional setting, but is most effectively reached by an objective check mark system rather than by social verbal reinforcement from the teacher.   The combination of learning characteristics we can hypothesize for our exceptional learners is almost endless, and no lock-step program or rigid formula for providing special educational services for all of them can be conceived.   But we can broadly define parameters of programs and guidelines for services which, hopefully, will allow us to individualize our efforts to a considerable degree.   Such is the goal of the Madison School Plan.

The Madison School Plan attacks the special versus regular class issue directly by attempting to offer the best of all possible worlds — full-time special class placement if necessary and limited part-time resource help if that is appropriate.   The swinging-door concept has been applied to all components of the program.   Placement in PA I, which for some may be a full-time setting, is not placement behind a closed door.   Rather, the option always exists for the child to move out to PA II and eventually to A I on a full-time or part-time basis and from there to move through the swinging door into a regular classroom.   The regular classroom door, which has in the past been closed and even locked to exceptional learners, has been replaced by a swinging door, which moves both ways.   Children with learning and behavior problems who are ready to profit from some experiences there may swing in on a part-time basis and then move freely out again for special educational help in the Learning Center.   Regular classroom children who are never classified as exceptional may also move out for part-time assistance in the Learning Center.   As it becomes apparent that a given child can profit from longer periods in the regular classroom, he can increase his time there; and conversely, if circumstances arise that indicate he should be removed from scheduled participation, he can increase his time in the Learning Center program. The extended resource program base for the Madison School Plan with its self-contained placement options has proven effective as a viable option to traditional either-or approaches.

No matter how well conceived and organized your viable option may be, if it eventually depends on a regular classroom door that swings in a free and easy manner based on the regular teacher's willingness to participate, all of your efforts may be for naught if such willingness simply does not exist. This brings us to the third and final issue — the merging of special and regular education. As barriers between special and regular education have been lowered due to court decisions, law changes, or innovative program strategies, the problem of how realistic it is to expect increased acceptance of children with learning and behavior problems into the regular classroom has had to be faced. We discussed the effect of such expectations on regular teachers, who may already see themselves as overburdened, in Chapter 10. Clearly, any merging of special and regular programs must have something for regular teachers beyond an opportunity to express their altruism or dedication to children. The Madison School Plan builds in one such something by offering assistance with non-classified children during those times children assigned to the Learning Center are integrated. In addition, materials and approaches utilized in the Learning Center have been shared with the regular classroom teacher. These have proven reasonably effective, but more is needed. Toward that end, the Santa Monica School Special Services Department has been exploring an in-service training program for regular school faculty called "Train and Trade."* It aims at increasing regular staff knowledge about exceptional learners and introducing them to the philosophy and strategy of this text. The program covers six to eight weeks and involves a weekly forty-five minute meeting held after school. The meetings include:

1. Six twenty-minute film strip presentations covering the following areas:
   a. Brief overview of the history of special education in the United States and the basis for current concerns with labeling and reliance on the self-contained class option

*Development of this in-service program has been made possible by Title VIb funds allocated by the State of California Department of Education, Department of Special Education.

    b. The determiners of capacity and experience as they relate to exceptional learners and the notion of all children as learners at varying levels of learning competence

    c. Consideration of the six levels of learning experience as references for describing the problems of exceptional learners

    d. Curriculum, conditions, and consequences as determiners of instructional effectiveness

    e. Implementation of the philosophy and specific instructional strategies outlined in this text in the regular classroom

    f. Discussion of the issues, questions, concerns, and possible resentments that arise among regular classroom teachers as they are confronted with the possibility of including exceptional learners in their classroom

2. A one-to-two full-day assignment as a teacher in the Learning Center for each member of the school staff. This includes the principal, vice-principal, nurse, coach, librarian, and other staff who work closely with the children in the school. Substitutes assume responsibility for regular classes during these Learning Center assignments.

3. Follow-up discussion centered around content in the film strips and actual experiences that the staff have during their Learning Center teaching assignments.

Evaluation of the in-service approach has not been completed, but it appears to open communication channels between Learning Center and regular school staff members and to provide meaningful information related to the regular class teacher understanding and acceptance of the exceptional learner. To facilitate interest and participation in the program, University extension course credit has been provided for the teachers involved in it. Even though this would not be a readily available possibility for all districts to offer since it entails a close involvement with a college or university special education program, it has been found to be extremely useful and is worth exploring. Eventually, the goal of the Train and Trade program is to have the school principal conduct the training sessions after he receives an orientation from the district special education department. If this is not feasible, in some instances a member of that department staff, such as the school psychologist, can assume the responsibility. There are many models that can be used on an in-service basis to narrow the gap between the special and regular educators. Regardless of the knowledge imparted or teaching approaches introduced during such in-service programs, the real bridge will emerge when an ongoing, practical, and productive working relationship develops and is maintained between the special educator in whatever guise — resource teacher, consultant, auxiliary teacher — and the regular classroom teacher.

This chapter and this discussion of real world issues and problems confronting all educators — special and regular — fittingly brings the transitional journey of this text to a close. At the onset, we set as our destination three goals:

1. A conceptual and organizational rearrangement of knowledge and practice in the field of special education
2. A shift in point of view regarding exceptional children that considers them first and foremost learners at varying levels of competence and that recognizes the similarities as well as the differences that exist among categories
3. A merging of special and regular education with respect to increased understanding of all children who are different along critical dimensions related to learning

In truth, to claim that a final destination has been reached in relation to each of these goals would be both presumptuous and premature. We must instead hope that new conceptual and organizational avenues have been opened up for more careful study and accessible travel. A field in transition, as is the field of special education at the present time, is a field on the move. More important than whether this text has taken the field to any final destination is the possibility that it will serve as a catalyst for change and as a facilitator of continuing movement.

Bibliography

ABEL, G. L. The blind adolescent and his needs. *Exceptional Children,* 1961, 27, 309–310, 331–334.

ACKER, L. Errorless discrimination training in autistic and normal children. Doctoral dissertation, University of California, Los Angeles, Department of Psychology, 1966.

AINSWORTH, S. *Speech correction methods.* Englewood Cliffs, N.J.: Prentice-Hall, 1948.

AINSWORTH, S. The education of children with speech handicaps. In W. M. Cruickshank and G. O. Johnson (eds.). *Education of exceptional children and youth.* Englewood Cliffs, N.J.: Prentice-Hall, 1967.

ALTSHULER, K. Z. Theoretical considerations in development and psychopathology of the deaf. In J. D. Rainer and K. Z. Altshuler (eds.). *Psychiatry and the deaf* (Social and Rehabilitation Service, #VRA 67-32). Washington, D.C.: U.S. Department of Health, Education, and Welfare, 1967.

ALTSHULER, K. Z., AND BAROFF, G. S. Educational background and vocational adjustment. In J. D. Rainer, K. Z. Altshuler, and F. J. Kallman (eds.). *Family and mental health problems in a deaf population.* Springfield, Ill.: Charles C. Thomas, 1969.

AMERICAN FOUNDATION FOR THE BLIND. *A teacher education program for those who serve blind children and youth.* New York: American Foundation for the Blind, 1961.

AMERICAN PSYCHIATRIC ASSOCIATION. *Diagnostic and statistical manual for mental disorders.* Washington, D.C.: American Psychiatric Association, 1952.

AMERICAN PSYCHIATRIC ASSOCIATION. *Planning psychiatric services for children in the community mental health program.* Washington, D.C.: American Psychiatric Association, 1964.

AMERICAN SPEECH AND HEARING ASSOCIATION'S COMMITTEE ON THE MID-CENTURY WHITE HOUSE CONFERENCE. Speech disorders and speech correction. *Journal of Speech and Hearing Disorders,* 1952, 17, 129–131.

ANDERSON, C. M., AND PLYMATE, H. B. Management of the brain damaged adolescent. *American Journal of Orthopsychiatry,* 1962, 32, 492–500.

ASHCROFT, S. Blind and partially seeing children. In L. Dunn (ed.). *Exceptional children in the schools.* New York: Holt, Rinehart, & Winston, 1963.

AUSUBEL, D. P. How reversible are the cognitive and motivational effects of cultural deprivation? Implications for teaching the culturally deprived child. In A. H. Passow, M. Goldberg, and A. J. Tannenbaum (eds.). *Education of the disadvantaged.* New York: Holt, Rinehart, & Winston, 1967.

AVERY, C. B. The education of children with impaired hearing. In W. M. Cruickshank and G. O. Johnson (eds.). *Education of exceptional children and youth.* Englewood Cliffs, N.J.: Prentice-Hall, 1967.

AYLLON, T., AND HAUGHTON, E. Control of the behavior of schizophrenic patients by food. *Journal of Experimental Analysis of Behavior,* 1962, 5, 343–354.

BAGLEY, C. R. The educational performance of children with epilepsy. *The British Journal of Educational Psychology,* 1970, 40, 82–83.

BALLER, W. R. A study of the present social status of a group of adults who, when they were in elementary schools, were classified as mentally deficient. *Genetic Psychology Monographs,* 1936, 18, 165–244.

BALLER, W. R., CHARLES, D., AND MILLER, E. Mid-life attainment of the mentally retarded: A longitudinal study. *Genetic Psychology Monographs,* 1967, 75, 235–329.

BARATZ, J. C. Teaching reading in an urban Negro school system. In F. Williams (ed.). *Language and poverty.* Chicago: Markham Publishing Co., 1970.

BARCLAY, W. *Train up a child.* Philadelphia: Westminster, 1959.

BAROFF, G. S. Patterns of socialization and community integration. In J. D. Rainer, K. Z. Altshuler, and F. J. Kallman (eds.). *Family and mental health problems in a deaf population.* Springfield, Ill.: Charles C. Thomas, 1969.

BARRISH, H. H., SAUNDERS, M., AND WOLF, M. Good behavior game: Effects of individual contingencies for group consequences on disruptive behavior in a classroom. *Journal of Applied Behavior Analysis,* 1969, 2, 119–124.

BARSCH, R. H. *A movigenic curriculum.* Madison, Wisc.: Bureau for Handicapped Children, 1965.

BATEMAN, B. Reading and psycholinguistic processes of partially seeing children. *CEC Research Monograph,* Series A, No. 5. Arlington, Va.: Council for Exceptional Children, 1963, 1–46.

BATEMAN, B. Learning disabilities — yesterday, today, and tomorrow. *Exceptional Children,* 1964, 31, 167.

BATEMAN, B. Visually handicapped children. In N. C. Haring and R. L. Schiefelbusch (eds.). *Methods in special education.* New York: McGraw-Hill, 1967.

BAUMAN, H. A., AND BAUMAN, R. J. *The checkered flag series.* San Francisco: Field Educational Publications, Inc., 1969.

BAUMEISTER, A. A. Learning abilities of the mentally retarded. In A. A. Baumeister (ed.). *Mental retardation: Appraisal, education, and rehabilitation.* Chicago: Aldine Publishing Company, 1967.

BAUMEISTER, A. A., URQUHART, D., BEEDLE, R., AND SMITH, T. Reaction times of normals and retardates under different stimulus intensity changes. *American Journal of Mental Deficiency,* 1964, 69, 126–130.

BEEZ, W. Influence of biased psychological reports on teacher behavior. Unpublished doctoral dissertation, Indiana University, 1968.

BEIER, D. C. Behavioral disturbances in the mentally retarded. In H. A. Stevens and R. Heber (eds.). *Mental retardation.* Chicago: The University of Chicago Press, 1964.

BEILIN, H. Teachers' and clinicians' attitudes toward the behavior problems of children: A reappraisal. *Child Development,* 1959, 30, 9–12.

BEILIN, H., AND GOTLEIN, L. Psychological issues in the development of mathematics curricula for socially disadvantaged children. In A. H. Passow, M. Goldberg, and A. J. Tannenbaum (eds.). *Education of the disadvantaged.* New York: Holt, Rinehart, & Winston, Inc., 1967.

BELMONT, J. M. Long-term memory in mental retardation. In N. R. Ellis (ed.). *Research in mental retardation.* New York: Academic Press, 1966.

BELTO, E. W. A comparative study of certain physical abilities of children with speech defects and children with normal speech. *Journal of Speech Disorders,* 1941, 6, 187–203.

BENDER, L. Psychological problems of children with organic brain disease. *American Journal of Orthopsychiatry,* 1949, 19, 404–441.

BENSBERG, C. J. The relationship of academic achievement of mental defectives to mental age, sex, institutionalization, and etiology. *American Journal of Mental Deficiency,* 1953, 58, 327–330.

BENTON, A. Psychological evaluation and diagnosis. In H. Stevens and R. Heber (eds.). *Mental retardation: A review of research.* Chicago: University of Chicago Press, 1964.

BEREITER, C., AND ENGLEMANN, S. *Teaching disadvantaged children in the preschool.* Englewood Cliffs, N. J.: Prentice-Hall, Inc., 1966.

BERKOWITZ, P., AND ROTHMAN, E. *The disturbed child: Recognition and psycho-educational therapy in the classroom.* New York: New York University Press, 1966.

BERKSON, G. Responsiveness of the mentally deficient. *American Journal of Mental Deficiency,* 1961, 66, 277–286.

BERNSTEIN, B. A sociolinguistic approach to socialization with some reference to educability. In F. Williams (ed.). *Language and poverty.* Chicago: Markham Publishing Co., 1970.

BERRES, F., COLEMAN, J., BRISCOE, W., AND HEWETT, F. *The deep sea adventure series.* San Francisco: Field Educational Publications, Inc., 1959–1971.

BERRY, M. F., AND EISENSON, J. *Speech disorders.* New York: Appleton-Century-Crofts, 1956.

BEST, H. *Public provision for epileptics in the United States.* New York: Thomas Y. Crowell Co., 1967.

BETTELHEIM, B. *Truants from life: The rehabilitation of emotionally disturbed children.* Glencoe, Ill.: The Free Press, 1955.

BIJOU, S. Experimental studies of child behavior, normal and deviant. In L. Krasner and L. Ullmann (eds.). *Research in behavior modification.* New York: Holt, Rinehart, & Winston, Inc., 1965.

BIJOU, S., AND BAER, D. *Child development: A systematic and empirical theory.* New York: Appleton-Century-Crofts, 1961.

BINET, A., AND SIMON, T. Upon the necessity of establishing a scientific diagnosis of inferior states of intelligence. *L'Annee Psychologique,* 1905, 11, 163–191. Reprinted in J. J. Jenkins and D. G. Patterson (eds.). *Studies in individual differences.* New York: Appleton-Century-Crofts, 1961, 81–90.

BIRCH, J. W., TISDALL, W., PEABODY, R., AND STERRETT, R. *School achievement and effect of type size on reading in visually handicapped children.* Cooperative Research Project No. 1766, Contract

No. OEC-4-10-028. Pittsburgh, Pa.: University of Pittsburgh, 1966.

BIRNBRAUER, J., BIJOU, S., WOLF, M., AND KIDDER, J. Programmed instruction in the classroom. In L. Krasner and L. Ullmann (eds.). *Case studies in behavior modification.* New York: Holt, Rinehart, and Winston, 1965.

BISHOP, V. E. *Teaching the visually limited child.* Springfield, Ill.: Charles C. Thomas, 1971.

BLACK, M. E. *Speech correction in the schools.* Englewood Cliffs, N.J.: Prentice-Hall, 1964.

BLACKMAN, L. The dimensions of a science of special education. *Mental Retardation,* 1967, 5, 7–11.

BLANK, H. R. Dreams of the blind. *The Psychoanalytic Quarterly,* 1958, 27, 158–161.

BLOCK, W. E. Personality of the brain-injured child. *Exceptional Children,* 1951, 21, 91–100.

BLOODSTEIN, O., JAEGER, W., AND TUREEN, J. A study of the diagnosis of stuttering by parents of stutterers and non-stutterers. *Journal of Speech and Hearing Disorders,* 1952, 17, 308–315.

BORTNER, M., AND BIRCH, H. G. Cognitive capacity and cognitive competence. *American Journal of Mental Deficiency,* 1970, 74, 735–744.

BOWER, E. M. A process for identifying disturbed children. *Child,* 1957, 4, 143–147.

BOWER, E. M. *Early identification of emotionally handicapped children in school.* Springfield, Ill.: Charles C. Thomas, 1960.

BOWER, E. M. Primary prevention in a school setting. In G. Caplan (ed.). *Mental disorders in children.* New York: Basic Books, 1961.

BOWER, E. M. The emotionally handicapped child and the school. In H. W. Harshman (ed.). *Educating the emotionally disturbed.* New York: Thomas Y. Crowell Co., 1969(a).

BOWER, E. M. Review of F. M. Hewett, *The emotionally disturbed child in the classroom. American Journal of Orthopsychiatry,* 1969(b), 39, 855–856.

BOWER, E. M., AND MESSENGER, J. F. Emotionally disturbed and brain damaged: Should we mix them? *Exceptional Children,* 1965, 32, 237–240.

BOWER, E. M., TASHNOVIAN, P., AND LARSON, C. *A process for early identification of emotionally disturbed children.* Sacramento, Calif.: State Department of Education, 1958.

BRADLEY, C. Characteristics and management of children with behavior problems associated with brain damage. *Pediatric Clinics of North America,* 1957, 4, 1049–1060.

BRIDGE, E. M. *Epilepsy and convulsive disorders in children.* New York: McGraw-Hill, 1949.

BRIELAND, D. M. A comparative study of the speech of blind and sighted children. *Speech Monographs,* 1950, 17, 99–103.

BRILL, R. B. Hereditary aspects of deafness. *Volta Review,* 1961, 63, 168–175.

BRILL, R. G. The relationship of Wechsler IQ's to academic achievement among deaf students. *Exceptional Children,* 1962, 28, 315–321.

BROIDA, D. C., IZARD, C. E., AND CRUICKSHANK, W. M. Thematic apperception reactions of crippled children. *Journal of Clinical Psychology,* 1950, 6, 243–248.

BROWNE, E. G. *Arabian medicine.* New York: Macmillan, 1921.

BRUININKS, R. H., AND RYNDERS, J. E. Alternatives to special class placement for Educable Mentally Retarded Children. In *Focus on exceptional children.* Denver: Love Publishing Co., 1971.

BRUNO, F. Life values, manifest needs, and vocational interests as factors influencing professional career satisfaction among teachers of emotionally disturbed children. *Dissertation Abstract,* 1969.

BRYANT, P. E. The transfer of positive and negative learning by normal and severely subnormal children. *British Journal of Psychology,* 1965, 56, 81–86.

BUELL, C. Motor perfection of visually handicapped children. *Exceptional Children,* 1950, 17, 69–72.

BURKE, B. The relative influence of nature and nurture upon mental development. In *Twenty-seventh yearbook National Society for the Study of Education.* Chicago: University of Chicago Press, 1928.

BURT, C. Creativity and intelligence. *British Journal of Educational Psychology,* 1962, 32, 292–298.

BURTON, J. L. Intelligence and intelligence testing. In M. Cowles (ed.). *Perspectives in the education of disadvantaged children.* Cleveland: The World Publishing Co., 1967.

CALIFORNIA STATE DEPARTMENT OF EDUCATION. *A master plan for special education in California.* Sacramento, 1973.

CARDWELL, V. *Cerebral palsy — Advances in understanding and care.* New York: Association for the Aid of Crippled Children, 1956.

CARLSON, J., AND MACMILLAN, D. Comparison of probability judgments between EMR and non-retarded. *American Journal of Mental Deficiency,* 1970, 74, 697–700.

CARRELL, J. A. A comparative study of speech-defective children. *Archives of Speech,* 1936, 1, 179–203.

CASTIGLIONI, A. *Adventures of the mind.* New York: Knopf, 1946.

CAVENESS, W. F., AND MERRITT, H. H. A survey of public attitudes toward epilepsy in 1964. *Epilepsia,* 1965, 6, 75–86.

CHANDLER, B. W. *Cowboy Sam series.* Benefic Press, 1959.

CHANNING, A. *Employment of mentally deficient boys and girls.* U.S. Department of Labor, Children's Bureau Publication No. 210. Washington, D.C., 1952.

CHARLES, D. C. Ability and accomplishment of persons earlier judged mentally deficient. *Genetic Psychology Monographs,* 1953, 47, 3–71.

CHOLDEN, L. A. *A psychiatrist works with blindness.* New York: American Foundation for the Blind, 1958.

CHRISTOPHOS, F., AND RENZ, P. A critical examination of special education programs. *Journal of Special Education,* 1969, 3(4), 371–380.

CLARIZIO, H. F. Stability of deviant behavior through time. *Mental Hygiene,* 1968, 52, 288–293.

CLEMENTS, S. D. *Minimal brain dysfunction in children.* NINDS Monograph No. 3. Public Health Service Bulletin No. 1415. Washington, D.C.: U. S. Department of Health, Education, and Welfare, 1966.

CLEMENTS, S., AND PETERS, J. Minimal brain dysfunction in the school age child. *Archives of General Psychiatry,* 1962, 6, 185–197.

COHEN, J. S., AND DeYOUNG, H. The role of litigation in the improvement of programming for the handicapped. In L. Mann and D. Sabatino (eds.). *The first review of special education.* Philadelphia: JSE Press, Buttonwood Farms, Inc., 1973.

COHEN, R. S. Therapeutic education and day treatment: A new professional liaison. *Exceptional Children,* 1965, 32, 23–28.

COLEMAN, J. C. *Abnormal psychology and modern life,* fourth edition. Glenview, Ill.: Scott, Foresman, 1972.

CONNERS, C. K. Psychological effects of stimulant drugs on children with minimal brain dysfunction. *Pediatrics,* 1972, 49(5), 702–708.

CONNOR, F. P. The education of children with chronic medical problems. In W. M. Cruickshank and G. O. Johnson (eds.). *Education of exceptional children and youth.* Englewood Cliffs, N.J.: Prentice-Hall, 1967(a).

CONNOR, F. P. The education of crippled children. In W. M. Cruickshank and G. O. Johnson (eds.). *Education of excep-*

tional children and youth. Englewood Cliffs, N.J.: Prentice-Hall, 1967(b).

CONNOR, F. P., RUSALEM, H., AND CRUICKSHANK, W. M. Psychological considerations of crippled children. In W. Cruickshank (ed.). *Psychology of exceptional children and youth.* Englewood Cliffs, N.J.: Prentice-Hall, Inc., 1971.

CORNFORD, F. M. *The republic of Plato.* New York: Oxford University Press, 1945.

COTZIN, M., AND DALLENBACH, K. M. Facial vision: The role of pitch and loudness in the perception of obstacles by the blind. *American Journal of Psychology,* 1950, 63, 485–515.

COWEN, F. L., UNDERBERG, R., VERILLO, R. T., AND BENHAM, F. G. *Adjustment to visual disability in adolescence.* New York: American Foundation for the Blind, 1961.

COWLES, MILLY (ed.). *Perspectives in the education of disadvantaged children.* Cleveland, Ohio: World Publishing Co., 1967.

CRATTY, B. J. *Motor activity and the education of retardates.* Philadelphia: Lea and Febiger, 1969.

CROMWELL, R. L. Personality evaluation. In A. A. Baumeister (ed.). *Mental retardation.* Chicago: Aldine Publishing Company, 1967.

CRONBACH, L .J. *Essentials of psychological testing, second edition.* New York: Harper & Row, 1960.

CROWTHER, D. L. Psychosocial aspects of epilepsy. *Pediatric Clinics of North America,* 1967, 14, 921–932.

CRUICKSHANK, W. M. Arithmetic vocabulary of mentally retarded boys. *Exceptional Children,* 1946, 13, 65–69.

CRUICKSHANK, W. M. Arithmetic work habits of mentally retarded boys. *American Journal of Mental Deficiency,* 1948(a), 52, 318–330.

CRUICKSHANK, W. M. Arithmetic ability of mentally retarded children: I. Ability to differentiate extraneous material from needed arithmetic facts; II. Understanding arithmetic processes. *Journal of Education Research,* 1948(b), 42, 161–170, 279–288.

CRUICKSHANK, W. M. A study of the relation of physical disability to social adjustment. *American Journal of Occupational Therapy,* 1952, 6, 100–109.

CRUICKSHANK, W. M. The education of the child with brain injury. In W. M. Cruickshank and G. O. Johnson (eds.). *Education of exceptional children and youth.* Englewood Cliffs, N.J.: Prentice-Hall, 1967(a).

CRUICKSHANK, W. M. The development of education for exceptional children. In W. M. Cruickshank and G. O. Johnson (eds.).

Education of exceptional children and youth. Englewood Cliffs, N.J.: Prentice-Hall, 1967(b).

CRUICKSHANK, W. M., BENTZEN, F., RATZEBERG, F., AND TANN-HAUSER, M. A. *Teaching method for brain-injured and hyperactive children.* Syracuse, N.Y.: Syracuse University Press, 1961.

CRUSE, D. The effect of distraction upon the performance of brain-injured and familial retarded children. In E. Trapp and P. Himmelstein (eds.). *Readings on the exceptional child.* New York: The Free Press, 1970.

CUBAN, L. *To make a difference: Teaching in the inner city.* New York: The Free Press, 1970.

CUTSFORTH, T. D. *The blind in school and society* (rev. ed.). New York: American Foundation for the Blind, 1951.

DAVIES, S. P., AND ECOB, K. G. *The mentally retarded in society.* New York: Columbia, 1959.

DAVIS, H. Audiometry: Pure tone and simple speech tests. In H. Davis and S. R. Silverman (eds.). *Hearing and deafness,* third edition. New York: Holt, Rinehart, & Winston, 1970.

DE HAAN, F., AND HAVIGHURST, R. J. *Educating gifted children.* Chicago: University of Chicago Press, 1957.

DELACATO, C. H. *The diagnosis and treatment of speech and reading problems.* Springfield, Ill.: Charles C. Thomas, 1963.

DE MILLE, R., AND MERRIFIELD, P. R. Creativity and intelligence. *Educational Psychology Measurement,* 1962, 22, 803–808.

DENNERLL, R. D., RODIN, E. A., GONZALES, S., SCHWARTZ, M. L., AND LIN, Y. Neurological and psychological factors related to employability of persons with epilepsy. *Epilepsia,* 1966, 1, 318–329.

DESPERT, J. L. *The emotionally disturbed child.* New York: Doubleday, 1965.

DEUTSCH, M. The disadvantaged child and the learning process. In A. H. Passow (ed.). *Education in depressed areas.* New York: Bureau of Publications, Teachers College, Columbia University, 1963.

DEUTSCH, M. *The disadvantaged child: Studies of the school environment and the learning process.* New York: Basic Books, 1967.

DEUTSCH, M., AND BROWN, B. Social influences in Negro-white intelligence differences. *Journal of Social Issues,* 1964, 20, 24–35.

Distar Instructional System. Chicago: Science Research Associates, 1971.

DOBZHANSKY, TH. Heredity, environment, and evolution. *Science,* 11, 1950, 161–166.

DOLL, E. The essentials of an inclusive concept of mental deficiency. *American Journal of Mental Deficiency,* 1941, 46, 214–219.

DOLL, E. A historical survey of research and management of mental retardation in the United States. In E. P. Trapp and P. Himmelstein (eds.). *Readings on the exceptional child: Research and theory.* New York: Appleton-Century-Crofts, 1962.

DOWNING, J. *The I.T.A. reading experiment.* Chicago: Scott, Foresman, 1965.

DOWNS, C. B. Teaching the mentally retarded. In R. Koch and J. C. Dobson (eds.). *The mentally retarded child and his family: A multi-disciplinary handbook.* New York: Brunner/Mazel, 1971.

DREGER, R. M., AND MILLER, K. S. Comparative psychological studies of Negroes and whites in the United States. *Psychological Bulletin,* 1960, 57, 361–402.

DUNCAN, M. H. Home adjustment of stutterers and non-stutterers. *Journal of Speech and Hearing Disorders,* 1949, 14, 255–259.

DUNLAP, J. M. The education of children with high mental ability. In W. M. Cruickshank and G. O. Johnson (eds.). *Education of exceptional children and youth.* Englewood Cliffs, N.J.: Prentice-Hall, 1967.

DUNN, L. M. *Peabody picture vocabulary test.* Circle Pines, Minn.: American Guidance Service, Inc., 1959.

DUNN, L. M. An overview. In L. Dunn (ed.). *Exceptional children in the schools.* New York: Holt, Rinehart, & Winston, 1963(a).

DUNN, L. M. School programs for trainable pupils. In L. Dunn (ed.). *Exceptional children in the schools.* New York: Holt, Rinehart, & Winston, 1963(b).

DUNN, L. M. Special education for the mildly retarded: Is much of it justifiable? *Exceptional Children,* 1968, 35, 5–22.

DUNN, L. M. (ed.). *Exceptional children in the schools,* second edition. New York: Holt, Rinehart & Winston, Inc., 1973.

DUNN, L. M., AND CAPOBIANCO, R. J. Studies in reading and arithmetic in mentally retarded boys. *Monograph of Society and Res. Child Development,* 1954, 19, No. 1. Lafayette, Indiana: Child Development Publications, 1956.

DUNN, L. M., AND SMITH, J. O. *Peabody language development kits,* Levels I, II, III. Circle Pines, Minn.: American Guidance Service, 1967, 1968, 1969.

DUNN-RANKIN, P. Personal Communication, 1967.

DUPONT, H. (ed.). *Educating emotionally disturbed children.* New York: Holt, Rinehart, & Winston, 1969.

DURANT, W. *Caesar and Christ.* New York: Simon & Schuster, 1944.

DURANT, W. *The age of faith.* New York: Simon & Schuster, 1950.

DURANT, W. *Our Oriental heritage.* New York: Simon & Schuster, 1954.

DURANT, W. *The reformation.* New York: Simon & Schuster, 1957.

DURANT, W. *The life of Greece.* New York: Simon & Schuster, 1966.

DURANT, W., AND DURANT, A. *The age of Louis XIV.* New York: Simon & Schuster, 1963.

DURANT, W., AND DURANT, A. *The age of Voltaire.* New York: Simon & Schuster, 1965.

EAMES, T. H. The relationship of reading and speech difficulties. *Journal of Educational Psychology,* 1950, 41, 51–55.

EDGERTON, R. B. *The cloak of competence: Stigma in the lives of the mentally retarded.* Berkeley: University of California Press, 1967.

EGLAND, G. O. *Speech and language problems: A guide for the classroom teacher.* Englewood Cliffs, N.J.: Prentice-Hall, 1970.

EISENBERG, L. Strengths of the inner city child. *Baltimore Bulletin of Education,* 1963–1964, 41, 10–16.

EISENSON, J. The nature of defective speech. In W. M. Cruickshank (ed.). *Psychology of exceptional children and youth.* Englewood Cliffs, N.J.: Prentice-Hall, 1963.

EISMAN, B. S. L. Paired associate learning, generalization, and retention as a function of intelligence. *American Journal of Mental Deficiency,* 1958, 63, 451–489.

ELDER, G. H., JR. *Adolescent achievement and mobility aspirations.* Chapel Hill, N.C.: University of North Carolina, Institute for Research in Social Science, 1962.

ELLIOTT, R. N. Meaningfulness in school tasks for EMR children. *Journal of Special Education,* 1970, 4, 189–197.

ELLIS, N. R. The stimulus trace and behavioral inadequacy. In N. R. Ellis (ed.). *Handbook of mental deficiency.* New York: McGraw-Hill, 1963.

ELLIS, N. R. Memory processes in retardates and normals. In N. R. Ellis (ed.). *International review of research in mental retardation,* volume IV. New York: Academic Press, 1970.

ENGELMANN, S. How to construct effective language programs for the poverty child. In F. Williams (ed.). *Language and poverty.* Chicago: Markham Publishing Co., 1970.

ERIKSON, E. H. *Childhood and society.* New York: W. W. Norton, 1950.

EVERHART, R. W. The relationship between articulation and other developmental factors in children. *Journal of Speech and Hearing Disorders,* 1953, 18, 332–338.

FARBER, B. *Mental retardation: Its social context and social consequences.* Boston: Houghton Mifflin, 1968.

FARBER, B., JENNE, W., AND TOIGO, R. Family crisis and the decision to institutionalize the retarded child. *CEC Research Monograph,* Series A., No. 1. Washington, D.C.: Council for Exceptional Children, 1960.

FASSLER, J. Reduced auditory input aids cerebral palsy children. *R.&D. News,* 1969, 1, 1–3, Teachers College, Columbia University, 1969.

FERNALD, G. M. *Remedial techniques in basic school subjects.* New York: McGraw-Hill, 1943.

FINDLAY, C. C. The Physical Science Study Committee. In J. J. Gallagher (ed.). *Teaching gifted students: A book of readings.* Boston: Allyn and Bacon, 1965.

FINELY, C. J. Arithmetic achievement in mentally retarded children: The effects of presenting the problem in different contexts. *American Journal of Mental Deficiency,* 1962, 67, 281–286.

FINESTONE, S., LUKOFF, I., AND WHITEMAN, M. *The demand for dog guides and travel adjustment of blind persons.* New York: Research Center, Columbia University, 1960.

FISHER, M. A., AND ZEAMAN, D. Growth and decline of retardate intelligence. In N. R. Ellis (ed.). *International review of research in mental retardation,* vol. IV. New York: Academic Press, 1970.

FITZGERALD, E. *Straight language for the deaf: System of instruction for deaf children,* 2nd edition. Washington, D.C.: The Volta Bureau, 1954.

FITZHUGH, K., AND FITZHUGH, L. *The Fitzhugh plus program.* Galien, Mich.: Allied Education Council, 1966.

FITZSIMONS, M. J. The predictive value of teacher's referrals. In M. Krugman (ed.). *Orthopsychiatry in the schools.* New York: American Orthopsychiatric Association, 1958.

FITZSIMONS, R. M. Developmental, psychosocial, and educational factors in children with articulation problems. *Child Development,* 1958, 29, 481–489.

FORCE, D. G., JR. Social status of physically handicapped children. *Exceptional Children,* 1956, 23, 104–107, 132.

FORD FOUNDATION. *Mental health.* New York: Ford Foundation, 1958.

FORNESS, S. Education of retarded children: A review for physicians. *American Journal of Diseases of Children,* in press.

FORNESS, S. Behavioristic approach to classroom management and motivation. *Psychology in the Schools,* 1970, 1, 356–363.

FORNESS, S. The mildly retarded as casualties of the educational system. *Journal of School Psychology,* 1972, 10, 117–125.

FORNESS, S., AND MACMILLAN, D. L. Reinforcement overkill: Implications for education of the retarded. *Journal of Special Education,* 1972, 6, 221–230.

FRANCIS, R. J., AND RARICK, G. L. *Motor characteristics of the mentally retarded.* Cooperative Research Bulletin, No. 1, USOE 35005. Washington, D.C.: Government Printing Office, 1960.

FREEMAN, F. S. *Theory and practice of psychological testing.* New York: Holt, Rinehart, & Winston, 1962.

FREEMAN, R. D. Drug effects on learning in children: A selective review of the past thirty years. *Journal of Special Education,* 1966, 1(1), 17–44.

FREEMAN, R. D. The myth of perfectability. *Journal of Special Education,* 1970, 4, 171–176.

FRIEDMAN, R. J., AND MACQUEEN, J. C. Psychoeducative considerations of physical handicapping conditions in children. *Exceptional Children,* 1971, 37(7), 538–539.

FRISINA, D. R. Hearing disorders. In N. G. Haring and R. L. Schiefelbusch (eds.). *Methods in special education.* New York: McGraw-Hill, 1967.

FROSTIG, M., AND HORNE, D. *The Frostig program for the development of visual perception.* Chicago: Follett Publishing Co., 1964.

FURTH, H. G. Linguistic deficiency and thinking: Research with deaf subjects 1964–1969. *Psychological Bulletin,* 1971, 76, 58–72.

GAETH, J. H. *Verbal and nonverbal learning in children, including those with hearing losses.* Cooperative Research Project 1001, Office of Education, U.S. Department of Health, Education, and Welfare, 1963.

GAGNÉ, R. M. *The conditions of learning.* New York: Holt, Rinehart, & Winston, Inc., 1970.

GALLAGHER, J. J. Social status of children related to intelligence, propinquity, and social perception. *Elementary School Journal,* 1958, 58, 225–231.

GALLAGHER, J. J. *The gifted child in the elementary school (What research says to the teacher),* no. 17, 1st ed. Washington, D.C.:

American Educational Research Association, N.E.A., Department of Classroom Teachers, 1959.

GALLAGHER, J. J. *Teaching the gifted child.* Boston: Allyn and Bacon, Inc., 1964.

GARRISON, K. C., AND FORCE, D. G. *The psychology of exceptional children,* 4th edition. New York: The Ronald Press, 1965.

GEARHEART, B. R. *Learning disabilities: Educational strategies.* St. Louis: Mosby, 1973.

GETMAN, G. N., AND KANE, E. R. *Developing learning readiness.* New York: McGraw-Hill, 1968.

GETZELS, J. W., AND JACKSON, P. W. *Creativity and intelligence.* New York: Wiley, 1962.

GIBSON, E. J. Perceptual development. In H. W. Stevenson (ed.). *Child psychology.* Yearbook National Society for the Study of Education, 1963.

GILBERT, T. R. Overlearning and the retention of meaningful prose. *Journal of General Psychology,* 1957, 56, 281–289.

GILLINGHAM, A., AND STILLMAN, B. *Remedial training for children with specific disability in reading, spelling, and penmanship,* 7th edition. Cambridge, Mass.: Education Publishing Service, 1965.

GLAVIN, J. P. Spontaneous improvement in emotionally disturbed children. Doctoral dissertation, George Peabody College for Teachers, Nashville, Tenn. *Dissertation Abstracts,* 1968, 28, 3503A, No. 9.

GLAVIN, J. P., AND QUAY, H. C. Behavior disorders. *Review of Educational Research,* 1969, 9, 83–102.

GOLDBERG, M. L. Factors affecting educational attainment in depressed urban areas. In A. H. Passow (ed.). *Education in depressed areas.* New York: Teachers College Press, 1963.

GOLDBERG, M. L. Methods and materials for educationally disadvantaged youth. In A. H. Passow, M. Goldberg, and A. J. Tannenbaum (eds.). *Education of the disadvantaged.* New York: Holt, Rinehart, & Winston, 1967.

GOLDMAN, R., AND FRISTOE, M. *Goldman-Fristoe test of articulation.* Circle Pines, Minn.: American Guidance Service, 1969.

GOLDSTEIN, B. *Low income youth in urban areas.* New York: Holt, Rinehart, & Winston, 1967.

GOLDSTEIN, H. *Construction of a social learning curriculum.* Unpublished manuscript, Yeshiva University, 1969.

GOODMAN, H., GOTTLIEB, J., AND HARRISON, R. H. Social acceptance of EMR's integrated into a nongraded elementary school. *American Journal of Mental Deficiency,* 1972, 76, 412–417.

GOODSTEIN, L. D. Functional speech disorders and personality:

A survey of the literature. *Journal of Speech and Hearing Research*, 1958, 1, 359–376.

GOTTLIEB, J., AND DAVIS, J. E. *Social acceptance of EMR's during overt behavioral interaction.* Cambridge, Mass.: Studies in Learning Potential (Research Institute for Education Problems), Volume 2, 1971.

GOWMAN, A. G. *The war blind in American social structure.* New York: American Foundation for the Blind, 1957.

GRACE, H. A., AND BOOTH, N. L. Is the gifted child a social isolate? *Peabody Journal of Education*, 1958, 35, 195–196.

GREEN, C., AND ZIGLER, E. Social deprivation and the performance of retarded and normal children on a satiation type task. *Child Development*, 1962, 33, 499–508.

GREENBAUM, J., AND BUEHLER, J. A. Further findings on the intelligence of children with cerebral palsy. *American Journal of Mental Deficiency*, 1960, 65, 261–264.

GROHT, M. *Natural language for deaf children.* Washington, D.C.: The Volta Bureau, 1958.

GRUENBERG, E. M. Epidemiology. In H. Stevens and R. Heber (eds.). *Mental retardation: A review of research.* Chicago: University of Chicago Press, 1964(a).

GRUENBERG, E. M. Some epidemiological aspects of congenital brain damage. In H. Birch (ed.). *Brain damage in children.* Baltimore: Williams & Wilkins, 1964(b).

GUILFORD, J. P. The structure of intellect. *Psychological Bulletin*, 1956, 53, 267–293.

GUILFORD, J. P. Traits of creativity. In H. Anderson (ed.). *Creativity and its cultivation.* New York: Harper & Row, 1959.

GUILFORD, J. P., AND MERRIFIELD, P. R. *The structure of intellect model: Its uses and implications.* Rep. Psychological Laboratory, No. 24. Los Angeles: University of Southern California, 1960.

HALL, M. Auditory factors in functional articulatory speech defects. *Journal of Experimental Education*, 1938, 7, 110–132.

HALL, R. V., LUND, D., AND JACKSON, D. Effects of teacher attention on study behavior. *Journal of Applied Behavior Analysis*, 1968, 1, 1–2.

HANSEN, B. F. The application of sound discrimination test to functional articulatory defectives with normal hearing. *Journal of Speech Disorders*, 1944, 9, 347–355.

HAPEMAN, L. B. Developmental concepts of blind children between the ages of three and six as they relate to orientation and mobility. *International Journal for the Education of the Blind*, 1967, 17, 41–48.

HARDY, W. G. *Children with hearing impairment.* Children's Bureau Publication No. 325. Washington, D.C.: Government Printing Office, 1952.

HARING, N. G. Cerebral palsy and emotional adjustment. *Exceptional Children,* 1959, 26, 191–194.

HARING, N. G., AND LOVITT, T. Operant methodology and educational technology in special education. In N. Haring and R. Schiefelbusch (eds.). *Methods in special education.* New York: McGraw-Hill, 1967.

HARING, N. G., AND PHILLIPS, E. L. *Educating emotionally disturbed children.* New York: McGraw-Hill, 1962.

HARING, N. G., AND PHILLIPS, E. L. *Analysis and modification of classroom behavior.* Englewood Cliffs, N.J.: Prentice-Hall, 1972.

HARLEY, R. K. Children with visual disabilities. In L. M. Dunn (ed.). *Exceptional children in the schools,* second edition. New York: Holt, Rinehart, & Winston, 1973.

HARLIN, V. K. Experiences with epileptic children in a public school program. *The Journal of School Health,* 1965, 35, 20–24.

HARTER, S. Mental age, IQ, and motivational factors in the discrimination learning set performance of normal and retarded children. *Journal of Experimental Child Psychology,* 1967, 5, 123–141.

HARTLAGE, L. C. Effects of chlorpromazine on learning. *Psychological Bulletin,* 1965, 64, 234–245.

HAVIGHURST, R. J. Who are the socially disadvantaged? *Journal of Negro Education,* 1964, 33, 210–217.

HAWKINS, J. E., JR. Iatrogenic toxic deafness in children. In F. McConnell and P. Ward (eds.). *Deafness in childhood.* Nashville, Tenn.: Vanderbilt University Press, 1967.

HAY, L. A. A new school channel for helping the troubled child. *American Journal of Orthopsychiatry,* 1953, 23, 676–683.

HAYES, S. P. *Contributions to a psychology of blindness.* New York: American Foundation for the Blind, 1941.

HAYES, S. P. Measuring the intelligence of the blind. In P. A. Zaac (ed.). *Blindness.* Princeton, N.J.: Princeton University Press, 1950.

HAYES, S. P. *First regional conference on mental measurement of the blind.* Watertown, Mass.: Perkins Institute for the Blind, 1952.

HEBER, R. A manual on terminology and classification in mental retardation. *American Journal of Mental Deficiency,* 1959, 64, monograph supplement.

HEBER, R. Modifications in the manual on terminology and classification in mental retardation. *American Journal of Mental Deficiency*, 1961, 65, 499–500.

HEGGE, T. G., KIRK, S. A., AND KIRK, W. D. *Remedial reading drills.* Ann Arbor, Mich.: George Wahr, 1936.

HEIDER, G. M. Adjustment problems of the deaf child. *Nervous Child*, 1948, 7, 1.

HEILMAN, A. Intelligence in cerebral palsy. *The Crippled Child*, 1952, 30, 12.

HEISS, W. E., AND MISCHIO, G. S. Designing curriculum for the educable mentally retarded. *Focus on Exceptional Children*, 1971, 3, 1–10.

HEJNA, R. J. *Developmental articulation test* (rev. ed.). Ann Arbor, Mich.: Speech Materials, 1959.

HERMELIN, B., AND O'CONNOR, N. *Speech and thought in severe subnormality: an experimental study.* New York: Macmillan, 1963.

HEWETT, F. M. Teaching reading to an autistic boy through operant conditioning.. *The Reading Teacher*, 1964(a), 17, 613–618.

HEWETT, F. M. A hierarchy of educational tasks for children with learning disorders. *Exceptional Children*, 1964(b), 31, 207–214.

HEWETT, F. M. Teaching speech to an autistic child through operant conditioning. *American Journal of Orthopsychiatry*, 1965, 35, 927–936.

HEWETT, F. M. *The emotionally disturbed child in the classroom.* Boston: Allyn and Bacon, Inc., 1968.

HEWETT, F. M., MAYHEW, D., AND RABB, E. An experimental reading program for neurologically impaired, mentally retarded, and severely emotionally disturbed children. *American Journal of Orthopsychiatry*, 1967, 37, 35–48.

HEWETT, F. M., QUAY, H., TAYLOR, F., AND WATSON, P. *EMR and EH placement inventory.* Santa Monica Unified School District, Santa Monica, California, 1973.

HEWETT, F. M., TAYLOR, F. D., AND ARTUSO, A. A. The Santa Monica project. *Exceptional Children*, 1968, 34, 387.

HILLIARD, L. T. *Mental deficiency.* Boston: Little, Brown, 1965.

HOBBS, N. Helping disturbed children: psychological and ecological strategies. *American Psychologist*, 1966, 21, 1105–1115.

HOBBS, N. The project on classification of exceptional children. *Journal of Abnormal Child Psychology*, 1(1), Jan.–March, 1973, 121.

HOLLINGWORTH, L. *Gifted children: Their nature and nurture.* New York: Macmillan, 1926.

HOLLINGWORTH, L. *Children above 180 IQ.* Yonkers-on-Hudson, N.Y.: World Book Co., 1942.

HOLT, J. *How children fail.* New York: Ditman Publishing, 1964.

HOPKINS, T. W., BICE, H. V., AND COLTON, K. C. *Evaluation and education of the cerebral palsied child.* Washington, D.C.: International Council for Exceptional Children, 1954.

HULL, F. M., AND HULL, M. E. Children with oral communication disorders. In L. Dunn (ed.). *Exceptional children in the schools,* second edition. New York: Holt, Rinehart, and Winston, 1973.

HULL, F. M., MIELKE, P. W., JR., TIMMONS, R. J., AND WILLEFORD, J. A. The national speech and hearing survey: Preliminary results. *Asha,* 1971, 13, 501–509.

HUNT, J. M. *Intelligence and experience.* New York: Ronald Press, 1961.

HUNT, J. M. The psychological basis for using preschool enrichment as an antidote for cultural deprivation. *Merrill-Palmer Quarterly,* 1964, 10, 209–248.

HURLEY, R. *Poverty and mental retardation: A causal relationship.* New York: Random House, 1969.

HURLEY, W. *Dan Frontier.* Benefic Press, 1959–1964.

INHELDER, B., AND PIAGET, J. *The early growth of logic in the child.* New York: Harper & Row, 1964.

ISCOE, I. The functional classification of exceptional children. In E. P. Trapp and P. Himmelstein (eds.). *Readings on the exceptional child.* New York: Appleton-Century-Crofts, 1962.

ITARD, J. M. G. *The wild boy of Aveyron.* New York: Appleton-Century-Crofts, 1962.

JACKSON, J. A. A survey of psychological, social and environmental differences between advanced and retarded readers. *Journal of Genetic Psychology,* 1944, 45, 113–131.

JACOBSON, S., AND FAEGRE, C. Neutralization: A tool for the teacher of disturbed children. *Exceptional Children,* 1959, 25, 243–246.

JARVIK, L. F., SALZBERGER, R. M., AND FALEK, A. Deaf persons of outstanding achievement. In J. D. Rainer, K. Z. Altshuler, and F. J. Kallmann (eds.). *Family and mental health problems in a deaf population.* Springfield, Ill.: Charles C. Thomas, 1969.

JENKINS, E., AND LOHR, F. E. Severe articulation disorders and motor ability. *Journal of Speech and Hearing Disorders,* 1964, 29, 286–292.

JENSEN, A. R. How much can we boost IQ and scholastic achievement? *Harvard Educational Review,* 1969, 39, 1–123.

JENSEN, A. R. A theory of primary and secondary familial mental retardation. In N. R. Ellis (ed.). *International review of re-*

search in mental retardation, volume IV. New York: Academic Press, 1970.

JOHNSON, D. L., AND MYKLEBUST, H. *Learning disabilities: Educational principles and practices.* New York: Grune & Stratton, 1967.

JOHNSON, G. O. Special education for the mentally handicapped — A paradox. *Exceptional Children,* October 1962, 62–69.

JOHNSON, G. O. The education of mentally retarded children. In W. M. Cruickshank and G. O. Johnson (eds.). *Education of exceptional children and youth.* Englewood Cliffs, N.J.: Prentice-Hall, 1967.

JOHNSON, G., AND BLAKE, K. *Learning performance of retarded and normal children.* Syracuse University Monograph No. 5, 1960.

JOHNSON, W. *Speech handicapped school children.* New York: Harper and Brothers, 1956.

JOHNSON, W., BROWN, S. F., CURTIS, J. F., EDNEY, C. W., AND KEASTER, J. *Speech handicapped school children,* 3rd edition. New York: Harper & Row, 1967.

JOHNSON, W., CURTIS, J., EDNEY, C. W., AND KEASTER, J. *Speech handicapped school children.* New York: Harper & Row, 1956.

JONES, J. W. The visually handicapped child at home and school. OE-3545, Bulletin 1963, No. 39. Washington, D.C.: Government Printing Office, 1963.

JONES, R. C., GOTFRIED, N. W., AND OWENS, A. The social distance of the exceptional: A study at the high school level. *Exceptional Children,* 1966, 32, 551–556.

JONES, R. L. Labels and stigma in special education. *Exceptional Children,* 1972, 38, 553–564.

JORDAN, L. Reading and the young mentally retarded child. *Mental Retardation,* 1963, 1, 21–27.

KANNER, L. Emotionally disturbed children: A historical review. *Child Development,* 1962, 33, 97–102.

KANNER, L. *A history of the care and study of the mentally retarded.* Springfield, Ill.: Charles C. Thomas, 1964.

KARNES, M., McCOY, G. F., ZEHRBACH, R. R., WOLLERSHEIM, V., AND CLARIZIO, H. F. *The efficacy of two organizational plans for underachieving intellectually gifted children.* Champaign, Ill.: Champaign Community Unified Schools, 1962.

KASS, C. Learning disabilities. *Review of Educational Research,* 1969, 39(1), 71–82.

KEATING, L. E. Epilepsy and behavior disorder in school children. *Journal of Mental Science,* 1961, 107, 161–180.

KELLER, H. A. *Teacher: Anne Sullivan Macy; A tribute by the foster-child of her mind.* Garden City, N.Y.: Doubleday, 1955.

KENMORE, J. R. *Associative learning by blind versus sighted children with words and objects differing in meaningfulness and identifiability without vision.* Doctoral dissertation, University of Minnesota. Ann Arbor, Mich.: University Microfilms, 1965, No. 66–3903.

KEOGH, B. K. Hyperactivity and learning disorders: Review and speculation. *Exceptional Children,* 38(2), October 1971, 101–109.

KEPHART, N. C. *The slow learner in the classroom.* Columbus, Ohio: Charles E. Merrill, 1971.

KERBY, C. E. A report on visual handicaps of partially seeing children. *Exceptional Children,* 1952, 18, 137–142.

KESSLER, J. W. *Psychopathology of childhood.* Englewood Cliffs, N.J.: Prentice-Hall, 1966.

KIDD, J. W. Pro — The efficacy of special class placement for educable mental retardates. Paper presented at the 48th Annual Convention of the Council for Exceptional Children, Chicago, April 1970.

KIRK, S. A. The influence of manual tracing on the learning of simple words in the case of subnormal boys. *Journal of Educational Psychology,* October 1933, 24, 525–533.

KIRK, S. A. Research in education. In H. Stevens and R. Heber (eds.). *Mental retardation: a review of research.* Chicago: University of Chicago Press, 1964.

KIRK, S. A. *Educating exceptional children,* second edition. Boston: Houghton Mifflin Co., 1972.

KIRK, S. A., AND BATEMAN, B. Diagnosis and remediation of learning disabilities. *Exceptional Children,* 1962, 29, 72.

KIRK, S. A., AND KIRK, W. D. *Psycholinguistic learning disabilities: Diagnosis and remediation.* Urbana: University of Illinois Press, 1971.

KIRK, S. A., McCARTHY, J. J., AND KIRK, W. D. *The Illinois Test of Psycholinguistic Abilities,* revised edition. Urbana, Ill.: University of Illinois Press, 1968.

KISATSKY, T. J. The prognostic value of the Carter-Birch Tests in measuring articulation skills of selected kindergarten children. *Exceptional Children,* 1967, 34, 81–86.

KOEGLER, R. R. Chronic illness of the adolescent. *Mental Hygiene,* 1960, 44, 111–114.

KOUNIN, J. Experimental studies of rigidity, I. The measurement of rigidity in normal and feebleminded persons. *Character and Personality,* 1941(a), 9, 251–273.

KOUNIN, J. Experimental studies of rigidity, II. The explanatory power of the concept of rigidity as applied to feeblemindedness. *Character and Personality,* 1941(b), 9, 273–282.

Kuhlmann-Anderson Intelligence Tests, seventh edition. Massachusetts: Personnel Press, Inc., 1963.

KVARACEUS, W. C., AND MILLER, W. B. *Delinquent behavior,* vol. I. Washington, D.C.: National Education Association, 1959.

LABOV, W. The logic of nonstandard English. In F. Williams (ed.). *Language and poverty.* Chicago, Ill.: Markham Publishing Co., 1970.

LAUFER, M. W. Cerebral dysfunction and behavior disorders of adolescents. *American Journal of Orthopsychiatry,* 1962, 32, 501–506.

LAUFER, M. W., AND DENHOFF, E. Hyperkinetic behavior syndrome in children. *Journal of Pediatrics,* 1957, 50, 463–474.

LENNOX, W. G., AND LENNOX, M. A. *Epilepsy and related disorders.* Boston: Little, Brown, 1960.

LEVIN, G., AND SIMMONS, J. Response to praise by emotionally disturbed boys. *Psychological Reports,* 1962, 11, 10.

LEVINE, E. S. Mental health clinic in New York. *Silent Worker,* 1956, 9, 7.

LEVISON, B. Understanding the child with school phobia. *Exceptional Children,* 1962, 38, 393–397.

LEWIN, K. *A dynamic theory of personality.* New York: McGraw-Hill, 1936.

LEWIS, W. Continuity and intervention in emotional disturbance: A review. *Exceptional Children,* 1965, 31, 465–475.

LEWIS, W. W. Project re-Ed: Educational intervention in discordant child rearing systems. In E. L. Cowen, E. A. Gardner, and M. Zax (eds.). *Emergent approaches to mental health problems.* New York: Appleton-Century-Crofts, 1967, 352–368.

LILLY, M. S. Special education: A teapot in a tempest. *Exceptional Children,* 1970, 37(1), 43–49.

LINDAMOOD, C., AND LINDAMOOD, P. *Auditory discrimination in depth* (A.D.D. Program 1). Boston: Teaching Resources, 1969.

LINDSLEY, O. *Precision teaching workshop.* Santa Monica Unified School District, Santa Monica, California, October 1970.

LIPSCOMB, D. M. Ear damage from exposure to rock and roll music. *Archives of Otolaryngology,* 1969, 90, 545–555.

LIVINGSTON, S. *Living with epileptic seizures.* Springfield, Ill.: Charles C. Thomas, 1963.

LIVINGSTON, S. What the teacher can do for the student with epilepsy. *National Educational Association Journal,* 1966, 55, 24–26.

LLOYD, L. L. Audiologic aspects of mental retardation. In N. R. Ellis (ed.). *International review of research in mental retardation*, vol. IV. New York: Academic Press, 1970, 311–374.

LORD, F. E. Identification of orientation and mobility skills relating to developmental tasks for young blind children. Los Angeles, Calif.: State College at Los Angeles, 1966.

LOVAAS, I. Building social behavior in autistic children by the use of electric shock. *Journal of Experimental Research in Personality*, 1965, 1, 99–109.

LOVAAS, I., BERBERICH, B., PERLOFF, B., AND SCHAEFFER, B. Acquisition of imitative speech by schizophrenic children. *Science*, 1966, 705–707.

LOVITT, T. C., AND CURTIS, K. A. Academic response rate as a function of teacher and self-imposed contingencies. *Journal of Applied Behavior Analysis*, 1969, 2, 49–53.

LOWENFELD, B. Psychological problems of children with impaired vision. In W. M. Cruickshank (ed). *Psychology of exceptional children and youth*, 2nd edition. Englewood Cliffs, N.J.: Prentice-Hall, Inc., 1963.

LOWENFELD, B. Psychological problems of children with impaired vision. In W. M. Cruickshank (ed.). *Psychology of exceptional children and youth*. Englewood Cliffs, N.J.: Prentice-Hall, 1971.

LOWENFELD, B., ABEL, G., AND HATLEN, P. *Blind children learn to read*. Springfield, Ill.: Charles C. Thomas, 1967.

LUKOFF, I. F., AND WHITEMAN, M. Attitudes toward blindness — some preliminary findings. *The New Outlook for the Blind*, 1961, 55, 39–44.

LURIA, A. R. Psychological studies of mental deficiency in the Soviet Union. In N. Ellis (ed.). *Handbook of mental deficiency*. New York: McGraw-Hill, 1963.

LUSZKI, W. A. Intellectual functioning of spastic cerebral palsied. *Cerebral Palsy Journal*, 1966, 27, 7–9.

MACFARLANE, J., ALLEN, L., AND HONZIK, M. *A developmental study of the behavior problems of normal children between 21 months and 14 years*. Berkeley: University of California Press, 1955.

MACMILLAN, D. L. The problem of motivation in the education of the mentally retarded. *Exceptional Children*, 1971(a), 37, 579–586.

MACMILLAN, D. L. Special education for the mentally retarded: Servant or savant? *Focus on Exceptional Children*, 1971(b), 2(9), 1–11.

MADSEN, C. H., JR., BECKER, W. C., AND THOMAS, E. R. Rules, praise, and ignoring: Elements of elementary classroom control. *Journal of Applied Behavior Analysis,* 1968, 1, 139–150.

MADSEN, M. C. Distribution of practice and level of intelligence. *Psychological Reports,* 1963, 13, 39–42.

MAES, W. R. The identification of emotionally disturbed elementary school children. *Exceptional Children,* 1966, 32, 607–609.

MANDLER, G., AND HEINEMANN, S. H. Effect of overlearning of a verbal response on transfer of training. *Journal of Experimental Psychology,* 1956, 52, 39–46.

MANDOLA, J. A theoretical approach to graphic aids for the blind. *International Journal for the Education of the Blind,* 1968, 18, 22–24.

MARSH, R. W. A statistical re-analysis of Getzel's and Jackson's data. *British Journal of Educational Psychology,* 1964, 34, 91–93.

MARTIN, W. E., AND STENDLER, C. B. *Child behavior and development.* New York: Harcourt, Brace, 1959.

MARTINSON, R. A. *Educational programs for gifted pupils.* Sacramento: California Department of Education, 1961.

MARTINSON, R. A. *Curriculum enrichment for the gifted in the primary grades.* Englewood Cliffs, N.J.: Prentice-Hall, 1968.

MARTINSON, R. A. Children with superior cognitive abilities. In L. M. Dunn (ed.). *Exceptional children in the schools,* second edition. New York: Holt, Rinehart, & Winston, 1973.

MASLAND, R. L. National Institute of Neurological Diseases and Blindness (NINDB) research profile No. 13 — Cerebral palsy. Public Health Service Publication No. 1671, 1967.

MASLAND, R., SARASON, S., AND GLADWIN, T. *Mental subnormality: Biological, psychological, and cultural factors.* New York: Basic Books, 1958.

MASLOW, A. H. Creativity in self-actualizing people. In H. Anderson (ed.). *Creativity and its cultivation.* New York: Harper & Row, 1959.

MATTHEWS, J. Communication disorders in the mentally retarded. In L. E. Travis (ed.). *Handbook of speech pathology and audiology.* New York: Appleton-Century-Crofts, 1971.

McCAFFEREY, I., AND CUMMING, J. *Behavior patterns associated with persistent emotional disturbances of school children in regular classes of elementary grades.* Onondaga County: Mental Health Researcher Unit, New York State Department of Mental Hygiene, December 1967.

McCARTHY, J. J. Research on the linguistic problems of the mentally retarded. *Mental Retardation Abstracts,* 1964, 1, 3–27.

McCARTHY, J. J., AND McCARTHY, J. F. *Learning disabilities.* Boston: Allyn and Bacon, Inc., 1969.

McConnell, F. Children with learning disabilities. In L. M. Dunn (ed.). *Exceptional children in the schools*, second edition. New York: Holt, Rinehart, & Winston, 1973.

McIntosh, D. K., and Dunn, L. M. Children with major specific learning disabilities. In L. M. Dunn (ed.). *Exceptional children in the schools*. New York: Holt, Rinehart, & Winston, 1973.

McManis, E. Marble sorting persistence in mixed verbal incentive and performance level pairings. *American Journal of Mental Deficiency*, 1967, 71, 811–817.

McNemar, Q. Lost: Our intelligence? Why? *American Psychologist*, 1964, 19, 871–882.

Meadow, K. P. Early manual communication in relation to the deaf child's intellectual, social, and communicative functioning. *American Annals of the Deaf*, 1968, 113, 29–41.

Medland, M. B., and Stachnik, T. Good-behavior game: A replication and systematic analysis. *Journal of Applied Behavior Analysis*, 1972, 5, 45–51.

Meerloo, L., and Meerloo, J. A. Some psychological problems in cerebral palsy children. *Quarterly Journal of Child Behavior*, 1950, 2, 381.

Mehler, J., and Bever, T. Cognitive capacity of very young children. *Science*, 1967, 158, 141–142.

Menkes, M. M., Rowe, J. S., and Menkes, U. H. A twenty-five year follow-up study on the hyperkinetic child with minimal brain dysfunction. *Pediatrics*, 1967, 39, 393–399.

Mercer, J. The meaning of mental retardation. In R. Koch and J. Dobson (eds.). *The mentally retarded child and his family*. New York: Brunner/Mazel, 1971.

Meyerowitz, J. H. Peer groups and special classes. *Mental Retardation*, 1967, 5, 23–26.

Meyerowitz, J., and Farber, B. Family background on educable mentally retarded children. In B. Farber (ed.). *Kinship and family organization*. New York: Wiley, 1966.

Miller, D. R., and Swanson, G. E. *Inner conflict and defense*. New York: Holt, Rinehart, & Winston, 1960.

Miller, E., and Rosenfeld, G. Psychological evaluations of children with cerebral palsy and its implications in treatment. *Journal of Pediatrics*, 1962, 40, 613–621.

Miller, R. V. Social status and socio-empathic differences among mentally retarded children. *Exceptional Children*, 1956, 23, 114–119.

Moed, M., and Litwin, D. The employability of the cerebral palsied. *Rehabilitation Literature*, 1963, 24, 266–277.

MONCUR, J. P. Parental domination in stuttering. *Journal of Speech and Hearing Disorders,* 1952, 20, 463–467.

MONTESSORI, M. *The Montessori method.* New York: Stroke, 1912.

MOORE, W. E., SODERBERG, G., AND POWELL, D. Relations of stuttering in spontaneous speech to speech content and verbal output. *Journal of Speech and Hearing Disorders,* 1952, 17, 371–376.

MORGENSTERN, M. Psychoeducational and vocational problems of the cerebral palsied child. In J. Hellmuth (ed.). *The special child in century 21.* Seattle: The Special Child Publications of the Sequin School, 1964.

MORLAN, J. Multisensory learning. In S. W. Tiedt (ed.). *Teaching the disadvantaged child.* New York: Oxford University Press, 1968.

MORLEY, M. E., *Cleft palate and speech,* 6th edition. Baltimore: Williams and Wilkins, 1967.

MORRIS, J. E. Relative efficiency of reading and listening for braille and large type readers. 48th American Biennial Conference of the American Association of Instructors of the Blind, Washington, D.C.: American Association of Instructors of the Blind, 1966.

MORSE, W. Working paper: Training teachers in life space interviewing. *American Journal of Orthopsychiatry,* 1963, 33, 727–730.

MORSE, W. C. The crisis teacher. In N. Long, W. Morse, and R. Newman (eds.). *Conflict in the classroom: The education of emotionally disturbed children.* Belmont, Calif.: Wadsworth, 1965.

MORSE, W. C. The education of socially maladjusted and emotionally disturbed children. In W. M. Cruickshank and G. O. Johnson (eds.). *Education of exceptional children and youth.* Englewood Cliffs, N.J.: Prentice-Hall, 1967.

MORSE, W. C., CUTLER, R. L., AND FINK, A. H. *Public school classes for the emotionally handicapped: A research analysis.* Washington, D.C.: The Council for Exceptional Children, 1964.

MORSE, W. C., CUTLER, R. L., AND FINK, A. H. Public school classes for the emotionally handicapped: A research analysis. *Exceptional Children Research Review,* 1968.

MORSE, W. C., AND SMALL, E. Group life space interviewing in a therapeutic camp. *American Journal of Orthopsychiatry,* 1959, 29, 27–44.

MOUSTAKAS, C. E. *Children in play therapy.* New York: McGraw-Hill, 1953.

MOUSTAKAS, C. E. The frequency and intensity of negative attitudes expressed in play therapy. *Journal of Genetic Psychology,* 1955, 86–87, 309–325.

MURPHY, A. T.   Attitudes of education toward the visually handi-
    capped. *The Sight Saving Review,* Fall, 1960, 30, 157–161.
MUTHARD, J. E., AND HUTCHISON, J. H.   Cerebral palsied college stu-
    dents. *The Journal of School Health,* 1969, 39, 317–321.
MYERS, P., AND HAMMILL, D. D.   *Methods for learning disorders.*
    New York: Wiley, 1969.
MYKLEBUST, H. R.   *Auditory disorders in children: A manual for dif-
    ferential diagnosis.* New York: Grune and Stratton, 1954.
MYKLEBUST, H. R.   Training aphasic children. *Volta Review,*
    1955, 57, 149.
MYKLEBUST, H. R.   *Psychology of deafness: Sensory deprivation,
    learning, and adjustment.* New York: Grune and Stratton, 1960.
MYKLEBUST, H. R.   Psychological and psychiatric implications of
    deafness. *Archives of Otolaryngology,* 1963, 78, 790–793.
MYKLEBUST, H. R.   Learning disorders: Psychoneurological dis-
    turbances in childhood. *Rehabilitation Literature,* 1964(a), 25,
    354–360.
MYKLEBUST, H. R.   *The psychology of deafness.* New York: Grune
    and Stratton, 1964(b).

NATIONAL ADVISORY COMMITTEE ON HANDICAPPED CHILDREN.   *Spe-
    cial education for handicapped children,* first annual report.
    Washington, D.C.: Department of Health, Education, & Wel-
    fare, Office of Education, 1968.
NATIONAL SOCIETY FOR THE PREVENTION OF BLINDNESS.   *Helping
    the partially seeing child in the regular classroom.* Publication
    No. P-300. New York: National Society for the Prevention of
    Blindness, Inc., 1965.
NEILL, A. S.   *Summerhill.* New York: Hart Publishing Co., 1960.
NEWGARTEN, B. L.   Social class and friendship among school chil-
    dren. *American Journal of Sociology,* 1946, 51, 305–313.
NEWMAN, R. G.   The assessment of progress in the treatment of
    hyperaggressive children with learning disturbances within a
    school setting. *American Journal of Orthopsychiatry,* 1959, 29,
    633–643.
NOLAN, C. Y.   Readability of large types: A study of type sizes and
    type styles. *International Journal for the Education of the Blind,*
    1959, 9, 41–44.
NOLAN, C. Y.   Reading and listening in learning by the blind. *Ex-
    ceptional Children,* 1963, 29, 313–316.

O'CONNOR, C. D.   Children with impaired hearing. *The Volta
    Review,* 1954, 56, 433–439.
OHIO COMMISSION ON CHILDREN AND YOUTH,   Committee on

Special Education. Children who are socially and emotionally maladjusted in school. In M. E. Frampton and E. D. Call (eds.). *Special education for the exceptional,* vol. 3. Boston: Porter Sargent, 1956.

O'LEARY, R. D., KAUFMAN, K. F., KASS, R. E., AND DRABMAN, R. S. Effects of loud and soft reprimands on the behavior of disruptive students. *Exceptional Children,* 1970, 37, 145–155.

ORTON, L. D., McKAY, E., AND RAINY, D. The effect of method of instruction on retention and transfer for different levels of ability. *The School Review,* 1964, 72, 451–461.

OSBORNE, J. G. Free time as a reinforcer in the management of classroom behavior. *Journal of Applied Behavior Analysis,* 1969, 2, 113–118.

PAIVIO, A., AND OKOVITA, H. Word imagery modalities and associative learning in blind and sighted subjects. *Journal of Verbal Learning and Verbal Behavior,* 1971, 10, 506–510.

PARKER, W. Science activities. In S. W. Tiedt (ed.). *Teaching the disadvantaged child.* New York: Oxford University Press, 1968.

PASSOW, A. H. Education in depressed areas. In A. H. Passow (ed.). *Education in depressed areas.* New York: Teachers College Press, 1963.

PATTERSON, C. R. An application of conditioning techniques to the control of a hyperactive child. In L. P. Ullman, and L. Krasner (eds.). *Case studies in behavior modification.* New York: Holt, Rinehart, & Winston, Inc., 1965.

PEGNATO, C. W., AND BIRCH, J. W. Locating gifted children in junior high school. *Exceptional Children,* 1959, 25, 300–304.

PELONE, A. J. *Helping the visually handicapped child in a regular class.* New York: Bureau of Publications, Teachers College, Columbia University, 1957.

PERKINS, F. L. L. *Teaching techniques for cerebral palsied children.* New York: Vantage Press, 1963.

PETERMAN, M. G. Convulsions in childhood: Twenty year study of 2500 cases. *American Journal of Diseases in Children,* 1953, 43, 452–459.

PETERSON, D. R. Behavior problems of middle childhood. *Journal of Consulting Psychology,* 1961, 25, 205–209.

PHELPS, W. M., AND TURNER, A. *The eartherist corner — An outline of the cerebral palsy problem in text and pictures.* Ohio: The National Society for Crippled Children and Adults, Inc., 1945.

PHILLIPS, E. L. Parent-child psychotherapy: A follow-up study comparing two techniques. *Journal of Psychology,* 1960, 49, 195–202.

PIERCE, J. W., AND BOWMAN, P. Motivation patterns of superior high school students. In *The gifted student,* Cooperative Research Monograph No. 2, Washington, D.C.: U. S. Office of Education, Government Printing Office, 1960, 33–66.

PINNEAU, S. R., TERMAN, L. M., AND MERRILL, M. A. *Stanford-Binet Intelligence Scale: Revised IQ Tables.* Boston: Houghton Mifflin Co., 1960.

PINTNER, E. M., EISENSON, J., AND STANTON, M. *The psychology of the physically handicapped.* New York: Appleton-Century-Crofts, 1945.

POSTMAN, L. Retention as a function of degree of overlearning. *Science,* 1962, 135, 666–667.

PREMACK, D. Toward empirical behavior laws: 1. Positive reinforcement. *Psychological Review,* 1959, 66, 219–233.

PRESIDENT'S COMMITTEE ON MENTAL RETARDATION. *Report to the president: A proposed program for national action to combat mental retardation.* Superintendent of Documents, U.S. Government Printing Office, Washington, D.C., October 1962.

PRESIDENT'S COMMITTEE ON MENTAL RETARDATION MR 67. *A first report to the president on the nation's progress and remaining great needs in the campaign to combat mental retardation.* Washington, D.C.: U.S. Government Printing Office, 1967.

PRESIDENT'S COMMITTEE ON MENTAL RETARDATION. *The six hour retarded child: A report on a conference on problems of children in the inner city.* Washington, D.C.: U.S. Government Printing Office, 1969.

PRESIDENT'S COMMITTEE ON MENTAL RETARDATION. *MR 70: The decisive decade.* Washington, D.C.: U.S. Government Printing Office, 1970.

PRESIDENT'S COMMITTEE ON MENTAL RETARDATION. *MR 71: Entering the era of human ecology.* Washington, D.C.: U.S. Government Printing Office, 1971.

PRESSY, S. L. Concerning the nature and nurture of genius. In J. L. French (ed.). *Educating the gifted.* New York: Holt, Rinehart, & Winston, 1960.

PRITCHARD, D. G. *Education and the handicapped: 1760–1960.* London: Routledge and Kegan Paul, 1963.

QUAY, H. C. Academic skills. In N. R. Ellis (ed.). *Handbook of mental deficiency.* New York: McGraw-Hill, 1963(a).

QUAY, H. C. Some basic considerations in the education of emotionally disturbed children. *Exceptional Children,* 1963(b), 30, 27–31.

QUAY, H. C. Remediation of the conduct problem child in the special class setting. *Exceptional Children,* 1966, 32, 509–513.

QUAY, H. C. The facets of educational exceptionality: A conceptual framework for assessment, grouping, and instruction. *Exceptional Children,* 1968, 35, 25–32.

QUAY, H. C., MORSE, W. C., AND CUTLER, R. L. Personality patterns of pupils in special classes for the emotionally disturbed. *Exceptional Children,* 1966, 33, 297–301.

RAMBEAU, J., AND RAMBEAU, N. *Morgan Bay Series.* Harr Wagner Publishing Co., 1962.

RAMONDA, R. Reading instruction. In S. W. Tiedt (ed.). *Teaching the disadvantaged child.* New York: Oxford University Press, 1968.

RAPPAPORT, S. R. (ed.). *Childhood aphasia and brain damage: A definition.* Narberth, Pa.: Livingston Publishing Co., 1964.

RAPPAPORT, S. R. In *Proceedings of the 1965 Pathway School Institute.* Narberth, Pa.: Livingston Publishing Co., 1966.

RAPPAPORT, S. R., HIRT, J. B., AND DECKER, R. J. Manifestations of the brain damage syndrome in school. In S. Rappaport (ed.). *Childhood aphasia and brain damage: A definition.* Narberth, Pa.: Livingston Publishing Co., 1964.

REDL, F. Strategy and techniques of the life space interview. *American Journal of Orthopsychiatry,* 1959, 29, 1–18.

REGER, R. *School psychology.* Springfield, Ill.: Charles C. Thomas, 1965.

REID, G. The etiology and nature of functional articulatory deficits in elementary school children. *Journal of Speech Disorders,* 1947, 12, 143–150.

REISSMAN, F. *The culturally deprived child.* New York: Harper & Row, 1962.

RHODES, W. C. The disturbing child. A problem of ecological management. *Exceptional Children,* 1967, 33, 449–455.

RIPPLE, R. E., AND MAY, F. B. Caution in comparing creativity and IQ. *Psychological Reports,* 1960, 10.

ROBBIN, J. *The reading fingers: Life of Louis Braille.* New York: American Foundation for the Blind, 1955.

ROBINS, L. N. *Deviant children grow up.* Baltimore: The Williams and Wilkens Co., 1966.

ROBINSON, H. B., AND ROBINSON, N. M. *The mentally retarded child.* New York: McGraw-Hill, 1965.

ROGERS, C. R.   Toward a theory of creativity.   In H. Anderson (ed.).   *Creativity and its cultivation.*   New York: Harper & Row, 1959.

ROGERS, M. E., LILIENFIELD, A. M., AND PASAMANICK, B.   *Prenatal and paranatal factors in the development of childhood behavior disorders.*   Baltimore: Johns Hopkins University Press, 1954.

ROSENTHAL, R., AND JACOBSON, L.   Teachers expectancies: Determinants of pupils' IQ gains.   *Psychological Reports,* 1966, 19, 115–118.

ROSENTHAL, R., AND JACOBSON, L.   *Pygmalion in the classroom.*   New York: Holt, Rinehart, & Winston, 1968.

ROSS, I.   *Journey into light: The story of the education of the blind.*   New York: Appleton-Century-Crofts, 1951.

RUBIN, E. Z., SIMSON, C. B., AND BETWEE, M. C.   *Emotionally handicapped children and the elementary school.*   Detroit: Wayne State University Press, 1966.

SARASON, S., AND GLADWIN, T.   *Psychological problems in mental deficiency.*   New York: Harper & Row, 1959.

SCHIEFELBUSCH, R. L.   Language studies of mentally retarded children.   *Journal of Speech and Hearing Disabilities.*   Monograph Supplement No. 10, 1963.

SCHLAEGEL, T. F.   The dominant method of imagery in blind as compared to sighted adolescents.   *Journal of Genetic Psychology,* 1953, 83, 265–277.

SCHOLL, G. T.   The education of children with visual impairments.   In W. M. Cruickshank and G. O. Johnson (eds.).   *Education of exceptional children and youth.*   Englewood Cliffs, N.J.: Prentice-Hall, 1967.

SCHONELL, F. E.   *Educating spastic children.*   London: Oliver & Boyd, 1956.

SCHRAGER, J., LINDY, J., HARRISON, S., McDERMOTT, J., AND WILSON, P.   The hyperkinetic child.   *Journal of American Academy of Psychiatry,* 1966, 5, 526–533.

SCHULTZ, E. W., HIRSHOREN, A., MANTON, A., AND HENDERSON, R.   Special education for the emotionally disturbed.   *Exceptional Children,* 1971, 38(4), 313–320.

SCHWITZGEBEL, R.   The science of learning and the art of teaching.   Paper presented at the First Annual Educational Engineering Conference, University of California, Los Angeles, 1965.

SHEEHAN, J. G.   Conflict theory of stuttering.   In J. Eisenson (ed.).   *Stuttering: A symposium.*   New York: Harper & Row, 1958.

Sheehan, J. G. (ed.). *Stuttering research and therapy.* New York: Harper and Row, 1970.

Shores, R. E., and Haubrich, P. A. Effects of cubicles in educating emotionally disturbed children. *Exceptional Children,* 1969, 36, 21–24.

Shuy, R. W. The sociolinguist and urban language problems. In F. Williams (ed.). *Language and poverty.* Chicago: Markham Publishing Co., 1970.

Sigerist, H. E. *Civilization and disease.* Chicago: Phoenix, 1943.

Siller, J. Socio-economic status and conceptual thinking. *Journal of Abnormal and Social Psychology,* 1957, 55, 365–371.

Silverman, S. R., and Lane, H. S. Deaf children. In H. Davis and S. R. Silverman (eds.). *Hearing and deafness,* 3rd edition. New York: Holt, Rinehart, & Winston, 1970.

Simpson, G. G. *Meaning of evolution.* New Haven: Yale University Press, 1949.

Singer, J. L., and Steiner, B. F. Imaginative content in the dreams and fantasy play of blind and sighted children. *Perceptual and Motor Skills,* 1966, 22, 475–482.

Skinner, B. F. *Science and human behavior.* New York: The Macmillan Co., 1953.

Skinner, B. F. *The technology of teaching.* New York: Appleton-Century-Crofts, 1968.

Slatoff, J. A combined educational and psychiatric approach to early primary grade learning problems. *Research Relating to Children,* 1968.

Smith, J. O. Speech and language of the retarded. *Training School Bulletin,* 1962, 58, 111–124.

Smith, R. M. *Clinical teaching: Methods of instruction for the retarded.* New York: McGraw-Hill, 1968.

Smoch, C., and Cruickshank, W. M. Responses of handicapped and normal children to Rosenzweig P-F study. *The Quarterly Journal of Behavior,* 1952, 4, 156–164.

Sommers, R. K. Case finding, case selection, and case load. In R. J. Van Hattum (ed.). *Clinical speech in the schools.* Springfield, Ill.: Charles C. Thomas, 1969.

Sommers, V. S. *The influence of parental attitudes and social environment on the personality development of the adolescent blind.* New York: American Foundation for the Blind, 1944.

Sontag, L. W., Baker, C. T., and Nelson, V. L. *Mental growth and personality development: A longitudinal study.* Society for Research in Child Development, Inc., Vol. 23, Serial No. 68, No. 2. Lafayette, Indiana: Purdue University Press, 1958.

SPIVAK, G., AND SWIFT, M. S. The Devereux Elementary School rating scales: A study of the nature and organization of achievement related disturbed classroom behavior. *Journal of Special Education,* 1966, 1, 71–91.

SPRADLIN, J. E. Language and communication of mental defectives. In N. Ellis (ed.). *Handbook of mental deficiency.* New York: McGraw-Hill, 1963(a), 512-555.

SPRADLIN, J. E. Parson's language sample. *Journal of Speech and Hearing Disorders,* Monograph Supplement, 1963(b), 10, 8–31.

SPRIESTERBACH, D. S., AND CURTIS, J. F. Misarticulation and discrimination of speech sounds. *Quarterly Journal of Speech,* 1951, 32, 483–491.

S.R.A. *primary mental abilities test.* Chicago: Science Research Associates, Inc., 1962.

STANCHFIELD, J. A study of boys' reading interests in relationship to reading achievement. Doctoral dissertation, University of California, Los Angeles, Department of Education, 1961.

STEINBECK, C. Report of the special class department, Cleveland, Ohio, 1918. Cited in Herbert Goldstein, Social aspects of mental deficiency. Unpublished Ed.D. dissertation, University of Illinois, 1957.

STEINZOR, L. V. School peers of visually handicapped children. *New Outlook for the Blind,* 1966, 60, 312–314.

STEWART, W. A. Toward a history of American Negro dialect. In F. William (ed.). *Language and poverty.* Chicago: Markham Publishing Co., 1970.

STONE, C. R., GROVER, C. C., AND ANDERSON, D. G. *New practice readers.* New York: Webster Division, McGraw-Hill, 1962.

STONE, F. B., AND ROWLEY, V. N. Educational disability in emotionally disturbed children. *Exceptional Children,* 1964, 30, 423–426.

STOUFFER, S. A., AND SHEA, P. D. *Your educational plans.* Chicago: Science Research Associates, Inc., 1959.

STRANG, R. Psychology of gifted children and youth. In W. Cruickshank (ed.). *Psychology of exceptional children and youth.* Englewood Cliffs, N.J.: Prentice-Hall, 1963.

STRANG, R., AND ROBERTS, R. *Teenage tales.* Boston: D.C. Heath and Company, 1964.

STRAUSS, A. A., AND KEPHART, N. C. *Psychology and education of the brain-injured child.* New York: Grune & Stratton, Inc., 1955.

STRAUSS, A. A., AND LEHTINEN, L. *Psychopathology and education of the brain-injured child.* New York: Grune & Stratton, 1947.

STUCKLESS, E. R., AND BIRCH, J. W. The influence of early manual communication on the linguistic development of deaf children. Part II. *American Annals of the Deaf,* 1966, 111, 499–504.

SULLIVAN, E. T., CLARK, W. W., AND TIEGS, E. W. *Manual: California test of mental maturity.* Los Angeles: California Test Bureau, 1957.

SUMPTION, M. R., AND LUECKING, E. M. *Education of the gifted.* New York: Ronald Press Co., 1960.

SYKES, D. H., DOUGLAS, V. I., AND MORGENSTERN, G. The effect of methylphenidate (Ritalin) on sustained attention of hyperactive children. *Psychopharmacologia* (Berl.), 1972, 25, 262–274.

SYKES, D. H., DOUGLAS, V. I., WEISS, G., AND MINDKE, K. K. Attention in hyperactive children and the effect of methylphenidate (Ritalin). *Journal of Child Psychology and Psychiatry,* 1971, 72, 129–139.

TABA, H., AND ELKINS, D. *Teaching strategies for the culturally disadvantaged.* Chicago: Rand McNally, 1966.

TALBOT, M. E. *Edouard Seguin: A study of an educational approach to the treatment of mentally defective children.* New York: Bureau of Publications, Columbia University, 1964.

TAMKIN, A. S. A survey of educational disability in emotionally disturbed children. *Journal of Educational Research,* 1960, 53, 313–315.

TARJAN, G., DINGMAN, H., AND MILLER, C. Statistical expectations of selected handicaps in the mentally retarded. *American Journal of Mental Deficiency,* 1960, 65, 335–341.

TAYLOR, F., ARTUSO, A., AND HEWETT, F. M. *Exploring our environment: Art tasks.* Denver: Love Publishing Co., 1973(a).

TAYLOR, F., ARTURO, A. A., AND HEWETT, F. M. *Exploring our environment: Science tasks.* Denver: Love Publishing Co., 1973(b).

TAYLOR, F., ARTUSO, A., SOLOWAY, M., HEWETT, F., QUAY, H., AND STILLWELL, R. A learning center plan for special education. *Focus on Exceptional Children,* May, 1972, 4(3).

TAYLOR, R. G. Personality traits and discrepant achievement: A review. *Journal of Counseling Psychology,* 1964, 11, 76–82.

TELFORD, C. W., AND SAWREY, J. M. *The exceptional individual.* Englewood Cliffs, N.J.: Prentice-Hall, 1967.

TEMPLIN, M. C., AND DARLEY, F. *The Templin-Darley tests of articulation.* Minneapolis: University of Minnesota Press, 1960.

TERMAN, L. M. *Genetic studies of genius, Vol. I.* Stanford, Calif.: Stanford University Press, 1925.

TERMAN, L. M., AND ODEN, M. H. *The gifted child grows up.* Stanford, Calif.: Stanford University Press, 1947.

TERMAN, L. M., AND ODEN, M. H. *The gifted group at mid-life.* Stanford, Calif.: Stanford University Press, 1959.

THORNDIKE, E. *Educational psychology.* New York: Columbia University Press, 1913.

TORRANCE, E. P. *Explorations in creative thinking in the early school years — VI, highly intelligent and highly creative children in a laboratory school.* Minneapolis: Bureau of Educational Research, University of Minnesota, 1959.

TORRANCE, E. P. *Guiding creative talent.* Englewood Cliffs, N.J.: Prentice-Hall, 1962.

TORRES, F. Convulsive disorders: A working classification and guidelines for diagnosis and treatment. *Medical Times,* 1969, 97, 152–156.

TREDGOLD, A., AND TREDGOLD, R. *A textbook of mental deficiency.* Baltimore: Williams & Wilkins, 1952.

TURNURE, J. Distractibility in the mentally retarded: Negative evidence for an orienting inadequacy. *Exceptional Children,* 1970, 37, 181–186.

TURNURE, J., AND ZIGLER, E. F. Outer directedness in the problem solving of normal and retarded children. *Journal of Abnormal and Social Psychology,* 1964, 69, 427–436.

TYMCHUK, A. J. Personality and sociocultural retardation. *Exceptional Children,* 1972, 38, 721–728.

UNITED STATES OFFICE OF EDUCATION. *Better education for the handicapped: Annual report, fiscal year, 1969.* Washington, D.C.: U.S. Government Printing Office, 1970.

VANE, J., WEITZMAN, J., AND APPLEBAUM, A. P. Performance of Negro and white children and problem and nonproblem children on the Stanford-Binet Scale. *Journal of Clinical Psychology,* 1966, 22, 431–435.

VAN RIPER, C. *Speech correction: Principles and methods.* Englewood Cliffs, N.J.: Prentice-Hall, 1954.

VAN RIPER, C. Historical approaches. In J. S. Sheehan (ed.). *Stuttering research and therapy.* New York: Harper and Row, 1970.

VAN RIPER, C. *Speech correction: Principles and methods.* Englewood Cliffs, N.J.: Prentice-Hall, 1972.

VAN RIPER, C., AND IRWIN, J. V. *Voice and articulation.* Englewood Cliffs, N.J.: Prentice-Hall, 1958.

VERNON, M. Fifty years of research on the intelligence of deaf and hard of hearing children: A review of literature and discussion of implications. *Journal of Rehabilitation of the Deaf,* 1968, 2, 1–12.

VERNON, M., AND BROWN, D. W. A guide to psychological tests and testing procedures in the evaluation of deaf and hard-of-hearing children. *Journal of Speech and Hearing Disorders*, 1964, 29, 414–423.

WALLIN, J. E. *Education of mentally handicapped children.* New York: Harper & Row, 1955.

WARDEN, S. A. *The leftouts.* New York: Holt, Rinehart, & Winston, 1968.

WATSON, R. I. *Psychology of the child.* New York: Wiley, 1959.

WEAVER, C. H., FURBEE, C., AND EVERHART, R. W. Articulatory competency and reading readiness. *Journal of Speech and Hearing Research*, 1960, 3, 174–180.

WEBB, C. E., AND KINDE, S. Speech, language, and hearing of the mentally retarded. In A. Baumeister (ed.). *Mental retardation: Appraisal, education, and rehabilitation.* Chicago: Aldine Publishing Company, 1967, 86–119.

WECHSLER, D. *Wechsler intelligence scale for children.* New York: The Psychological Corporation, 1949.

WECHSLER, D. *Wechsler adult intelligence scale.* Baltimore: The Williams & Wilkins Co., 1958.

WECHSLER, D. *Wechsler preschool and primary scale of intelligence.* New York: The Psychological Corporation, 1967.

WEISS, G., MINDE, K., WERRY, J. S., DOUGLAS, V., AND NEMETH, E. Studies of the hyperactive child VIII: Five year follow-up. Paper presented to American Psychiatric Association, Bal Harbor, Florida, 1969.

WEST, R. A historical review of the American literature in speech pathology. In R. W. Rieber and R. S. Brubaker (eds.). *Speech pathology.* Philadelphia: J. B. Lippincott Co., 1966, 25–41.

WESTLAKE, H., AND RUTHERFORD, D. *Cleft palate.* Englewood Cliffs, N.J.: Prentice-Hall, 1966.

WHELAN, R. F. The relevance of behavior modification procedures for teachers of emotionally disturbed children. In P. Knoblock (ed.). *Intervention approaches in educating emotionally disturbed children.* Syracuse: Syracuse University Press, 1966.

WHELAN, R. F., AND HARING, N. G. Modification and maintenance of behavior through systematic application of consequences. *Exceptional Children*, 1966, 32, 281–289.

WHIPPLE, G. The culturally and socially deprived reader. In A. H. Passow, et al. (eds.). *Education of the disadvantaged.* New York: Holt, Rinehart, & Winston, 1967.

WHITE, M., AND HARRIS, M. *The school psychologist.* New York: Harper & Row, 1961.

WHITE, S. The Physical Sciences Study Committee: A planning conference report. *Contemporary Physics*, October 1960, 39–54.

WICKMAN, E. *Children's behavior and teachers' attitudes.* New York: Commonwealth Fund, 1928.

WILLIAMS, F. Some preliminaries and prospects. In F. Williams (ed.). *Language and poverty.* Chicago: Markham Publishing Co., 1970.

WILSON, M. Children with crippling and health disabilities. In L. M. Dunn (ed.). *Exceptional children in the schools,* second edition. New York: Holt, Rinehart, & Winston, 1973.

WILSON, R. C. Creativity. In N. B. Henry (ed.). *Education for the gifted.* Chicago: University of Chicago Press, 1958.

WISHIK, S. M. Handicapped children in Georgia: A study of prevalence, disability, needs, and resources. *American Journal of Public Health,* 1956, 46, 195–203.

WOLF, M. M., GILES, D. K., AND HALL, R. V. Experiments with token reinforcement in a remedial classroom. *Behavior Research and Therapy,* 1968, 6, 51–64.

WOLF, M. M., RISLEY, T., AND MILLS, H. Application of operant conditioning procedures to the behavior problems of an autistic child. *Behavior Research and Therapy,* 1964, 1, 305–312.

WOLFE, W. G. A comprehensive evaluation of fifty cases of cerebral palsy. *Journal of Speech and Hearing Disorders,* 1950, 15, 234–251.

WOLFENSBERGER, W. Counseling the parents of the retarded. In A. Baumeister (ed.). *Mental retardation: Appraisal, education, and rehabilitation.* Chicago: Aldine Publishing Company, 1967.

WOODCOCK, R. W., AND DUNN, L. M. *Efficacy of several approaches for teaching reading to the educable mentally retarded.* U.S. Office of Education Project No. 5-0392. Nashville: George Peabody College for Teachers, 1967.

WOODEN, H. Z. Deaf and hard of hearing children. In L. M. Dunn (ed.). *Exceptional children in the schools.* New York: Holt, Rinehart, & Winston, 1963.

WOODS, F. J., AND CARROW, M. A. The choice-rejection status of speech defective children. *Exceptional Children,* 1959, 25, 279–283.

WOODS, G. E. A lowered incidence of infantile cerebral palsy. *Developmental Medical Child Neurology,* 1963, 5, 449–450.

WOODY, R. H. The use of electroencephalography and mental abilities tests in the diagnosis of behavioral problem males. Unpublished doctoral dissertation, Michigan State University, 1964.

WOODY, R. H. Diagnosis of behavioral problem children: Mental abilities and achievement tests. *Journal of School Psychology,* 1968, 6, 111–116.

Woody, R. H. *Behavioral problem children in the schools.* New York: Appleton-Century-Crofts, 1969.

Worcester, W. *The education of children of above-average mentality.* Lincoln: University of Nebraska Press, 1956.

Worchel, P., and Andies, J. G. The perception of obstacles by the blind. *Journal of Experimental Psychology,* 1950, 40, 170–176.

Worchel, P., and Dallenbach, K. M. Facial vision: Perception of obstacles by the deaf-blind. *American Journal of Psychology,* 1947, 60, 502–553.

Worchel, P., and Mauney, J. The effect of practice on the perception of obstacles by the blind. *Journal of Experimental Psychology,* 1951, 60, 746–751.

Wright, S., and Tarjan, G. Mental retardation: A review for pediatricians. *American Journal of Diseases of Children,* 1963, 105, 511–526.

Wrightstone, J. W., Justman, J., and Moskowitz, S. *Studies of children with cardiac limitations.* New York: Board of Education of the City of New York, 1953.

Wrightstone, J. W., Justman, J., and Moskowitz, S. *Studies of children with physical handicaps II: The child with orthopedic limitations.* New York: Board of Education of the City of New York, Bureau of Educational Research, 1954.

Zeaman, D., and House, B. The role of attention in retardate discrimination learning. In N. Ellis (ed.). *Handbook of mental deficiency.* New York: McGraw-Hill, 1963.

Zigler, E. F. Social deprivation and rigidity in the performance of feebleminded children. *Journal of Abnormal and Social Psychology,* 1961, 62, 413–421.

Zigler, E. F. Rigidity and social reinforcement effects in the performance of institutionalized and noninstitutionalized normal and retarded children. *Journal of Personality,* 1963, 31, 258–269.

Zigler, E. F. Research on personality structure of the retardate. In N. Ellis (ed.). *International review of research in mental retardation, Volume I.* New York: Academic Press, 1966.

Zigler, E. F. Developmental vs. difference theories of mental retardation and the problem of motivation. *American Journal of Mental Deficiency,* 1969, 73, 536–556.

Zigler, E. F., and Butterfield, E. C. Motivational aspects of changes in IQ test performance of culturally deprived nursery school children. *Child Development,* 1968, 39, 1–14.

Zilboorg, G., and Henry, G. W. *A history of medical psychology.* New York: W. W. Norton, 1941.

ZINTZ, M. V. Problems of classroom adjustment of Indian children in public elementary schools in the Southwest. *Science Education,* 1962, 46, 261–269.

ZWEIBELSON, I., AND BARG, C. F. Concept development of blind children. *New Outlook for the Blind,* 1967, 61, 218–222.

Subject Index

Name Index